DARKNESS AND DESIRE, 1804–1864

KABUKI PLAYS ON STAGE

See page 396 for a complete list of plays in these volumes.

VOLUME 3

Kabuki Plays On Stage

DARKNESS AND DESIRE, 1804–1864

EDITED BY JAMES R. BRANDON AND SAMUEL L. LEITER

UNIVERSITY OF HAWAI'I PRESS

HONOLULU

Publication of this book has been assisted by
grants from the Nippon Foundation

and

Shiseido Co, Ltd., and the International
Communications Foundation through
the Association for 100 Japanese books.

University of Hawai'i Press books are printed on acid-
free paper and meet the guidelines for permanence
and durability of the Council on Library Resources.

Design by Stuart McKee Design, San Francisco

Printed by Friesens

Library of Congress Cataloging-in-Publication Data

Kabuki plays on stage / edited by James R. Brandon
    and Samuel L. Leiter.
        p.   cm.
    Includes bibliographical references and indexes.

    Contents:
        v. 1 Brilliance and bravado, 1697–1766
        v. 2 Villainy and vengeance, 1773–1799
        v. 3 Darkness and desire, 1804–1864
        v. 4 Restoration and reform, 1872–1905
    1. Kabuki plays—Translations into English.
I. Brandon, James R.   II. Leiter, Samuel L.

PL782.E5 K36 2002
895.6'2008—dc21   2001027912

    ISBN 0–8248–2403–2 (v. 1. : alk. paper)
    ISBN 0–8248–2413–x (v. 2. : alk. paper)
    ISBN 0–8248–2455–5 (v. 3. : alk. paper)
    ISBN 0–8248–2574–8 (v. 4. : alk. paper)

This series is dedicated to Professor Torigoe Bunzō
and his strong vision of kabuki
as an international theatre.

CONTENTS

CONTENTS

CONTENTS

The kabuki theatre of Japan, one of the world's greatest dramatic traditions, presently has an active repertory of 250 to 300 plays and dances, of which less than 20 have been translated into English. In addition, somewhat more than a dozen texts of the puppet theatre (widely known as *bunraku*), later adapted by kabuki, have been translated. Even taken together, this small number does not compare with the hundreds of translations of *nō* and *kyōgen* plays. Our intention in these four volumes is to begin to redress this gap by bringing to the reader translations of 51 previously untranslated kabuki plays. It is the first time in over twenty years that a collection of new kabuki translations is being published.

There are many reasons for this lack of translations, including the linguistic difficulty of understanding kabuki's ever-changing colloquial vocabulary, the complexities of transposing kabuki's elaborate verbal gymnastics and declamatory meter into another language, and the problem of establishing authentic texts in a domain where, in principle, the script of each production was newly written. Even today, as our experience working on this project often demonstrated, there are likely to be significant variations among certain scripts used by different actors. Moreover, as a practical matter, many of the plays are long. Finally, translation of the composite art of kabuki must take into account music, dance, acting, and staging as well as language.

The plays translated in these four volumes were selected with several criteria in mind. Most of all, the plays chosen by the editors and translators have exciting stories and charismatic characters; they are powerfully written and are brilliantly theatrical on stage. It often was difficult to limit our selection because many other plays also deserve translation.

The plays chosen for inclusion are also representative of major playwrights, chronological periods of playwriting, play types (history, domestic, and dance dramas), and performance styles. Plays from both Edo (Tokyo) and Kamigata (Osaka and Kyoto) kabuki are included.

All the chosen plays are in the current repertory, are regularly staged, and have not been previously translated. If only certain scenes or acts from a long play are presented today, then those scenes or acts have been translated. In a few cases, long plays, with their important scenes intact, have been slightly reduced in length, and where possible, a brief summation of the deleted passages has been provided by the translator.

We had not initially planned a four-volume effort, but as we combed kabuki's wonderfully rich repertory and as we consulted with our translators, the number of "must translate" plays grew beyond one, or two, or even three volumes. In the end, we selected fifty-one plays that we felt deserved translation, would be interesting to read, and might even be performed in English. The translations have been written by the editors and twenty contributors from Japan, England, Canada, Australia, and the United States, each person doing one or more plays. In addition to their love for kabuki and deep knowledge of its performing traditions, the translators share one vital quality: a passionate desire to transform these plays of two and three centuries past into living theatrical English. The translators bring different viewpoints to their work: some are scholars of literature and drama, some are practitioners of kabuki music and dance, some are kabuki theatre experts. As editors, we value each translator's unique voice and style of writing, and we hope the reader will enjoy the variety of tone and style within the series. We have, of course, made suggestions to the translators, but our major efforts have been to regularize the format and work for consistency of form.

As the series title implies, the plays are translated as if "on stage," with stage directions indicating major scenic effects, stage action, costuming, makeup, music, and sound effects. In some cases, complex stage action—such as stage fights— require several pages of careful description. We hope that such passages will read as clearly and interestingly as the dialogue. One translator may emphasize music and another action or scenic effects, according to the nature of the play and his or her interests. Each translation is based on the translator's choice of a text that approximates a performance on stage today (often this is an unpublished performance script), supplemented by attending public performances and by viewing performance videotapes. Because each performance is different, a translation reflects one performance example; it cannot reflect them all.

Each play is illustrated with a woodblock print *(ukiyo-e)*, sometimes a series of them, and several stage photographs. The *ukiyo-e* artist commonly included on the print the name of the actor or character and, occasionally, a poem, commentary, or section of dialogue. These inscriptions, translated in the captions, are indicated by quotation marks.

Voice in kabuki is often sculpted into definite rhythmic measures. Narrative portions are sung or chanted by musicians on- or offstage (*takemoto* and *ōzatsuma* are two such styles). In the translations, the end of a phrase of sung or chanted lyric is indicated by a slash (/) between phrases, which we hope will suggest the original's general structure. Some translators directly reproduce the Japanese seven-five meter *(shichigochō)* in English, while others seek only to suggest the rhythmic structure of such lines.

The theatre, city, and date of the first production are mentioned before each translation. Stage directions are given in the standard way, from the actor's point of view: when facing the audience, right is the actor's right and left is the actor's left. Personal names are given in the Japanese fashion, with family name first, followed by the given name. A dozen or so Japanese terms that are generally known —kimono, obi, sake, samurai, daimyo, shamisen, and others—are not translated into English nor included in the glossary. In all other cases, translations of Japanese terms are given in the text. To facilitate reading, we have eschewed footnotes within the translations wherever possible in favor of including the pertinent information in the body of the translation, the stage directions, or the introduction. In years prior to 1873, months are given according to the lunar calendar; thus "first month 1865" means the first lunar month of 1865 (early to mid-February on the Western calendar). Dates after 1873, when the Japanese government adopted the Western calendar, are given in Western style (e.g., January 1899).

Translations are arranged in chronological order, and each translation is introduced by its translator. For each volume, the editors have written a general introduction, focusing on the historical development of kabuki drama, and have compiled a bibliography of sources and a glossary of terms. (For more detailed definitions of terms, see Samuel L. Leiter, *New Kabuki Encyclopedia: A Revised Adaptation of* Kabuki Jiten [1997].)

The editors wish to thank the many institutions, scholars, artists, and friends who have supported this undertaking. Publication of the four volumes is supported in part through a major grant to the University of Hawai'i Press from The Nippon

Foundation, for which we are enormously grateful. The Japan Foundation provided a six-month research fellowship to James R. Brandon for study in Tokyo, from January through June 1999, to get the project underway. A grant from the University of Hawai‘i Research Council provided support for computer assistance and photo digitizing. Samuel L. Leiter received two PSC-CUNY Research Foundation grants that allowed him to work on the project in Tokyo in January 1999 and May 2000. A grant from the Asian Cultural Council assisted his research in January 1999. He also was awarded an Ethyle Wolfe Institute for the Humanities Fellowship that allowed him to spend a year working on the project free from teaching and administrative duties. Professors Torigoe Bunzō, former director, and Ito Hiroshi, current director of the Tsubouchi Memorial Theatre Museum of Waseda University (Waseda Daigaku Tsubouchi Hakase Kinen Engeki Hakubutsukan) and their staff generously opened the museum's vast kabuki collection to us. In particular, Suzuki Yoshio, Kozuka Kumi, Terada Shima, and Ikawa Mayuko searched out and provided 229 *ukiyo-e* prints and stage photographs as illustrations. Asahara Tsuneo, secretary-general of the Japan Actors' Association (Nihon Haiyū Kyōkai), kindly extended permission to use photographs under the association's jurisdiction. Hayashi Yukio, managing director of Engeki Shuppansha, and Umemura Yutaka, chief photographer of that theatrical publishing house, kindly provided many needed photographs that we were unable to obtain elsewhere. Karashima Atsumi and Orita Kōji of the National Theatre of Japan, Miyazaki Kyoichi of the Kabuki-za, Abiko Tadashi and Nakazato Takeshi of the Shōchiku Company, and chief librarian of the Shōchiku Otani Library, Ogawa Akiko, generously helped locate and obtain research materials. Among our colleagues, we are especially indebted to professors Kei Hibino of Seikei University for being an indefatigable negotiator on our behalf and, at the University of Hawai‘i, Julie Iezzi for sharing her wide knowledge of kabuki music, Kakuko Shōji for writing English translations of many woodblock inscriptions, and Alexander Vovin for transcription assistance. Professors Kawatake Toshio, Mori Mitsuya, and Furuido Hideo; Kono Takashi of the *Nihon Keizai* newspaper; Konaka Yotarō, managing director of the Japan P.E.N. Club; and Fujita Hiroshi, general-secretary of the Japan Theatre Association (Nihon Engeki Kyōkai), have been staunch supporters of the project, opening many doors for us. Patricia Crosby, our executive editor, and Ann Ludeman, our production editor, have been pillars of support and understanding throughout this arduous project, and we cannot thank them enough for all their help. And we are, as ever, indebted to our wives, Reiko Mochinaga Brandon and Marcia Leiter, for their limitless patience and support.

James R. Brandon
Samuel L. Leiter

INTRODUCTION

Samuel L. Leiter and James R. Brandon

The fourteen plays in this volume mark an extreme point of development in kabuki dramaturgy. The plays are quite remarkable, even within kabuki, for their intense theatricality, gutsy individualism of character, cold-blooded and ferocious violence, realism pushed into fantasy and grotesquery, novelty for novelty's sake, sexual aggressiveness, and assertion of female will. The plays depict a society in extremis, the end of an era, a time often marked by unmitigated darkness and desire.

Like Volume 1, the plays covered here span seven decades. It was a time in Japanese history when local rebellions, rural famine, and urban lawlessness became the cruel fruit of a rapidly failing feudal social order. Eleven times the Tokugawa shogunate changed the historical period name, often after only two or three years, in symbolic attempts to rejuvenate society. With some exceptions, the plays in this volume directly mirror major developments within the larger feudal society that was in the process of disintegration. The Kasei era (1804–1830, its name derived from the last syllables in the contiguous Bunka [1804–1818] and Bunsei [1818–1830] periods) is generally characterized as a time of cultural decadence. Six Kasei plays included here are entirely or partially by Tsuruya Nanboku IV (1755–1829) and feature scenes filled with flamboyant grotesquery, cruelty, murder, madness, and magic. During the Tenpō period (1830–1844), which immediately followed, draconian government reform edicts, called the Tenpō Reforms (*Tenpō no kaikaku*), attempted to restore order to society and sanity to government finances. The two plays translated here from this middle period feature impressive spectacle and dance. The final two decades, beginning just before Commodore Matthew Perry's arrival off the coast of Japan in 1853—precipitating the abandonment of Japan's long-standing isolation policy—and concluding with the violent overthrow of the Tokugawa shogunate in 1868, comprise the era of the "late military regime," or *bakumatsu*. Four plays written by Kawatake Mokuami (1816–1893) and Segawa Jokō III (1806–1881) during this epoch-ending age depict men and women struggling to survive and find their paths—even if by criminal acts—in a collapsing social order.

Almost all the plays here mirror an uneasiness and insecurity about the future. The old feudal values that had anchored characters in early times now bring hollow results. In extremely popular plays, such as *The Scandalous Love of*

Osome and Hisamatsu (1813, hereafter *Osome and Hisamatsu*); *The Execution Ground at Suzugamori* (1823, hereafter *Suzugamori*); *Kasane* (1823); *The Ghost Stories at Yotsuya on the Tōkaidō* (1825, hereafter *Ghost Stories at Yotsuya*); and *The Three Kichisas and the New Year's First Visit to the Pleasure Quarters* (1860, hereafter *Three Kichisas*), we see that characters are motivated again and again by overpowering greed and lust and often show a heart-chilling ruthlessness toward others. To a great extent, then, the plays in this volume portray an overripe age of moral darkness and unbridled human desire.

Two plays stand out as exceptions. *Sanbasō with His Tongue Stuck Out* (1812, hereafter *Sanbasō*) is a felicitous dance that eschews the strong emotional coloring of other dance plays in this volume. The celebratory meeting of the symbol of happy old age, Okina, with Senzai and Sanbasō has been staged in numerous dance variations since at least the Genroku period (1688–1704). The version translated here, and still often performed, was written by Sakurada Jisuke II (1768–1829). The second play, *The Tale of the Martyr of Sakura* (1851, hereafter *Martyr of Sakura*), was written by Segawa Jokō III near the end of the feudal era and is famed as kabuki's only overt political protest play. The sole play that dramatizes a peasant revolt, it depicts directly the terrible suffering of poor farmers who are powerless within the feudal system. Sōgo, the village head, is an honest, sincere man who willingly gives up his life in order to present a petition for redress to the shogun in person. The scene in which he parts from his children knowing they will be executed for his actions is exceptionally poignant but uplifting in its nobility, a far cry from other plays of its time.

This volume's works show the complete dominance of Edo playwrights and producers during the nineteenth century—all the plays were by Edo playwrights and first produced in Edo theatres. The plebeian arts of kabuki, popular literature, visual art, scholarship, publishing, and other cultural manifestations flourished, if unevenly, during the period covered in this volume. Woodblock printing benefited from such giants as Katsushika Hokusai (1760–1849) and Utagawa Hiroshige (1797–1858). In popular fiction, Jippensha Ikku (1765–1831) was known for his series of comic travelogues, the first being *A Shank's Mare's Tour of Tōkaidō* (Tōkaidōchū Hizakurige). The historical novelist Takizawa Bakin (1767–1848) was famous for his immensely long, didactic, and highly conservative Confucianist novel *Satomi and the Eight Dogs* (Satomi Hakkenden). Both stories were frequently dramatized in kabuki.

The nineteenth century produced two playwrights considered kabuki's most gifted ever: Tsuruya Nanboku IV and Kawatake Mokuami. Each was a prolific writer of all types of plays, including dances (*shosagoto* or *buyōgeki*), spectacular history plays, and, especially, realistic and sometimes fantastic domestic dramas about the daily life of contemporary commoners. Nanboku wrote more than 120 plays, while Mokuami is credited with 360 works of all dramatic types. In all-day plays (*tōshi kyōgen*) such as Mokuami's *Gorozō the Gallant* (1864), translated in this volume, authors continued to use the old Edo convention of *naimaze* (mixing), in which the play was divided into a first-part (*ichibanme*) history section (*jidaimono*) tenuously linked to a second-part (*nibanme*) domestic section (*sewamono*). Other plays were constructed following the example of playwright Namiki Gohei I (1747–1808), who in 1794 had brought to Edo the Kamigata (Osaka and Kyoto area) custom of writing the first and second parts as two independent plays (see introduction to Volume 2). For example, Nanboku's *Osome and Hisamatsu* and Mokuami's *Three Kichisas* were written as domestic plays from beginning to end. The former is a second part written in three acts, and the latter is an all-day play in eight acts. The writing of Nanboku and his successors, Jokō and Mokuami, helped spark renewed interest in kabuki at a time of great population growth. Despite rampant crime, poverty, and occasional famine, substantial portions of the urban citizenry had more time and money to spend on leisure activities.

Nanboku assumed his name in 1811 at the age of fifty-six, after having spent his early years as a beginning and then supporting dramatist, learning his trade and polishing his writing skills. He developed a tendency toward realism more fully than any previous playwright. In plays that sharply reflected the speech and customs of Edo's contemporary townsmen—especially those on society's lower rungs —he pioneered the "raw" or "pure" domestic play, the *kizewamono* ("*ki*" may mean raw or uncooked, or pure and unadulterated), in which gangsters and thieves, both male and female, were turned into popular antiheroes. The performative flavor of these works was wonderfully enhanced by a new "musical" style of composition and performance based on dialogue written in alternating phrases of seven and five syllables (*shichigochō*); this technique was further developed in the plays of Jokō and Mokuami. Nanboku also was adept at mingling the high "worlds" (*sekai*) of grand, posturing historical figures with lower-class *kizewamono* worlds, thereby heightening the contrast through the "mixing" convention of overlaying one with the other. Nanboku structured *Ghost Stories at Yotsuya* in a daringly unconventional manner: the squalid world of the murderer Yoemon and the streetwalker Oiwa was connected to the classic samurai revenge play *The Treasury of Loyal Retainers* (Kanadehon Chūshingura, 1748, trans. Keene 1971 and Brandon 1982). Acts of the two plays were performed on alternate days, a juxtaposition that pointed up the sharp differences between their moral universes. In 1827, Nanboku mixed five worlds together in a single play, creating one of the most complex examples of this technique. Whereas there had been plays with several worlds intertwined before, Nanboku's combinations were far more complex and surprising than their predecessors.

Nanboku's *kizewamono*—inhabited by a palpable atmosphere of darkness and desire—typify the tone of decadence, even corruption, of Kasei-period society. In such plays as *Osome and Hisamatsu*, *Kasane*, and *Ghost Stories at Yotsuya*, Nanboku shows himself to be a master manipulator of scenes depicting sexuality (*nureba*), murder (*koroshiba*), torture (*semeba*), and extortion (*yusuriba*), to say nothing of insanity, incest, and suicide. Desire is sometimes expressed through illicit cravings for power or money or position. For example, in *Ghost Stories at Yotsuya*, while the neighbor woman, Oume, is consumed by lust for Iemon, he is motivated to marry her and desert his wife, Oiwa, out of hunger for greater financial rewards and higher social standing. Oume and Iemon's alliance is partly responsible for the death of Oiwa, who relentlessly pursues vengeance even from beyond the grave.

As in the case of Oume, the desire that pulses through the bloodstream of Nanboku's works is often strongly sexual. A sympathetic sexual longing drives the action of the lyrical dance *Yasuna* (1818), in which the handsome Yasuna wanders the fields in a state of madness caused by the suicide of his beloved. Considerably more typical of Nanboku, desire in its darkest forms suffuses *Kasane*, in which the eponymous pregnant heroine suffers unbearable jealousy caused by Yoemon's unfaithfulness. Earlier, Yoemon has fulfilled his sexual desire with Kasane's mother and has viciously killed Kasane's father for interfering with Yoemon's illicit relationship.

The Buddhist-based theme of unsatisfied desire is, of course, not unique to kabuki. Unrequited love and the anguish of slain warriors were persistent themes in *nō* drama. One of the principle teachings of Buddhism is that human desire is the cause of emotional pain and suffering. Numerous kabuki plays have expressed this belief, if not always with the brutal outcomes found in Nanboku's works. Two plays in this volume present sexual desire and its attendant suffering in sublimated form. *Wisteria Maiden* (1826) expresses unrequited desire through the lyrical dance movements of a young woman surrounded by wisteria blossoms. *Nagauta* musicians delicately sing her words of pique and sorrow, "What is hateful in a man's heart is that, although he promised by the gods never to meet another woman, he may be worshipping someone else." In the multipart dance play *Six Poet Immortals* (1831), sexual longing is subtly intimated in the revelation of five famous poets—among them an old man and a priest—who are drawn by the magnetic sexual lure of the exquisite poetess Ono no Komachi, perhaps the closest thing in classical Japanese legend to an icon of male desire. The Buddhist theme of desire's evil consequences is clearly stated in the opening scene, when Henjō, a learned priest, says, "[T]hat which wreathes about my person is a mantle of desire! For this, for all eternity, the Buddha's punishment . . . I'll receive."

The *bakumatsu*-period plays in this volume revert to the dark vision of the Kasei years and stand in contrast to the aristocratic elegance of the court poets in *Six Poet Immortals* and the ethereal vision of a fragile beauty in *Wisteria Maiden*. In *Martyr of Sakura*, the policies of a corrupt and failing Tokugawa government are directly challenged and harshly criticized, something never before attempted in kabuki drama. The title character in Mokuami's *Gorozō the Gallant*, once a samurai, is disgraced and trapped in a life of poverty; his villainous opponent, Doemon, is also a former samurai now reduced to commoner status. All the characters in Mokuami's *Scarface Otomi* (1864) are closely connected to the criminal class, living on the outer edges of society, and the three main characters in Mokuami's *Three*

Kichisas are self-professed thieves and swindlers. These four plays are representative of the amoral, imprisoning darkness of the closing years of feudalism.

In the commoners' world dramatized by kabuki, the most brilliant topos for desire was the licensed quarters, a constant point of reference even when not shown onstage. Yasuna's late beloved is likened to a courtesan in her beauty and allure. The "Bunya" section of *Six Poet Immortals* strongly evokes the aura of the quarters. In *Masakado* (1836), Princess Takiyasha takes on the guise of a lady of pleasure in her attempt—unsuccessful, it turns out—to seduce and overcome Mitsukuni. The lyrics in these scenes are rich in sensual, even erotic, imagery. For example, the *tokiwazu* sings these words of Takiyasha in *Masakado*, as rendered by Leonard C. Pronko:

> Softly, gently, the sparrows / chirp in the ruined palace. / Watchmen extinguish / the torches of the night. / Beyond the screen, lovers, / whispering sweet nonsense, / can still be heard. / From our beautiful dream / I tore myself away, / for it is time to part, / to put on again my obi. / In a playful mood, / you've hidden it— how endearing! / Midst the fragrance of / your lingering perfume, / we share more lovers' cups / of sake. One more? / The shamisen has one string / broken, but let's see / if we can play it with but two. / Changing hearts on changing pillows, / we may never meet again. /

Prostitutes and geisha who appeared in earlier plays had status, however menial, within the brothel world. Kotoura in *Summer Festival: Mirror of Osaka* (see Volume 1) was a geisha working in the unlicensed quarter of Fukugawa, and Umegawa in *A Message of Love from Yamato* and Okon in *The Ise Dances and Love's Dull Blade* (see Volume 2) were licensed prostitutes. The quarters possessed a certain elegance and refinement, and the women in them were able to leave when their contract expired or was purchased by a lover. But the Yoshiwara licensed quarter shown in *Gorozō the Gallant* is a tawdry place. And Otose in *Three Kichisas* is a common streetwalker, a "nighthawk" who plies her trade in seedy thoroughfares, carrying her own floor mat with her. In her unquenchable thirst for Jūzaburō, she unknowingly is guilty of desire's darkest manifestation—incest, which lurks in the background of *Ghost Stories at Yotsuya* and *Scarface Otomi* as well.

Love scenes, in which desire is fulfilled, are perhaps less common than one might expect given the importance of romantic affairs in kabuki domestic plays. Japanese critics railed against the "pornography" of the love scenes in the plays of Nanboku and Jokō. Certainly as the plays are performed today, lovemaking is implied rather than shown. When lovers meet, they may indulge in flirtation and erotic banter, but scenes end before physical intimacy occurs. This pattern is illustrated in the "Dream" scene in *Ghost Stories at Yotsuya* where Oiwa's ghost, in the guise of an innocent yet seductive country maiden (a refreshing departure from the usual courtesan-as-temptress image), meets her unknowing husband Iemon. He is sexually aroused, they engage in an aggressive flirtation, make mutual pledges of love, and she suggestively leans her body against his, preparatory to lovemaking. At this point they pose and stagehands lower a blind hiding them from view.

Ghost Stories at Yotsuya is a famous ghost play (*kaidan mono*), a *kizewamono* subgenre created in the Kasei period, in which wronged spirits of the dead return to exact vengeance on their tormentors. Audiences thrilled to the startling sight of fantastic supernatural beings magically materializing within grittily naturalistic surroundings. The spirits of the dead had often appeared within historical plays, which generally were less realistic than domestic dramas, and their purpose was not necessarily to horrify the audience; in the new *kaidan mono,* authors and actors consistently presented the most frightening aspects of these fearsome visitors from beyond the grave. The presence of vengeful ghosts in otherwise mundane—even squalid—surroundings was a major breakthrough in the psychological manipulation of spectators' innermost fears.

The earliest of the *kaidan mono* was Nanboku's 1804 *The Tale of Tokubei from India* (hereafter *Tokubei from India*), translated here. In this work, the ghostly presence of Tokubei's father is not intended to frighten his son but to guide him in his quest to overthrow Japan. This ghost appears in a dream scene, which kabuki dramatists recognized as an excellent device for the expression of suppressed fears and desires. *Tokubei from India,* produced in the summer, when business was traditionally slow and leading actors were on vacation, proved an unexpected smash. Its success gave rise to the practice of regularly producing ghost plays during the hot weather, plays that became increasingly focused on frightening the audience. Some assert such plays did best in the summer because bone-chilling scenes offered swel-

tering spectators a kind of psychological air conditioning. A more likely explanation is that they were appropriate during July and August because this was the time
of the Buddhist Obon festival, when worshippers welcomed back the souls of departed family members.

With summer becoming the conventional season for ghost plays (although
other dramatic types were also seen during this season), the term *natsu kyōgen*
(summer play) came to be most closely associated with ghost dramas. Audiences
loved *kaidan mono* in part because physically disfigured and obsessively vengeful
women like Oiwa and Kasane were portrayed through intriguing stage devices and
acting tricks (*keren*). The ghost of Oiwa appears through walls and out of a burning
lantern. She floats overhead and drops from the ceiling. She draws a strangled
body high into the air. An extremely gruesome example of *keren*, known as the
"raindoor flip" (*toitagaeshi*), is used in *Ghost Stories at Yotsuya* to show in quick succession two decaying corpses played by the same actor. The villain, Iemon, pulls a
raindoor from the canal on which Oiwa's body is nailed; when he turns the door
over, Kohei, played by the same actor, is instantly revealed. Kasane, possessed by
the spirit of her murdered father, behaves like a living ghost, demonstrating her
power over Yoemon by making unearthly hand movements that manipulate him
like a puppet and draw him back, no matter how far he flees.

Some of the eerie atmosphere of a ghost play touches *Masakado,* a dance-
drama set in a ruined and supposedly haunted castle peopled with powerful historical figures from the past. Princess Takiyasha is a sorceress with mystic powers who
takes on the form of the courtesan Kisaragi. Her magical appearance on the small
hanamichi trap (*suppon*) to chilling flute music (*netoribue*) sends shivers down one's
spine. Takiyasha, like Tokubei, is also adept at black magic, a feature of several
plays from this period, and both characters use their dark powers to conjure up
a familiar whose form is that of a monstrous, supernatural, fire-breathing toad.
Doemon, the wicked samurai boss in *Gorozō the Gallant*, possesses magical powers
as well (shown in scenes not translated here).

Death casts a dark shadow on play after play of this era. It is hard not to be
shocked by the prevalence of chilling scenes of deliberate slaughter: blood flows as
Kasane and Yoemon hack at one another in *Kasane;* Iemon is grimly slain by
Yomoshichi in *Ghost Stories at Yotsuya;* a brother and sister are decapitated in *Three*

A two-panel *ukiyoe* print by Utagawa Kunisada I (Utagawa Toyokuni III, 1786–1864) showing the sensational "raindoor switch" *(toitagaeshi)* trick staging device *(keren)* used in the "Onbō Canal" scene of *Ghost Stories at Yotsuya* at the Ichimura-za in Edo in the eighth month of 1831. The caption on each panel reads, "Old and new, a smashing success, the raindoor switch: Oiwa and Kohei by Onoe Kikugorō; Tamiya Iemon by Seki Sanjūrō." The two panels illustrate the quick change of character that made the raindoor switch so popular with audiences. In the left panel, the skeletal remains of Oiwa are played by Onoe Kikugorō III; a moment later, in the right panel, Kikugorō is playing the corpse of Kohei, the servant Iemon had murdered. (See translation p. 198.) The two prints are made from the same block, except the figure nailed on the board has been recarved. (Tsubouchi Memorial Theatre Museum of Waseda University)

Kichisas; Otomi fatally slashes Yasu in *Scarface Otomi;* and Gorozō mistakenly annihilates an innocent courtesan in *Gorozō the Gallant.* These plays depict both hand-to-hand mortal combat and large-scale choreographed battles (*tachimawari*). In *Martyr of Sakura, Three Kichisas,* and *Scarface Otomi,* heroes and heroines engage in desperate struggles against squads of police and constables. Elegant choreography ensues in *Tokubei from India* and *Masakado*, when Tokubei and Princess Takiyasha employ supernatural powers to baffle their attackers. In *Suzugamori*'s grotesquely comic *tachimawari*, the robbers' body parts sliced off by Gonpachi take on a life of their own. Women can be just as violent as men in kabuki, and they give tit for tat in *Kasane, Ghost Stories at Yotsuya, Scarface Otomi,* and *Six Poet Immortals.* A beautiful flowering branch may be used as a weapon in a courtly play like *Six Poet Immortals,* but razor-sharp swords remain the weapon of choice in most battle scenes. Moreover, the gritty *kizewamono* of this period—like *Kasane* and *Scarface Otomi*—allow hazardous everyday implements such as kitchen knives and sickles to play their gory parts.

Countless kabuki plays make use of suicide as a crucial dramatic device. Onstage suicide methods vary, ranging from *seppuku,* the Japanese ritual suicide in which a person slits his or her belly, to a variety of less noble approaches. *Seppuku* appears only once in this volume's plays, when Sōkan, in *Tokubei from India,* performs it in recompense for having allowed a precious sword to be stolen. In several cases that might not technically be deemed suicide, characters willingly accept their own deaths at others' hands as punishment for their own actions. Thus in *Three Kichisas,* the incestuous brother and sister, Otose and Jūzaburō, allow Oshō to slay them, aware that their forbidden love has led them to this juncture. Also, the hero of *Martyr of Sakura* accepts his imminent death calmly, knowing that when he petitioned the shogun on his community's behalf, he, his wife, and his children would swiftly be executed. Occasionally, characters are set on suicide but are prevented from carrying it out, as when Obō and Ojō are dissuaded from dying in *Three Kichisas.* Similarly, in *Osome and Hisamatsu,* the lovers of the title are about to end their lives in despair, only to be stopped by others. *Kasane* concerns a lovers' double suicide that turns into murder. Suicide is also important when it occurs prior to a play's action, as in *Yasuna,* whose hero goes insane after his mistress kills herself. Moreover, scenes not translated here from *Gorozō the Gallant* and *Three Kichisas* show the title figures eventually choosing death, Gorozō because he slew the wrong woman and the Kichisas (who take each others' lives) because their arrest is imminent.

The obvious brutality of murder and suicide is counterbalanced by kabuki's passion for stage beauty. Realistic stage blood may be used occasionally, but more typically, blood is presented symbolically. In *Kasane*, for example, a serious wound is represented by a design of tiny red leaves on a pure white undergarment. During the nineteenth century, the established conventions of lyrical background singing, exquisite music, choreographed movement, and beautiful costumes and makeup were taken to ever-greater levels. Such performing techniques applied to scenes of cruelty in the *kizewamono* of Nanboku, Jokō, and Mokuami are the ultimate expression of kabuki's "aesthetic of cruelty" (*zankoku no bi*) (see Volume 2 for a fuller discussion).

Kabuki's long-standing conventions of self-referentiality and metatheatricality served to distance the apparent truthfulness of enacted events. It was easy for a spectator to become totally engrossed in a play, especially in a *sewamono* where people ate real food and discussed the ingredients, drank, shaved, sewed, dressed their hair, did their accounts, and attended to other homely tasks. But in *Osome and Hisamatsu*, when Oroku says, upon exiting, "I can't think of any other example of a play in which a husband and wife make an exit like this," the spectator is reminded that this is a stage work, not reality. The names of the actors performing —as well as past actors—are mentioned in *Suzugamori*, whose comic spirit can be expected to support the references, but even in the grim *Kasane*, the evil Yoemon is told he looks just like "the kabuki actor Danjūrō," who originated the role, reminding the spectator that the people onstage are actors as much as characters. In *Six Poet Immortals* an actor's home address is provided, while in *Three Kichisas* not only are the names of the actors playing Obō and Ojō mentioned, but the scene concludes with the actors turning to the audience and saying, "And this is where we must end today's performance," a conclusion that both Mokuami and Nanboku used in scores of plays.

Metatheatricality, of course, disrupts suspense. But suspense remains a preeminent goal of the period's dramatists, whose dangerous villains keep audiences fearful of the evil they might wreak around them. Darkness, of course, shades the intentions of many characters in this volume's plays, among them Doemon, Yoemon, Iemon, Takiyasha, and (despite their raffish charm) the three Kichisas. But the tool of darkness was also used quite directly and literally by nineteenth-century playwrights to express their deeply somber vision. Of the fourteen plays translated here, nine are set mainly at night. The pathetic death of the courtesan Oshū in *Gorozō the Gallant* happens only because the scene occurs in the dark: she is wearing Satsuki's robe, and Gorozō, mistaking her for Satsuki, kills her by mistake. *Kasane* and *Ghost Stories at Yotsuya* contain suspenseful nighttime pantomimic scenes (*danmari*) in which the participants search in the gloom for a desired object. In *danmari* scenes the terror of the dark is softened by the slow pace, beautiful music, dancelike movements, and formal tableaus. In current productions of *Masakado*, black-garbed stagehands (*kurogo*) hold up to Takiyasha's face "spotlights" of burning candles mounted at the end of long, thin poles. This nineteenth-century device also happens to be a theatrically effective way to cast an eerie glow upon her face. Play after play shows dimly lit scenes of desolation and poverty, heightening our sense of foreboding. A gory scene in *Scarface Otomi* is set in a ruined graveyard; dusky riverbanks are the sites of violence in *Ghost Stories at Yotsuya* and *Three Kichisas,* the latter also containing a shadowy scene set in a decrepit temple; *Masakado* takes place at a dilapidated castle at night; a gruesome fight occurs at a crumbling graveyard in *Scarface Otomi;* and *Suzugamori* is enacted at the famed execution grounds of the play's title on a pitch-black evening. We see characters living or working in broken-down homes, shops, cottages, or hermitages. Moreover, playwrights add intemperate weather to intensify characters' troubles, as when rain lashes Kasane and Yoemon in *Kasane* and a brutal snowstorm impedes Sōgo's secret return home in *Martyr of Sakura*. Meanwhile, the offstage beating of ominous *dorodoro*, wind, and rain patterns on the large drum (*ōdaiko*) and the tolling of a lonely temple bell fill the air with sounds of ominous melancholy.

The dance-plays *Sanbasō, Yasuna, Six Poet Immortals,* and *Masakado* bring historical backgrounds to the stage, and historical elements are found in *Tokubei from India*. Yet it is notable that domestic plays predominate in this volume. While this period's playwrights created "realistic" depictions of society's outcasts in *Suzugamori, Osome and Hisamatsu, Kasane, Ghost Stories at Yotsuya, Three Kichisas, Scarface Otomi,* and scores of other plays, they also took a sideshow-like interest in the odd, the bizarre, the deviant, and the grotesque. Playwright Fukumori Kyūsuke I (1767–1818) startled spectators in 1815 with a play showing a gruesomely realistic crucifixion scene based closely on the recent public execution of a woman who had murdered her husband. Audiences were attracted, as well as horrified, by the savageness of many *kizewamono*. We cringe when we see the hideously ruined faces of Oiwa and Kasane, whose beauty has been destroyed by malicious men. In *Kasane*, the skull with a sickle thrust in its gouged-out eye socket makes an indelibly fearsome image. Equally shocking is the sight of Oiwa and Kohei's corpses floating down the river, nailed to opposite sides of a raindoor. One can hardly conceive a better physical example of the "aesthetic of cruelty" than the white face and body of Otomi in *Scarface Otomi* bearing seventy-five precisely placed scars. And certainly the gigantic toads of *Tokubei from India* and *Masakado* are bizarre—even horrific—stage figures.

Audiences were able to tolerate such sights in part because dark humor was inextricably woven into *kizewamono* scenes. The stylized savagery of Gonpachi's attack on the robbers in *Suzugamori* is distanced by the grotesque humor of his victims dancing offstage carrying a severed arm or leg. The scene in *Osome and Hisamatsu* in which the "corpse" of Kyūta is kicked out of its coffin, manhandled, and even shaved and dressed to resemble someone else is both barbaric and funny. It is even odder when the corpse turns out to be alive after all. Similarly, the business in *Three Kichisas* with the severed heads and with Genji flailing about with a coffin must have made spectators laugh even as they shuddered.

Kabuki plays are rich in dramatic circumstances that recognize the ambiguous nature of human character—an ambiguity that is highly theatricalized in scenes of character transformation. Such scenes occur frequently in history or dance-plays because of their legendary sources. In *Tokubei from India*, for example, before our amazed eyes the giant toad-familiar changes into its real form, the human Tokubei. Audiences in the Kasei period must have gasped when Mitsukuni in *Masakado* reveals his character's true inner strength by instantly changing his costume from somber black to brilliant gold, and when Kisaragi, admitting her identity as Takiyasha, shows her demonic nature through instant hair and costume changes. Such climactic revelations of a character's true identity are called *jitsu wa* (in reality).

Plays specifically written to show an actor playing several different characters through rapid quick-change techniques (*hayagawari*) have been described in

Volume 1. During the Kasei period, the audience's taste for variety and surprise led to the development of "transformation dances" *(hengemono* or *henge buyō),* in which a single actor played many strikingly different roles, dazzling viewers with his virtuosity. Transformation dances, normally focused on a star performer, often depicted contemporary urban customs and manners, making them "genre" studies of everyday life. It was possible to dance five major roles in sequence in *Six Poet Immortals* through instantaneous costume changes, which could involve fully removing an outer kimono in one movement *(hikinuki)* or dropping the top kimono half around the hips to reveal a new kimono beneath it *(bukkaeri),* thereby dazzling the audience with seemingly magical transformations. *Yasuna* and *Wisteria Maiden* are also derived from the *hengemono* tradition. Originally, both were part of much longer works and now are appreciated as solo dances in and of themselves (*Yasuna* included seven changes of character in its premier performance, and *Wisteria Maiden* was originally a five-character transformation dance). Today, *Six Poet Immortals* is the only transformation dance still occasionally performed in its entirety, although it, too, is more likely to be seen in excerpt form. The term *"hengemono,"* it should be noted, is reserved for dances in which the star plays several different roles. Thus a 1937 version of *Wisteria Maiden* created by Onoe Kikugorō VI (1885–1949) in which the dancer makes several offstage quick changes but remains the same character is not considered *hengemono.*

Transformation dances developed rapidly during the Tenpō period. Originally these works featured five or seven characters that the actor delineated in brief, thematically linked dances. Then plays were written in which an actor played twelve characters, one for each month or sign of the zodiac. Although there were rare exceptions when even more characters were introduced, twelve was generally considered the upward limit. A primary impetus for the popularity of transformation dances during the Kasei and Tenpō periods was the fiery rivalry between two specialists in the genre, Edo's Bandō Mitsugorō III (1773–1831) and his Kamigata counterpart, Nakamura Utaemon III (1778–1838). Utaemon made three memorable, extended incursions to the eastern city, in 1808–1812, 1814–1815, and 1817–1819. Devoted fans turned up by the thousands to compare and argue their favorites' talents. Two especially prolific transformation dance playwrights, Segawa Jokō

II (1757–1833) and Sakurada Jisuke II, wrote new pieces for the two stars. (Jisuke also authored this volume's auspicious dance-play, *Sanbasō*.) In these new genre dances, playwrights broadened the range of female characters beyond elegant historical figures and the romantic, doomed lovers of earlier dances to include commoners such as country girls, nursemaids, boat women, prostitutes, and maidservants. As was noted in Volume 2, with the staging of *The Barrier Gate* in 1784, dance for the male-role specialist was introduced. In the new genre dances of the nineteenth century, not only did the male-role specialist come to the fore by playing both male and female roles through quick changes, he was provided with interesting new male roles, many of them commoners—mendicant priests, plasterers, entertainers, apprentices, street vendors, and the like.

Dance, in general, was greatly enhanced by Kiyomoto Enjudayū I's (1777–1825) 1814 founding of a new school of kabuki narrative music called *kiyomoto*, known for its high-pitched sound and the great emotional power of its singing. Enjudayū was inspired by the Kasei period's dance plays, and his music quickly became a favorite accompaniment for actors, choreographers, and playwrights who were creating new dance pieces. *Kasane, Sanbasō,* and *Six Poet Immortals* are normally accompanied by *kiyomoto* music. A number of dance plays can be staged using one or another musical style, according to the taste of the lead actor. *Sanbasō* and *Six Poet Immortals* may be staged with *kiyomoto* alternating with either *nagauta* or *tokiwazu*, a convention called *kakeai* (exchange). Each musical ensemble sits on its own platform placed onstage as part of the dance spectacle.

Whatever the play, fans loved to see a favorite actor showing off his virtuosity by performing multiple roles. Crowds flocked to see stars like Utaemon III and Mitsugorō III play six roles in *Yoshitsune and the Thousand Cherry Trees* (Yoshitsune Senbon Zakura, 1747), seven roles in *Sugawara and the Secrets of Calligraphy* (Sugawara Denju Tenarai Kagami, 1746), or nine roles in *The Treasury of Loyal Retainers*. In the Kasei period, Nanboku devised dialogue plays like *Osome and Hisamatsu*, popularly known as *The Seven Roles of Osome* (Osome Nanayaku), that called for the star to alternate twelve or fifteen times among seven characters. The tradition of playing multiple roles to demonstrate versatility is carried on today by the talented actor Ichikawa Ennosuke III (b. 1939).

Experiments with quick-change techniques went hand in hand with new mechanical stage devices (*karakuri*). Many of the quick changes and mechanical effects used in *Tokubei from India* became standard in subsequent ghost plays. Onoe Matsusuke I (later Onoe Shōroku I, 1744–1815), already sixty when he premiered the role of Tokubei, stepped into the limelight with the role of Tokubei after a long career as a supporting player. He devised many original effects as Nanboku's creative collaborator. His specialty became the family art (*ie no gei*) of his Onoe family successors, especially his adopted son, Onoe Kikugorō III (1784–1849), who also collaborated extensively with Nanboku in creating the unforgettable roles of Kasane and Oiwa.

One of Matsusuke's most fascinating effects in *Tokubei from India* was seen when Tokubei disappeared into an onstage body of water, only to reappear moments later at the rear of the theatre on the *hanamichi*, totally dry and transformed into a completely different character. It proved so awesome that the actor and playwright became the subject of an official investigation into whether they were practicing magic learned from secret Christians or Dutch traders.

Theatre technicians in Edo advanced kabuki stagecraft significantly in the nineteenth century. Earlier advances, such as elevator traps *(seri)* and the revolving stage *(mawari butai),* had been developed chiefly in Kamigata (see Volume 2). Plays like *Tokubei from India* and *Masakado* presented the spectacle of an entire palace collapsing *(yatai kuzushi)* before spectators' eyes. The closing scene of *Three Kichisas* required a large lift to bring onto the stage the town's roofs, where the final action took place.

Most of the major technical advances of the period are associated with the ingenuity of technician–set designer Hasegawa Kanbei XI (1777–1841). As a wigmaker, he created trick wigs from which clumps of hair, dripping with blood, were pulled when Oiwa combed her long tresses in *Ghost Stories at Yotsuya*. Among other examples in this volume, Takiyasha reveals her true identity in *Masakado* when her beautifully coiffed hair suddenly comes undone and falls to her shoulders. Kanbei also invented impressive stage devices. He created a dual stage revolve, called the bullseye revolve *(janome mawashi)*, that allowed an actor standing on the small central revolve to then cross onto a larger revolve around it, each revolve moving in the opposite direction. The bullseye revolve opened new possibilities for scene changing and actor movement. Kanbei devised many of the technical tricks for *Ghost Stories at Yotsuya* through which, as noted earlier, Oiwa's ghost appears and disappears. Nanboku's son, Naoeya Jūbei (1781–1831), created the raindoor trick in *Ghost Stories at Yotsuya*, alluded to earlier. Scenery, props, and wigs grew increasingly illusionistic, while costumes became ever more sumptuous, contributing to the growing production costs that plagued the era's managers. For the first time, the stage technician–designer's name appeared on theatre posters alongside those of the star and dramatist.

For more than a century, each kabuki actor had specialized in one type of role, such as leading man *(tachiyaku)*, villain *(katakiyaku)*, comic *(dōkeyaku)*, or female-role specialist *(onnagata)*. Throughout his career an actor could move from one specialty to another—from young female *(wakaonnagata)* to middle-aged woman *(kashagata)*, for example—although actors strove to achieve the highest level of skill within each role type. The new plays in which an actor played many roles of a deliberately different nature conflicted with this long-standing system of role types *(yakugara)*. For example, Iwai Hanshirō V (1776–1847), who was one of the most beautiful and talented *onnagata* in kabuki's history, also played to great acclaim the refined male role *(nimaime)* of Gonpachi in the premier of *Suzugamori*. The previous distinction between the acting styles for male and female roles began to break down during this period, which, in the opinion of some, altered the nature of kabuki art from that time to the present.

Playing multiple roles had an economic impact on kabuki as well. Under the so-called "additional role" *(kayaku)* system, an actor playing a role outside his specialty was paid an allowance for the new costumes required (kabuki actors owned, and paid for, their own costumes in the nineteenth century). For example, when, as mentioned above, Hanshirō played the male-role Gonpachi in *Suzugamori*, his income was raised. Thus the more role types an actor played, the more bonus money *(yonai)* he earned. As a consequence, popular actors had an enormous economic incentive to play multiple roles.

Theatre managers, who competed intensely with other theatres, hated to pay multiple-role bonuses to their stars, but they also believed they had to provide

crowd-pleasing versatility in order to draw large audiences. An actor skilled at playing a variety of role types was known as a "double-duty actor" *(kaneru yakusha)*. He
was, we might say, an actor with a thousand faces, able to transform himself instantly into a character who was male or female, young or old. As we have seen,
among the first famous multirole actors were the fierce rivals Mitsugoro III and
Utaemon III. Other multirole specialists of this period include Seki Sanjūrō II
(1786–1839), who danced the five roles in the first production of *Wisteria Maiden*;
Kikugorō III, who starred in the original transformation dance in which *Yasuna*
was included and who also played Oiwa and two other roles in *Ghost Stories at Yotsuya*; Nakamura Shikan II (later Utaemon IV, 1796?–1852); and Bandō Mitsugorō
IV (1800–1873).

    The leading "man with a thousand faces" of the age, equally skilled at dance
and drama, was Ichikawa Danjūrō VII (1791–1859). Short of stature but famed for
his large eyes and golden voice, he was brilliant in his family's flamboyant bravura
style *(aragoto)*. He was skilled in transformation dances and *kizewamono* and could
play villains as well as male and female romantic leads. His remarkable breadth can
be seen in the variety of roles that he premiered among the plays translated here:
the chivalrous townsman *(otokodate)* Banzuin Chōbei in *Suzugamori*, farmer Kyūsaku in *Osome and Hisamatsu*, and the villainous Yoemon in *Kasane* and Iemon in
Ghost Stories at Yotsuya. The latter two roles represented an important new character type, the erotic villain *(iroaku)*. Dressed in black, exposed arms and legs as
white as his handsome face, and with eyes, brows, and mouth flatteringly outlined
in black, this new role type could make evil dangerously attractive. A bushy yet stylish
wig suggested tonsorial casualness and a fall from better days. Typical of a number
of actors at the top of their careers, Danjūrō VII in 1832 passed his name on to his
son, who became Danjūrō VIII (1823–1854), while he became Ichikawa Ebizō VI.
(To avoid confusion, he is referred to below as Danjūrō VII.)

    One of Danjūrō VII's signal accomplishments was creating the *Eighteen Famous
Kabuki Plays* (Kabuki Jūhachiban), a collection of the Ichikawa family's most popular pieces, two of which—*Just a Minute!* and *The Medicine Peddler*—are translated
in Volume 1. After consultation with various persons, Danjūrō VII created a preliminary list of plays in 1832, calling it the Edo Ichikawa-Style Kabuki Eighteen Group-

ing *(Edo Ichikawa-ryū Kabuki Gumi Jūhachiban)*. The word "eighteen" *(jūhachiban)* here was used in a broader meaning than as just a number; it suggested a group of favorites—which could be more or less than eighteen—of one sort or another. The listing was not made official, however, until Danjūrō VII formally announced it onstage in 1840, the final version being somewhat different from that of eight years earlier. The occasion for the announcement was his premier performance as Benkei in *The Subscription List* (Kanjinchō, trans. Scott 1953 and Brandon and Niwa 1966), a dance-drama based closely on a *nō* play. It was the only member of the collection never previously performed. Following the success of *The Subscription List*, other *nō* and *kyōgen* plays were adapted into kabuki as dance-dramas, borrowing elements of music, dance, and staging from the two earlier theatre forms, including settings that suggested a *nō-kyōgen* stage, hence the name *matsubame mono*, or "pine board plays" (see detailed discussion in Volume 4). The impetus for the collection seems to have been Danjūrō VII's concern that kabuki's old conventions were breaking down, as well as his desire to strengthen his family's position within the acting profession. Later actors in other families would create collections of their own "family art," which may refer either to the plays closely associated with a family or to the acting specialty those plays exemplify.

Despite the widespread emphasis on versatility, some actors—while often capable of playing a broad variety of types—are remembered primarily for their ability in a certain line. Matsumoto Kōshirō V (1764–1838), for example, was indispensable when Nanboku needed a realistic urban villain *(jitsuaku)* in his *kizewamono*. This great star created Naosuke Gonbei in *Ghost Stories at Yotsuya* and the rascally Kihei in *Osome and Hisamatsu*.

Several *onnagata* were renowned for developing a new type of role, the *akuba*, literally "wicked woman," a coarse, sometimes profane, lower-class female also known as "poison woman" *(dokufu)*. Its prototype, a kind of tomboy called *ochappi*, was first created by Iwai Hanshirō IV (1747–1800) in 1792, but—with the addition of a certain depraved charm—was developed for Nanboku's *kizewamono* by the actor's son, Hanshirō V, "the actor with the million dollar eyes" *(mesenryō no yakusha)*. He helped establish the *akuba* when he created the erotic, ponytailed snake handler Dote no Oroku (Oroku of the Canal) in the premier of *Osome and*

Hisamatsu. Despite the name *akuba*, the conniving Oroku is not truly wicked, for, typical of these seemingly perverse women, it is revealed that she had served in a samurai household and that her attempt at extortion is not selfish but rather intended to redeem her clan's stolen sword. Nanboku wrote the *akuba* role of Otomi in *Scarface Otomi* for Sawamura Tanosuke III (1845–1878), an actor of great physical beauty who was only nineteen years old at the time. Otomi, too, engages in extortion, not because of an evil or depraved nature, but out of moral impulses to help her clan.

Playwrights found a ready source of dramatic material for a number of new *kizewamono* in the cheap popular fiction *(gesaku)* that flourished in this period: *yomihon* (didactic historical novels with Buddhist or Confucian leanings), *sharebon* ("smart" books, often about the pleasure quarters), and *gōkan* (popular illustrated tales and romances). With Kamigata's puppet theatre now moribund, kabuki playwrights turned to these popular prose narratives for stories that could be put on the stage. At the same time, kabuki influenced these stories, with pictures of actors on stage illustrating some *gōkan*, for example, while other *gōkan* were written in the form of play scripts. Works in this volume derived entirely or in part from popular fiction include *Suzugamori, Masakado, Three Kichisas, Martyr of Sakura,* and *Gorozō the Gallant.*

Kabuki's presence pervaded Japanese society in the nineteenth century. It was even said that "[n]owadays kabuki doesn't imitate the world, rather the world imitates kabuki." Rare was the city home without an actor print by Utagawa Toyokuni I (1769–1825) or one of his followers. Rare was the traveler to Edo who failed to bring a kabuki print home as a souvenir. Partly as a consequence of hard economic times at Edo's three large licensed theatres (Edo *sanza*), troupes of touring actors took kabuki to some 130 theatres throughout the country, thereby making familiar across the land the names and faces of the city's midcentury stars.

The hereditary managers *(zamoto)* of Edo's three major licensed theatres—the Nakamura-za, the Ichimura-za, and the Morita-za—found it increasingly difficult to pay the mounting costs of staging a yearly season of five or six plays. A provision of the 1794 government regulation, the "Contract of the Agreement for the Control of Theatres" (Kyōgen Za Torishimari Gijō Shōmon), described in Volume 2, declared that if one of the three theatres failed to find financial backing for a season, its actors were to be hired by the other two theatres. This was intended to provide stability to the production system, but it also set a precedent for actors to break the traditional yearly contract with a theatre. By the late 1820s, the system of contracting actors on an annual basis to form a theatre company was no longer universally followed in Edo, and actors felt increasingly free to move from theatre to theatre during the season.

Kabuki in Edo survived because of the alternate theatre *(hikae* [or *kari]* *yagura)* system (described in Volume 2)—a system that faced its ultimate test when, in 1793 and 1797, Edo's three hereditary theatre managers all failed to find financial backers. Production rights for the Nakamura-za, the Ichimura-za, and the Morita-za were transferred to alternate producers and the theatres were renamed the Miyako-za, the Kiri-za, and the Kawarasaki-za (or Kawarazaki-za). Producers continued to lose money through the first half of the nineteenth century. The Morita-za, the smallest and most troubled of the major theatres, faced particular hardship. Between 1800 and 1868, five generations of the producing family, Morita Kanya VIII–XII, attempted without success to run the theatre profitably: the Morita-za was replaced by the Kawarasaki-za for forty-two of those sixty-eight years, and for five years the theatre was either dark or saw its season halted midway due to poor houses. When Ichimura Uzaemon XII (1812–1851) could not raise money to open the season in 1815, his license was transferred to Kiri Chōkiri, producer of the Kiri-za. Two years later, this theatre was deeply in debt and had to pass its license to a third producer, Miyako Dennai. His management failed the following year, and the license passed from the Miyako-za to a fourth producer, Tamagawa Hikojūrō. Within three years the management of the Tamagawa-za had gone deeply into debt as well, and the troupe disbanded in midseason. Finally, in 1821, the Ichimura-za was able to revive its license. Such instability had been unheard of before. During the period covered by this volume, only the Nakamura-za survived intact.

The principal reason that managers fell into tremendous debt was the prodigality of their expenditures. For decades, leading actors had demanded and received astronomical salaries of a thousand or more gold pieces *(ryō)* per year (see Volume 2). The actors, in turn, lavished their money on gorgeous costumes to please and attract fans. Because of intense professional rivalry, each actor sought to vanquish his opponents by the splendor of his appearance, a common occurrence in the theatre in any country where actors are responsible for their own costuming. The Kansei Reforms of the late 1790s had attempted to cap actor salaries at 500 gold pieces a year. During the Kasei period, actors upped the ante, purchasing ever more expensive costumes and demanding salaries exceeding the legal limit. The outside financiers *(kinshu)* who backed the theatres as an investment naturally sought to create hits, so they gathered the top casts available, further raising costs: it was a vicious cycle. Including bonuses for playing multiple roles, a versatile actor could easily cost a producer 1,000 gold pieces. When Kikugorō III asked for 1,200 in 1827, it sparked a dispute with two other stars that culminated in his leaving the company.

During this period, the financier Ōkubo Kinsuke took an active interest in producing as well as providing generous financial support. He arranged for Utaemon III's immensely successful visit to Edo in 1808 and was largely responsible for a remarkable two-decade string of hits at the Nakamura-za during the 1810s and 1820s. He would pay almost anything to have the right actor, giving Utaemon 300 gold pieces in 1818 for appearing in a single play—200 for acting and another 100 for costumes. In 1819, Kinsuke simultaneously supported two theatres, the Tamagawa-za and the Nakamura-za, earning a windfall when, in the third month, he pitted two of the era's most popular actors, Danjūrō VII and Kikugorō III, against each other in rival productions of *Sukeroku: Flower of Edo* (Sukeroku Yukari no Edo Zakura, 1713, trans. Bowers 1952 and Brandon 1975).

In 1828, Edo's three theatres almost did not open the new season. Managers argued that if they continued to pay exorbitant salaries, income would fall short of annual expenses by 1,000 gold pieces, even if they had hit productions. Further, whereas past actors had received one-third of their annual salary at the season-opening *kaomise* (face-showing) production, actors now expected to be paid 60 percent of their annual earnings at the first production. Unable to raise this much "up front" money, managers of the Edo *sanza* were able, at the last minute, to open the season only because city authorities agreed to return to the 1790 salary cap. The great stars Danjūrō VII, Kōshirō V, Mitsugorō III, and Shikan II received the top salary allowed, that is, 500 gold pieces plus 200 for a multiple-role bonus. Supporting actors received 100–150 gold pieces with no bonus; minor actors were paid 10–15 gold pieces for their year's work.

During the Kasei through *bakumatsu* periods, the frequent loss of theatres to fire caused much financial distress, as it had in previous times (see Volume 2). During the twenty-seven-year Kasei period alone, a total of ten fires destroyed the Edo *sanza*, with all three theatres being incinerated in 1829 in a single blaze. Stars survived by touring or joining provincial troupes. Other actors took temporary jobs with minor theatres—a practice the authorities grudgingly allowed, under limited conditions. Some of these theatres were set up in shrine or temple grounds *(miyaji shibai* or *miya shibai); other small theatres (koshibai)* were scattered throughout the city at busy transportation hubs (see Volume 2). Such secondary theatres charged lower admissions and paid lower salaries to actors, yet they were serious competition to the major theatres (known as *ōshibai,* or large theatres), leading their producers to constantly petition the authorities to close the small theatres. In 1829, before the three major theatres were rebuilt, the three principal shrine/temple companies *(sanza no miya shibai)*—at Ichigaya Hachiman Shrine, Shiba Jinmei Shrine, and Yūjima Tenjin Shrine—were allowed to jointly operate a combined company at the Hanazono Inari Shrine in Shinjuku. For a brief time, this theatre was permitted to use the *hanamichi,* draw curtain, and other technical amenities normally reserved for the majors.

Needless to say, theatres in Osaka and Kyoto were also victims of fire and bankruptcy. Our discussion of the situation in Edo simply serves to emphasize the above-noted dominance of Edo kabuki during and after the Kasei period. Kyoto became little more than a destination for Osaka productions, and the number of new plays fell dramatically in Osaka once the long-dormant domestic plays of Kamigata playwright Chikamatsu Monzaemon (1653–1725) began to be staged again in revised versions, beginning in the 1840s.

Changing economic and social conditions were the proximate cause of the gradual decline of kabuki in Kamigata, where production system arrangements had always been more open and informal than in Edo. The distinction between major theatres and second-class theatres (the latter called *chūshibai* and *hama-*

shibai) began to break down, and actors moved rather freely among theatres and troupes. Unlike in Edo, an Osaka or Kyoto producer's license was not hereditary. An interested person could buy the license to produce and become a theatre manager, or *nadai* (literally "name"). When business was slow, the manager would change the troupe, headed by a central actor (*zamoto,* the term used in Edo for producer or manager). It was common in the Bunka period for a theatre in Osaka or Kyoto to have up to four or five different central actors and their troupes pass through during a single season. During the Bunsei period, acting companies moved with increasing frequency from playhouse to playhouse, as many as eight times in a season.

The nation's cash economy was centered in Osaka. Excellent highways connecting cities and towns made it easy and lucrative for Kamigata's stars to tour the provinces. Touring was considered a natural part of Kamigata theatre life, and when local business conditions proved too weak to sustain a company, it quickly went on the road in search of audiences. Provincial castle towns that were the seat of daimyo rule were important calling places for troupes, which often left Osaka in midseason, thus wreaking havoc on the city's theatre schedules. The troupe head might even be a child actor or an actor chosen for his popularity rather than his business acumen. The fact that Osaka theatre customs, such as the elaborate *kaomise* boat parade, were gradually abandoned after the Kasei period was a sign of the faltering conditions.

As some Kamigata customs declined, others arose. One of the most far-reaching changes involved play scheduling. During the Kasei era Osaka producers inaugurated the practice of choosing scenes from several successful older works and putting them on the same program. This system of performing excerpts was called *midori,* meaning "see" and "take." Audiences at an excerpt program were treated to the highlights of several long plays, in effect getting more for their money. Producers found such programs attractive, as it was safer to revive popular known works than produce untried ones, and it was usually cheaper to stage them. All-day plays were still written, but excerpt programs became increasingly popular both in Kamigata and Edo. Many of the plays translated in this volume are *midori* versions of longer plays; they consist of the major scenes that are now commonly staged.

As popular as programming excerpts was, it had an immediate deleterious effect on new playwriting in Kamigata. Osaka's two chief playwrights of the early nineteenth century, Chikamatsu Tokuzō (1751–1810) and Tatsuoka Mansaku (1749–1809), died at the end of the first decade; their plays fell from favor and are no longer revived.

A significant by-product of the new programming was that actors were stimulated to create new and varied stage business *(kata)* in order to make constantly repeated plays interesting to audiences who were ever more familiar with them. More and more, from the mid-nineteenth century "acting was all." Ultimately, a new kind of audience connoisseurship evolved: fans were encouraged to compare great actors' performances of canonical roles, while actors endeavored—within an ever-hardening tradition—to offer fresh insights and approaches.

The top Osaka actors of the first half of the nineteenth century were the highly versatile Utaemon III, already mentioned, and the male-role specialist Arashi Kichisaburō II (later Arashi Rikan II, 1769–1821). Others included Kataoka Nizaemon VII (1755–1837) and Ichikawa Danzō V (1788–1855). Their careers were managed by clever backers (*ginshu* in Kamigata) who selected roles for them and fostered actor rivalries. Backers actively promoted the growing interchange of actors between Kamigata and Edo, with actors from one area occasionally spending considerable time in the other. For example, Osaka's Kataoka Nizaemon VIII (1810–1863) remained in Edo for eight years in the 1850s and became as popular there as in his hometown. Ichikawa Kodanji IV (1812–1866) began his career in Edo, developed it in Osaka, and returned to Edo to find stardom. And Edo's Mitsugorō IV had as fiery a rivalry with Osaka's Utaemon IV as did their identically named predecessors; both actors made several significant trips to their rival's home cities.

Between 1837 and 1844, the government harassed kabuki with a series of petty and annoying restrictions as part of the Tenpō Reforms. For example, actors were ordered not to earn a living in the provinces (1837), but of course they did. Settings at the Ichimura-za were deemed too extravagant (1838); kabuki dancers could not perform at patrons' homes and professional actors could not associate with amateurs (1842); actors could not be depicted on woodblock prints (1842); and actors were told to wear deep straw hats in order to hide their faces in public

(1842). More significant, Edo's Yūjima Shrine theatre was ordered demolished in 1840; in 1842, the town's other shrine theatres were abolished. In the same year, the authorities, incensed by Danjūrō VII's ostentatious style of living, banished him from Edo for seven years. He was forced to tour the provinces and Kamigata, bringing his luminosity to Osaka in 1843. In a similar case, as part of the Tenpō Reforms in Kamigata, Nakamura Tomijūrō II (1786–1855) was banished from Osaka. For two years (1843–1845) he was compelled to make his living in Sakai, with occasional forays to Kyoto and Nagoya.

Although the great Danjūrō VII had his share of flops during his artistic exile, Osaka audiences were especially fascinated by his revivals of the Eighteen Famous Kabuki Plays and productions about the Soga brothers, who were unknown in Kamigata theatre. In 1854, while performing in Osaka with his father, Danjurō VIII killed himself, some say because of crushing debts and the shame of his father's banishment. Perhaps because of the unsettled times, no new Danjūrō was named for a full generation.

The most egregious act of government control over kabuki during the Tenpō Reforms was the 1842 order that forced the three major theatres of Edo to move from their established downtown locations in Sakai-chō, Fukiya-chō, and Kobiki-chō, near where the Kabuki-za stands today, to a newly developed area on the edge of the city—where the present Asakusa is located—not far from the New Yoshiwara (Shin Yoshiwara) pleasure quarters. Prior to that, when the Nakamura-za and Ichimura-za, as well as neighboring puppet theatres, burned down late in 1841, a bureaucrat had asked the powerful city magistrate Tōyama Saemonojō whether kabuki should be allowed to continue. Tōyama—subsequently respected as kabuki's savior—rejected this suggestion. Nonetheless, a year later the shogunate council ordered the theatres to move to the new neighborhood, renamed Saruwaka-chō after the seventeenth-century theatre manager Saruwaka Kanzaburō. Theatre teahouses (shibaijaya) registered a formal petition against the move, but they were promptly fined for their impertinence. In their new setting, far from their old audiences, a few days of rain could spell financial catastrophe for the three theatres, making them struggle more than ever for survival. The Tenpō Reforms, devised by the shogun's chief minister, Mizuno Tadakuni (1794–1851), touched on all aspects of urban life, not just kabuki. By 1844 it became apparent that the reforms were causing an economic depression, and Mizuno was removed from office, thus bringing an end to the reforms. Unfortunately, however, the theatres were not allowed to move back to their cherished former locations. The government was satisfied that they were less of a threat to social order if they remained where they were. Four plays in this volume premiered between 1851 and 1864 at the newly built theatres in Saruwaka-chō: *Martyr of Sakura* at the Nakamura-za, *Three Kichisas* and *Gorozō the Gallant* at the Ichimura-za, and *Scarface Otomi* at the Morita-za.

In Kamigata, the Tenpō Reforms initiated restrictions that lasted in some cases for years afterward. The sale of books or items with the pictures or crests *(mon)* of actors was banned, publication of the annual Kamigata actor critiques *(yakusha hyōbanki)* was forbidden, actors' tombstones were removed from shrine burial grounds, shrine theatres were forbidden (until 1858), and actors' likenesses were banned from votive offerings. Finally, only five major and second-ranking theatres were allowed in Dōtonbori, Osaka's chief entertainment district.

Times were difficult in Saruwaka-chō. In 1849, even the great virtuoso of versatility, Utaemon IV, failed to draw audiences in the ninth-month production at the Ichimura-za. Worried, the managers of the three main Edo theatres postponed the eleventh month's season-opening ceremonies until the New Year's production of 1850 and offered ordinary presentations in their stead. Symbolically, at least, this marked the end of the old annual contract system in which the members of a troupe were determined each fall at the start of the theatre season. As has been mentioned, actors were now changing theatres during the season. The formal *kaomise* production, in which a new troupe had been introduced, began to seem an anachronism and gradually declined in significance.

During the final years of the shogunate, skilled authors Kawatake Mokuami (then called Kawatake Shinshichi II), Segawa Jokō III, and Sakurada Jisuke III (1802–1877) wrote new, quality plays despite the theatre's economic problems. Like their immediate predecessors, they drew their dramatic material from storytelling arts that had reached their artistic pinnacle. Artists who told the humorous *rakugo* tales (sometimes called *ninjō banashi*) and the serious *kōdan* narratives performed at variety theatres *(yose)* were themselves in competition with kabuki. *Ghost*

Stories at Yotsuya was one of the first kabuki plays influenced by *kōdan*. In addition to borrowing stories, kabuki playwrights adapted from *rakugo* and *kōdan* their concrete, everyday, realistic dialogue, which had never been heard on the stage before. For example, Otomi in *Scarface Otomi* begins one speech thus, as translated by Valerie L. Durham:

> Mere woman though I be, I am known far and near as the bold and fearless "Scarface." Yet were it not for these scars, I'd wear painted eyebrows and set myself up as a geisha, or take a patron. I'd have a lover, too, and enjoy a life even more rich and stylish than the eels they serve at Wada and Ōwada. But thanks to the seventy-five stitches of these scars, the world of love and romance has passed me by, there in my house by the cliff at Satta Pass.

This kind of bold, frank talk, especially from a woman, was new to the Japanese stage.

Mokuami, the most prolific, versatile, and consistently successful playwright in kabuki history, refined and developed the *kizewamono* genre introduced by Nanboku and Jokō III. His collaboration with actor Kodanji IV produced a decade-long (1856–1866) series of hits, including *Three Kichisas* and *Gorozō the Gallant*. Mokuami often combined genres and subgenres in the same work. *Three Kichisas*, for example, is a *kizewamono*, a "dashing outlaw play" (*shiranami mono*, literally "white wave play"), and a "fate play" (*ingamono*) as well. Mokuami was notably adept at the latter two subgenres, both new to kabuki, and was even called "the outlaw dramatist," while Kodanji IV was "the outlaw actor." Mokuami's plays are filled with brash and attractive young urban outlaws—thieves, gamblers, murderers, extortionists, cross-dressers, and bandits. The three Kichisas are especially compelling characters who combine several of these attributes. Like Depression-era movie gangsters, these antiheroes struck a chord of familiarity with audiences, who saw in them flawed but somehow admirable and believable persons with whom they could identify.

Characters in fate dramas are bound to one another through a seemingly inescapable network of blood relationships that dooms them to a dark karma (*inga*). A tragic outcome is inevitable, but only after they have repented their immoral deeds. Thus the incestuous siblings in *Three Kichisas* meet their deaths after their sinful relationship is exposed. The symbolic link that ties the seemingly disparate souls of these plays together, revealing their hidden relationships, is often a precious object or a sum of money, as with the hundred gold pieces in *Three Kichisas*. The word "fate" is a litany running through many of these works, including those by Nanboku, Mokuami's predecessor. A good example of a fate-centered speech is in Nanboku's *Kasane*, when Yoemon says to Kasane, as translated by Mark Oshima, "Listen to the workings of fate. . . . I killed Suke, the husband of your real mother, Kiku. The punishment for that crime has gone around and around and now has destroyed your face. This is all determined by our karma from previous lives. I am your father's murderer. All this too is karma, so be resigned to your fate." In Mokuami's *Three Kichisas*, an exemplar of the fate drama, the concept is mentioned again and again. Here are Oshō and Obō speaking, as translated by Kei Hibino and Alan Cummings:

OSHŌ: That we three should meet is indeed a strange twist of fate. Our ap-
        pearances so different, but we share the same thief's heart.
OBŌ: They say a baby who is born in the Year of the Monkey will grow up to
        be a thief. This is the Year of the Monkey.

Otose says, "I almost drowned, but fate must have been on my side because Jūza's father, Kyūbei the greengrocer, pulled me out. He saved my life." And in Oshū's words: "Look at them, so happy and so innocent of what fate has brought them! This, too, must be heaven's retribution for my father's crimes. Ah, truly one cannot do wrong . . ." Characters insist over and over that their circumstances are the result of fate, ultimately weakening their personal responsibility for the extortion, murder, and incest in which they are involved. Fate dramas bear a burden of determinism every bit as heavy as those soon-to-appear European naturalistic dramas that insist that people's natures are formed by environment and heredity.

Collaborating with Kodanji IV, Mokuami gradually deemphasized and even abandoned the deeply ingrained custom of dramatic worlds, or *sekai*, in favor of freshly conceived characters existing in their own contemporary environment. Nanboku's leading figures, such as Dote no Oroku, Iemon, and Gonpachi, created only a generation earlier, were *sewamono* characters still conventionally linked to a historical world—often through being, in reality *(jitsu wa)*, someone other than they claimed, or by the plot device of a stolen clan heirloom. In *Scarface Otomi*, which is based on an earlier play, Mokuami continues this older pattern, relating Otomi to a samurai household, but in *Three Kichisas* and *Gorozō the Gallant* the major characters belong to the domestic world of the play itself. In *Three Kichisas*, an older world, that of Yaoya (Greengrocer) Oshichi, is briefly introduced, but primarily as an inside joke, with little dramaturgical connection to the story. And the ubiquitous stolen heirloom device that appears in the same play does not bear its traditional dramatic function of justifying the relation of *sewamono* characters to a historical world. Mokuami's focus is on the much more immediate idea of a burglarized purse, sought for pressing personal reasons not related to other worlds, typifying the way in which fate works to connect seemingly random souls.

Further enhancing the unique combination of realism and theatricality found in his plays, Mokuami mastered traditional performance conventions such as the ornate, musical rhetoric of monologues called *yakuharai* (or *yakubarai*), delivered in rhythmic seven-five meter and replete with delightful wordplay. He introduced into some of his later plays a new convention called "somewhere else music" *(yosogoto jōruri)*, beautiful background music rationally motivated as emanating from neighborhood musicians rehearsing in a room or building just offstage. He wrote scenes that used puppet-style narrative chanting and music *(takemoto)* to provide character insight and to heighten emotions, as in the first and final sections of *Three Kichisas*. Puppet-derived kabuki plays naturally included *takemoto* narrative music, but it was unusual to use this music in a new play written for kabuki.

One of Mokuami's chief collaborators, Kodanji IV, was a great character actor, a man of unprepossessing appearance who had ascended from the lowest ranks of nonacting theatre employees. His ordinariness was symptomatic of the theatre's changing tastes. He was especially gifted at acrobatics and special effects *(keren)* and awed spectators with aerial tricks *(chūnori)* and quick changes. He became an Edo star with his down-to-earth portrayal of the self-sacrificing village headman in *Martyr of Sakura*, wearing an ordinary kimono rather than a more conventionalized costume. Audiences found his lack of pretension in the role refreshing, and the play was a long-run hit of more than a hundred performances.

One special Kamigata feature during the *bakumatsu* period was the wide popularity of troupes of child actors who performed kabuki *(kodomo shibai)* for adult audiences. Children often play significant roles in kabuki, as they do in this volume's *Martyr of Sakura*. Kabuki, of course, had a long tradition of adolescent male actor-prostitutes *(wakashu)* going back to the early 1600s. Many members of the nineteenth-century children's troupes were kabuki actors' sons, usually under the age of fifteen. By 1757, Kamigata child actors were popular enough to warrant their own annual published critiques. Throughout the nineteenth century, acting in a children's troupe was the first step in an ordinary kabuki actor's career. The best child actors then went on to secondary theatres after the age of fifteen and, with luck, to the majors when they became adults. The first children's theatres in Osaka sprang up on shrine grounds (the term *"miya shibai"* long implied children's theatre). Some low-ranking adult actors, termed "kid actors" *(chinko yakusha)*, were restricted to performing in shrine-ground theatres and consequently sometimes acted in children's troupes alongside the boys. Interestingly, the sons of Kamigata's star actors rarely joined children's troupes, instead receiving their training alongside their fathers in the large theatres.

At this point we must leave behind the benign world of children and step into a zone where giant toads belch sulfurous fumes, where jealous ghosts will not rest until their bloodlust is slaked, and where shapes shift magically before astonished eyes. This volume's plays and dances take us to places where night blankets acts of horror, love's loss inspires pathetic madness, maimed women claim vengeance on cruel men, and oppressed peasants are crucified for seeking redress. Nightmares become reality, swords carve into human flesh, and passionate lovers are revealed as long-lost siblings. In short, in these plays we enter a kabuki realm of darkness and desire.

Three-panel woodblock print by Utagawa Kuniyoshi (1797–1861). Ichimura-za, Edo, seventh month 1847. A rewrite of Nanboku's play by Sakurada Jisuke III and Namiki Gohei III, titled *A Singular Tale of Onoe Kikugorō* (Onoe Kikugorō Ichidaiki), in which the troupe star, Onoe Kikugorō III, played ten roles in honor of the thirty-third anniversary of the death of his adoptive father, Onoe Shōroku I. "Young Man from India" (Onoe Kikugorō III), center, "Princess Karashi" (Bandō Shuka I), right, and "Shiba Zaemon" (Sawamura Sōjūrō V), left, strike a powerful group pose *(hippari mie)* before a herd of magical toads, the largest of which comically squashes two men. Tokubei wears a foreign-influenced costume: a deep blue open robe exotically fringed with gold tassles and decorated with large golden Chinese dragons. Zaemon, dressed for battle, wears full samurai armor and carries two swords and a baton of military command. (Tsubouchi Memorial Theatre Museum of Waseda University)

The Tale of Tokubei from India
Tenjiku Tokubei Ikoku-Banashi

Tsuruya Nanboku IV
TRANSLATED BY PAUL B. KENNELLY

YOSHIOKA SŌKAN'S MANSION

Yoshioka Sōkan Yashiki no Ba

TOKUBEI'S MAGICAL SHIP

Tokubei no Gensōbune no Ba

RETURN TO YOSHIOKA SŌKAN'S MANSION

Moto no Yoshioka Sōkan Yashiki no Ba

THE DESTRUCTION OF YOSHIOKA SŌKAN'S
MANSION

Yatai Kuzushi no Ba

THE SLUICE GATE AT THE REAR
OF YOSHIOKA SŌKAN'S MANSION

Urate Suimon no Ba

1804　KAWARASAKI-ZA, EDO

The Tale of Tokubei from India

INTRODUCTION

This play was first produced at the Kawarasaki-za in the seventh lunar month of 1804 as a five-act summer play *(natsu kyōgen)*. Its title was written with characters spelling out *Otonikiku Tenjiku Tokubei*, but it was meant to be read as *Tenjiku Tokubei Ikoku-Banashi* (The Tale of Tokubei from India), which is how it is usually rendered today. The original Sino-Japanese characters preceding the words *Tenjiku Tokubei* (Tokubei from India) are for "sound" *(oto)* and "chrysanthemum" *(kiku)*, a play on words in which the character for chrysanthemum is substituted for the homonymous *kiku*, meaning "to hear" (a sound). This kind of wordplay is common in kabuki titles, making them maddeningly difficult to translate.

Tokubei from India enjoyed outstanding popularity and established its author, Tsuruya Nanboku IV (1755–1829), as the preeminent playwright of his generation. Nanboku drew on an established genre of Tokubei plays that were, in turn, largely based on a verbatim narrative ascribed to the Edo merchant mariner Takamatsu Tokubei, who had returned from India to Nagasaki on a Dutch ship in 1633. For decades, these plays had been performed in summer as so-called water plays *(mizu kyōgen)*, which used real water to distract audiences from the heat. Nanboku also used the water and added numerous spectacular tricks *(keren)* to emphasize his transformation of the tale into a, at times, chilling ghost play *(kaidan mono)*, in tune with the summer Obon *(bon)* festival in which the spirits of the dead were briefly welcomed home by their families.

The success of the 1804 production of *Tokubei from India* not only resulted in a series of revivals but also ushered in a whole slew of ghost plays. Previously, ghosts had appeared in kabuki to express the yearning of a departed soul. Nanboku—inspired by the new taste of theatregoers for the bloodthirsty and bizarre, an effect of the Bunka-Bunsei (Kasei) era's (1804–1830) social decadence—wrote a series of ghost plays that aimed to terrify audiences. His masterpiece in this vein is *The Ghost Stories at Yotsuya on the Tōkaidō*, translated in part in this volume. In the 1850s, ghost plays began to adopt a more psychological emphasis, and by the early Meiji era (1868–1912), Kasei-style ghost plays such as *Tokubei from India* had fallen from favor.

In the original production, Onoe Matsusuke I (1744–1815), an expert actor in ghost roles and quick-change techniques *(hayagawari)*, many of which he created, starred as Tokubei. The Tokubei acting tradition he established has been continued by the Onoe family line as their family art *(ie no gei)*. The play is renowned for its spectacular tricks and unusual costumes, which represent magic and foreign influences on Japan. The play is also unusual for the multiple and rapid scene changes that contribute to the sense of supernatural uncertainty.

In Act II, which provides the play's major dramatic interest and which is translated here, Tokubei first appears as a ship's captain during a stopover on a return journey from India. He wears a padded costume showing the influence of the Ainu, the natives of northern Japan, who had a reputation for exotic appearance and fierce demeanor. Tokubei regales the Sōkan household with tales of India and unwittingly jogs Sōkan's memory of his lost son. Sōkan is, in fact, a Korean warrior who has failed in his life's aim: to assassinate the shogun. He possesses a sword (Namikirimaru) and mirror, representing two of the three sacred imperial regalia, which enable him to perform "toad magic."

Committing suicide to avoid discovery, Sōkan passes the sword, mirror, magical incantations, and his mission on to Tokubei. Tokubei's dream of flying in a ship and of the magical destruction of Sōkan's mansion are staged as breathtaking spectacle. During the mansion's destruction, produced through a stage technique called *yatai kuzushi*, Tokubei, mounted on a gigantic, fire-breathing toad, appears with Sōkan's head dangling from his mouth. Also deserving mention is Tokubei's swift underwater transformation from blind musician to imperial envoy in Act V. According to a famous anecdote, a local magistrate investigated a rumor, probably spread by Nanboku and Matsusuke I, that Christian sorcery was being used in the play.

The concentration on foreign elements and forbidden topics in *Tokubei from India* is relatively unique in kabuki and explicable by two factors: declining popular interest in kabuki since the late 1780s and a relaxation of official censorship. The policy of national seclusion *(sakoku)* introduced in the 1630s prohibited journeys overseas and the entry of foreigners by ship. Only delegations arriving from China, Korea, and the Netherlands were officially sanctioned. Thus Tokubei's journey was a rarity and bound to capture national attention. Furthermore, his Korean-Japanese nationality and the exotic destination of India were sure to excite the popular imagination, as Korea became well known after two Japanese invasions of Korean kingdoms in the 1590s, ordered by Toyotomi Hideyoshi (1537–1598). Accounts of exotic customs in Indian ports gleaned from Dutch merchants began to trickle into Japan in the early 1700s; to these elements Nanboku added Christianity and Tokubei's Ainu appearance. Christianity, officially prohibited in the 1600s, was associated with miraculous powers.

36

The large Japanese toad (*gama*), which can grow to over a foot in length, is covered with warts and has a glaring expression considered frightening. The Ainu were reputed to believe that lunar eclipses were caused by a toad swallowing the moon. Popular belief holds that the toad can exhale poisonous gas when threatened and that it possesses supernatural powers. Many folktales and plays (including this volume's *Masakado*) exploit this belief, sometimes with a leading character mastering the toad's magic and, with the toad at the character's side, using its powers to overcome enemies.

The play is remarkable not only for preposterous magic and visually brilliant special effects, but also for the dramatic concept of supernatural chaos, which Nanboku continued to explore in plays such as this volume's *Ghost Stories at Yotsuya*.

A text is available in Toita Yasuji et al., eds., *Meisaku Kabuki Zenshū*, vol. 9. Also consulted were videotapes of performances at the Kokuritsu Gekijō (National Theatre of Japan) in May 1972 and the Kabuki-za in July 1990.

CHARACTERS

TENJIKU TOKUBEI, *in reality* DAINICHIMARU, *son of* YOSHIOKA SŌKAN

YOSHIOKA SŌKAN, *in reality the Korean warrior* MOKU SŌKAN, *father of* TENJIKU TOKUBEI

YŪNAMI, *wife of* YOSHIOKA SŌKAN

SASAKI KATSURANOSUKE, YOSHIOKA SŌKAN's *lord*

OKIEMON, *village headman*

SHŪNO UTANOSUKE, *arch-enemy of* YOSHIOKA SŌKAN

YAMANA TOKIGORŌ, *servant of* SHŪNO UTANOSUKE

ATTENDANT

SOLDIERS

STAGE ASSISTANTS, *black-garbed* kurogo

Yoshioka Sōkan's Mansion

(*Offstage musical accompaniment as the curtain is pushed open. The set is the veranda of* YOSHIOKA SŌKAN's *mansion flanked by a manicured brushwood hedge. A large, elegantly painted golden screen stands center, masking a rear door, with low screens right and left.* YŪNAMI, *an old woman dressed in a purple kimono, is at right, and* SASAKI KATSURANOSUKE, *coat draped over somber-colored* hakama, *is at left, in the place of honor, as a foppishly attired* ATTENDANT *enters right to drumbeats.*)

ATTENDANT: A message for my lady!

YŪNAMI: What is it?

ATTENDANT: A merchant ship from Otakejima entered the harbor last night. The captain, Tokubei, is from Takasago in northern Japan. Five years ago he was blown off course and landed in India. He requests permission to visit while he awaits fair weather to return home.

YŪNAMI (*Beside herself with excitement*): He's crossed the seas all the way to India! Surely Lord Katsuranosuke wants to hear wondrous tales of foreign lands!

KATSURANOSUKE (*Jocularly*): It'll be fun to hear some exotic tales! Call him! By all means, call him!

YŪNAMI: Summon him!

ATTENDANT: Yes, madam!

> (*He exits via the* hanamichi. *Lively shamisen and rhythmic sea song are heard.* OKIEMON, *attired in ceremonial kimono and holding a stylish fan, enters leading* TENJIKU TOKUBEI, *long-haired, wearing a loose-fitting ship captain's coat and pants, hands covered with mittens.*)

OKIEMON (*Officiously*): Hurry up! Hurry up!

TOKUBEI: Where are you taking me?

OKIEMON: To the mansion of Lord Yoshioka Sōkan, chief retainer of the Sasaki clan! (*Venomously.*) You proclaimed yourself a mystery man who has traveled far and wide, but after you've spilled your tale it'll be back to oar-pulling for you!

TOKUBEI (*Troubled*): Hmm! This means trouble! They'll yank and jerk me just like the kimono a man wears when he adopts his wife's surname. And they'll stare at me as if I'm a freak!

> (OKIEMON *jealously ad-libs* [sutezerifu] *about* TOKUBEI*'s celebrity status. They reach the door.*)

OKIEMON (*Entering respectfully*): I am Okiemon, headman of Otakejima, and this is Tokubei, a ship's captain, who has traveled to India!

YŪNAMI: Oh! Wonderful! This is Lord Sasaki Katsuranosuke! (*Unable to contain herself.*) Come close, Tokubei! I want to see your costume!

OKIEMON (*Enjoying* TOKUBEI's *discomfort*): Don't be shy, Tokubei! Tell us your tale!

TOKUBEI: Very well. I am Tokubei, ship's captain, originally of Takasago.

YŪNAMI (*Impatiently*): Yes, yes! Tell us your tale!

> (*The* ATTENDANT *spreads a straw mat, and* TOKUBEI *sits cross-legged, center.*)

TOKUBEI: Five years ago I packed all my belongings, set sail, and was blown across the perilous oceans all the way to India and China! Finally, I reached land and immediately felt homesick!

YŪNAMI (*Beside herself*): Get on with the story!

TOKUBEI (*Realizing his power over the audience and slowing his delivery*): Patience! India is a vast country! At first I sailed about one thousand leagues from Nagasaki to

Toronka Island, an evil place! *(Tartly addressing* OKIEMON.*)* I guess you won't want to stay for this!

OKIEMON *(Entranced in spite of himself):* Of course I do! Go on! Go on!

TOKUBEI *(Pompously):* Then pay attention! *(Languid shamisen.)* Toronka Island was Buddha's birthplace. I continued my journey until I landed on another island four thousand leagues from Nagasaki. I climbed a mountain peak where Kōbō Daishi, the great Buddhist teacher, and Bunji, the wise man, held a contest of wisdom.

OKIEMON: What happened then?

TOKUBEI: The ruins of the head monk's villa were inside a huge temple to the Indian god Debi. I walked twenty leagues from the temple door just to reach the villa entrance! Three halls at the end of three corridors, each thirty leagues long, had pillars so large that a seventy-fathom rope would not have encircled one-third. The first hall contained a standing Buddha, the next a sitting Buddha, and the third a sleeping Buddha. The standing Buddha was thirteen leagues high, and his little finger alone was one hundred feet long! *(He pauses, relishing the entranced audience.)* Then I visited the Ryōjusan District where Buddha delivered his first sermon. The merchants set up their stalls on the fourth evening of every month, so it was called the Fourth Day Bazaar, a lively place with kabuki, puppet theatre, and wrestling!

OKIEMON *(Overenthusiastically):* I'll bet the Indian actors were giants, Tokubei!

TOKUBEI *(Testily):* Not at all! They were only half the size of temple steeples in Japan!

OKIEMON: Well, I never!

TOKUBEI: There were three annual rice harvests, and in summer even poor people could afford to burn aloe wood to drive away mosquitoes! *(Slyly.)* I saw more extraordinary things, but, alas, my throat is running dry. Some tea!

OKIEMON: Certainly! *(To the* ATTENDANT.*)* A cup of tea!

(The ATTENDANT *serves tea.)*

TOKUBEI: Anyway, that's what I saw!

KATSURANOSUKE: That was certainly an entertaining tale!

YŪNAMI: Delightful! Another tale, Tokubei! I'll have a word with my husband, Sōkan, to have your ship provisioned.

TOKUBEI *(Enjoying his celebrity status):* Hmm! Shall I stay after all?

YŪNAMI: Please! Stay and drink all you want!

TOKUBEI: Oh, all right!

OKIEMON: You're a lucky man, Tokubei! You can dine like a lord on the splendid fish feast before you! *(With new respect.)* What do you want me to do?

TOKUBEI: Take care of my ship!

OKIEMON: Yes sir! *(He exits right.)*

YŪNAMI: Come indoors!

KATSURANOSUKE: Let's enter together!

YŪNAMI: Certainly, my lord! Come, Tokubei!

> (*Song.* KATSURANOSUKE *and* YŪNAMI *exit via the rear door.* TOKUBEI *peeks through after them.*)

TOKUBEI: No parlor in all of India or Japan rivals this!

> (*He sits cross-legged and strikes a self-satisfied* mie.)

SŌKAN (*Inside the parlor*): Tokubei! Are you there? We must talk! (YOSHIOKA SŌKAN, *wearing a magnificent ceremonial kimono and the two swords of a samurai, enters.*) Tell me of your adventures in India, Tokubei, and I'll allow you to proceed home without a customs inspection.

TOKUBEI: Thank you! Are you Yoshioka Sōkan, lord of the mansion?

SŌKAN: Indeed, I am!

TOKUBEI: I thought so! (*Staring at* SŌKAN's *face.*) You have the face of a man who will perish by the sword before day's end! Oh! What a calamity!

SŌKAN (*Startled*): What's that? Death's shadow hangs over Sōkan?

TOKUBEI: Yes!

SŌKAN: Absurd! I control the heavens and the earth, good and evil, life and death! I am a magician! (*Imperiously.*) You, an ignorant ship's captain, dare deliver such a pronouncement! How can you know life's course? Speak up, Tokubei!

TOKUBEI: I, Tenjiku Tokubei, wandered India for five years learning many things, and although I cannot say exactly where I learned of your fate, I merely warn you to defend yourself!

SŌKAN: Impossible! I am invincible! (*Suddenly recognizing* TOKUBEI *as his lost son, his tone softens.*) Come within and we'll talk.

TOKUBEI: I'll come, but may I ask how you can escape your fate?

SŌKAN (*Nodding sagely*): I'm an old man but not a coward! I'll tell you later, Tokubei.

TOKUBEI: Yes sir!

SŌKAN: Come! This way!

> (*Offstage musical accompaniment. They exit rear, and the curtain closes to* ki *clacks. Soon, the curtain is pushed open to accelerating* ki *clacks, which gradually fade. A single loud* ki *clack. We are in* SŌKAN's *inner sanctum. Vertical panels of orange, purple, and green alternate in the background broken only by the drawing of a gracefully curved willow tree on a light-grey panel at right. A waist-high gold screen, with a picture of a crouching toad, stands in front of the tree.* YŪNAMI *sits center.*)

VOICE OFFSTAGE: An envoy!

> (SŌKAN *enters and sits right of* YŪNAMI. *Lively shamisen and drumbeats.* SHŪNO UTANOSUKE, *attired in the refined golden ceremonial robe of a high-ranking samurai, and* YAMANA TOKIGORŌ, *in brown* hakama, *enter grandly along the* hanamichi.)

40

SŌKAN *(Rising)*: Welcome, Lord Shūno Utanosuke and undervassal Yamana Tokigorō! Please enter my humble home!

UTANOSUKE: I, Shūno Utanosuke, am here on business!

TOKIGORŌ: I, Yamana Tokigorō, accompany my lord!

SŌKAN: Come in, then!

BOTH: We shall!

(Offstage narimono. *They enter and sit right as honored guests.)*

SŌKAN: What is your business?

UTANOSUKE *(Imperiously)*: I come from my lord to recover the precious sword, Namikirimaru, which you lost and were given one hundred days to recover. Time's up! Produce the sword now!

SŌKAN *(Bristling)*: I confess that you entrusted me with Namikirimaru.

UTANOSUKE: Excellent! And the sword?

SŌKAN: I'm still searching.

UTANOSUKE: What?

TOKIGORŌ: Ha, ha, ha! Foolish Yoshioka Sōkan! Again you say that you can't produce Namikirimaru! *(Menacingly.)* The sword!

SŌKAN *(Resolutely)*: All right! *(To* YŪNAMI.*)* Bring Namikirimaru here at once!

YŪNAMI: Yes, my lord!

(Offstage music. YŪNAMI *goes inside and reappears carrying a ritual suicide set, which she carefully places before* SŌKAN.*)*

TOKIGORŌ: What's this? Implements for ritual suicide instead of Namikirimaru? Ah! You can't produce the sword so it's suicide for you!

SŌKAN: I accept responsibility.

*(*SŌKAN *straightens his posture and clutches his long samurai sword, blade pointed at his belly. His attire, a long, loose white shirt and pale brown* hakama, *together with his shoulder-length grey hair, pointed grey beard, and mustache, completes the image of a dignified old man steeled to face death.)*

UTANOSUKE *(Gloating)*: Your life rushes to its end!

*(*SŌKAN *leans forward and plunges the sword into his belly. He strikes a* mie *of intense agony to two* tsuke *beats. His frame collapses, lurching to the side.)*

SŌKAN *(Speaking laboriously through immense pain)*: I was born Moku Sōkan, a Korean vassal. I came to Japan to lead a rebellion against the shogun to avenge Japan's cruelty toward Korea. *(Offstage percussion accompaniment. Head bowed and teeth clenched in determination,* SŌKAN *draws the sword from left to right across his abdomen. A black-robed* STAGE ASSISTANT [kurogo] *relieves* SŌKAN *of the sword and passes to him a circular, magical pouch.* SŌKAN *applies the pouch to the wound and makes a magical gesture with his thumb and forefinger pressed together.)* I mastered toad magic in order to kill the shogun, but I have failed! I must order my lost son, Tokubei, to carry on this mission!

Tenjiku Tokubei (Onoe Shōroku II), kneeling left, is amazed to see his father, Yoshioka Sōkan (Kataoka Nizaemon XIII) commit suicide with the sword brought out by Sōkan's wife, Yūnami (Onoe Kikujirō IV). (Tsubouchi Memorial Theatre Museum of Waseda University)

(*Ominous* dorodoro *drum pattern.* **SŌKAN** *faces right. He raises the pouch over his head and throws it behind the screen. Loud* dorodoro. *A toad, played by a child actor in a costume* [nuigurumi], *bursts through the screen, red tongue lolling from its mouth. The toad faces* **UTANOSUKE** *on the left, who rises in amazement and hurriedly moves right. The toad follows. Stopping in front of* **TOKIGORŌ**, *it cuts a* mie, *slapping its right front leg down and rotating its head to double* tsuke *beats. Rising, it shows its underbelly. It twists its head diagonally and, in a flash, shoots a stare at* **UTANOSUKE**, *posing in a* mie *to double* tsuke *beats.*)

UTANOSUKE: Incredible! To think that Sōkan has kept this secret!

TOKIGORŌ: What magic!

(**SŌKAN**, *teeth bared, sits erect and poses to* tsuke *beats. He summons the toad. In four jumps it reaches its master and rests its leg on* **SŌKAN**'s *knee, gesturing with its right front leg.* **SŌKAN** *painfully pulls himself up on his left knee and poses in a* mie *to double* tsuke *beats. To percussion music he grasps the sword blade and painfully pulls it near as the curtain is closed to regular* ki *clacks.*)

Tokubei's Magical Ship

(*The set is changed, and in a few moments the curtain is pushed open to loud, continuous* ki *clacks. A single loud clack signals the action to begin. At right and left, high ocean waves lap against a ship that extends almost the entire length of the stage. Right is a large, rectangular sail. In the center of the deck* TOKUBEI *is seated on a chair placed before a blue three-panel screen with climbing white flowers. At* TOKUBEI's *elbow is a small earthenware bowl atop a large bamboo cistern.* TOKUBEI *wears a heavy kimono suggesting the powerful geometric patterns of the Ainu. Over this is a long wine-red coat cut in Chinese style, decorated with large green motifs of mythic beasts and red tongues of flame. Enormous sleeves depict with variegated colors scenes of people in hell. Both garments accentuate* TOKUBEI's *foreignness.*)

TOKUBEI: Is this a dream? Where am I?

(Dorodoro. TOKUBEI *bows his head. Drumbeats accelerate. The torso of* SŌKAN's *ghost in white kimono appears amid the waves at left.*)

SŌKAN: Tokubei! Tokubei!

TOKUBEI (*Looking left*): Who's there?

(*Eerie offstage music of flute and shamisen portend communication between ghost and human.*)

SŌKAN: I am your father!

TOKUBEI: This is frightening! How can you be my father?

SŌKAN (*To continuous soft* dorodoro): In my disguise as a *rōnin*, I fell in love with a highborn Japanese maiden and secretly fathered a child. I could not claim you as my son because my true identity would have been exposed. When you turned three we could no longer keep you hidden and had to give you away.

TOKUBEI: So that's what happened!

(SŌKAN *produces the Namikirimaru sword wrapped in orange brocade. The sword, on a black pole* [sashigane] *manipulated by a* STAGE ASSISTANT, *flies from* SŌKAN *to* TOKUBEI, *who catches it and attaches it to his waist.* TOKUBEI *takes out a round, cloth-covered mirror, which he holds in his right hand, shoulder high.*)

SŌKAN: I learned toad magic to evade capture as a Korean spy. You must learn the same magic to carry on my mission! The mirror can make you invisible or alter your appearance. Together, the mirror and Namikirimaru can summon toad magic. But beware! The blood of a man born in the hour, day, and year of the serpent can thwart toad magic! Beware!

TOKUBEI: Yes, father!

(*He poses in a* mie *to two* tsuke *beats. Receiving a small prop toad from a* STAGE ASSISTANT, SŌKAN *throws it toward* TOKUBEI. *It lands in the bowl to one* tsuke *beat. The bowl flips over, and a smaller toad appears in its place.* TOKUBEI *recoils. Smoke puffs up from the cistern. Dorodoro.*)

Tenjiku Tokubei (Onoe Shōroku II) mounts a small platform to better display the recovered sword Namikirimaru. In this production at the Kokuritsu Gekijō (National Theatre of Japan), Tokubei's enemy, holding up the magical mirror, is Hosokawa Masamoto (Kataoka Nizaemon XIII). (Tsubouchi Memorial Theatre Museum of Waseda University)

TOKUBEI: What's this?

SŌKAN: Toad magic! It is time to learn!

        (TOKUBEI *quickly removes his coat to fully reveal his exotic Ainu kimono, and a* STAGE ASSISTANT *spirits it away.* TOKUBEI *jumps erect, arms raised high. He leaps and strikes a* mie, *legs spread far apart, fingertips joined at the waist, to two*

44 tsuke *beats. Emphasized by slow percussion music,* SŌKAN *raises his hands high in front of his face. He drops his hands, indicating that* TOKUBEI *is to follow his example. Regular drumbeats set a ritual atmosphere.* SŌKAN's *fingertips touch, and then, with his right index finger, he swiftly draws three triangles with bases at shoulder height, right and left. After each triangle is completed,* TOKUBEI *imitates his father in the stiff manner of a novice.* SŌKAN *draws arcs right and left, which* TOKUBEI *repeats one by one.* SŌKAN *makes the figure eight, and* TOKUBEI *copies. Both then clasp their hands in prayer to signify the passing of the magic from father to son. The music stops. Silence. As they assume a pose, soft, ominous* dorodoro *begins.)*

SŌKAN: Abracadabra!

TOKUBEI: Abracadabra!

SŌKAN: Heavens wake!

TOKUBEI: Heavens wake!

SŌKAN: Presto!

TOKUBEI: Presto!

(TOKUBEI's *hands sweep wide, and then he brings his outstretched palms together. He rotates his palms twice, nods his head, and leaps erect, arms by his side. His face quivers.)*

SŌKAN: You have the power!

TOKUBEI: I feel the magic! Now for a test! *(Offstage percussion accompaniment. He makes the magic sign and, stepping toward the toad, extends his left index finger. Smoke rises from around the toad.)* Wonderful! I'll soon bring Japan to its knees! The gutters will run with blood! I understand the magic, Father!

(Dorodoro. SŌKAN *hypnotizes* TOKUBEI *to ensure his devotion to the vendetta.)*

SŌKAN: I am content.

TOKUBEI: I'll ruthlessly rove the seas. I'll hide in the clouds and in the water. Magic will be my life!

(TOKUBEI *drops gratefully to his knees, facing front. He places his hands on the ground and bows his head.)*

SŌKAN: Lead the rebellion!

(*Loud drums and* tsuke *beats as the ghost of* SŌKAN *descends into the waves.* TOKUBEI *stands, raising and lowering his right hand to summon a magical beast.* Tsuke *beat. A giant serpent, on a pole operated by a* STAGE ASSISTANT, *emerges right and sinuously flies left.)*

TOKUBEI: Now I'm a magician!

(*A stylized combat scene* [tachimawari] *begins in which* TOKUBEI *demonstrates his supernatural invincibility. One* SOLDIER *enters right and another left. They move to attack* TOKUBEI, *who extends both arms. As he makes the magic hand gesture right and left, the first* SOLDIER *collapses; the second falls on top of the first.* Tsuke *beats.* TOKUBEI *places his right foot on the back of the second* SOLDIER, *draws a magic line with his right index finger in the air, extends both arms, clasps his hands before him, and poses in a fierce* mie *to double* tsuke *beats. Two more* SOLDIERS *lunge from either side. They retreat.* TOKUBEI *lifts his foot and spreads his arms. The* SOLDIERS *leap up.* TOKUBEI's *right arm slices downward. The* SOLDIER *at right somersaults backward and lands in front of* TOKUBEI. Mie *to double* tsuke *beats.* TOKUBEI *briefly scuffles with both* SOLDIERS *and then casts them into the sea at front, one after the other. Two, and then four more,* SOLDIERS *enter right and left.* TOKUBEI *tosses them all into the sea. Lively drum and flute music. During the battle, images of the sea, islands, temples, castles, and famous places in Japan pass below and in front of the action, creating the impression that* TOKUBEI *is flying through the air in his ship at supernatural speed.* TOKUBEI *makes the magic sign. Silence. He poses alone in a triumphant* mie *to two* tsuke *beats.)*

TOKUBEI *(To loud, insistent drums):* I'll rule land and sea! I'm invincible! Death and destruction to all Japan! *(He strides right and faces rear while a black cloth drops and Mount Fuji, capped with snow, appears in the distance. Rotating front, he discovers himself on his old ship with its cistern center at the foot of the mast and a long hut right.)* I can even level Mount Fuji!

*(*TOKUBEI *takes a huge compass with a long wooden handle from the top of the cistern. Transferring it to his left hand, head high, he stamps his right foot, causing Mount Fuji to vanish.* Tsuke *beat.* Mie. *Two more* tsuke *beats and drums. He drags the compass across his belly, magically steering the ship onto a new course. He removes his coat to reveal the upper half of a Dutch ship captain's uniform. A white ruff plunges down a dark-blue silk shirt emblazoned with multicolored emblems to a wide, pale-green sash. He strides to the prow, reveling in his supernatural power. He spreads and drops his arms, staring left, then right, then center. He spreads his arms shoulder high before the palms of his hands spring to his chest. His arms rise swiftly above his head, palms stretched backward, and he extends his neck to an arrogant tilt. His diaphragm relaxes and then fully inflates, forcing his head backward to face the sky. After a preliminary forward-backward shoulder movement, he cuts a* mie *to double* tsuke *beats. Slow percussion before drumbeats accelerate. He poses, gazing with egomaniacal ferocity into the ocean as the ship sweeps across the sea. To* ki *and drums the curtain is pushed closed.)*

Return to Yoshioka Sōkan's Mansion

(Large drums and chanting as the curtain is pushed open. The setting is the parlor inside SŌKAN's *mansion. Large circular flower emblems adorn each of the golden background panels. Three steps at center ascend to the mansion.* UTANOSUKE,

46   TOKIGORŌ, *and a band of* SOLDIERS, *ignorant of* SŌKAN's *suicide, have arrived at lower level left to arrest him and* TOKUBEI. TOKUBEI, *at the head of the steps, is attired in a short-sleeved white half-coat, padded knee-length culottes, and baggy black trousers, which trail several feet behind him in an outlandish fashion. The sleeves and chest of a black mesh undershirt are visible. With his bushy black hair and black makeup delineating his eyes and lips, he cuts a terrifying figure.)*

UTANOSUKE: Tokubei! Stop where you are!

TOKIGORŌ: Don't move!

(UTANOSUKE and TOKIGORŌ draw their bowstrings.)

TOKUBEI: You can't harm me! *(Concentrating.)* Abracadabra! Heavens wake! Presto!

(TOKUBEI makes the magic sign. Dorodoro. The bowstrings snap and the bows break. UTANOSUKE and TOKIGORŌ are stunned.)

BOTH: Hey! What's this?

TOKUBEI: Lost your courage?

BOTH: You shall pay heaven!

(TOKUBEI draws magic diagrams in the air with expansive gestures to ominous drumbeats, then poses in a fierce mie, *praying for power, to two* tsuke *beats. Dorodoro grow louder, and to loud* tsuke *beats, a toad of monstrous size crashes through the golden doors at the rear of the room, smoke billowing around it.* UTANOSUKE *points in horror. The toad forces its way into the room behind* TOKUBEI, *who looks proudly at it. Its mouth opens and closes, its head and body rise and fall, with continuous* tsuke *beats accompanying the movements.* TOKUBEI *commandingly sweeps his right leg in front of the toad, raising both arms wide, and brings his hands together. Fast drumbeats.* TOKUBEI *rolls his head and strikes a* mie. *Double* tsuke *beats. The toad raises its head, opens its mouth, props its front legs on the top step, and breathes fire. As the toad advances farther into the room to furious* dorodoro *and* tsuke, TOKUBEI *mounts its back. Gazing fiercely at his opponents, he performs a long* mie, *hands clasped in prayer before him, eyes wide and glaring at the* SOLDIERS, UTANOSUKE, *and* TOKIGORŌ, *to accelerating* tsuke *beats* [uchiage].*)*

ALL: Incredible!

TOKUBEI: I am a magician! *(Gloating, he makes the magic sign.)*

UTANOSUKE: How weird!

TOKIGORŌ: It's magic!

TOKUBEI *(Menacingly)*: Exactly! Ha, ha, ha, ha!

(Eerie offstage flute and loud dorodoro. *The toad's eyes open and flames rush from its mouth, forcing the* SOLDIERS *to retreat. A single* ki *clack signals the end of the scene. To offstage musical accompaniment and accelerating* ki *pattern, the curtain is pulled closed on this incredible sight.)*

Tenjiku Tokubei (Onoe Shōroku II) poses in a fierce *mie*, kneeling on top of his monstrous toad familiar that, through magic, he has summoned to destroy Sōkan's mansion. (Tsubouchi Memorial Theatre Museum of Waseda University)

The Destruction of Yoshioka Sōkan's Mansion

(The curtain opens, revealing the roof of SŌKAN's *mansion.* TOKUBEI *bestrides the huge toad,* SŌKAN's *decapitated head dangling from its teeth. Two bands of four* SOLDIERS, *led by* UTANOSUKE *at right and* TOKIGORŌ *at left, are mounting an attack.* TOKUBEI *plants himself defiantly, left arm extending outward, palm raised. Double* tsuke *beats. The toad breathes fire on the band of* SOLDIERS *at right and then at left. They recoil. Deafening* dorodoro *drums and continuous* tsuke *beats. The mansion begins to collapse [yatai kuzushi]. Pillars cave in, walls tumble, and the roof dangles.* TOKUBEI, UTANOSUKE, TOKIGORŌ, *and the* SOLDIERS *strike a beautifully balanced tableau [hippari mie] to two* tsuke *beats. The curtain is pulled closed to accelerating* ki *that crescendo in time to accompanying music. Silence.)*

The Sluice Gate at the Rear of Yoshioka Sōkan's Mansion

(Chanting and drums as the curtain is pushed open. The scene is the rear of SŌKAN's *mansion showing a palisade atop a stone wall with a water sluice gate center flanked by pine trees. A man-sized toad appears from the open sluice gate. It*

is confronted by eight SOLDIERS [hana yoten] *dressed in simple but colorful leggings and short tunics with flower designs. The toad self-importantly waddles center and, facing front, makes a kind of self-introduction* [nanori] *through simple, deliberately paced gestures, wiping its face, opening its mouth, and moving its head from side to side. The* SOLDIERS *attack, first one at a time, then in groups. In a comic parody of the kabuki hero defeating a host of opponents, the toad easily deflects each thrust and strike with a deliberate, minimal gesture. Stately drumbeats and* tsuke *give the fight a grotesque, ritual quality.* SOLDIERS *attack singly from left and right. Each time, the toad places a foot on the spearhead and drives off the* SOLDIER *to one* tsuke *beat. Two* SOLDIERS *from opposite sides leap over the toad, which drops both hands and, like a puppet master pulling strings, compels the* SOLDIERS *to somersault forward onto their backs. A* tsuke *beat accompanies each fall. The toad attacks three* SOLDIERS *standing left in single file with spears at the ready. Several times it defiantly raises and drops each leg in turn, stands on its front legs, and kicks its rear legs in the air, routing the* SOLDIERS. *A line of three* SOLDIERS *standing right charges the toad. Nonchalantly, the toad defeats them all to double* tsuke *beats. The* SOLDIERS *regroup left, but the toad casts a spell to continuous, loud* tsuke *beats* [uchiage], *which destroys their resolve. Victorious, the toad waddles confidently right and poses. In an instantaneous costume change* [hayagawari], *the toad is revealed to be* TOKUBEI *in magical transformation.* Tsuke *beats cease abruptly as* TOKUBEI *strides to* shichisan, *resplendent in shining gold costume with indigo coat and black pants. Namikirimaru is securely fixed within a turquoise sash tied in front. He has long, thick black hair, which extends to the middle of his back and is tied with a luxurious gold ribbon.)*

TOKUBEI *(Triumphantly):* Ha, ha, ha, ha, ha!

(To loud drums the curtain closes behind the posing TOKUBEI. *Two blue-coated* SOLDIERS *attack* TOKUBEI *from the rear. He flips them forward in somersaults to sharp* tsuke *beats. He whirls and, in a demonstration of his magic power, raises his arms overhead, and the* SOLDIERS *fall backward, their legs in the air.* TOKUBEI *strikes a powerful* mie *with his right arm above his head, his left arm stretched waist high in front, and his legs together as a continuous* tsuke *pattern* [uchiage] *is played. To strong stick drum, large drum, and song, he forces the* SOLDIERS *back step by step, until they charge past him once, and then again. He gestures, and both* SOLDIERS *drop to their left knees:* TOKUBEI *poses with his foot on the closest* SOLDIER *to double* tsuke *beats.* TOKUBEI *pushes the* SOLDIERS *away. His arms circle wide and return to the center of his chest, in preparation for his final* mie. *He poses, ramrod straight, eyes glaring with an air of invincibility, to furious* tsuke *beats* [uchiage]. *Drums and shamisen music and* tsuke *beats accelerate as* TOKUBEI *makes a leaping "six directions"* [tobi roppō] *exit. He gathers speed and bounds down the* hanamichi, *leaping from one foot to the other until he is out of sight.)*

Three-panel woodblock print by Utagawa Toyokuni III (1786–1864). "*Felicitous Celebratory Sanba* [sō]" (Kotobuki Shiki Sanba [sō]), a version of the dance staged at the Nakamura-za, first month 1859. "Senzai" (Onoe Kikugorō IV), right, holds up a black lacquered box decorated with gold actors' crests that contains the old man, or Okina, mask. "Okina" (Ichikawa Ebizō V, previously Ichikawa Danjūrō VII), center, wears an elegant court robe. He holds out his opened fan toward "Sanbasō" (Nakamura Fukusuke I), left, posed with his tongue stuck out. Sanbasō's raised toe, typical of a *mie* pose, is clearly seen. (Tsubouchi Memorial Theatre Museum of Waseda University)

Sanbasō with His Tongue Stuck Out
Shitadashi Sanbasō

Sakurada Jisuke II (text); Itō Tōsaburō and Kineya Shōjiro I (music);
Fujima Kanjūrō (choreography)

TRANSLATED BY MARK OSHIMA

1812   NAKAMURA-ZA, EDO

Sanbasō with His Tongue Stuck Out

INTRODUCTION

During the Tokugawa period, every kabuki program began at dawn with a sophisticated ritual dance featuring the character of Sanbasō. Performed by a low-ranking actor, the dance was built around three short scenes *(dan):* "waving sleeves and stamping" *(momi no dan),* the conventional "jumping like a crow" *(karasutobi),* and the "bell-tree" *(suzu no dan),* in which the dancer shakes a wand covered with small bells. It would be hours before the major stars appeared and the main play began, so only the most determined fans would attend. Today the dance is performed regularly for the New Year's production, and occasionally at other times as well.

Kabuki's various Sanbasō dances have their origin in the ritual *nō* play *Okina,* which in turn derives from early agricultural rituals intended to ensure prosperity. *"Okina"* means "old man," and the central character symbolizes longevity and eternal youth. *Okina* exhibits many features that are different from *nō* proper, marking it as sui generis: the main actor *(shite)* puts on his mask in front of the audience; the steps at the front of the stage are used for an entrance; the music includes percussion patterns not found in any other *nō* play; and the dance has no plot. The *nō* performance begins with Senzai, played by the secondary actor *(waki),* taking the Okina mask from a small onstage altar. After the *shite* dons the Okina mask, he performs a short, solemn dance and leaves the stage. An actor of comic *kyōgen* roles playing Sanbasō then dances a light-spirited imitation or parody of Okina's movements. Sanbasō is known as the "black Okina," since he wears a black version of the old-man mask.

In old-time kabuki, a more or less faithful imitation of *Okina,* with the addition of kabuki music, was performed on ceremonial occasions such as the dedication of a new theatre or the celebration of an actor taking a prestigious name. However, the *nō* was considered the exclusive property of the samurai class. For kabuki to imitate or borrow from *nō* carried risks. On the other hand, *kyōgen* farces were closely related to early kabuki, and the two forms shared a deep kinship. It was far more appropriate for kabuki actors to perform the *kyōgen* role of Sanbasō than to hazard the *nō* play. As a result, the Sanbasō dance became kabuki's single most important ceremonial dance. In time, it was developed into a variety of independent dances that incorporated all kinds of humorous and entertaining episodes. *Sanbasō with His Tongue Stuck Out* was the first of these variations.

Sanbasō was first performed by Osaka actor Nakamura Utaemon III (1778–1838) in the ninth lunar month of 1812 at Edo's Nakamura-za as homage to the great actor-dancer Nakamura Nakazō I (1736–1790). Its formal title was *Spring Again and Time for Planting the Turnips* (Mata Kuru Haru Suzuna no Tanemaki). The lyrics refer to Nakazō by name and incorporate his nickname *(yagō)*, Sakae-ya, into the text. Utaemon was just concluding a successful series of performances in Edo and was about to return to the Kamigata area. His performance was considered a *nagori kyōgen*, the conventional "farewell" by a visiting out-of-town star, typically given in the ninth and tenth months before the new season began in the eleventh month with the *kaomise* (face-showing) production. In *Sanbasō*, Utaemon recalled his youthful experience of seeing Nakazō perform as Sanbasō in Osaka. On going to Edo, he discovered little trace of Nakazō's dance style and noticed that Nakazō's venerable Shigayama dance school *(ryū)* had seriously declined. He therefore asked Sakurada Jisuke II to write lyrics for a Nakazō-style Sanbasō dance, which resulted in the present work.

Nakazō's Sanbasō dance was distinctive not only for its Shigayama-school style, but because Sanbasō stuck out his tongue in one section. It is said that Nakazō imitated a traditional child's toy, modeled after a humorous character's head whose tongue sticks out when a string is pulled. When Sanbasō, absorbed in the joy of his dance, sticks out his tongue, it greatly enhances his comic charm. This tongue-sticking-out business also became an important part of Nakazō's villain roles, where the tongue is painted bright red for emphasis. Sekibei in *The Barrier Gate*, translated in Volume 2, provides an example. Sticking out the tongue may also incorporate a spell to ward off evil spirits.

The texts of early versions of *Sanbasō* are so obscure as to be untranslatable, being derived from the ritualistic *Okina*. The text of the version translated here is much more understandable; it began a trend of more popular and accessible variations in which Sanbasō is a marionette whose strings get tangled, or competes in athletic and comic routines, or visits the pleasure quarters.

Utaemon III's performance of Jisuke II's new version of *Sanbasō* encapsulated three stages in the history of kabuki dance. From early kabuki through the middle of the eighteenth century, dance had been considered essentially decorative and the exclusive property of female-role specialists *(onnagata)*. The present play pays homage to this traditional role of dance by referring to the Shigayama school at the Nakamura-za, which perpetuated *onnagata* dance. Then, Nakazō I, adopted son of the Nakamura-za's dance teacher, revolutionized kabuki by creating dance roles for male-role specialists. Later, as explained in this volume's introduction, leading male-role specialists *(tachiyaku)* Utaemon III and Bandō Mitsu-gorō III (1773–1831) helped advance the genre of "transformation dances" *(hengemono* or *henge buyō),* in which one actor played a variety of widely contrasting characters, male and female, in quick succession. They also introduced common everyday characters, which until then had been considered alien to the spirit of dance.

If we look at kabuki dance overall, most consist of the actor gracefully illustrating through mime, in both direct and subtle ways, the images or themes of lyrics sung by a musical ensemble. Sometimes the dancer precisely mimes the words; other times the narrative is carried solely by the singers while the dancer moves in abstract patterns or is totally motionless. In other words, the dance actions do not necessarily occur at exactly the same time as the sung lyrics. The link between text and movement is fully broken in a dance's lively conclusion, known as the "dance section" *(odoriji).* Here the movements are rhythmical and largely abstract, probably reminiscent of kabuki's earliest days.

Sanbasō moves through a great variety of moods and methods, from solemn and ritualistic sequences to a folklike atmosphere of work songs to comic and romantic sections. The piece also employs an early example of *kakeai,* the use of two or more contrasting styles of music in the same work, providing musical variety: the rhythmic and melodic *nagauta* music contrasts with the heavier narrative *kiyomoto* music. *Sanbasō* is considered particularly important for *kiyomoto*-school musicians in that it was the first piece performed by Kiyomoto Enjudayū I (1777–1825), the founder of *kiyomoto,* after he had split away from the rival, and now defunct, *tomimoto* school.

In Utaemon III's 1812 premier of this work, the setting imitated a *nō* stage, a tradition largely followed in current performances. This predated the tradition of producing *nō*-originated plays on kabuki's version of a *nō* stage *(matsubame mono),* which began with *The Subscription List* (Kanjinchō) in 1840. At the premier of *Sanbasō,* part of the set suddenly opened to reveal, first, the *kiyomoto* ensemble, then the *nagauta.* Today, *Sanbasō* may be performed with both ensembles or with only *nagauta* or *kiyomoto,* hence the distribution of the music between the two ensembles may differ considerably from one production to another. In the first production, the Okina section preceded Sanbasō's dance, an arrangement rarely seen today except when the dance is performed to commemorate an important ceremonial occasion. Senzai can be played as either a pure *onnagata* role, dressed in a woman's long trailing kimono, or as a delicate, adolescent youth *(wakashu)* wearing a man's kimono and formal *hakama.* Overall, the emphasis is on the old-fashioned elements of the dance and on the imitation of Nakazō. When, on occasion, a modern interpretation of the dance is staged, an abstract set and a less flamboyant Sanbasō costume are used. In such cases, even though the choreography does not change much, the mime is deemphasized, and the representational movements become more abstract.

The translation here is based on the text in Gunji Masakatsu, ed., *Buyoshū*, in *Kabuki On-Sutēji*, Vol. 25, and on professional *kiyomoto* scores.

CHARACTERS

SANBASŌ
SENZAI
STAGE ASSISTANT, *formally dressed* kōken
KIYOMOTO, *one of the two musical ensembles accompanying the action*
NAGAUTA, *one of the two musical ensembles accompanying the action*

(The set is the kabuki version of the nō *stage. A* KIYOMOTO *ensemble of four singers and three shamisen players sits on a single platform* [yamadai], *left, which is covered with a red cloth. A* NAGAUTA *ensemble with five or six singers and an equal number of shamisen players sits along the back of the stage, with singers and shamisen players on a platform* [hinadan] *covered with a red cloth. Also on a red cloth is the* NAGAUTA *flute and percussion ensemble seated directly in front of the singers and shamisen players. To the accompaniment of the* nō *flute and percussion in the* NAGAUTA *ensemble,* SENZAI *enters carrying a lacquered box, which is not used in the dance, but instead recalls the role of* SENZAI *in the original* nō *ritual as the carrier of the box holding Okina's mask.* SANBASŌ *wears a black kimono with auspicious designs and a large robe* [suō] *decorated with a fancifully colored crane arranged so the wings extend along the sleeves. He wears a tall court cap* [eboshi] *decorated on each side with horizontal black-and-gold stripes and a large red sun. The character is plump and round-shouldered, evoking the presence of Nakamura Nakazō I. His face is made up in a* kumadori *pattern, with comically rounded eyebrows high and quizzical, downward-turning red lines at the outside corners of his eyes, and a broad band of red running under each cheekbone, somewhat like a handlebar mustache.* SENZAI, *whether played as a female or as a gentle youth, is costumed in a kimono decorated with numerous felicitous designs worn under a large purple* suō. *On his head is a small black court cap* [eboshi] *with a decorative crown of red and white plum blossoms. The following introductory passage* [okiuta] *may be omitted.)*

56

KIYOMOTO:

Once long ago the great actor Nakazō / traveled to perform in Kamigata. Then, as a child, I was privileged / to learn dancing in the venerable Shigayama style. / Those movements that I learned in my youth remain faintly, / almost forgotten, today. / Oh, the Sanbasō and its wonderful ancient moves! / Ah, Nakazō! May the heirs to your art grow and flourish / as I recall your dance on this stage.

(The flute and percussion players [hayashi] *within the* NAGAUTA *ensemble begin a pattern unique to the Sanbasō tradition. From a seated position,* SANBASŌ *puts his arms straight in front of him and moves his head so as to write the characters for "full house"* [ōiri] *three times. Then he stands and stamps twice, quickly, before moving vigorously in a circle and delivering the fixed opening call of the Sanbasō dance.)*

SANBASŌ: All hear! All hear! Let there be joy! Let there be joy! I will perform the auspicious dance! I vow not to give this wonderful duty to anyone else!

(The shamisen begin playing. This section [momi no dan] *consists of a fixed set of ritual movements in which* SANBASŌ *waves his sleeves, holds them by his shoulder, and stamps vigorously.)*

NAGAUTA:

Like painting with fake purple, / the images produced by this brush cannot possibly equal the original. / This dance is no more than a rough tracing. / It is like a stone tortoise in the water that cannot have life. / Truly it is like a scrawny crow / trying to fly like a magnificent cormorant.

(With sleeves held at his shoulders, SANBASŌ *leaps once, twice, as though trying to fly, then drops to the stage in a humorous pratfall. The music becomes slow and labored as he tries to stand and, in pain, rubs his legs. To energetic music, he sticks out his tongue, waving his head back and forth. Set to traditional music, the lyrics describe Utaemon III in the original performance when he was about to return to the Kamigata region.* SANBASŌ *bows to the audience.)*

KIYOMOTO:

How overwhelmingly welcome, / the warm patronage of the good people of flowery Edo, / the warm weight of their reception / is like the weight of this ceremonial court hat that I wear.

*(*SANBASŌ *sits upstage facing the rear wall. A formally dressed* STAGE ASSISTANT [kōken] *helps him take off the outer robe and cap to reveal* SANBASŌ*'s special wig in the style of a low-ranking samurai servant. The shaved top of the head and narrow side pieces evoke Nakazō I. The* NAGAUTA *ensemble plays slowly and graciously as* SENZAI *dances with a fan, using abstract formal movements vaguely reminiscent of a Shinto shrine performance* [kagura].*)*

NAGAUTA:

Ah, the famous stone cave of ancient legend, / recited in the *kagura* shrine dances. / So does *kagura* give its name to the eleventh month, / the month of celebrating children.

(SENZAI *depicts the first ceremonial visit of children to a shrine at the auspicious ages of seven, five, and three at the Seven-five-three Celebration* [Shichi-go-san no Oiwai]. *Throughout the performance the numbers seven, five, and three are a continuing motif.*)

How old are the children? / Indeed, five, seven, and three. / Their long ceremonial kimonos are covered / with all sorts of auspicious embroidered designs. / Pictures of bamboo, / full of wishes for eight thousand ages of good fortune.

(SENZAI *withdraws to the side of the stage, sitting facing forward in the position of the* waki *actor in* nō. *In the following section,* SANBASŌ *gestures with his fan and a short wand with small bells* [suzu]. SANBASŌ *rhythmically shakes the wand, ringing the bells, suggesting planting seeds. With it, he mimes the images in the song.*)

KIYOMOTO:

The evergreen pine lives for thousands and thousands of years. / The crane and tortoise are models of unchanging longevity. / The sea bream jumps energetically, / while the tail of the lobster curls with good fortune.

(SANBASŌ *mimes these symbols of good fortune. He holds the fan behind him like the tail of a lobster.* SENZAI *comes and sits center while* SANBASŌ *stands right, holding the wand as though it were the rudder of a boat.*)

NAGAUTA:

Symbols of good fortune and / the coming of the legendary treasure boat.

(*Solo singers from the two ensembles alternate singing the plaintive strains of a boat song. The treasure boat is supposed to appear at New Year's from a lucky direction bearing the seven lucky gods and a boatload of treasures. This section combines the image of this legendary boat with the real boats of Tokugawa-period daily life.*)

KIYOMOTO:

Yara, yara. How auspicious!

NAGAUTA:

The four seas are untroubled by wind and waves.

KIYOMOTO:

And the branches of the evergreen pine swell / with luxurious bunches of green needles.

(*Again the music becomes vigorous. In a rush, the singers describe other auspicious images that might be found on the kimono of children during their first shrine visit.*)

Sanbasō (Bandō Mitsugorō IX) dances, shaking a wand of bells and waving his fan behind him like the tail of a lobster. Sanbasō's yellow *tabi* indicate the character's origin in *kyōgen* theatre. (Umemura Yutaka, Engeki Shuppansha)

A carp vigorously swimming up a waterfall. / Chinese lions playing among the peony blossoms. / Vistas of slim Chinese pines.
(SANBASŌ *and* SENZAI *dance together, evoking the festive atmosphere at the shrine on that occasion.*)
What a sight! What a sight!
(*With his fan,* SANBASŌ *suggests a child is perched on his shoulders.*)

NAGAUTA:

> Indeed, what a sight. / The craftsmen have spared no trouble. / What
> an achievement, this fine kimono for a good child. / Put it on and let's
> go! / The little child in an outsize kimono / sits on the shoulder of a
> big man!

KIYOMOTO:

> Put the boy on his shoulders and / let's go to the shrine of our family god. /
> *(Moving rhythmically,* SENZAI *suggests the drums.)* The shrine maiden plays the
> drums with a rat-tat-tat-tat-tat.
>
> *(*SENZAI *mimes playing the flute.)*

NAGAUTA:

> And there is the sweet sound of the bamboo flute, / sounding clearly through
> the air.
>
> *(The singers move from the beauty of the flute to describing a beautiful young girl,
> setting the stage for the story of an auspicious marriage.)*
>
> How clear and beautiful, the eyes of a young girl, / the middle daughter, oh,
> the middle daughter! / The wealthy man of Hitachi says / that he wants her
> to become his bride.
>
> *(The* KIYOMOTO *ensemble plays a slow, deliberate shamisen interlude accompa-
> nied by percussion and bamboo flute. The melody is one often used in kabuki dances
> based on* kyōgen *farces. With exaggerated solemnity,* SANBASŌ *mimes a samurai
> retainer getting ready to act as messenger with a marriage request. First he mimes
> carrying a tray holding ceremonial clothes. He puts on a formal wing-like vest
> [kataginu]* and dons *hakama. Then he puts two swords in his obi and attaches a
> bag with a pipe and tobacco pouch at the back. He mounts an imaginary horse and
> rides off. The elaborate preparation makes the actual message a kind of humorous
> anticlimax.)*

KIYOMOTO:

> Tōnai Jirō gets on a chestnut horse. *Ei, Ei, Ei. (Whipping the horse on its way.)*
> Riding slowly and importantly, he goes on this important errand, giving the
> message of his lord requesting a marriage.
>
> *(As the singers introduce the next section,* SANBASŌ *and* SENZAI *prepare, facing
> the back of the stage.)*

NAGAUTA:

> When the match has been arranged, / an auspicious day is selected for the
> ceremony / and the bargain is sealed with an exchange of lavish gifts.
>
> *(*SANBASŌ *and* SENZAI *mime the array of gifts.)*
>
> What are the gifts? / A jeweled makeup case, a coral comb, / all in a carrying
> box of crystal. / How impressive, all of these boxes and bundles / and the
> great procession carrying them!

(To a rhythmical interlude by the NAGAUTA *shamisen,* SANBASŌ *and* SENZAI *stamp rhythmically and mime carrying a framework on a bamboo pole containing presents to seal the marriage arrangement. Finally, they mime putting down their burden, then pose. To music suggesting the work song of baggage porters, they suggest an old couple together, signifying a wish for long years of happy married life.)*

KIYOMOTO:

May we be together until I am a hundred and you are ninety-nine.

NAGAUTA:

As husband and wife, we will be happy together / with one another, until our hair grows white.

(The next sequence, sometimes omitted, is a lamentation [kudoki], which expresses the feelings of a female character. Very short, it shows the sexual directness typical of kabuki's female characters, connecting the image of fertility with that of marriage and children. It is danced by SENZAI, *who illustrates the narrative with appropriate movements directed to an imagined partner and occasionally to* SANBASŌ.*)*

KIYOMOTO:

Even though she has grown old enough to go as a bride, / still, she knows nothing of the world. / As she is carried in a palanquin to her new home, / her thoughts go anxiously to what awaits her. / She worries, bashful and afraid of doing the wrong thing. / The new pillow of the first shared bed, / what words should be exchanged, what she should do, as mouth and mouth meet.

NAGAUTA:

The sake of the wedding toast—she cannot drink, / but her husband encourages her, and her ears grow bright pink. / Her face as well takes on the crimson of the leaves in autumn. / As her face colors, even so does she change her kimono / to robes of different colors for different parts of the ceremony. / Then they go toward bed. / She is full of fear, but half overcome with joy. / She does not have the courage to walk fast / and dawdles, lingering behind.

KIYOMOTO:

They grasp each other's hands and there is the sound of birds at dawn, / urging them together as the morning sky grows white and the moon slowly fades.

(The singers progress quickly through the following lyrics while SANBASŌ *and* SENZAI *remain still.)*

NAGAUTA:

Bride and groom are now husband and wife, / and in six short months she wears a maternal sash.

KIYOMOTO:

Eventually there are grandchildren and great-grandchildren. / Can there be any greater joy? / The heart jumps with a lively dancing song.

(The final sequence, the lively "dance section" [odoriji], is performed with hand gestures.)

NAGAUTA and KIYOMOTO:

The flowers have blossomed, blossoms of pure gold. / They are at their height and bloom fragrantly. / How fabulous, these golden flowers.

KIYOMOTO:

If you want some flowers, / I will give them to you. / Here, I will break off a branch. / Who shall this go to? *(SENZAI mimes a courtesan on parade while SANBASŌ mimes the attendant holding a parasol above her.)* The blossoms will adorn the hair of an adorable courtesan. / It is a world of love.

NAGAUTA:

Truly, it is a world of love.

NAGAUTA and KIYOMOTO:

How wonderful!

(SANBASŌ comes forward with his fan and bell tree for the bell-tree section [suzu no dan], one of the most important parts of the ritual. Shamisen music begins slowly and gradually grows faster. SANBASŌ holds the fan and bell tree high in front of him and shakes the bells sharply as he brings down fan and bell tree. First he makes seven strokes of the bell tree, then brings it together with the fan back to the top with a big, round sweeping gesture. Then five strokes of the bell tree, then up again, and finally three more strokes. Ringing the bells constantly, he now backs up three steps, circles the stage, and poses. The brief concluding section [odoriji] brings the dance back to the original performance style.)

KIYOMOTO:

Soon I must leave Edo and its wonderful audiences.

NAGAUTA:

I hope again to spread these felicitous seeds here / for a thousand springs, ten thousand ages . . .

KIYOMOTO:

Ages and ages to the end of time . . .

NAGAUTA and KIYOMOTO:

Now in this festive, auspicious age. / Here ends the dance.

(SANBASŌ and SENZAI come forward and pose as the curtain closes.)

Two-panel woodblock print by Utagawa Toyokuni III (1786–1864). Ichimura-za, fifth month 1848. "Farmer Kyūsaku" (Ichikawa Uzaemon XII), left, peddles chrythanthemum leaves to "Oroku of the Canal Bank," (Ichikawa Kodanji IV), standing. Oroku's husband, "Demon's Gate Kihei" (Ichikawa Danjūrō VIII), smoking a pipe, looks on contemptuously. All the characters wear sober, indigo-dyed cotton kimono appropriate to commoners; in typical kabuki fashion the designs are nonetheless elegant and eye-catching. (Tsubouchi Memorial Theatre Museum of Waseda University)

The Scandalous Love
of Osome and Hisamatsu

Osome Hisamatsu Ukina no Yomiuri

Tsuruya Nanboku IV

TRANSLATED BY VALERIE L. DURHAM

THE KOUME TOBACCO SHOP

Koume Daichi Tabakoya no Ba

THE KAWARAMACHI ABURAYA PAWNSHOP

Kawaramachi Aburaya no Ba

1813   MORITA-ZA, EDO

The Scandalous Love
of Osome and Hisamatsu

INTRODUCTION

The Scandalous Love of Osome and Hisamatsu was first performed at the Morita-za in Edo in the third lunar month of 1813; it proved such a hit that the run was extended into the following month. In its entirety, it consists of three acts in eight scenes. The chief playwright for Acts I and II (including the scenes translated here) was Tsuruya Nanboku IV (1755–1829).

Written when Nanboku was fifty-eight, *Osome and Hisamatsu* is considered one of his masterpieces and continues to be performed regularly. It belongs to a group of plays that gain inspiration from the tragic love story of Osome, an Osaka merchant's daughter, and Hisamatsu, a young apprentice serving in her family's household. The most famous is the 1780 puppet play *The Balladeer's New Tale* (Shinpan Utazaimon), the source for *Nozaki Village* (Nozaki Mura), translated in Volume 2. Nanboku's 1813 play uses many of the role names and situations standardized by this earlier work, while resetting the tale in Edo. A more literal rendering of the title would be *Osome and Hisamatsu: Their Scandal as Spread by Broadsheets.* "Broadsheets" *(yomiuri)* is an allusion to the *utazaimon* in the title of the 1780 play; both *yomiuri* and *utazaimon* refer to ways in which, before the advent of modern newspapers, the latest news and scandals were spread by woodblock-printed broadsheets, the contents of which were publicized by itinerant balladeers.

Although the play is customarily performed in its entirety, this translation consists only of the last scene from Act I ("The Koume Tobacco Shop") and the first scene of Act II ("The Kawaramachi Aburaya Pawnshop"), which focus on the husband and wife extortion team of Kimon no Kihei and Dote no Oroku. A brief synopsis of the preceding scenes is necessary to understand the excerpt translated here.

Hisamatsu was the son of a samurai family but lost his position when his father was forced to commit suicide in atonement for the loss of the sword Goō Yoshimitsu, a treasure of the clan in which he served as a samurai retainer. Hisamatsu has become an apprentice at the Aburaya Pawnshop in hopes that he will be able to find the lost sword. He has fallen in love with Osome, the daughter of his employer, who has been betrothed against her will to Yamaga Seibei, an apothecary.

The theft of the Yoshimitsu sword was engineered by Yachūta, a samurai serving the same clan as Hisamatsu. His lackey, Kihei, however, then pawned it at the

Aburaya and pocketed the money for himself. Kihei's wife, Oroku, once served in the same clan mansion as maid to Takekawa, Hisamatsu's older sister. When Oroku and Kihei eloped, Takekawa intervened and saved them from punishment, and the couple now eke out a living running a tobacco shop on the outskirts of the city. The section translated here revolves around the attempt of Oroku and Kihei to raise the one hundred gold pieces needed to redeem the Yoshimitsu sword.

In the opening scenes that precede the excerpt translated here, the farmer Kyūsaku comes to the Myōken Shrine to sell *yomena*, a kind of wild chrysanthemum with edible leaves. Also at the shrine is Zenroku, the head clerk of the Aburaya, who is plotting to take over the pawnshop. As a first step toward that goal, he has gained possession of the Yoshimitsu sword's certificate of authenticity. Kyūta, an apprentice at the Aburaya, learns of Zenroku's plot, and Zenroku tries to get rid of him by giving him money so he can elope with a maid. But Kyūta instead uses the money to eat blowfish *(fugu)*. Unfortunately, Kyūta has also just eaten glutinous rice—commonly believed to be fatal when eaten with blowfish—and apparently has died. Zenroku temporarily hides the sword's certificate in a bunch of Kyūsaku's chrysanthemum greens, but when Kyūsaku refuses to sell him this bunch, a fight ensues in which Kyūsaku is wounded and his jacket ripped. As recompense, the Aburaya employees give him a used kimono. Both this kimono and the bunch of chrysanthemum greens play important roles in the acts translated here.

Although most plays using the world *(sekai)* of Osome and Hisamatsu depict the lovers committing double suicide *(shinjū)*, this work ends on a congratulatory note, with Hisamatsu killing Kihei to gain repossession of the Yoshimitsu sword, thus ensuring that he will be reinstated to his former position and united at last with Osome.

Osome and Hisamatsu was written during an age when quick role changes *(hayagawari)* by actors playing multiple roles in the same play were in vogue. As hinted by the play's alternate title, *The Seven Roles of Osome* (Osome no Nanayaku), this play features a virtuoso performance by the main actor in seven different roles. The original version had the actor playing Osome, Hisamatsu, Oroku, Takekawa, Osome's mother Teishō, Hisamatsu's fiancée Omitsu, and the farmer's wife Osaku, changing roles more than thirty times. (Modern productions often substitute the role of the geisha Koito for that of Osaku as the seventh role played by the actor.) Many of these role changes take place onstage, in split-second transformations that never fail to delight the audience.

The scenes translated here do not derive their impact from such quick role changes; they succeed as pure drama and are counted among the best and most representative of Nanboku's oeuvre. The scenes are examples of the "raw domestic play" *(kizewamono)* form that Nanboku made famous—grittily realistic depictions of the life of the lower classes. The main characters, Dote no Oroku and her ne'er-do-well husband Kimon no Kihei, are also quintessential Nanboku character types. "Dote" refers to the banks by the canals leading to the Yoshiwara licensed quarter, where Oroku once ran a teahouse. "Kimon," or "Demon Gate," refers to the north-easterly direction, considered unlucky; it alludes to the location of the Osaka house of the historical Osome. Both nicknames symbolize the characters' current status as social outsiders.

The character of Dote no Oroku is of historical significance as the first well-known example of the *akuba* role type, characteristic of late Edo-period kabuki. Although the characters for *akuba* literally mean "evil old woman," such figures are not old, nor are they truly evil. Rather, *akuba* are attractive women in their prime, and unlike earlier kabuki representations of feminine evil, characters like Oroku are heroines in their own right, rather than simply foils for a male protagonist. The evil acts they commit are always for some higher cause, usually involving a lover or feudal lord.

The crime most closely associated with the *akuba* is extortion, and the highlight of the typical *akuba* play is the extortion scene *(yusuriba),* which culminates in the *akuba*'s bravado speech of defiance, called a *tsurane.* (See the discussion of kabuki's most famous *tsurane* in the introduction to *Just a Minute!,* translated in Volume 1.) Somewhat contradictorily, the noticeably comic element of the second scene in this translation is another characteristic of *akuba* plays: it serves to remind the audience that the *akuba* and her male cohort are not completely evil.

Osome and Hisamatsu standardized the conventions of both the *akuba* and the extortion scene. The play's influence can be seen clearly in such later works as the 1864 *Scarface Otomi* (Kirare Otomi) by Kawatake Mokuami, translated in this volume. The role of Oroku herself proved so popular that Nanboku wrote another play featuring Oroku, *Even the Irises Are Dyed with Edo Purple* (Kakitsubata Iro mo Edozome), in 1815.

Dote no Oroku was originally played by Iwai Hanshirō V (1776–1847), whose father, Hanshirō IV (1747–1800), is generally credited with having invented the *akuba* role. Famous both for his beauty (he was given the nickname "Mesenryō," literally Eyes Worth a Thousand Gold Pieces) and his dramatic skill, Hanshirō V starred in many of Nanboku's productions. Hanshirō V's performance of this role still influences modern actors, particularly in Oroku's *tsurane* in the extortion scene.

Another of Nanboku's favorite actors, Matsumoto Kōshirō V (known as "Big-Nosed" [Hanadaka] Kōshirō, 1764–1838), played the evil yet not entirely unlikable Kimon no Kihei. Ichikawa Danjūrō VII (1791–1859) rounded out the cast in the secondary but pivotal role of Kyūsaku.

In later years, this Edo play was performed almost exclusively in the Kamigata region. It reentered the standard repertoire with a 1934 revival by the Zenshin-za troupe, starring Kawarasaki Kunitarō V (1909–1990) and using a script adapted by Atsumi Seitarō (1892–1959), which became the standard version used today. Other actors who have starred in this play include Nakamura Utaemon VI (1917–2001), Nakamura Jakuemon IV (b. 1920), Bandō Tamasaburō V (b. 1950), Ichikawa Ennosuke III (b. 1939), and Nakamura Fukusuke IX (b. 1960).

This translation is based primarily on the scripts for a 1993 production at the Kabuki-za and a 1999 production at the Nissei Gekijō. Reference was also made to scripts in Tsubouchi Shōyō and Atsumi Seitarō, eds., *Ō Nanboku Zenshū*, Vol. 6; Urayama Masao and Matsuzaki Hitoshi, eds., *Nihon Koten Bungaku Taikei*, Vol. 54; Fujio Shinichi, ed., *Tsuruya Nanboku Zenshū*, Vol. 5; and the Atsumi Seitarō adaptation in Toita Yasuji et al., eds., *Meisaku Kabuki Zenshū*, Vol. 15. Stage directions in the scripts have been augmented by observation of live and videotaped productions, in particular a 1977 production at the Kabuki-za and the 1999 production at the Nissei Gekijō.

CHARACTERS

DOTE NO OROKU, *proprietress of the tobacco shop at Koume*
OKATSU, *maid of* TAKEKAWA
ICHI, *an outcast*
KYŪTA, *apprentice at the Aburaya Pawnshop*
KIMON NO KIHEI, DOTE NO OROKU*'s ne'er-do-well husband*
GONPEI, *lackey of* YACHŪTA
KYŪSAKU, *farmer from Iozaki*
KAMEKICHI, *hairdresser*
TARŌSHICHI, OSOME*'s uncle, the master of the Aburaya*
ZENROKU, *head clerk of the Aburaya*
KUSUKE, *employee at the Aburaya*
CHŌTA, *apprentice at the Aburaya*
YAMAGAYA SEIBEI, *apothecary and fiancé of* OSOME
SHOP ASSISTANTS
TWO PALANQUIN BEARERS

The Koume Tobacco Shop

(The stage is dark as the scene changes, and the large stick drum [ōdaiko] *plays the* tsunagi *pattern linking this scene with the previous one. The* ōdaiko *then stops and the background musicians begin* giri to nasake *[duty and compassion], slow and somber music meant to evoke the atmosphere of a lower-class neighborhood. A spotlight comes up to focus on two actors sitting center. At the signal of a single, sharp* ki *clack, the song stops, with only the shamisen accompaniment continuing. Now the lights come up to reveal a run-down, thatch-roofed cottage in Koume, on the outskirts of Edo. This is the dwelling of* KIMON NO KIHEI *and* DOTE NO OROKU, *which also serves as a tobacco shop. Right, on the raised* tatami *platform inside the house, is a large box decorated with a tobacco-leaf design. Above it, tobacco leaves have been hung to dry on a line strung inside the shop, and a sign made of three diamond-shaped boards hung vertically on the veranda pillar, right, advertises tobacco. The walls are stained; center, a split curtain hides the interior of the cottage from view. At left is a low folding screen, and next to the veranda stands a small towel rack. At right is a shed connecting with the cottage. A barrel-shaped coffin stands next to the shed; a sign on the pole next to it describes the corpse it contains as that of a nameless young boy who has died by the wayside. Next to the coffin, the outcast* ICHI *is taking a nap. It is twilight, and the darkness and desolate setting, combined with the outcast and a coffin, create a mood of foreboding.* OROKU, *seated center inside the cottage, is reading a letter from her former mistress,* TAKE- KAWA. *The letter has been brought by* OKATSU, TAKEKAWA's *maid, who sits left.* OROKU *wears a brick-colored kimono with a bold white check pattern and a black satin collar. Underneath, she wears a flowered cotton kimono, its edges visible at the hem, and underneath that an underskirt of very light blue. Her black satin obi is tied in front in a simple, tab-like bow, revealing an underside in the black-and-yellow plaid check known as* kihachijō. *In the manner typical of a woman of the lower classes, she wears no under-collar, and her hair is tied back in the simple "horse-tail"* [uma no shippo] *style, the only ornament a half-moon-shaped boxwood comb inserted in the side locks on the right side of her head. Her shaved eyebrows and blackened teeth announce* OROKU's *status as a married woman. As is typical of the* akuba *role type, the hair above the forehead, parted in the middle, has been cut short in bangs that stick up in the "cockscomb"* [tosaka] *fashion.* OKATSU *wears the costume typical of maids at samurai mansions, with a black-and-yellow checked kimono and a black satin obi tied in a straight diagonal bow.)*

OROKU: Thank you, Okatsu, for coming all this way. And how fares my lady Takekawa?

*(*OROKU *speaks in the low-pitched voice of a woman of the lower classes, but the extreme politeness of her diction as she talks to* OKATSU *reflects her former position in a samurai household.)*

OKATSU: After visiting the shrine at Yanagishima today on a pilgrimage on behalf of her lady, she wrote that letter for you as she was waiting for the return boat.

OROKU: I see. *(Rolling up the letter.)* Please be so kind as to inform your mistress that I shall soon visit her at the mansion to speak with her in more detail. *(Puts the rolled-up letter in the bosom of her kimono.)*

OKATSU: Certainly, ma'am. I do not know the nature of your business, but I shall give Lady Takekawa your message. *(Bows slightly.)*

OROKU: Please do. *(She fastens the cords of the now-empty letter box and returns it to* OKATSU.*)*

OKATSU: Yes, ma'am.

*(*OKATSU *bows politely, with the fingers of both hands on the floor. The outcast* ICHI *suddenly stands up and yawns, then comes over to the women. He is barefoot and dressed in rags. His closely cropped hair is dull and unhealthy looking, and he keeps scratching himself, as if suffering from a skin disease or vermin.)*

ICHI: Missus, I'm going to get a drink. Would you mind looking after this stiff until I get back?

(As she turns to address him, OROKU *raises one knee and crosses her arms over it in a casual pose. She now reverts to lower-class speech patterns.)*

OROKU: What? The dead traveler? You've got to be kidding!

ICHI: I'll just be a minute.

OROKU: Who was he, anyway?

ICHI: A boy, just fifteen or sixteen, still with his forelock. He kept saying, "My stomach hurts, my stomach hurts!" and then he suddenly dropped dead. Looks like blowfish poisoning.

OROKU: Poor thing!

ICHI: I'd be much obliged if you'd keep an eye on him.

OROKU: Hurry back, then.

ICHI: Be back before you know it! Oh, I could really use a drink!

(Ad-libbing, "Be back soon!" ICHI *exits right to shamisen accompaniment.)*

OKATSU: Life is so . . . *exciting* around here, isn't it?

OROKU: I am ashamed that you had to see that.

OKATSU: And where is your honorable husband today?

OROKU: "Honorable husband"? *(At first she doesn't understand that* OKATSU *is speaking of* KIHEI; *then she titters, amused to have her husband referred to in such a polite manner.)* That's a good one. My old man's at the bathhouse right now.

OKATSU: Please give him my regards. *(Bows lightly.)* Well, it is time for me to take my leave. *(Bows again, this time more deeply.)*

OROKU: Must you go already? I'm sorry I couldn't have shown you the proper hospitality.

70   OKATSU *(Taking up the letter box and rising)*: Thank you for your kindness. *(Steps down from the raised platform of the house and puts on her sandals.)* Mistress Oroku, we shall meet again soon. *(Bows.)*

OROKU *(Rising on her knees)*: Okatsu—please convey my greetings to everyone back at the mansion. *(Sits down again and bows politely.)*

OKATSU *(Standing left, by the veranda)*: Yes, ma'am, I shall.

    (The two exchange parting bows, and OKATSU, *carrying the letter box, exits left to* giri to nasake. *The music then stops as* OROKU *takes out the letter from the bosom of her kimono and unfolds it once more. She glances at it briefly before she begins to speak.)*

OROKU: It seems that my lady's younger brother, Master Hisamatsu, who now serves in a townsman's household, has located the clan's heirloom sword that he has been seeking. But he will not be able to gain possession of the sword without the one hundred pieces of gold necessary to redeem it. Now my lady asks me to help get the money. But when even my lady herself cannot raise such a sum, how can I and my husband hope to, living hand-to-mouth as we do? *(Pause.)* But she is my former mistress, to whom I owe my life. (OROKU *lowers her eyes briefly in respect, remembering her debt of gratitude to her former mistress.)* Oh, certainly there must be some way to raise those hundred pieces of gold *(pause)*, mustn't there?

    (Voice and shamisen now begin "Higashi Kazusa" ["Eastern Kazusa"], *another slow and gloomy tune evoking the atmosphere of life in the poorer quarters. Deep in thought,* OROKU *exits inside through the divided curtain. Meanwhile,* KIHEI *enters along the* hanamichi, *returning from the public bath. He wears a kimono in a large dyed check of black and grey with a black collar. His obi is of rough beige home-spun, and his bare feet are thrust into wooden clogs. His topknot is luxuriant and worn on a diagonal; that, and the grown-out hair on his pate, tells us that he now lives on the fringes of society. Heavy black makeup marks his eyebrows, eyes, lips, and chin, hinting at hidden evil in his character. In his left hand, hanging from a cord, is an earthenware jug of sake and a small packet wrapped in bamboo bark; the cotton hand towel* [tenugui] *he used at the bath is thrown jauntily over one shoulder. He is followed by* YACHŪTA's *lackey,* GONPEI, *who wears the usual lackey's costume of a black kimono hitched up in back and small triangular patches* [kyahan] *tied around his legs directly beneath his knees. They stop,* KIHEI *at* shichisan *and* GONPEI *behind him.)*

GONPEI *(Half-crouching in an aggressive pose, as if ready to spring at* KIHEI *)*: Hey, Kihei! Does this mean that you're not going to return the Yoshimitsu sword?

KIHEI *(Facing the stage, speaking insolently over his shoulder to* GONPEI *)*: Your master, Yachūta, ordered me to steal it, and so I did. But then I pawned it at the Aburaya—and spent all the money. Tell Yachūta that if he wants the sword, he'll have to cough up the hundred pieces of gold to get it out of hock. Bunch of fools!

GONPEI: No, Kihei, he's not going to like that at all.

KIHEI: Like it or not, you can't get water from a dry well.

GONPEI: You'd better watch it! *(He raises his fist, about to strike* KIHEI, *but when* KIHEI *turns around to glare at him,* GONPEI *thinks better of it. Turning around, he runs back up the* hanamichi.*)* I'm not going to forget this!

(The musical accompaniment momentarily ceases.)

KIHEI: Gone, is he? Well, I may talk big, but I never should've embezzled the money of my ancestral lord. Now I'm hounded every day for the sword's return. If only I could get my hands on a hundred pieces of gold and dig myself out from this mess! *(*"Higashi Kazusa" *begins again, with song and shamisen, and* KIHEI *proceeds to the stage. When he steps onto the stage proper, the song stops, with only the shamisen continuing.)* Wife! I'm back!

OROKU *(Emerging from inside):* What, already? That was a quick bath. *(She goes right, where she kneels and begins preparing* KIHEI's *dinner tray.)*

KIHEI: You know me, three shakes and I'm out. *(Removes his clogs and steps up into the room, going to stand center, to* OROKU's *left.)* I bought some sake. *(Hands her the jug.)*

OROKU: That's nice. And what did you get to eat?

KIHEI: The usual—mud snails with miso and pepper-leaf sauce.

OROKU: What? That again?

(He hands OROKU *the packet wrapped in bamboo bark, and they pause briefly in a stylized pose,* KIHEI *standing as he hands down the packet and* OROKU *sitting as she receives it.* OROKU *then begins preparing* KIHEI's *dinner tray while he goes to hang his hand towel on the towel rack, left. To shamisen accompaniment of* yotsu-dake aikata *[*bamboo castanets*]* KYŪSAKU *enters right, dressed as a farmer. He wears a dark kimono hitched up in back, and under it, shin-length trousers in light blue. His* tabi *are black, and he wears sandals [*zōri*]. He carries yoked baskets, empty except for a single bunch of edible chrysanthemum greens—the same bunch of greens in which* ZENROKU, *the head clerk of the Aburaya, hid the certificate of authenticity for the Yoshimitsu sword in the play's first scene.* KYŪSAKU's *jacket [*hanten*] is ripped, and his forehead bears a fresh wound from the quarrel that broke out when he refused to sell his chrysanthemum greens to* ZENROKU. KYŪ-SAKU *glances at the coffin and the sign next to it as he passes by, then peers into the shop.)*

KYŪSAKU: Excuse me, but I'd like some tobacco. *(Sets his yoked baskets down by the side of the cottage, right.)*

OROKU: Just a moment. *(Goes left to the large box decorated with the tobacco-leaf design and gets out some tobacco.)* There you are. *(Hands tobacco to* KYŪSAKU.*)*

KYŪSAKU (Giving OROKU a coin): Much obliged. (Takes a look inside and sees KIHEI's dinner tray.) Oh, I see it's time for your evening sake. What're you having with it?

KIHEI (Standing left): Snails with miso and pepper-leaf sauce.

KYŪSAKU: I've got something better than snails. There's a leftover bunch of chrysanthemum greens in my basket. I'll sell them to you cheap. How about eating them boiled?

KIHEI: Chrysanthemum greens? That's nothing special, but show me what you've got.

KYŪSAKU (Picking up the greens): Here you are.
(Hands KIHEI the chrysanthemum greens; he takes a look.)

KIHEI: What's this? The leaves have all turned red. I can get as much of this stuff as I want by the ditch over there.

KYŪSAKU: But I'll let you have it cheap.

KIHEI: I wouldn't want it even for free. (Rudely tosses it down on the veranda. Shamisen accompaniment momentarily stops.)

KYŪSAKU: I just can't seem to get rid of this bunch of chrysanthemum greens!
(Picks up the bunch of greens from where KIHEI threw it and puts it back in his basket. KIHEI sits down to his dinner, with OROKU serving him. Shamisen accompaniment resumes as KAMEKICHI enters left. He wears a dark kimono and wooden clogs with white tabi. A hairdresser's rat-tail comb is stuck in his hair; in his right hand he carries a folded cotton kimono, and in his left a wooden box containing his hairdressing tools.)

KAMEKICHI: Hey, boss! Can I do you?

KIHEI: My hair? It's too late today. Come back tomorrow, early.

KAMEKICHI (Bowing): Will do. (To OROKU.) Missus, this cotton kimono has gotten pretty grimy. I'd like to have you wash it for me, and also mend it where it's ripped.

OROKU: Sure. I'm busy during the days, but I'll work on it in the evenings.

KAMEKICHI: I appreciate it. (Goes right, toward KYŪSAKU.)

KYŪSAKU: Excuse me there, hairdresser. Would you mind fixing my hair a bit for me?

KAMEKICHI: A country man, I see. Well, it's almost dark, but if it's just your hair, I'll fix it up a bit.

KYŪSAKU: I'd be much obliged. Just a quick job will be fine.

KAMEKICHI: Boss, do you mind if I put my tools here? (Gestures to the edge of the veranda, right.)

KIHEI: Put them wherever you like.

KAMEKICHI: Thanks. (Places his toolbox on the edge of the veranda.) But there's no place to sit. (Looks around him, then has an idea and slaps his knee.) We're in luck. There's a straw mat right over here. (Takes up the straw mat that has been placed *on top of the coffin.)* Here, you can sit on this. *(Spreads it on the ground in front of the coffin.)* Have a seat.

KYŪSAKU: Isn't that the mat that was on top of the coffin of that dead traveler?

KAMEKICHI: So what? We'd better get a move on before it gets too dark to see.

KYŪSAKU *(Dubiously):* That may be true, but it still gives me the creeps.

KAMEKICHI: You sure have a lot to say! What does it matter, anyway? Come on, let's get started.

(KIHEI and OROKU watch from inside, KIHEI drinking and OROKU smoking a long-stemmed pipe, as KYŪSAKU kneels on the straw mat upstage right. KAMEKI-CHI takes his hand towel and places it over KYŪSAKU's shoulders. He then notices the wound on KYŪSAKU's forehead.)

KAMEKICHI: What's that, a cut on your forehead? Your jacket's torn, too. Were you in a fight or something?

KYŪSAKU *(Chuckling wryly):* Yes, that's right. I was in a little quarrel with some Edo people today at Yanagishima, and I got hit.

KAMEKICHI *(Fixing KYŪSAKU's hair):* And what was the quarrel about?

(As they talk, he straightens KYŪSAKU's topknot and then smoothes the side locks.)

KYŪSAKU: It was just a silly thing, really. It all started because they wanted me to sell them a bunch of chrysanthemum greens, and I refused. So they hit me, and that was how I got this cut.

KAMEKICHI: That was a piece of bad luck! They hit you and ripped your jacket—did you let them get away with it?

KYŪSAKU: Well, then another fellow stopped the quarrel. He gave me a silver coin to buy ointment for my injury and a lined kimono in place of the jacket that had been ripped. *(Thinking.)* From what I heard just now, it seems that the missus here takes in sewing. Is that right?

OROKU: Well, I'm no good with expensive silk kimonos, but I'll do it if it's made of cotton.

KYŪSAKU: Well, then, I wonder if you could alter that kimono for me.

OROKU: Yes, I'll do it when I've got some extra time.

KYŪSAKU: No hurry. And could you also mend my ripped jacket?

OROKU: Just leave them here when you go.

(Gestures with her pipe to the veranda in front of her. KAMEKICHI takes the towel from KYŪSAKU's shoulders.)

KAMEKICHI: Your hair's done. *(Begins putting away the towel and tools.)*

KYŪSAKU *(Standing):* Much obliged. *(Opens his purse and offers KAMEKICHI some coins.)* Hairdresser, please settle for this.

KAMEKICHI: What? That's all?

KYŪSAKU: I'm a country man. Be a good fellow and give me a discount.

KAMEKICHI: You drive a hard bargain! *(Chuckles good-naturedly and accepts the money. He folds up the straw mat and puts it away by the side of the cottage.)* By the way, show me the kimono you got.

(KYŪSAKU gets the kimono and shows it to KAMEKICHI.)

KYŪSAKU: This is it.

KAMEKICHI: That's a nice stripe. *(Looks more closely.)* Oh, the tag's still on it. Let me see. Hey, this is from the Aburaya Pawnshop in Kawaramachi in Asakusa. It must have been an unredeemed pledge.

KYŪSAKU *(To himself):* The Aburaya in Kawaramachi—that's the shop where young Master Hisamatsu is in service. I had no idea. . . . I should never have gotten into a fight with them.

KAMEKICHI *(Slaps his knee, remembering):* Oh, I forgot! I've got a loan association meeting tonight. *(Hands kimono back to KYŪSAKU. To KIHEI.)* Boss, do you mind if I leave this toolbox here until tomorrow morning?

KIHEI: Sure, go right ahead.

KYŪSAKU: And I'll just leave my jacket and kimono over here. *(Places them in front of OROKU.)*

OROKU: Sure. Come back for them in a couple of days.

KYŪSAKU: I surely appreciate it. *(Picks up his yoked baskets and their solitary bunch of chrysanthemum greens.)* Well, it's time to go home and get some supper.

KAMEKICHI: Until tomorrow, then. *(Bows.)*

KYŪSAKU: Good-bye.

(To shamisen accompaniment, KYŪSAKU exits right and KAMEKICHI left. The shamisen accompaniment stops, and a temple bell sounds in the distance, signaling both the fall of evening and the beginning of a new section in the scene. KIHEI and OROKU are lost in thought, contemplating how to raise the one hundred gold pieces that each needs—KIHEI to pay off YACHŪTA and OROKU to give to TAKE-KAWA. Suddenly, they both hit on the same idea at the same time. OROKU drops her pipe and picks up KYŪSAKU's ripped jacket, rising to her knees. The dialogue that follows is in rhythmic, stylized "seven-five meter" style [shichigochō], each line growing louder until climaxing at "We need to be free of debt.")

OROKU: If we use as evidence this jacket's torn sleeve . . .

KIHEI: And the wound on the forehead that that man suffered . . .

OROKU: And if we can also use this lined kimono . . .

KIHEI: That he received as payment for being struck . . .

OROKU: As proof for the claim we make, then we can blackmail . . .

KIHEI: Indeed, extort, the hundred pieces of gold . . .

OROKU: We need to be free of debt.

(They look at each other, startled to realize that they each have been thinking the same thing. OROKU drops the jacket and sits down again, twisting her body slightly away from KIHEI.)

KIHEI: Wife, it's time to light the lantern.

OROKU: Yes, dear.

(The temple bell tolls once more. A light drum pattern indicating the sound of the wind [kazaoto] rattling the wooden frame of the house begins and continues throughout the scene, adding to the sinister atmosphere. KIHEI sits, thinking, as OROKU gathers up KYŪSAKU's ripped jacket and striped kimono. Standing, she poses briefly, the garments folded over her left arm, holding KIHEI's dinner tray with her right hand. A single, very faint beat of the tsuke marks her pose. She goes inside to get the lantern. Now KIHEI also stands up and, stepping down barefoot from the raised platform of the house, goes over to the coffin, right. He lifts the lid and puts it to one side. Placing his right hand on the rim of the coffin, he puts his left hand in the breast of his kimono and looks inside the coffin with an exaggerated, stylized motion. The temple bell tolls again. Spotting KAMEKICHI's toolbox on the veranda, KIHEI goes over and takes out a straight razor. He holds it up to look at the blade, rejects it, and chooses another. He then goes to the shed behind the coffin, right, and brings out a whetstone and a small wooden basin. Placing the basin on the ground in front of the coffin, he hitches up his kimono and crouches before it. The temple bell sounds again. KIHEI moistens the whetstone and begins to sharpen the razor blade. He looks left, then right, to make sure that he is not being watched. The temple bell sounds. KIHEI takes a hair from his head and tests the razor on it. Satisfied that the razor is sharp enough, he puts the basin away on the veranda. Then, holding the razor between his lips, he goes over to the coffin. He glares at it for a moment, then kicks it over with a sudden, violent movement. The corpse rolls out, the motion emphasized by loud clacks of the tsuke. Holding the front flaps of his kimono up and away from his legs to facilitate movement, KIHEI goes to shichisan as the tsuke plays the batabata pattern symbolizing running. There, with the razor still held between his lips, he poses in a mie, marked by three strong beats of the tsuke, followed closely by another sounding of the temple bell. Shamisen accompaniment and kazaoto resume. Still at shichisan, KIHEI looks around cautiously as he tucks the back hem of his kimono into his obi. He then returns to the corpse. He unties the corpse's obi; as he does so, the corpse rolls over and over on the ground to beats of the tsuke. KIHEI poses in a mie, holding one end of the obi with both hands and thrusting his left leg forward. Three beats of the tsuke are heard, followed by the temple bell. Throwing down the obi, KIHEI lifts the corpse into a sitting position facing the audience, in the same position that KYŪSAKU sat when KAMEKICHI fixed his hair. KIHEI removes the corpse's kimono, leaving it in light-blue trousers and pink under-jacket with a black collar and sleeves in an indigo and light-blue flax-flower pattern. KIHEI brings over the basin and sets it on the ground next to the corpse. He wets the corpse's forehead in a gesture recalling KAMEKICHI's ministrations to KYŪSAKU earlier. Then, taking the razor from his mouth, he shaves off the corpse's forelock. He puts the basin back on the veranda but keeps the whetstone in his hand.

A production by the Zenshin-za troupe of the "Koume Tobacco Shop" scene. Kimon no Kihei (Kawarasaki Chōjūrō II) poses beside the corpse of Kyūta while Dote no Oroku (Kawarasaki Kunitarō V) attempts to hide his action by covering the lamp with his cloak. (Tsubouchi Memorial Theatre Museum of Waseda University)

Next, he spins the corpse around so it is facing him. The shamisen accompaniment stops. He prepares to wound the corpse on the forehead with the whetstone, first posing in a mie *with the whetstone brandished above his head to two* tsuke *beats. The temple bell booms. Then, to a loud beat of the* tsuke, KIHEI *gives the corpse a single, sharp blow to the forehead. The corpse collapses with the force of the blow.* OROKU *comes back out from inside the cottage. She is now wearing a short blue-and-white* hanten *with a bold design associated with the acting family of the actor playing* OROKU.)

OROKU: Kihei, what are you doing with that corpse?

KIHEI: Wife, hold your tongue.

（ICHI *returns, right.*）

ICHI: Hey, what are you doing to that stiff?

（*Seeing that* KIHEI *is up to something,* ICHI *attacks him. They scuffle briefly in a stylized fight* [tachimawari] *marked by beats of the* tsuke. ICHI *is played by an acrobat; when* KIHEI *kicks him,* ICHI *does a back flip and balls himself up as if he has been knocked out.*）

KIHEI: Wife!

OROKU: Kihei!

KIHEI: Watch out!

> (KIHEI *swiftly places the coffin over* ICHI, *then jumps on top of the coffin and sits cross-legged, grabbing his left foot with his right hand and thrusting out his left arm, the hand in a fist. At the same time,* OROKU *takes off her jacket, red lining out, and drapes it over the lantern to cut the light. A single, sharp clack of the ki [ki no kashira] signals the end of the act. They pose in a "pulling tableau" [hippari mie] to two beats of the tsuke. The shamisen accompaniment resumes, along with the repeated clacking of the ki [kizami] that signals the closing of the curtain. The large drum is sounded as the curtain is run shut.)*

The Kawaramachi Aburaya Pawnshop

> (*Before the curtain opens, a lively accompaniment of* "Shitō Kokoro" ["The Longing Heart"] *begins, the shamisen and song joined by bamboo flute [shinobue] and stick drum [taiko] playing a pattern meant to recall the sound of festival music. This creates an atmosphere appropriate to the next scene, set in a bustling downtown neighborhood. The curtain opens to accelerating ki clacks, revealing the Aburaya Pawnshop in Kawaramachi, near Asakusa in Edo. The shop has two tatami-floored levels, one at stage level, the other a platform raised above it. Left can be seen the outside wall of the whitewashed storehouse in which the pledges are stored. A sliding door at center separates the shop from the inner rooms of the establishment. Cupboards line the wall at left center. Right, several oil barrels are visible in an earthen-floored area level with the stage, as the Aburaya is an oil shop—the literal meaning of its name—as well as a pawnshop. Hanging above this area is an indigo-dyed curtain with white characters reading* "Abura" [Oil]. *A similar, smaller curtain hangs over the shop's entrance, represented by a door frame set at right angles to the stage. Inside the shop at right is a low desk where* ZENROKU, *the head clerk, is doing the accounts with the pawnshop proprietor,* TARŌSHICHI, OSOME's *uncle. At left sits* KUSUKE, *who is checking the paper-wrapped pledges. Next to him sits the boy apprentice* CHŌTA. *They are all dressed in the manner typical of tradesmen, in sober kimono and white tabi.* ZENROKU, KUSUKE, *and* CHŌTA *wear black half aprons, and* CHŌTA, *in the manner of a boy apprentice, wears light-blue trousers under his kimono.* TARŌSHICHI, *as befitting his status as proprietor, wears a haori.* ZENROKU's *hair is in the standard style for slightly comic head clerks, with his topknot arranged in a circular shape.* CHŌTA, *who has not yet come of age, still wears his forelock.)*

TARŌSHICHI: Next.

ZENROKU: Number 3171. Pawned by Kisuke, guarantor Kyūhachi. A lined kimono of striped Santome cotton. Pawned for one silver coin and four hundred coppers.

78

KUSUKE: Right.

ZENROKU: Number 3465. Pawned by Denbei, guarantor Kyūshichi. A mosquito net and three unlined kimonos. Pawned for two silver coins.

KUSUKE: Right.

ZENROKU *(To TARŌSHICHI):* Let's stop here.

TARŌSHICHI: Good idea.

ZENROKU *(To KUSUKE):* Kusuke, it's time for a break.

KUSUKE: Yes, sir. *(Bows politely.)*

ZENROKU *(Accompaniment stops briefly. To CHŌTA):* Boy, bring us some tea.

CHŌTA *(In a high-pitched, drawn-out voice):* Y-e-e-e-e-e-s.

(CHŌTA goes inside. "Shitō Kokoro," with shamisen, song, bamboo flute, and stick drum, resumes as YAMAGAYA SEIBEI enters along the hanamichi. *He is dressed in the sober manner of a respectable merchant, with a brown kimono, blue* haori, *white* tabi, *and straw sandals [*zōri*]. The singing stops when he reaches the shop entrance, with the shamisen accompaniment continuing.)*

SEIBEI: Good day. It is I, Yamagaya Seibei.

TARŌSHICHI *(Putting away the accounts book):* Well, well. Please come in. *(Still seated, he bows and gestures for SEIBEI to enter.)*

SEIBEI: Thank you.

(SEIBEI removes his shoes and enters the shop. He goes to seat himself on the upper level, in the position of honor, left, KUSUKE sitting to SEIBEI's left.)

TARŌSHICHI: Well, Master Seibei. How good of you to come. *(Facing SEIBEI, he bows politely.)*

SEIBEI: Tarōshichi, I heard from the go-between, Master Sashirō, that you had a little problem yesterday at Yanagishima.

KUSUKE: Please be so kind as to convey to Master Sashirō my thanks for his coming to my aid. *(Bows.)*

SEIBEI: Yes, I will. *(Avuncularly.)* You're a good worker, but you've got to watch that quick temper of yours.

KUSUKE *(Bowing deeply):* I humbly beg your pardon.

SEIBEI: And now I must meet with Mistress Teishō.

TARŌSHICHI *(Bowing and gesturing toward the inner rooms):* Please go right in.

(SEIBEI bows lightly, rises, and exits through the sliding doors. The shamisen accompaniment momentarily ceases. TARŌSHICHI rises and goes to sit left in the position vacated by SEIBEI, where he takes out his pipe and begins to smoke.)

ZENROKU: Boy! Where's that tea?

CHŌTA *(From inside, in the same high-pitched, drawn-out voice):* C-o-o-o-o-o-ming!

(Comes out with the tea. A new tune, "Kokorozukushi" ["That Letter, Written from the Heart"], begins, with song and shamisen and a lively accompaniment of bamboo flute and stick drum, signaling the entrance of OROKU along the

hanamichi. *She is now wearing a kimono in a bold black-and-white check, and over it the short* hanten *from the previous act. Her obi is also the same black-and-yellow plaid obi from the previous act, but it is now tied in a large, pendulous bow in front so that more of the yellow plaid side is visible. She wears thick-soled sandals on bare feet and carries a cloth-wrapped bundle. After a brief pause at* shichisan *she steps onto the stage, where she stops at the entrance to the shop.*)

OROKU *(In polite tones, her voice more high-pitched than it was in the last scene):* Pardon me. Is this the pawnshop known as Aburaya Tarōbei's of Kawaramachi?

KUSUKE: *(Coming to the door):* Yes, this is the Aburaya. How may we be of service?

OROKU *(Diffidently):* I've come on a little matter of business.

KUSUKE: I see. You've come to pawn something, right?

OROKU: No, that's not it. I've got something here that I'd like you to take a look at.

KUSUKE *(Puzzled):* Something you want us to look at? Well, in any event, if you will be so kind as to come in. *(He politely motions her inside.)*

OROKU: Thank you, I will.

KUSUKE: Please come this way.

　　　(OROKU *bows briefly and enters. Demurely, she seats herself on the* tatami *of the lower level of the shop at right.* KUSUKE *sits to her left.*)

KUSUKE: So, what might it be that you wish to show us?

　　　(Opening the cloth-wrapped bundle, OROKU *takes out the lined kimono from the previous scene.)*

OROKU: I would like to know if this kimono came from your shop. Please be so kind as to take a look. *(She slides the kimono toward him over the floor.)*

KUSUKE: Let me see what you've got. *(When he begins to unfold the kimono, he is puzzled to recognize it. He goes left to where* TARŌSHICHI *sits on the upper level.)* Say, Uncle. Isn't this the kimono we gave to that country fellow yesterday at Yanagishima?

　　　(The shamisen accompaniment briefly stops.)

TARŌSHICHI *(Putting away his pipe):* Let me see.

KUSUKE: Please take a look. *(Hands him the kimono and sits left.)*

TARŌSHICHI *(Examining the tag):* Yes, this is definitely the kimono we gave to that chrysanthemum greens peddler. *(To* OROKU.*)* Who are you, and how did you happen to come by this?

OROKU: I am honored to make your acquaintance. *(Bows politely with her fingers touching the floor. Shamisen accompaniment resumes.)* I come from Kasai, where I live with my younger brother. Last night, when he came home, he said that today, at the Myōken Shrine in Yanagishima, he'd gotten into a little fight over some trifling matter. He received a slight wound to the forehead, and it seems the other party felt sorry about this, because they gave him one silver coin and that lined kimono. Or so he said. *(Her tone suddenly darkens.)* We're poor folk, and I wondered if this kimono might really have been stolen from somewhere. I was so worried that I couldn't sleep even a wink last night. So that is the reason I have come here today, to ask you in person. *(She again bows politely, with her fingers touching the floor.)*

TARŌSHICHI: Oh, is that it? Yes, it's just as your brother said. Yesterday, he had a slight disagreement with Kusuke here at Yanagishima. There was a little scuffle, and so we gave him that kimono and one silver coin in apology.

(Shamisen accompaniment stops.)

OROKU *(Makes an exaggerated gesture of surprise. Loudly):* What? So it's true that you hit my brother!

TARŌSHICHI *(A bit reluctantly):* "Hit" might be putting it a bit strongly, but . . .

OROKU *(Her voice lowers and her eyes take on a cold gleam):* You struck him, did you, sir? *(Suddenly, her attitude changes from obsequiously polite to menacing; her speech grows louder, and she begins to speak in the vernacular of the lower classes. She shifts her pose from a polite posture with her legs tucked under her to a more casual backward slouch.)* So, you beat him up, did you? Well, I've brought him here to thank you in person. Please be so kind as to meet with him. *(She rises and exits the shop. Facing the far end of the* hanamichi, *she calls out in a loud voice.)* Hey! This is the place!

(She raises her hand to beckon to her companions. Another lively tune, "Tanda Ute Ya" ["Just Beat the Drums"], begins, with shamisen, voice, and an accompaniment of bamboo flute and stick drum. From along the hanamichi *enter two* PALANQUIN BEARERS. *They wear their kimono hitched up like short jackets over their loincloths and are barefoot. Twisted towels tied around their foreheads serve as sweatbands. They are led by* KIHEI, *who now wears a kimono with large brown-and-white check, a blue striped* hanten, *and wooden clogs* [geta].*)*

KIHEI: Wife! You're sure this is the right place?

OROKU: That's what they said, so it must be true.

KIHEI: Well, then, you guys with the palanquin—carry him into the shop.

PALANQUIN BEARERS: Right, boss!

(They carry the palanquin through the gate and onto the lower level of the shop. KIHEI *follows them in. Meanwhile,* OROKU *remains outside the gate, where she removes her jacket.)*

KUSUKE *(Standing up):* What do you mean, bringing a palanquin in here like that?

KIHEI: Shut your traps. *(To the* PALANQUIN BEARERS.*)* Dump him over there!

PALANQUIN BEARERS: Sure thing.

(To tsuke *beats that accentuate the action, they tip the palanquin sideways and unceremoniously dump out the corpse from the previous scene. The body lies face upward, limbs outstretched. Tied around its forehead is the triangular patch of white cloth identifying it as a corpse.* ZENROKU, KUSUKE, *and* CHŌTA *come over to look at him.* OROKU *now comes back into the shop.)*

KIHEI: Just leave the palanquin over there. You can come pick it up later.

PALANQUIN BEARERS: Will do.

> *(They leave the palanquin outside the entrance and exit right. A light shamisen accompaniment continues.)*

KUSUKE: Oh, no—it's the chrysanthemum greens peddler from yesterday.

ZENROKU: If that peddler's dead, how am I going to get the sword certificate back? *(Suddenly realizing that he shouldn't have said this, he covers his mouth.)* What am I going to do? Oh my, oh my!

KIHEI *(Standing in the middle of the shop and looking around):* Hey, you've got quite a nice spread here. *(To* OROKU.*)* Wife, get them to give us some tea.

OROKU *(To* KIHEI*):* Yes, dear. *(*OROKU *goes center, a sign that she is taking charge of the negotiations.* KIHEI *sits right, his arms tucked inside his kimono. Standing,* OROKU *now addresses the shop employees in an insolent fashion. The low pitch of her voice and her lower-class diction are in contrast to her earlier polite demeanor.)* Hey, you!

KUSUKE: Yes, ma'am? *(He comes over and kneels in front of* OROKU.*)*

OROKU: Sorry to *bother* you, but could you let us have a cup of tea? And there's nothing to light my pipe with. *(*KUSUKE *stares at her with horrified fascination, too overcome by shock to move.)* What're you just lollygagging around like that for? I said give us some tea. And a light for my pipe. I said I need a light! What's this —*(the shamisen accompaniment stops, and there is a pause as she tosses down her* hanten *and sneers)*—afraid of fires or something?

> *(She flicks the hems of her kimono between her legs with an unladylike gesture and sits, raising one knee and crossing her arms over it. Meanwhile,* ZENROKU *surreptitiously signals for* CHŌTA *to get* SEIBEI, *and* CHŌTA *discreetly goes inside.* KUSUKE *timidly brings over the smoking tray and places it in front of* OROKU.*)*

KUSUKE: Here you are, ma'am, your smoking tray.

> *(*KUSUKE *bows, then retreats left, as far from* OROKU *as possible, to where* ZENROKU *is sitting next to the corpse. Now* TARŌSHICHI *stands and looks at the corpse, then at* OROKU.*)*

TARŌSHICHI: This brother of yours—isn't he dead?

> *(*OROKU *faces front and speaks over her shoulder to the shop employees.)*

OROKU: That's right, he's dead. Or, to put it another way—he went and died. *(Shamisen accompaniment resumes.)* Not that he wanted to die, mind you. But you folks ganged up and beat him until he was dead. And who was it who decided that the going rate for murder is an old kimono and one silver coin? I'd like to make his acquaintance. *(She shifts position again, sitting once more with her legs beneath her.)* I said, I want to meet him! Bring him here to me!

> *(*KIHEI *faces forward, looking at neither* OROKU *nor the shop employees as he speaks. He still wears his jacket and keeps his arms inside his kimono.)*

KIHEI: Wife, keep your voice down. This is a pawnshop, and people will think that you're dickering over the amount of a loan. The neighbors will talk.

OROKU (*Speaking with exaggerated gestures*): But they killed my little brother! Oh, the injustice of it! I'm so angry I don't know what to do!

KIHEI: I understand how you feel. After all, any brother of yours is my brother, too. But let me be the one to get revenge. (*Loudly.*) Hey! (*KUSUKE and ZENROKU jump.*) There must be a neighborhood association around here. I want to meet your landlord!

TARŌSHICHI: Yes, indeed, we have a landlord, and there is a neighborhood association. But first, before bringing them into this, couldn't you wait for us to consult with the other members of the household?

KIHEI: Idiot! You think we have time to wait for a household meeting? Wife—I'm going to go report this to the authorities. (*Rises.*) Wait for me here. Don't go anywhere, now.

(*Accompaniment stops.*)

OROKU (*Sarcastically*): Wherever would I go?

KIHEI: I'm going to see all of you in ropes!

(*KIHEI is about to go off when SEIBEI comes out from inside, accompanied by CHŌTA.*)

SEIBEI: Excuse me there, sir. If you would be so kind as to wait just a moment.

KIHEI: Are you talking to me?

(*Shamisen accompaniment resumes as SEIBEI sits left on the upper level, on a cushion put out for him by CHŌTA, and TARŌSHICHI goes to sit behind the accounts desk. KIHEI again sits to OROKU's right, once more putting his arms inside his kimono. Meanwhile, OROKU takes out her pipe and begins to smoke. ZENROKU is left, next to the corpse, and KUSUKE and CHŌTA are to his left.*)

SEIBEI: That's correct. I am a member of this household, so you may speak to me without reserve.

KIHEI: Better than having me tell you what happened, why don't you ask those guys? They know exactly what happened at Yanagishima yesterday.

TARŌSHICHI: It's like this, Master Seibei. Yesterday at Yanagishima, Kusuke got into a quarrel with a man selling chrysanthemum greens. Fortunately, Master Sashirō stepped in and patched things up. Be that as it may, the peddler looked perfectly fine at the time. . . .

KIHEI: That's my brother-in-law for you—can't do anything right. He doesn't die when he gets hit, like he's supposed to. No, he has to wait until after he gets home to say "It hurts!" and keel over dead.

SEIBEI: I am very surprised to hear that. But our involvement with your brother ended yesterday. Whatever happened after that is not any affair of ours. For all we

Kimon no Kihei (Kataoka Takao, later Kataoka Nizaemon XV) and Dote no Oroku (Bandō Tamasaburō V) confront Yamagaya Seibei (Ichikawa Omezō V, later Ichikawa Sadanji IV), master of the Aburaya pawnshop, over the "death" of Oroku's little brother. Brandishing a pipe, Oroku denys her criminal intent: "No matter how wretched and mean my life may be, never would I stoop to extortion or blackmail." (Tsubouchi Memorial Theatre Museum of Waseda University)

know, he died of illness. *(Slyly.)* Hearing you talk this way, it almost sounds as if you're trying to blackmail us.

(At the word "blackmail" OROKU *turns to glare at him, still holding her pipe. The shamisen accompaniment stops.)*

OROKU: Wait! Wait just one minute there! What's that you say? "Blackmail"? How dare you! *(Shamisen accompaniment resumes. There is a pause, marked by the sharp sound of* OROKU *hitting her pipe against the ashtray, twice, to clear it of tobacco. The following conventionalized speech* [tsurane] *is both the high point of* OROKU's *role and the climax of the act. The lines are spoken in rhythmic seven-five meter style, although the speech patterns retain a relatively realistic flavor. As she speaks,* OROKU *sits with one knee raised and gestures with her pipe. Throughout her speech, there is a shamisen accompaniment,* tsurane no aikata, *typical of extortion scenes.)* No matter how wretched and mean my life may be, never would I stoop to extortion or blackmail. You would not suppose it, to look at me now, but once I ran a teahouse by the Sanya Canal, sending on customers to the lesser houses of the Yoshiwara. "Oroku of the Canal Bank" I was called; I would sometimes even pay the way for those too poor to do anything else but look. But my glory days are gone. Now, in Koume, I run a little shop barely nine feet across. While my husband is doing odd jobs in Edo, I stay at home, taking in laundry and selling "Old Lady Tobacco." *(The speech reaches its climax, and the actor speaks loudly, carefully enunciating each syllable.)* Well spoken of are we . . . *(reverting to a more realistic voice)* known to all as honest and hard-working merchants. So, sir, you have no call to take that tone with us. *(To* KIHEI.*)* You're right, Kihei. The only way we can clear our names is to take this case to court.

KIHEI: Let me talk a minute, will you? *(To* SEIBEI.*)* So, you insist that you didn't kill him, eh?

SEIBEI: Regardless of whether he died of his wounds or illness, wouldn't it have been usual to call in a doctor?

KIHEI: Oh, yes. And we did. After all, he's my wife's brother. We tried internists, surgeons, acupuncturists, even a doctor in the service of a samurai lord. But they all said that there was nothing they could do.

SEIBEI: That's too bad. But, in fact, I'm an apothecary by trade and know a little something about medicine. Just to be sure, let's check his pulse.

(As SEIBEI *speaks,* ZENROKU *discreetly goes to the upper level of the shop, to where* TARŌSHICHI *sits by the accounts desk. After the two confer,* ZENROKU *wraps some coins in paper.)*

KIHEI: Don't bother. What's the use of checking the pulse of someone who's already stiff and cold?

SEIBEI: As the proverb says—"A fool's bolt may sometimes hit the mark." *(He stands up and steps down to where the corpse lies on the lower level and begins his examination.)*

TARŌSHICHI *(Still on the upper level of the shop and bowing politely):* I can well understand your anger. But if you take this matter to the courts, it will damage the good name of the Aburaya.

*(*ZENROKU *comes down to the lower level and sits next to* OROKU, *offering her the packet of money by placing it on the floor next to her and bowing deeply. Music stops.)*

ZENROKU: It's only a small amount, but please take it and buy a memorial stone.

OROKU *(Still sitting in her insolent pose, with one knee raised, speaking in scornful tones):* What's this? Money? *(She looks over her shoulder at him.)*

KIHEI *(Disinterestedly):* How much?

TARŌSHICHI *(Timidly):* Fifteen gold pieces.

KIHEI *(Raising his voice):* Fool! Do you think we're going to leave for a lousy fifteen pieces of gold?

OROKU: That's right! I need *(loudly)* at least a hundred myself.

(*Behind her,* TARŌSHICHI *starts in surprise at her audacity.*)

KIHEI: Mister, just think about it for a minute. (*Tsurane no aikata resumes.* TARŌ-SHICHI *discreetly signals for* ZENROKU *to return to his place left, next to the corpse. What follows is* KIHEI*'s equivalent of* OROKU*'s tsurane above, although the seven-five rhythm is not adhered to as rigidly.*) With but a measly ten or twenty pieces of gold, do you really think it possible to buy a human life? If that were the case, I'd be the one doing the buying. I'd stock up on people's lives and make a killing as a wholesaler of men's souls. I am Kimon no Kihei, an honest merchant, and this is the first I've ever heard of such a business. I'm sorry, but I see no choice but to go to court.

SEIBEI: Don't be so hasty. It looks like he's not quite dead yet. (*The shamisen accompaniment stops.* SEIBEI *has an idea and slaps his knee.*) Right! (*To the employees.*) Moxa should work for this. Try burning some moxa on him.

(ZENROKU *bows as* SEIBEI *returns to his seat on the upper level.*)

ZENROKU: Oh, I'm so glad to hear that! If he were really dead, I'd never be able to get back that bunch of chrysanthemum greens!

KUSUKE: And I'd be charged with his murder!

ZENROKU: Apprentice! Get out the moxa!

CHŌTA (*Drawing out the word*): Y-e-e-e-e-s!

(CHŌTA *steps up to the upper level of the shop and goes inside to get the moxa.* ZENROKU *turns his back to the audience and prepares for the moxa treatment by tying a hand towel around his head for concentration and lowering the right sleeve of his kimono for ease of movement.*)

KIHEI (*Scornfully*): Burning moxa on someone even the doctors couldn't help—what good can that possibly do? Bunch of fools!

OROKU: Just leave them be. When he doesn't come back to life, that'll just strengthen our position.

KIHEI (*Amused*): You have a point there.

(CHŌTA *comes from inside with moxa and some incense sticks with which to light it, then goes back down to the lower level where the corpse lies.*)

ZENROKU: Time for the moxa treatment!

(*A rhythmic and amusing musical accompaniment called* kome arai [*rinsing the rice*] *commences, with shamisen, metal gong* [kane], *and* kankara, *a kind of stick drum* [taiko] *that produces a sharp, dry sound.* OROKU *and* KIHEI *sit quietly at right,* KIHEI *smoking and* OROKU *bent over, facing the floor. The focus is now* ZENROKU *and* CHŌTA *as they prepare to burn moxa on the corpse.* ZENROKU *opens the corpse's jacket and under kimono, exposing his abdomen and yellow belly-band.* ZENROKU *then puts a large lump of moxa on the corpse's stomach and lights it with an incense stick, fanning it with his folding fan to keep it burning.*)

This comic interlude contains topical ad-libs that vary according to the production. While ZENROKU *is busy burning moxa on the corpse,* CHŌTA *puts a big lump of moxa on* ZENROKU *'s bald pate and lights it.* ZENROKU *doesn't notice at first, but then he suddenly realizes that his head is being burned.)*

ZENROKU: Ouch, that's hot! *(Frantically, he brushes off the smoldering moxa.)* That's my head you're burning there!

(To a rustic and somewhat humorous accompaniment with large stick drum [ōdaiko], shamisen, and song, KYŪSAKU *enters along the* hanamichi, *carrying the bundle of chrysanthemum greens from the previous scene. He comes to the front entrance and the song stops, with the shamisen accompaniment continuing.)*

KYŪSAKU: Excuse me! Is anyone home?

ZENROKU: Kusuke, someone's at the door.

KUSUKE: Oh, what a bother. A customer's the last thing we want right now. What is it you want—oil? To pawn something? *(Goes to the door and recognizes* KYŪSAKU.*)* Oh! You're the chrysanthemum greens peddler from yesterday at Yanagishima! *(At this,* OROKU *and* ZENROKU *start in surprise.)* Zenroku, that chrysanthemum greens peddler is here!

ZENROKU: Don't talk nonsense. I'm giving the peddler a moxa treatment right now!

KUSUKE: There's no mistake. It's the fellow from yesterday, all right.

ZENROKU *(Rising and going to the door to see for himself):* What? You expect me to believe that? *(Takes a look at* KYŪSAKU.*)* Oh! It's the chrysanthemum greens peddler from yesterday! *(His surprise turns to delight when he realizes that he now has a chance to get back the sword certificate.)* I'm *so* glad to see you! Come right in! *(Takes* KYŪSAKU*'s hand and leads him to sit in the center.* KIHEI *and* OROKU *avoid looking directly at him as he passes by.)*

KYŪSAKU *(Spotting* TARŌSHICHI*):* Thank you for your great kindness yesterday.

(Kneeling, he puts down his bunch of chrysanthemum greens and bows politely.)

TARŌSHICHI: You're the chrysanthemum greens peddler from yesterday. How good of you to come!

KYŪSAKU: Please allow me to introduce myself. I am Kyūsaku of Iozaki, who served as the guarantor of your apprentice, Hisamatsu, when he entered service here.

*(*OROKU *sits up in surprise at the mention of* HISAMATSU*'s name.)*

OROKU: "Your apprentice Hisamatsu"? Then this must be the shop where the young master serves as an apprentice. But—does that mean his guarantor is—? *(She rises to her knees and looks directly at* KYŪSAKU *for the first time; he also rises to his knees and looks at her. They are startled to recognize each other.)*

KYŪSAKU *(Delighted):* Oh! And you're the woman I left my kimono with yesterday for alterations!

(With frantic gestures, OROKU *futilely signals for him to keep quiet.)*

OROKU: Please—you must stop—please stop . . .

KYŪSAKU: But it's true. You're the one who . . .

OROKU: Oh! *(Trying to draw attention away from what* KYŪSAKU *is about to say, she holds up her pipe and exclaims in a loud voice.)* Stop, stop . . . this pipe's all— *stopped* up!

(OROKU *throws down her pipe and crouches over, hiding her face in shame.* KYŪSAKU *now spots the kimono where it is still lying folded, center.)*

KYŪSAKU: That's the kimono I was given yesterday. *(He then notices the corpse and stands up to get a better look.)* And why is that fellow asleep over there wearing my ripped jacket?

SEIBEI: That fellow "asleep" over there is a chrysanthemum greens peddler who got into a quarrel at Yanagishima. No sooner had he reached home than he dropped dead. It is not for us to know when our time will come. *(Ironically.)* You, too, had best be careful.

KYŪSAKU *(Puzzled):* Everything you say sounds just like what happened to *me* yesterday. *(He falls to his knees and bows to* SEIBEI.*)* Will you take a good look at me and make sure that I'm not dead?

SEIBEI: There's no need for worry. That "dead man" is going to come back to life.

ZENROKU: I just burned moxa on him, so if luck's with us, he'll revive. *(Looking carefully at the corpse's face for the first time.)* You know, I think I've seen this corpse somewhere before.

KUSUKE: I've been thinking the same thing.

CHŌTA *(Standing and looking):* Master Zenroku, it's Kyūta, our apprentice!

ZENROKU: You're right. If you look closely, you can see that it's Kyūta, all right.

ZENROKU, KUSUKE, and CHŌTA *(All standing and pointing at the body):* It's Kyūta, it's Kyūta!

ZENROKU *(To* KIHEI *and* OROKU *):* How dare you try to blackmail us, pretending our apprentice Kyūta was your brother? Get out of here, and take him with you! *(*ZENROKU *pulls* KYŪTA *up to a sitting position and then kicks him over to a loud beat of the* tsuke. *At this,* KYŪTA *begins to groan and suddenly sits up.)*

KUSUKE: The dead man spoke!

(KYŪTA *opens his eyes and looks dazedly around him, rubbing his newly shaven pate. He is shocked to recognize* ZENROKU.*)*

KYŪTA: Master Zenroku!

ZENROKU: Is that you, Kyūta?

KYŪTA: Master Zenroku, I've been had! I've been had! *(Removes the triangular white corpse tag around his forehead.)*

ZENROKU: You were supposed to have eloped yesterday. Where did you go? And how did you die?

KYŪTA: How can you ask me that, Master Zenroku? For you're the one who—who . . . *(He briefly assumes an effeminate pose, half-crouching, with his sleeves held away from his body. Then he sits, and a new, somewhat humorous, shamisen melody begins. The speech that follows, in rhythmic seven-five meter, may include ad-libs.)* Yesterday, you told me to elope with the maid and gave me a silver coin for the journey. But instead I went to a pub in Koume. There, though it was out of season, I ate my fill of blowfish. Little did I know that the rice I ate earlier had been glutinous rice, fatal when eaten with blowfish. Poor ignorant wretch I was indeed, for the blowfish and rice went to battle in my stomach, and when it was all over, Kyūta was dead. *(He briefly places his hands together as if offering a prayer for the dead.)* I have no idea what happened after that, but I can tell, when I rub my head, that someone's gone and shaved off my forelock. Master Zenroku, I've always depended on you as my "elder brother," but surely now you'll find me unattractive with my grown man's bald pate. That's why I'm sad, so very sad. *(Crouching, he poses again in a feminine posture, pointing accusingly at* ZENROKU. *The accompaniment stops.)*

ZENROKU: Shut up! Go over there and drop dead again!

KYŪTA: And to think I came back to life for *this!*

(ZENROKU *shoves* KYŪTA *far left, where he goes to sit down next to* KUSUKE *and* CHŌTA. ZENROKU *straightens his clothing and sits down again.)*

KIHEI *(To* OROKU *)*: It looks like it wasn't such a good idea to use that little squirt, huh.

OROKU: I thought something like this might happen.

KIHEI: Well, if we hang around here any longer, they're going to put us where the sun don't shine.

OROKU: Let's just cut our losses and go home.

(They prepare to leave, KIHEI *putting away his pipe and* OROKU *picking up her jacket. She stands and heads for the door, where she puts on her sandals and waits for* KIHEI. *He, meanwhile, goes to the center of the room and, with an exaggerated gesture, bends down and grabs the packet of money, which he then stashes in his sleeve.)*

TARŌSHICHI: Hey, you. What are you doing with that money?

KIHEI *(Threateningly)*: What? You got some objection to our *borrowing* it?

TARŌSHICHI *(Backing down immediately)*: No, not if you put it that way.

KIHEI *(Turning around and glaring at* KYŪSAKU *)*: Fool! *(To* tsuke *beats, he kicks over* KYŪSAKU. *Then, putting on his clogs, he follows* OROKU *out the door.)*

OROKU *(Pointing to the palanquin that has been left by the entranceway)*: Kihei, the palanquin's still here.

KIHEI: It'd be like throwing money after a thief to just leave it. Wife, you take one end.

OROKU *(Shocked)*: Me? You want me to help carry it? You've got to be kidding!

("Passed-along dialogue" [watarizerifu], in seven-five meter, ensues between the couple and the people inside the Aburaya.)

SEIBEI: What, does this mean that you must be leaving us so soon?

KYŪSAKU: To think that if it had been later when I arrived . . .

KIHEI: Our little job would have been a splendid success!

OROKU: But just because you had to come, our great fortune . . .

TARŌSHICHI: Ended up a measly fifteen pieces of gold.

KIHEI: One day we will come back, to thank you properly.

SEIBEI: If you have some claim to make, you're welcome any time.

KIHEI: Well, wife.

OROKU: Kihei.

> (*The two pick up the palanquin,* OROKU *staggering under its weight, and they proceed to* shichisan, *where they stop. A single, sharp clack of the* ki [ki no kashira] *is sounded, signaling the end of the play.*)

OROKU: What a puzzle we must look!

> (*Accompaniment resumes, with shamisen, voice, bamboo flute, and stick drum as the curtain closes behind them to a steadily accelerating series of* ki *clacks* [kizami]. OROKU *and* KIHEI *are left alone on the* hanamichi. *When the curtain has closed, the accompaniment momentarily ceases. The following is an example of an "outside-the-curtain exit"* [maku soto no hikkomi].)

OROKU: Kihei, put down the palanquin, put it down. It's too heavy for me to carry. (*They put down the palanquin, and* OROKU *rubs her shoulder.*) Oh, that hurts! (*Turning to* KIHEI.) See, Kihei, what a waste of effort that all was, and just because of that hayseed. The two of us really messed up today but good.

KIHEI: Anybody watching us would wonder why we have to carry home this palanquin ourselves.

OROKU: Yes. I can't think of any other example of a play in which a husband and wife make an exit like this.

KIHEI (*Chuckling*): Nor I.

OROKU: But Kihei, be that as it may, when I heard that that was the shop where Lady Takekawa's younger brother, Hisamatsu, is serving, I broke out in a cold sweat. (*Bows her head briefly in respect when mentioning* TAKEKAWA *and* HISAMATSU.)

KIHEI: Oh? Well, seeing as you're already sweating, you might as well sweat some more and help me get this palanquin back. Wife—let's go!

OROKU: Yes, Kihei dear!

> (*They pick up the palanquin once more,* OROKU *again staggering under its weight. They pose briefly. The accompaniment, with song, shamisen, bamboo flute, stick drum, and large stick drum, resumes as the couple exit down the* hanamichi *ad-libbing,* OROKU *occasionally losing her footing under the palanquin's weight.*)

Three-panel woodblock print by Toyohara Kunichika (1835–
1900). Kabuki-za, July 1897. Yasuna, lying on the ground,
occupies the full three panels, shared only with a portion of a
kiyomoto shamisen player seated on a red platform. Yasuna's
derangement, caused by the death of his beloved, is indicated
by his unkempt hair and trailing kimono. Referring to Yasuna's
mental condition and the spring season of the play, the left
panel reads, "Dance finale, *Breeze of Madness, Rape Blossom
Butterflies*, Abe no Yasuna, Onoe Kikugorō" V. (Tsubouchi
Memorial Theatre Museum of Waseda University)

Yasuna

Chikuda Kinji and Tsuruya Nanboku IV (text); Kiyozawa Mankichi (music);
Fūjima Ōsuke (choreography)

TRANSLATED BY MARK OSHIMA

1818   MIYAKO-ZA, EDO

Yasuna

INTRODUCTION

Yasuna, especially the modern version created by Onoe Kikugorō VI (1885–1949) in 1922, is one of the most popular dances in today's kabuki repertory. The figure of a handsome man driven mad by the suicide of his lover, with his hair hanging loose, wearing a beautiful formal robe and long, trailing trousers *(nagabakama)* and embracing his lover's garment as he wanders through a field of yellow blossoms, continues to be a familiar kabuki image. The character of Abe no Yasuna and the subject of this mad scene originate in the puppet play *A Courtly Mirror of Ashiya Dōman* (Ashiya Dōman Ōuchi Kagami, 1734). In that play, Yasuna is the father of the famous diviner Abe no Seimei, and Yasuna's mad scene occurs just before he saves the life of the fox that becomes his wife. The only part of this play commonly performed today is *Lady Kuzunoha* (Kuzunoha), dealing with the parting of the fox Kuzunoha from her son Seimei. It is translated in Volume 1.

The dance *Yasuna*, starring Onoe Kikugorō III (1784–1849), was first performed in the third lunar month of 1818 at Edo's Miyako-za (one of Edo's alternate, or *hikae yagura*, theatres) as one of a series of seven dances dealing with the four seasons. The work's formal title was *Both Flowers and Shapely Trees on Mi Mountain* (Miyama Hana Todokane Edaburi). The four seasons was a conventional theme in transformation pieces *(hengemono)*, designed to display a performer's protean abilities. The spring section included three dances. The first featured a high-ranking courtesan and the second a blind musician playing a Chinese-style xylophone, both accompanied by *nagauta* music. The third—performed to *kiyomoto* accompaniment—was a mad scene showing a man carrying a kimono. The summer segment consisted of a single *nagauta* dance devoted to Gama Sennin, an ascetic immortal who mastered the magic of toads *(gama)*, a traditional subject found in two other plays in this volume, *Tokubei from India* and *Masakado*. Autumn had two dances: one, to *tokiwazu* music, showed Tamamo-no-mae, the magical fox that disguised itself as a beautiful court woman to topple the realm; the other, to *nagauta* music, presented a gallant Edo fireman. Finally, winter featured a skeleton dressed as a beautiful young girl in long, flowing kimono sleeves. All that remains, though, is the third dance of the spring section. This is *Yasuna*.

The *Yasuna* dance soon disappeared, and only its *kiyomoto* music survived as one of the early masterpieces of the style. The singing was created by Kiyomoto

Enjudayū I (1777–1825), the first *kiyomoto* master; the piece is credited with having gained *kiyomoto* its first widespread recognition, thus making it highly respected among *kiyomoto* devotees. Much of the dance text used by Enjudayū was inspired by the old puppet play and included the appearance, at the end of the dance, of Yasuna's footman, worried about his master. The *kiyomoto* version drops the specific story (and the footman's appearance) and replaces it with a flow of fantastic images of love and beauty taken from contemporary Edo culture and the Yoshiwara pleasure district.

Yasuna was revived as a kabuki dance in 1886 by Ichikawa Danjūrō IX (1838–1903). Stage assistants *(kōken)* manipulated butterflies dangling from long poles *(sashigane),* and in the dance's lively final section, two samurai footmen appeared, a reference to a moment in the puppet play where the footman is doubled by a fox in human disguise.

Kikugorō VI, son of the great Onoe Kikugorō V (1844–1903), was heir to the Kikugorō tradition; he was also, however, a student of Danjūrō IX, hence he was deeply steeped in these two very different traditions. While keeping Danjūrō's basic choreography, Kikugorō transformed *Yasuna* into an abstract, psychological dance. The background was changed from a representation of a shrine to an abstract field of yellow blossoms, the field gradually appearing from total darkness as the music began. The butterflies disappeared and were instead evoked by the actor's eye movements. The samurai footmen also disappeared, and instead of concluding with Yasuna, holding the kimono of the deceased Sakaki no Mae and posing handsomely, the dance followed the final words of the song that describe him collapsing in madness. At the end, Yasuna covered himself with the kimono and sank to the stage, a moment said to have been inspired by Anna Pavlova's "Dying Swan," which Kikugorō viewed during the Russian ballerina's visit to Japan.

The text of *Yasuna* contains several obscure references that should be noted. One is to Konishi Raizan, a famous haiku poet of the Genroku period (1688–1704) who lived in the Imamiya District of Osaka. He loved dolls of beautiful women and always kept several on his desk. He also wrote an essay in praise of dolls and their quiet beauty and their lack of the inconvenient emotional excesses of real women. Passages from Raizan are quoted simply because Yasuna in his madness describes his love in similar terms.

Later in the piece, Yasuna's encounter with his love is described in terms of a patron and courtesan in Edo's Yoshiwara pleasure district. Every year, the cherry trees that lined the central avenue of Yoshiwara were planted anew. In this dance the planting becomes the occasion for the first meeting of a man and his lover.

Finally, the section toward the end evoking the image of a man traveling on a pleasure boat with his lover derives from a very old poetic form called *hinda bushi;* similar lyrics appear in several other dances as well. It is likely that this is one of the songs used in the *kyōgen* farces that accompanied very early kabuki dance.

This translation is based on the text in the volume devoted to Japanese dance edited by Gunji Masakatsu in the *Kabuki On-Sutēji* series (Vol. 25) and the *kiyomoto* practice books used for today's productions. The stage directions are based on a performance by Onoe Kikugorō VII (b. 1942), who received the tradition from Kikugorō VI through his father Onoe Baikō VII (1915–1995), in recent years the foremost performer of Yasuna. Although the Kikugorō interpretation is most common nowadays, from time to time features of Danjūrō IX's staging, like the use of butterflies or the presence of the samurai footman, are revived by other performers.

CHARACTERS

YASUNA, *a handsome young man driven mad by the loss of his wife*
STAGE ASSISTANTS, *formally dressed* kōken
KIYOMOTO, *the musicians and singers who accompany the action*

(When the curtain rises, the stage and auditorium are pitch-black. The music begins in darkness, and gradually, like a sunrise, the lights come up onstage, revealing a background suggesting a field of bright yellow rape blossoms and, center, the silhouette of a tree, eventually revealed to be a cherry tree in full bloom.)

KIYOMOTO:

"Love, oh love. / I feel a void inside like the empty sky. / Ah, this is a love that should not be." The wind of love comes and blows through my sleeves / making them fly wildly about. / As the wind blows, it separates a couple in love. / So does a storm blow through the cherry trees / scattering the blossoms in a mad cloud of pink petals. / Now my heart is hollow with loneliness. / Wherever I go, I ask people on the road where my love is, / but there is never any answer. / I feel as though I have encountered a powerful gush of water that penetrates stone; / so have events pierced my being. / My heart shatters and falls in pieces, / a shower like my unstoppable tears. / I weep and tears soak my sleeves. / I wander sleeping on a single spread-out sleeve, / a single, unrequited love.

(To the drum and flute pattern [kakeri] *used for the entrance of mad characters,* YASUNA *enters on the* hanamichi. *He wears a brocaded kimono and long purple* nagabakama *that trail behind on the ground. The right sleeve of his kimono has*

been dropped to reveal his under kimono, and he carries a woman's orange kimono over his left shoulder. In his right hand is a fan with black ribs. His hair hangs loose and he wears a purple headband tied with the knot on his left, indicating illness. He walks swiftly along the hanamichi *as though following someone, or as though blown about by the winds of love. When he gets to* shichisan, *which is decorated with clumps of yellow rape flowers, he turns around, as though the person he is seeking is there, then backs up slowly toward* shichisan *and stands still, closing his eyes. His closed eyes move as though in his mind he is still following something floating through the fields. Even though the lyrics describe his mental and physical disorder, and his poses lack the formal perfection of someone sane, he is seen as a cultured and handsome man whose great attractiveness shines through.)*

Somewhere, like his mind, his looks have become disordered as well, / his hair hanging loose in tangles. / *(He languidly brushes his hair aside.)* Who will comb out his hair?

(Unobtrusively, he opens his fan, rests the kimono on it, and gazes at it, recalling his love.)

Who will speak to him here in the midst of a field of bright yellow rape blossoms?

(Seeing butterflies fluttering nearby, he tries to brush them away.)

Here there are only pairs of amorous butterflies, / flying crazily together.

(He sees the butterflies resting on the flowers and walks stealthily toward them to try to catch them, but just as he does so they fly away, and he waves his fan at them in vain. He follows the butterflies, walking rhythmically to the music of the shamisen. Finally, he poses, arms outstretched, like a butterfly gazing soulfully at its mate.)

They rub their wings together in ecstasy as they fly.

(He waves his arms like a butterfly in flight and poses, now as one butterfly, then as another.)

Oh, how I envy them.

(He follows the butterflies with his fan, raises his fan to hail them, then plays hide-and-seek with them.)

He walks through the clouds of small insects and spring grasses and flowers.

(He looks out at the field and with his fan suggests the clouds of small insects that shimmer over the fields.)

He walks about madly in his court robe and long trousers.

(He makes a few dance steps that emphasize the outlandish sight of a man in such formal clothing walking through the empty fields.)

So wandering, Yasuna has arrived.

(He follows the butterflies around. Then, as though seeing his lover in the distance, he continues on his way, moving onto the main stage. He walks to far left, drops the orange kimono, and faces right as though someone has spoken to him.)

YASUNA: What, my lover is over there? *(Takes a few anxious steps forward.)* Where? Where? Where! *(Disappointed, he takes a few steps back.)* Ah, another lie. Don't speak such cruel, senseless things.

KIYOMOTO:

There, ah, look over there. *(Dreamily points into the distance, then sits.)* / Just as Raizan, the old man of Imamiya, described in his writing, / a clay doll of a beautiful young woman.

(He mimes writing on his fan and gazes at it, then stands with one sleeve at his mouth, fan at his side. He takes a few steps and poses as a beautiful young woman.) She is like a precious flower high in the mountains.

(He gazes up at the mountains and then looks at the flowers, waving his fan at them.)

How delicate and quiet she is. / She does not pick and destroy the flowers. / Weeping: no, *she* never, ever weeps.

(He is about to burst into tears but controls himself.)

She never gets angry.

(He throws his hands pensively to the side, then, suddenly light and coquettish, he moves rhythmically in a beckoning gesture.)

She is never jealous and is always quiet and well-mannered.

(He mimes a woman holding her lover by his kimono collar and forcing him to sit and listen to her complaints, counting them out, one by one. Then he turns and sits formally, hands quietly placed in his lap, showing how well-mannered she is. Gradually, he beats out a rhythm with his fan in pleasure at such a perfect lover, but then the rhythmical movement of the fan seems to suggest something falling apart, as with an illusion that has been shattered.)

Wait, was it really so? Our bond as husband and wife.

(He poses sitting handsomely, one long nagabakama *leg trailing in front of him, holding his closed fan tightly in both hands by his side.)*

My love, you probably have forgotten.

(He points with his fan in the distance and takes a few steps right. He twirls the fan winsomely and then, as though he has forgotten it, drops it. He notices the orange kimono and goes to it, sits, and, holding it up with his left hand, gazes lovingly at it, as though this were the woman he loves.)

Last year when the cherry blossoms were unveiled in the pleasure quarters: / that was when we first met.

(He drapes the kimono around his shoulders and, with a flourish of each hand, puts it on, finally standing looking out at the cherry blossoms. He holds the long hem of the kimono with his right hand and holds out his left sleeve, posing as a beautiful courtesan. He walks dreamily.)

In a state approaching madness, Abe no Yasuna (Nakamura Baigyoku IV) kneels
beside the kimono of his dead wife as he looks longingly into the distance for her.
(Umemura Yutaka, Engeki Shuppansha)

After that first meeting, I could not bear even a single day passing / without a
message of love from you.
*(He turns around and suggests the brevity of a single day, then mimes unrolling a
love letter and reading it.)*
I would wander aimlessly, awake through the night.
*(Hands in sleeves, he walks unsteadily, preoccupied with his love. Then he sits and
poses, gazing lovingly at the kimono, as though spending the night thinking of his
lover.)*
 Possessed with love, I could not sleep even in the day.
*(He takes off the orange kimono and puts it on the ground again. Then he goes
running toward it, clapping joyfully as though going to a meeting with his lover.)*
Oh, the joy of the rare nights when we met.
*(He sits and mimes exchanging a drink of sake with his lover, but before he drinks,
he catches a glimpse of the full moon in the sky and stands, posing as he looks
up at it.)*

98

On nights when we stopped drinking and talked intimately, / the dawn came sooner than ever.

(He mimes a man after a meeting with a courtesan, tying on his hakama, *confronting the courtesan who insists that he stay longer.)*

"I must leave" "Don't go!" / I was happily deceived by even the simple lying words / uttered by every courtesan. / On a bright moonlit night, / the crows can be fooled into crying as though it is morning.

(He mimes looking up at the moon and waves his arms to suggest a crow deceived by the bright moon into thinking that it is morning. He points at the moon, then lies down and poses, pillowing his head on one arm and facing up as though gazing at the moon.)

I ignore the calls of the birds at morning telling me that I must leave. / I stay on and on until the coming of the sun.

(He opens his fan and, as though it is a sake cup, drinks to pass the time.)

I try to rest but cannot fall asleep.

(The music becomes slow and moody, and he languidly twirls his fan as he wanders aimlessly in circles.)

I resent the fact that I cannot sleep, / wandering endlessly under the sky of the lonely traveler.

(Finally, he sits and stares vacantly. Suddenly, he notices that the kimono is no longer on his shoulder. He rushes around the stage, desperately searching for it. From time to time his movements are punctuated by a single stroke of an open shamisen string [kara ni]. *Then he sees the kimono. He rushes to it, clapping his hands joyously. The movements are accompanied by continuous music from the solo shamisen. He picks up the kimono and walks in a circle, fanning it happily. At last he sits, holding the kimono up with his left hand, his fan in his right hand miming the oar of a boat. It is as though he were rowing a pleasure boat together with his love. During the preceding section, a solo shoulder drum* [kotsuzumi] *player has come onstage and taken his seat in front of the* KIYOMOTO *musicians. This final section is a rhythmical "dance section"* [odoriji] *and is enlivened by the solo drum player.)*

"Tonight's lodging, where will we spend the night."

(He mimes rowing the boat, then walks, making beckoning gestures with his fan.)

"Spreading grass and pillowing my head on my arm, my arm for a pillow."

(He drops the kimono and mimes spreading out grass for a bed and holding his head with his hand. Then he wakes and stamps rhythmically together with the beats of the shoulder drum.)

Waiting through the night alone, how sad.

(He is in tears as he spends the night alone.)

Oh, how sad!

(He is overcome with tears and hides his face with his fan. Then he lets the fan down and waves it playfully with elegant dance gestures during this short instrumental passage.)

Inside a curtained enclosure in the fields.

(With large, welcoming gestures, he suggests a curtained enclosure for a banquet out in the fields.)

The face of the one I loved long ago, her enchanting fragrance.

(He happily welcomes anyone and anything that reminds him of his love.)

That face . . . has vanished like the dew.

(But mention of the dew reminds him that she is gone forever, and he sits and covers his face in grief.)

"Tell me if there is anyone who looks like her."

(He beckons on every side for the assistance of passersby.)

So saying he clutches her robe and collapses in madness.

(He holds the kimono over his head, looks around, and cowers at the outside world, using the kimono to hide his face. Finally, lost in mad grief, kimono draped over him, he sinks to the ground, and the drop curtain slowly falls.)

白井權八

若井半四郎

五柳亭德升

江戸ツ子

足滑を滑の人目三重
そ ず神の橋ハを民芸記
胡えをむ神沢弘
いせの國へ内の神相
成田の子勧かしまん
辿鳴るり車三の引く歩も
記くをもするの上アぼう迠辺
江戸辺の妻義年に三ずの
宝板付口でもろうさを
みせんうくそてぬらう一

歌川國貞画

Two-panel woodblock print by Toyohara Kunichika (1835–
1900). Premier performance at the Ichimura-za, third month
1823. "Banzui Chōbei" ("Ichikawa Danjūrō" VII), right, and
"Shirai Gonpachi" ("Iwai Hanshrō" V), left, discover a dropped
letter. Chōbei strikes an inquisitive *mie*, eyes crossed (*nirami*),
feet together (*soku*), right hand thrusting out a lantern. Gonpachi, crouching, leans into the light to read the letter. The
inscription above Gonpachi begins with poetic imagery of
moonlight on a lake, Yoshino's cherry blossoms, flowers in an
alcove, and the purple mists of spring, ending with the abrupt

The Execution Ground at Suzugamori

Suzugamori

Tsuruya Nanboku IV

TRANSLATED BY RONALD CAVAYE

claim that "while the weakling is swept away, a willow frond in the wind, the true Son of Edo smashes the strong." The inscription above Chōbei alludes to the actor, Danjūrō, playing the role. It reads, in part, "You may well ask what sort of man am I. Riding the spring breeze, brilliant kin of the Ichikawa, emperor of kabuki, Edo's Banzui Chōbei of Hanakawadō, fruit of my father's loins, christened in Tama River waters, thanks to the teachings of my ancestors, I am undaunted." (Tsubouchi Memorial Theatre Museum of Waseda University)

1823   ICHIMURA-ZA, EDO

The Execution Ground at Suzugamori

INTRODUCTION

The Execution Ground at Suzugamori, first performed at the Ichimura-za, Edo, in the third lunar month of 1823, is part of a nine-act drama entitled *Ukiyozuka Hiyoku no Inazuma,* regarded as one of Tsuruya Nanboku IV's (1755–1829) finest plays. The title of the full-length play—which could be translated as *The Floating World's Pattern and Matching Lightning Bolts*—is a series of puns that reflect the lightning-shaped birthmark on the cheek of a maid who plays a part in the main story, and the important pairing of two sets of characters: Chōbei and Gonpachi in *Suzugamori,* and Nagoya Sanza (Sanzaburō) and Fuwa Banzaemon in the equally famous scene known as "The Scabbard Crossing" (Saya-ate).

Apart from *Suzugamori,* "The Scabbard Crossing" is the only act still regularly performed. In fact, one version is considered an independent play and, indeed, belongs to the famous *Kabuki Jūhachiban* (Eighteen Famous Kabuki Plays) collection of the Ichikawa Danjūrō line. "The Scabbard Crossing" consists of a simple plot in which rivals Nagoya Sanza and Fuwa Banzaemon confront each other on the Nakanochō main street of Edo's Yoshiwara pleasure quarters. Their identities are concealed under large straw hats, and the scabbards of their swords brush together as they pass—an act considered offensive by the samurai class. (A similar scene can be found in *Gorozō the Gallant,* translated in this volume.) Although the plot is slight, the play is celebrated as a display piece, especially because of the sparkling antiphonal dialogue *(warizerifu)* between the two characters as they announce their names and boast of their exploits.

Suzugamori is usually presented under the title *The Well-Known Suzugamori* (Gozonji Suzugamori), the first word a conventional term attached to several other popular plays as well. The story deals with an entirely fictitious meeting between two frequently dramatized characters from the annals of Edo history, Banzuin (sometimes spelled Banzui) Chōbei and Shirai Gonpachi. The role of Gonpachi was first performed in this particular work by Iwai Hanshirō V (1776–1847), who was a famous female-role specialist *(onnagata).* Today, the part may be taken either by a young male-role specialist *(nimaime)* or an *onnagata.* The role of Banzuin Chōbei was played in 1823 by Ichikawa Danjūrō VII (1791–1859).

A young samurai, Shirai Gonpachi, who has killed his uncle because of an insult to his father, is escaping to Edo from his distant hometown of Inshū. As he travels along the great Tōkaidō Highway he reaches Suzugamori—near present-day Shinagawa, Tokyo—a grim place, used as Edo's execution ground.

The play falls into three sections. We are first introduced to a band of robber palanquin bearers who discover that there is a bounty on the head of Gonpachi, who enters borne in a palanquin. The robbers recognize the crest on his costume and attempt to capture him.

The second section consists of one of kabuki's most celebrated fight scenes *(tachimawari)*, which lasts ten to fifteen minutes. As the action proceeds in the dead of night, the robbers grope around, trying to lay hands on Gonpachi, who effortlessly foils them with feats of elegant swordsmanship. As the action moves from sequence to sequence, the fighting is highlighted by dramatic poses *(mie)*. Little real physical contact takes place, and such movements as somersaults (which indicate a kill), and the clashes between swords, are symbolically indicated by the beating of the *tsuke*.

To a large degree, realism is suspended in all *tachimawari*, but in this particular example a comic element compounds the sense of fantasy. Various humorous tricks are employed to show the wounds of Gonpachi's enemies; these comic elements are juxtaposed against the relative reality of the grim execution ground setting. Comic moments include a severed leg that hops along after its hapless owner, a torso cut in half, and a cutaway mask *(sogimen)* that opens to show a sliced-off face. Grotesque though these may seem, the lack of reality in the mask face, for example, the way in which the cut is revealed, and the crab-wise, moaning exit of the victim are played as comedy and always make the audience laugh. The grotesque is an important element in Nanboku's oeuvre—a reflection of the plebeian tastes prevalent during the Kasei period (1804–1830), the most celebrated example being the disfigurement suffered by Oiwa in *The Ghost Stories at Yotsuya on the Tōkaidō*, translated in this volume.

In the third and final section of the piece, Gonpachi meets the chivalrous townsman, Banzuin Chōbei, who has been watching his swordsmanship with admiration. Chōbei introduces himself in a well-known speech largely in seven-five meter rhythm *(shichigochō)* telling of the journey that has led him here. In a famous bit of staging that follows, Chōbei closely examines the blade of Gonpachi's sword, then discovers that Gonpachi is wanted for murder. Disregarding this, however, he agrees to help Gonpachi, and they depart for the city. Ultimately, in later scenes not translated here, Gonpachi becomes romantically involved with an Edo courtesan, various tragic circumstances intervene, and Gonpachi commits suicide.

Banzuin Chōbei is a larger-than-life hero whose deeds became the inspiration for a great number of plays produced throughout kabuki's history, among them *The Renowned Banzui Chōbei*, translated in Volume 4. Although a mere townsman and not a samurai, he is an *otokodate,* or chivalrous commoner. Chōbei, portrayed in a stylized, romantic manner, is a Robin Hood–like figure. Strong and brave, he defends the townsmen from the excesses of the arrogant samurai class. In this play, Chōbei chooses to take on the cause of a samurai. Although the text offers no explanation, it seems that Chōbei sympathizes with Gonpachi, who has been unjustly accused. The chivalrous commoner always fights for justice and knows no prejudice.

The historical characters of Chōbei and Gonpachi lived at different times, and a meeting between them would, in fact, have been impossible. This play lets the audience see how they *might* have befriended each other—rather like the conjecture of who would win a tennis match between stars of different generations.

The enduring popularity of *Suzugamori* may be explained by the eerie setting, the juxtaposition of the dramatic and comic in the long *tachimawari,* and, above all, the contrast in character between the boyish samurai (he still wears an adolescent's forelock) and the mature townsman. Chōbei's sparkling speeches, in particular, certainly thrilled the Edo patrons at the premiere and are still greatly enjoyed by audiences today.

While most of the dialogue is in a style that would have been the standard discourse of the day, Chōbei's opening speech, for example, is well-known for its rhythmic seven-five meter. The consonant-vowel, consonant-vowel pairings of the Japanese language are ideally suited to this form of rhythmic recitation, and I have translated this speech into *shichigochō* in order to keep the flavor of the original.

As the 1823 production was such a success for Hanshirō V, *onnagata* who perform Gonpachi usually adopt Hanshirō's stage business *(kata)* and wear a similar light yellow-green kimono. When male-role actors *(tachiyaku)* play Gonpachi, they wear a refined black kimono over a bright red undergarment.

This translation largely follows the script used for a production in May 1999 at Tokyo's Kabuki-za. Other performance details, including the *tachimawari,* are based on a videotape of a 1977 performance by Matsumoto Kōshirō VIII (Hakuō I) (1910–1982) as Chōbei and Nakamura Kankurō V (b. 1955) as Gonpachi.

CHARACTERS

BANZUIN CHŌBEI, *a chivalrous commoner*
SHIRAI GONPACHI, *a young samurai in his late teens*

BAND OF ROBBER PALANQUIN BEARERS
COURIER
PRIEST, *in league with the* ROBBER PALANQUIN BEARERS
TWO PALANQUIN BEARERS, *from the Tsurugaya Teahouse*
STAGE ASSISTANT, *black-garbed* kurogo

> (*Two* ki *clacks* [naoshi] *signal the start of offstage music* [geza], *a song of a pack-horse driver* [mago no uta] *and horse bells* [ekiro] *suggestive of the atmosphere of a busy highway. To accelerating* ki *pattern the curtain opens to reveal the Tōkai Highway at Suzugamori. Offstage drumbeats represent the sound of the waves* [nami no oto] *breaking on the nearby shore. A black backdrop signifies night. Center is a large memorial stone on a broad plinth dedicated to the souls of executed criminals. Etched into the stone in florid writing is the prayer "Praise to the Lotus Sutra." On either side of the stone are bushes and sparse trees. It is evening, between the hours of seven and nine—the Hour of the Dog—marked by the sounding of the fifth temple bell. A large group of dirty and poorly dressed robber palanquin bearers is seated on the ground drinking. A shamisen melody and wave pattern continue.*)

FIRST ROBBER: It seems the nights are getting shorter, ain't they? Sundown must be about the time of the fifth bell.

SECOND ROBBER: But in our line of business the nights are just what we need.

THIRD ROBBER *(Spotting someone coming):* But even now there seems to be a plump duck coming this way . . .

ALL: To help feather our nests!

> (*A dirty and disheveled temple* PRIEST, *in league with the thieves, enters to a rapid* tsuke *pattern* [batabata] *imitating the sound of running feet.*)

PRIEST: Hey everyone, so you're here, so you're here.

FOURTH ROBBER: Oh, it's the priest, is it? Any nice work to be had?

PRIEST: In Kawasaki there was this courier saying he was from Kamakura or some-where. He was carrying three hundred pieces of gold. Has he come this way?

FIFTH ROBBER: Nobody like that's passed through here.

SIXTH ROBBER: Well, there's only one road. He's bound to come by soon.

FIRST ROBBER: So we'll just hang around here . . .

ALL: And see what we can get!

> (COURIER *enters along the* hanamichi. *Offstage shamisen music indicates running* [idaten]. *He runs with smooth, flowing strides emphasized by the* batabata tsuke *beats. He wears a smart black tunic decorated with the crest of his employer. His legs are bare except for black calf leggings.*)

COURIER *(Rhythmically, as he runs):* One, two, three . . . one, two, three . . .

FIRST ROBBER: Hey! Want a cheap ride? Get in the palanquin and we'll take you.

COURIER *(Surprised):* What? Get in the palanquin? Whoever heard of a courier doing half his trip by palanquin?

SECOND ROBBER: That's as may be, but being carried by four legs will sure be quicker than walking on two.

THIRD ROBBER: How about it? Get in and we'll take you.

COURIER: My, my. How persistent! I said I won't get in!

FIRST ROBBER *(Threateningly):* Like it or not, you'll get in because we're not leaving you here!

SECOND ROBBER: Or just show us your cash and we'll forgive you and let you pass.

THIRD ROBBER: This is your first stop in hell. There won't be another!

FOURTH ROBBER: Just cut the chatter. Get out what you've got . . .

ALL: And lay it down here!

COURIER *(Shocked):* So, you're a pack of thieves! I knew this highway was dangerous when I set out alone. You won't get my package! I want to go home! I want to go home! *(Shaking with fear.)* I'll get away!

FIRST ROBBER: Shut your mouth! *(Turning to his men.)* Get him!

ALL: Right, let's do it!

COURIER *(Petrified):* Oh, forgive me! What can I do?

(They attack him, taking his gold and stripping him to his comical blue-and-pink underwear.)

ALL: Stupid fool!

COURIER *(Pathetically):* Oh, you don't care! Now this has happened I can't go home and I can't go on to Edo, either. Do you expect me to parade along undressed like this? *(Suddenly has an idea.)* Say, say ! Don't you think you could possibly let me join your group?

FIRST ROBBER: We're not saying you can't join us, but have you got anything to put up?

COURIER: What do you mean, "put up"?

SECOND ROBBER: When anyone joins our band they have to hand over something to prove they're okay.

COURIER *(Pathetically):* But I haven't got anything!

THIRD ROBBER: Without anything you can't join up.

COURIER: Well, I haven't got a penny in cash, but I have got something that might make a profit.

FOURTH ROBBER: You've got something good? If you have, get it out! Get it out!

COURIER *(Producing a letter):* Here you are.

FIRST ROBBER: What? This is a letter, isn't it? I don't know if it will do us any good, but let's read it! Let's read it!

SECOND ROBBER: *(Taking the letter):* We can't read! *(Calling out.)* Priest! Read it out to us! Read it out to us!

PRIEST: What, what? *(Reading formally.)* "Hereby be aware of this urgent communication. By act of malice, Honjō Suketayū, of this province, has been struck down and left dead. The scoundrel responsible is the son of Shirai Heiemon, a creature by the name Shirai Gonpachi. With regard to Edo, the seat of legislature, we hereby appeal at this time for his capture. To the constabulary of Edo from the constabulary of this province."

FIRST ROBBER: Very good, with this information then how can we . . .

ALL: Make some money?

COURIER: It's written there. If you can catch the samurai, Shirai Gonpachi, and deliver him to the court, you'll be able to name your reward. Don't you think that's good enough?

PRIEST: Very well. But what about this man's bearing and appearance? About how old is he?

COURIER: He's about seventeen or eighteen. He's a good-looking boy, still with his forelock. And he looks just like the actor Kankurō! *(The name of the actor playing Gonpachi is inserted here.)*

ALL: So, an attractive young man!

FOURTH ROBBER: And is there any special sign that we can identify him by?

COURIER: The crest on his clothing. The crest is the character "i" from Shira-i in a circle. That should confirm that he's the man.

FIRST ROBBER: So, the character "i" within a circle. *(Calling the men to pay attention.)* Hey! Everyone! Come here, come here!
(Many more ROBBERS appear from the bushes.)

ROBBERS *(Gathering round):* What is it? What is it?

SECOND ROBBER: Listen, if a samurai comes along wearing a kimono with a crest of the character "i" in a circle and we arrest him we'll get money. Everybody, keep your eyes peeled!

FIRST ROBBER: So we'll just hang around here . . .

ALL: And see what we can get!

COURIER *(Foolishly adopting a fighting stance):* So we'll just hang around and see what we can get!

ROBBERS *(Ribbing their new partner):* Just what do you think you're saying!
(Offstage singing, lively packhorse music, and horse bells. The robbers hide in the bushes. A palanquin enters along the hanamichi *carrying* SHIRAI GONPACHI. *The* PALANQUIN BEARERS *wear headbands and have their kimono tucked up, showing their bare legs. They carry sticks and walk briskly and rhythmically. They stop on main stage right.)*

FIRST BEARER: Master, this is the place we promised to bring you to.
(The SECOND BEARER places footwear before the palanquin.)

SECOND BEARER *(With great politeness):* Please, would you care to alight?

(GONPACHI *gets out of the palanquin. His elegant kimono, either black or lime-green, is decorated with his family crest on the back, breast, and sleeves. He wears bright red leggings and pure white* tabi. *In his obi he carries the two swords of a samurai. Indications of his youth and samurai breeding are his high-pitched and gentle voice, his pure white face makeup, and his dressed forelock* [maegami].*)*

GONPACHI: This must, therefore, be the place in front of Kannon Temple.

(GONPACHI *is deeply suspicious because he has asked them to take him to Edo's famous Asakusa District temple dedicated to the deity Kannon. They are clearly nowhere near this bustling center. The* BEARERS *move the palanquin to the background.)*

FIRST BEARER: Yes, indeed.

GONPACHI *(Looking around and facing the audience):* Now I see that we have journeyed round a bay.

SECOND BEARER: During the day you can see the whole of Awakazusa. The view from here is really good.

FIRST BEARER *(Bowing deferentially):* Well, Master, we've done your bidding. If we might just take our fee . . .

GONPACHI: Of course. As it is nighttime and because I have made you especially hurry, please take this with many thanks. *(Takes out money and pays the* FIRST BEARER.*)*

FIRST BEARER *(Gratefully):* Thank you very much indeed. *(Turning.)* Hey, partner, thank the gentleman.

SECOND BEARER: Thank you very much.

FIRST BEARER *(Looking at the money, annoyed):* Is this two hundred?

GONPACHI: I realize the rate should be six hundred in copper, but with many thanks, I give you this. *(Realizing he is nowhere near his destination, he has no intention of paying the agreed sum.)*

FIRST BEARER: What? "With many thanks" you give us just two hundred? You must be joking! If we get two or even four hundred, we've sweated, carrying that palanquin all night! If you want it . . . *(makes to throw the money at him)* there it is! *(Throws the money to the ground in disgust.)*

SECOND BEARER *(Foolishly picking up the money):* Oh, what a waste! I'll have it!

GONPACHI *(With dignity):* In that case, how much would you like to receive?

FIRST BEARER: As you've had a ride in our palanquin, we'll just have all you've got.

SECOND BEARER: Take off everything . . .

BOTH: And give it here!

GONPACHI *(Turning to face them, hand to his sword):* So, you are just a pair of thieves!

SECOND BEARER *(Angry, threatening):* What! Thieves! Thieves! *(Grabbing both lapels of* GONPACHI'*s kimono.)* What do you mean by that?

(Wave pattern [nami no oto]. GONPACHI *merely brushes him off, but the* SECOND BEARER *somersaults from the force of the blow to strong* tsuke *beats.)*

FIRST BEARER: Eh! You've knocked him down! Well, well, you won't get away with that! You won't get away with that!

(They prepare to attack GONPACHI *with their sticks. The* ROBBERS *appear and stop them.)*

FIRST ROBBER: Hey, hey! Just a minute. You two, just leave things to me. *(Shamisen accompaniment. He speaks politely to* GONPACHI.*)* Well. Well, master samurai. Those two have committed such an impertinence, you have every right to be really angry.

SECOND ROBBER: However, their blows were like those of sick men.

THIRD ROBBER: So, please understand . . .

ALL: And forgive them.

GONPACHI: Well, well, all of you, I am most grateful for your intervention. However, their demands were surely exorbitant

BOTH BEARERS *(Very angrily):* What? What? Is that exorbitant?

(They make to attack him but are pushed back in the bushes.)

FIRST ROBBER *(To* GONPACHI, *very politely):* You are perfectly correct. Leave these two to us and do not trouble yourself further.

SECOND ROBBER *(Bowing formally):* Well, sir, to where might you be traveling?

GONPACHI: You appear to be from this part of the world. From here to Edo . . . about how far is it?

THIRD ROBBER *(Politely):* Edo is only about two or three leagues away. Please, feel free to continue on your journey.

GONPACHI: I am most grateful for your help. *(Makes to set off.)*

FOURTH ROBBER: One moment, young man. Before you go, wouldn't you care for a smoke?

GONPACHI: Me? I care little for tobacco.

FIFTH ROBBER: What? You don't like tobacco! Whoever heard of going to a festival without tobacco!

SIXTH ROBBER *(Becoming angry):* It's because we're only palanquin bearers. I suppose you say that accepting a light from us will get you dirty or something.

FIRST ROBBER: Like it or not, we'll have you smoke! We'll have you smoke!

ALL: Yes, yes. Make him smoke! Make him smoke!

GONPACHI *(Kindly):* Well, you are harassing indeed! I do not know whether you are palanquin bearers or what you are. I simply hate tobacco. I told you that I did not want any. What is the matter with that?

(Gathering round, they notice the crest on his kimono.)

COURIER *(Shocked):* Look, the character "i" in a circle! The character "i" in a circle!

ALL *(Coming closer):* The character "i" in a circle! The character "i" in a circle!

GONPACHI (*Long, drawn out*): Wait, wait, wait! (*He pushes them aside and poses with arms outstretched.*) My crest of the character "i" in a circle . . . (*quickly covering the crests on his sleeves with his hands*) what does that matter to you?

FIRST ROBBER: Well, well. Now we can . . .

ALL: Get some money!

GONPACHI: What?

FIRST ROBBER: The wanted man . . .

ALL: Shirai Gonpachi!

GONPACHI (*Startled at being recognized*): Oh!

FIRST ROBBER: Arrest him!

ALL: Let's do it!

(*Drums, bells, and* tsuke *accompany their attack on* GONPACHI. *In the rapid fight* [tachimawari] *that follows,* GONPACHI *casts one* ROBBER *to the ground, places his right foot on him, and poses. Another takes* GONPACHI *'s sword from its scabbard, but he immediately retrieves it.* GONPACHI *turns in a circle, holding one* ROBBER *by the back of his kimono collar. The others circle around him, slashing ineffectually with their sticks.* GONPACHI *strikes at the group on the left and then on the right, chasing them off. All but two disappear into the bushes.* GONPACHI *chases them onto the* hanamichi, *their running feet accompanied by rapid* tsuke *beats* [batabata]. *They fall to the ground in fear. At* shichisan GONPACHI *poses in a* mie *to two* tsuke *beats, right foot thrust forward, his sword pointed back. A temple bell sounds. The mood changes. Slow, languorous flute and shamisen music* [shinoiri no aikata] *gives the scene an air of pathos and unreality. All movements are now slow, languorous, and graceful. In the pitch-dark,* GONPACHI *moves cautiously back to the main stage. The* ROBBERS *intermittently call out to each other, looking for him. Occasional tolling of the temple bell. Offstage drum wave pattern continues throughout. A stick is thrust in front of* GONPACHI. *He parries, blocking the blow, and then suddenly releases, making his opponent fall forward. Two attackers strike at once, but he deflects both sticks upward into the* ROBBERS *' eyes. They exit comically, tapping their sticks in front of them like blind men. More solitary blows miss him in the dark, each blow marked by* tsuke *beats. Two attack, and their deflected sticks form a mountain shape above* GONPACHI. *Dropping his stick, one* ROBBER *places a trick mask* [sogimen] *over his face and turns toward* GONPACHI, *who slices down with his sword and cuts off the* ROBBER *'s face. The mask, hinged at the jaw, falls open, revealing the interior, which is painted red to represent blood. Comically, the victim exits left, crab-wise and moaning. Striking to the right,* GONPACHI *cuts off the face of a second robber. As if in a dream,* GONPACHI *strikes slowly and effortlessly, seemingly unaware of his consummate swordsmanship. He moves to the center and two* ROBBERS *follow him, carrying the palanquin. They push the roof into his back, but he ducks down and they lift the palanquin over his head. He strikes at them and they grope about in the dark, being narrowly missed by his slashing sword. One finds him and grabs his outstretched left arm.* GONPACHI *pulls it from him and the robber flies forward, knocking over the palanquin. Meanwhile, the other grasps the back of* GONPACHI *'s kimono collar, but he turns quickly and the* ROBBER *is cast aside.* GONPACHI *stands alone at center, with his sword held out. A third* ROBBER *strikes at him with a stick, but* GONPACHI *takes it from him and thrusts the stick into his stomach. Moaning, the* ROBBER, *impaled, staggers backward into the palanquin seat, and the other two carry him off, crying out in fear. Another* ROBBER *enters and attacks with arms outstretched, trying to find* GONPACHI, *who slashes slowly to the left and right, and the* ROBBER *executes a back flip. The two edge backward and bump into the memorial stone.* GONPACHI *slices his assailant through the middle. Leaping into a hole so only his torso is visible, the* ROBBER *appears to be cut in two.* GONPACHI *edges cautiously left, looking around in the dark. The* PRIEST *enters, grabs the back of* GONPACHI *'s kimono, and is cast aside by an idle shrug of* GONPACHI *'s shoulder.* GONPACHI *forces him to his knees in front of him. In mime, the* PRIEST, *flapping his hands on either side of his body like a fish, begs pathetically for his life.* GONPACHI *raises his sword to run him through but instead casts him into the bushes, cutting off his buttocks as he does so. A flap on the priest's kimono is pulled aside to reveal red cloth indicating blood. Another* ROB-BER *enters and forces* GONPACHI *to crouch by pressing the end of his stick down on* GONPACHI *'s shoulder. They briefly pose.* GONPACHI *shrugs him off and slices through his arm. The* ROBBER *poses to* tsuke *beats with the severed arm still grasping the stick held high above his head. He slowly looks up, seeing his severed arm for the first time. Looking down at his stump he moans pathetically and, placing the stick and arm over his shoulder like a bundle, goes off into the bushes.* GONPACHI, *briefly alone, circles the stage, still looking cautiously around. Another* ROBBER *enters from the right, dressed in comical green child's underwear. Bumping into* GONPACHI *'s glinting sword blade, he cowers in fear, but, mesmerized, he follows the blade as* GONPACHI *slowly circles the stage. The sword is lowered and he thinks he is saved, but suddenly* GONPACHI *slices off his nose. He staggers off crying. A* ROBBER *enters holding a large, flat, circular straw hat. Comically, he tries to catch* GONPACHI *under it as if* GONPACHI *were the size of an insect. Thinking he hears a sound, the* ROBBER *carefully lifts it to see whether he has caught* GONPACHI. *This is repeated two or three times. Finally,* GONPACHI *sees him and raises his sword to strike. Crouching before him, the* ROBBER *holds the hat up for protection and forces* GONPACHI *backward.* GONPACHI *slashes and the* ROBBER *moves behind him, holding the hat in front of* GONPACHI *'s belly. Finally,* GONPACHI *cuts off the* ROBBER *'s leg below the knee. The* ROBBER, *moaning, hops off, pointing to his severed leg, which hops along after him. The actor holds his stump out of sight behind the hat while the severed leg is held on a black pole* [sashigane] *by a* STAGE ASSISTANT [kurogo]. *Another assailant enters from the right carrying a long, thin branch. In the darkness he strikes with it and circles round trying to find* GONPACHI. *He poses to* tsuke *beats with the branch held in outstretched arms above his head. Seeing him,* GONPACHI *places the blade of his sword on the middle of the branch, between the* ROBBER'*s hands, and forces him to his knees. He withdraws his sword, and the* ROBBER *lifts the branch up and down and runs the fingers of his right hand along it to check whether the sword is still there. He gets slowly to his feet, and they both strike with sword and branch to left and right.* GONPACHI *forces him backward up onto the plinth of the memorial stone. The* ROBBER *somersaults forward, and* GONPACHI *mounts the plinth and poses. The* ROBBER'*s head appears to be forced down into his body, and he goes off crying. To create this effect he lifts a slender frame within his kimono that raises up the shoulders.* GONPACHI *slowly edges out of sight around to left of the memorial stone, while the* COURIER *appears from the opposite side. The* COURIER *walks cautiously as far as the bushes. Drumbeats. Something moves and shakes the bushes. Carefully, he moves to the right, where the same occurs again. He moves to the left and then to the right, to the left, then right, and finally turns in a tight circle at center. The* tsuke *beats accelerate, preparing for the pose as two more* PALANQUIN BEARERS *appear from the bushes on left and right. The three pose in a* mie *accompanied by two* tsuke *beats. The mood changes as the three dance in a manner reminiscent of a kabuki pantomime* [danmari]. *The music* [kaminari] *is livelier and comical, and the movements are closer to real dance than in the previous fight section. The* FIRST BEARER *carries the long, thin branch, sweeping it before him. The* COURIER *and the two* BEARERS *now perform a comic dance using the branch as a prop. They seesaw the branch up and down, with the* COURIER *holding the center. The* COURIER *then ducks down under the branch and all three pose, the* BEARERS *holding the branch between them and the* COURIER *posing in front. They dance foolishly again, the* COURIER *tripping and falling onto his back as he does so. They push the branch down onto his chest, trapping him, but he forces it up and they both fall backward in front of the memorial stone. All three get up and, crouching, arms extended, grope around looking for* GONPACHI. *They sweep the air with extended hands and finally join hands, center. They dance and circle around, facing outward. They finally bump their heads together, and all three, clutching their heads in pain, sink down to their knees in front of the memorial stone. Groping, they find each other again and, with the* COURIER *in the center, grasp each other by the ears. Letting go, they sink to their knees. As* GONPACHI *reappears behind them, the three childishly clap their hands in front of them three times in a parody of the Japanese celebratory clapping ritual* [teuchi]. *They then assume the famous "hear no evil, see no evil, speak no evil" pose. With his sword,* GONPACHI *strikes each in turn on the head. The mood suddenly becomes lively, and the* tachimawari *resumes with quick and animated movements accompanied again by drums, bells, and* tsuke *beats.* GONPACHI *is attacked by two groups of* ROBBERS *from the left and right.* GONPACHI *slashes at them, killing each* ROBBER *as they strike at him in turn. He chases one group to the left and the other to the right. During the fight another palanquin enters along the* hanamichi. *From it hangs a paper lantern decorated with the crest of the Tsurugaya Teahouse whence its passenger is returning.* GONPACHI *chases the* ROBBERS *into the bushes on the left and right. The* BEARERS *set the palanquin down and open the side flap to reveal a middle-aged man dressed in a brown-and-white checked* haori *over a black kimono. He watches with folded arms. One* ROBBER *remains. His back and thighs are heavily tattooed, and he is wearing only a loincloth. He grasps* GONPACHI*'s sword arm, and* GONPACHI *swings him up onto the stone plinth and slashes at his back. A gaping red wound appears, and the man falls from the plinth onto his back.* GONPACHI *stands over him, thrusts his sword into the man's throat to finish him off, and poses. The temple bell tolls and a rapid, repeated, high-pitched staccato shamisen note* [shinobi sanjū] *gradually slows and fades away as* GONPACHI *withdraws his sword and, sinking to his knees, takes the dead man's neckerchief to wipe the blood from his sword. He kicks the body away and, still in darkness, slowly feels with his foot for his scabbard. He cautiously examines the blade of his sword and then, catching sight of the lantern on the front of the palanquin, decides to examine his sword for damage. He moves quickly over toward it and poses, examining the sword by the light of the lantern. The bell tolls and the* shinobi sanjū *shamisen motif is played again.* GONPACHI *then catches sight of the passenger and starts up, ready to run off. The passenger calls out to him. Music stops.)*

CHŌBEI *(Remaining seated with arms folded):* Young man! Wait just a moment.

GONPACHI *(Warily):* I can't tell whether you are a traveler, but is it me whom you wish to detain?

CHŌBEI: Yes, indeed. *(He delivers the following in seven-five meter.)* Among the stately mansions, / of Kamakura, / there I have my business and, / oft I come and go. / With this excuse I travel, / but for pleasure, too. / Going from Enoshima, / up to Katase, / the day before yesterday, / at Kanagawa, / I paused to enjoy myself. / Stopping at Shinagawa, / from Kawabata, / by palanquin I go home. / Here in Suzugamori, / as I pass this way, / I see this young man. / His swordsmanship is dazzling. / Such ability! / I am indeed astounded / by the skill I see. *(Resuming normal rhythm.)* But this matters naught. Please *(he drops his footwear to the ground and the temple bell tolls)* . . . put up your sword. *(Shinobi sanjū shamisen pattern as before.* GONPACHI *turns to face* CHŌBEI, *who alights from the palanquin and puts on his sandals.* CHŌBEI *moves to center*

Banzui Chōbei (Ichimura Uzaemon XVII), sitting with folded arms in his palanquin,
halts Shirai Gonpachi (Onoe Kikugorō VII), who is approaching with drawn sword,
"Young man! Wait just a moment." (Umemura Yutaka, Engeki Shuppansha)

holding the lantern to get a closer look at GONPACHI, *who holds his sword out,
pointed at* CHŌBEI. *The temple bell tolls and the pair warily circle each other.*
CHŌBEI *lifts his left hand to his forehead in a gesture of deference, and* GON-
PACHI *extends the sword toward him in an elegant pose.* CHŌBEI *examines the
sword, holding the lantern in his left hand and the sleeve of his robe over his mouth
to avoid letting the moisture from his breath damage the blade. They pose, and the
temple bell tolls again. The* shinobi sanjū *shamisen pattern is repeated. Satisfied,*
CHŌBEI *gestures for* GONPACHI *to put up his sword and moves to the left to
hang the lantern on the branch of a tree.* GONPACHI *moves to the right and kneels
down, wiping the blade of his sword with a white cloth as he speaks.)*

GONPACHI: Compared to samurai of the past my skills are still immature. I am
embarrassed.

CHŌBEI *(Kindly):* As I see, you are a samurai but yet have your forelock. Is your journey
a solitary one? From where to where do you travel?

GONPACHI *(On one knee):* Your concern is most kind. As you see, unsure of my way, I
am bound for the east *(looks out toward the audience),* traveling from afar from
the midcountry. Moreover, arriving at this bay alone I was insulted by those

insolent palanquin bearers whom I have roundly defeated. I knew I was taking their lives, but they were too insolent. This was avoidable, but by chance I have also aided other would-be victims. *(Smiling, he quotes a famous proverb and stands, taking a few steps forward, brushing his hands together as though after hard work, very pleased with himself.)* However, "The pheasant would not be caught but for its cries." I gained nothing, but I have taken life.

CHŌBEI: Oh, that's of no consequence. You have killed five or six of these ruffians, yet you were but one. I hope I am not being impertinent, but a skilled hand in one so young is impressive indeed. You say you come from the midcountry, but where exactly is the place of your birth, and for what reason do you travel to Edo?

GONPACHI: I would not have come except for the unjust aspersion cast upon me by my stepmother that I lack filial piety. I was born in Inshū. I could not prevent my father from casting me out, and, hearing tell of the great bustling city of Edo, I am making this unexpected journey to seek an official position in the house of a samurai. As I see, you appear to be a citizen of Edo. *(Somewhat embarrassed.)* Your words have been so kind and I lack any letter of introduction. If it please you to assist me through your good offices *(bowing),* I would be most grateful.

CHŌBEI: Having heard of your general circumstances, I will indeed. Depending on the situation, I will undertake to assist you in whatever way I can. Now let me move these ruffians to the side of the road where they can be food for the dogs. *(Shinobi sanjū shamisen pattern is repeated.* CHŌBEI *throws the bodies into the bushes. He moves a large stone to center, takes off his haori, folds it, and, sitting on the stone, places it over his knee.)*

CHŌBEI: You may rest assured that I shall never speak of this matter.

GONPACHI *(Gratefully):* Those kind words are so true to the spirit of Edo. In what strange circumstances may one find a companion! Before you favor me with details of your household, please allow me to introduce myself. *(Looks around nervously to check that he is not being overheard.)* From Inshū, now a masterless samurai, my name is Shirai Gonpachi.

CHŌBEI: So, you are Gonpachi?

GONPACHI *(Urgently):* That said, what of your own house?

CHŌBEI *(Self-deprecatingly):* You ask, but I can introduce myself only as a person of little importance. I was born in the east of the capital and live in the vicinity of the Sumida River. Coming and going, I have seen much of life. The talk of Edo, from Hanakawado *(very grandly),* I am called Chōbei of the house of Banzuin! *(Self-deprecating again.)* Just a cheap fellow!

GONPACHI *(Very surprised):* What? Even as far as the midcountry your fame goes before you. You are that Banzuin! . . .

CHŌBEI: Oh, no! The man whose name echoes as far as the midcountry was my ancestor. (*Actors here include references to great performers of the past and possibly also to their own ancestry.*) If you thought I was that Chōbei you are mistaken. There is a big difference! A big difference! The man whose fame spreads as far as the midcountry is the Chōbei with the very long nose. (*This alludes to a famed performer of the role, Matsumoto Kōshirō V.*) That's the real Banzuin Chōbei. Furthermore, here in the great city of Edo, the man known for his great big eyes (*an allusion to Danjūrō VII*) was Chōbei, my father. However, thanks to being nurtured on water from the waterways of Edo, we are a strong-willed people. For the weak we step aside. The strong we meet face to face. Even confronted by a fierce god, dressed in a robe of hide and mounted on a wild steed, we would not turn a hair. I'm only a humble man of the streets. But those crows who haunt the Awaza whorehouses among the reeds of Naniwa Bay! Those wild warblers, born of the back alleys of the capital! Compared to them, the sparrows of Edo's Yoshiwara soar high! To be a man in Edo is to be a man among men! (*Very grandly.*) Come to visit whenever you wish! With a table ready set for our guests, we await your pleasure!

GONPACHI: Your words are most compassionate. However, Chōbei, if you would be kind enough to assist me, I commend my affairs to your discretion.

CHŌBEI (*Kindly*): Of course. If I undertake your cause we may not be boarding a very grand boat, but at least we will be in a skiff! Well, that's all settled. Let's get on our way.

GONPACHI (*Very politely, bowing*): I do not know how to express my deepest gratitude.

CHŌBEI (*Kindly, smiling*): What? I am only doing you a little favor. You have no need to feel indebted to me. We sons of Edo are like that! Well, let's be getting on our way. Come with me.

(CHŌBEI *rises. A black-garbed* STAGE ASSISTANT *removes the stone. Sound of waves.* CHŌBEI *retrieves the lantern and, starting to lead* GONPACHI *away, sees the warrant for* GONPACHI*'s arrest, dropped by the robbers.*)

CHŌBEI: What have we here? Something of yours, is it not?

(*They drop to one knee as* GONPACHI *reads.*)

GONPACHI: "Hereby be aware of this urgent communication. Be it known that on the twentieth day of this third month, by act of malice, Honjō Suketayū, of this province, has been struck down and left dead. The scoundrel responsible is . . ." (*Suddenly realizing that it refers to him,* GONPACHI *quickly turns to prevent* CHŌBEI *from seeing it.*)

CHŌBEI (*Holding out his hand*): Just show me, please. Come, come! Show it to me!

(GONPACHI *hands him the letter.*)

CHŌBEI: What have we here? What have we here? (*Reading.*) "Hereby be aware of this urgent communication. Be it known that on the twentieth day of this third month, by act of malice, Honjō Suketayū, of this province, has been struck down and left dead. The scoundrel responsible is the son of Shirai Heiemon . . ." That's all. The rest is torn away. The name is missing. *(Suddenly realizing.)* But that is Gonpachi's surname is it not?

GONPACHI *(Starts):* Ah!

CHŌBEI *(Kindly):* What! Of this . . . of this we shall say nothing! *(He burns the letter in the lantern's flame.)*

(GONPACHI, deeply impressed by this townsman's gesture, slaps his thigh.)

GONPACHI: Would that a samurai could be so magnanimous!

(CHŌBEI looks down into a puddle of water.)

CHŌBEI *(Quickly):* Ah! In this puddle, a shadow reflected! . . .

(He spots a man in a tree behind him and quickly blows out the lantern's flame. GONPACHI throws a stone at the man, who springs from the tree.)

ROBBER: Stop right there!

(He attacks GONPACHI. A brief fight occurs accompanied by beats of the tsuke and the drum wave pattern. GONPACHI holds him by the collar of his kimono.)

CHŌBEI: Without doubt that is . . .

GONPACHI: One of their accomplices!

(He throws the ROBBER toward the memorial stone and slashes him across his back with his sword. The ROBBER freezes, and GONPACHI holds the sword embedded in his back.)

CHŌBEI *(Slapping his thigh):* Yes, indeed, a skilled hand!

GONPACHI: Chōbei!

CHŌBEI: Gonpachi!

(GONPACHI withdraws the sword, turns to face the audience, and runs the blade through the lower part of his kimono, cleaning it.)

GONPACHI: At leisure in Edo . . .

(A single ki clack [ki no kashira]. At once the backdrop falls to reveal a country scene as dawn breaks. The ROBBER somersaults, dead. GONPACHI and CHŌBEI pose, GONPACHI putting away his sword and CHŌBEI throwing his robe over his shoulder and raising his right hand in a triumphant gesture.)

BOTH: Let us meet again!

(They pose, looking about them, and slowly begin the journey to Edo, moving left, as the offstage musician sings the packhorse song and we hear the horse bells and drum wave pattern. To a soft and accelerating ki pattern [hyōshi maku], the curtain is run across the stage.)

Two-panel woodblock print by Utagawa Toyokuni III (1786–1864). At the Nakamura-za in the first month of 1853, the dance *Kasane* was woven into a long play, its title, *The Licensed Quarters and the Ichikawa Family Close to the Date Clan* (Kozotte Kuruwa Mimasu no Datezome), calling upon three elements of the play: Kasane's sister had been a courtesan, the crest of Ichikawa Danjūrō was three nested rice measures (*mimasu*), and the Kasane-Yoemon story was placed in the world (*sekai*) of the Date clan. With one hand, "Kinegawa Yoemon" (Ichikawa Danjūrō VIII) seizes a mirror to show Kasane her disfigured face. At Yoemon's feet lies the sickle with which he soon will murder her. (Tsubouchi Memorial Theatre Museum of Waseda University)

Kasane

Tsuruya Nanboku IV and Matsui Kozō II (text); Kiyomoto Saibei (music)

TRANSLATED BY MARK OSHIMA

1823   MORITA-ZA, EDO

Kasane

INTRODUCTION

As a showcase for two attractive performers, *Kasane* is one of the most popular dances in both the kabuki and classical Japanese dance repertories. It was first performed in the sixth lunar month of 1823 at the Morita-za in Edo as part of the long play *A Surplice-Hanging Pine and the Sharp Sword of Narita* (Kesa Kakematsu Narita no Riken), a summertime ghost play *(kaidan mono)*. Tsuruya Nanboku IV (1755–1829) served as the head playwright *(tatesakusha)*, and the play starred Ichikawa Danjūrō VII (1791–1859) as Yoemon and Onoe Kikugorō III (1784–1849) as Kasane; these great young actors were central to Nanboku's later plays. Although Nanboku probably did not write the actual lyrics, filled as they are with difficult poetic language, the dance perfectly embodies the atmosphere of Kasei-period kabuki (1804–1829) and Nanboku's theatrical style. It combines a grotesque and violent tale of ghosts and sexual jealousy with a beautiful and highly polished surface, along with generous doses of humor.

The legend of Kasane is very old and originally was told as a tale of the holy power of Yūten Shōnin (called Yūnen in this play), a Pure Land Buddhist priest who, in 1692, exorcised the vengeful ghost of Kasane in Hanyū Village in present-day Ibaragi Prefecture, northeast of Tokyo. Yūten Shōnin later became abbot of Edo's Zōjō Temple, the temple of the Tokugawa family, and is remembered in the name of Yūten Temple on the outskirts of Tokyo. The original story is quite complex and begins with a farmer named Yoemon, who married several times and had a one-eyed son, Suke. Yoemon killed Suke, only to have his son's deformities repeated in his daughter, Kasane. One day, when Kasane went out to harvest beans with a sickle, Yoemon tortured her to death by filling her mouth with river stones and holding her under water until she drowned. Kasane's vengeful ghost then possessed Kiku, Yoemon's daughter by his fifth wife. This is the ghost exorcised by Yūten Shōnin.

Kasane, Yoemon, Kiku, and Suke are names that appear in numerous dramatizations of the story; also reappearing are the dramatic devices of Kasane's limp, her one-eyed blindness, and the sickle, the latter representing an alteration in the method by which Kasane meets her death. In the original story she drowns, but the dramatizations add the element of a sickle—which becomes a murder weapon—because she was going to use it to cut beans. This is reflected in the full title that

Nanboku gave to the dance scene, "Sensual Colors, Going to Cut Beans" (Iro Moyō Chotto Karimame).

The many versions of the tale in kabuki are known as *Kasane mono* (Kasane plays). Most notable are those plays that made the story of Kasane part of the world *(sekai)* of disturbances in the Date clan of Sendai, best known from the play *The Precious Incense and Autumn Flowers of Sendai,* translated in Volume 2. In that world, Kasane is the sister of the courtesan Takao, who is killed because she is regarded as the source of Lord Yorikane's dissipation, which originally caused the clan's disturbances.

In Nanboku's play, Kasane is transformed from a homely countrywoman to an elegant lady-in-waiting in a samurai mansion who then falls in love with a samurai named Yoemon, unaware that he had an affair with her mother, Kiku, and killed Kiku's husband, Suke, when he discovered the couple together. Yoemon stabbed Suke in the leg, and Kiku gouged out one of his eyes with a poker. In the dance, Suke's vengeful spirit possesses Kasane, making her lame and disfiguring her face terribly. Although there is a physical justification for Kasane's transformation, her gruesome appearance perfectly symbolizes her bitter feelings after being betrayed by Yoemon.

In *Kasane,* Nanboku and his cowriter transformed a violent and grotesque story into an elegant dance, in the process creating a play that is a prime example of kabuki's "aesthetic of cruelty" *(zankoku no bi).* The drama's horrific depiction of hell is couched in poetic lyrics that suggest the surface beauty of a Japanese-style screen painting of a natural scene, full of charming representations of fragile plants and flowers. Further, the *kiyomoto* narrative singing accompanying the dance adds a tone of sensuous refinement.

The love suicide plays of Chikamatsu Monzaemon (1653–1725) include a travel scene *(michiyuki)* of stylized romanticism in which a couple, usually wearing matching black kimono, flees the torment of the mortal world to be united in the afterlife. Chikamatsu's poetry bridges our world and the next. In Nanboku's play, death offers no escape: Kasane becomes the image of a living demoness. Compared to Chikamatsu, Nanboku writes with a kind of fresh realism. Instead of the stylized costumes of an earlier era, Yoemon wears the kimono of a samurai or a simple cotton kimono *(yukata),* exposing his bare legs. He embodies the image of the handsome villain *(iroaku),* a role type that was developed by Nanboku in such plays as *The Ghost Stories at Yotsuya on the Tōkaidō,* translated in this volume.

The atmosphere of the dance is intimately related to the *kiyomoto* singing style. *Kiyomoto* began in the early nineteenth century with Kiyomoto Enjudayū I

(1777–1825), who split off from the *tomimoto* style. *Tokiwazu, tomimoto* (which no longer survives in kabuki), and *kiyomoto* are narrative musical styles *(jōruri)* sharing the same roots but possessing important differences. *Tokiwazu* is a straightforward style of singing in a relatively fixed time, and its texts usually make grammatical sense. But the singing of *kiyomoto* is highly embellished and the rhythm quite flexible. Often, a single word can be drawn out for several seconds with the addition of all kinds of melodic flourishes, making it possible to amplify the poetic images of the text. For example, the singer may be describing green maple leaves, or the white flowers called "evening faces" *(yugao).* For emphasis the word is drawn out, often in conjunction with a pose held by the dancer. Usually, the pose does not illustrate the image directly. Sometimes there is an indirect relation to the image and sometimes not; however, the poetic image in the music and the pose in the dance join together to emphasize individual words in a way that a simple reading of the text does not make apparent. A series of vivid images flow into each other dreamily without following the usual grammatical rules. For example, the first words of the text are "*moi o mo kokoro mo hito ni somaba koso, koi to yugao*" (thoughts and heart, as they are dyed in a person, love is what it is called / evening faces). Rather than a coherent sentence, it is a series of potent images of loving thoughts, the human heart, the overwhelming influence of the beloved. Finally, the conclusion is a pun, "*koi to iu*" (called love) and "*yugao*" (evening faces). Instead of being a logical statement, the line ends with the ambiguous but beautiful image of these white flowers. Such poetic devices are common throughout *kiyomoto* texts. A text of this nature cannot be translated into English exactly, and the reader should imagine that each concrete poetic image in English refers to a much more potent image in Japanese.

Although the play is excellent, it was not revived on the professional kabuki stage during the Edo period. The music was preserved and became one of the most famous *kiyomoto* pieces. Finally, in the Meiji period (1868–1912), *Kasane* was revived as a dance and given a new staging. It reached its definitive form with a 1922 revival starring Ichimura Uzaemon XV (1874–1945) and Onoe Baikō VI (1870–1934), a famous acting combination of the day, and the singer Kiyomoto Enjudayū V (1862–1943). To show off Enjudayū's voice, a languourous song was added that accompanies Yoemon's fight with the men sent to capture him. The *ero-guro* (erotic-grotesque) tastes of the Taishō period (1912–1926) blended perfectly with Kasei kabuki to provide a popular dance that has been performed constantly ever since.

Among performance variations that have become common is the opening, which, unlike that given here, may begin with the scene hidden by a light-blue curtain *(asagimaku)* before which appear the arresting officers, who reappear later in the dance; they say that they carry a letter of arrest for Yoemon, accused of Suke's murder. Then, with a clack of the *ki*, the curtain drops to reveal the scene, and the play proper commences. Afterward, Yoemon sometimes enters on the dike that forms part of the set, instead of from the secondary *(kari) hanamichi*, which alters some of the blocking described in the translation. Present-day versions of the extended fight between Yoemon and Kasane are more stylized than they were in Nanboku's time, and today Yoemon wears a black formal kimono rather than the simple *yukata* as in the past. Contemporary productions are based either on the 1922 Baikō and Uzaemon version, known as the "Baikō version," or the 1925 approach of Onoe Kikugorō VI (1885–1949) and Morita Kanya XIII (1885–1932), called the "Kikugorō version."

This translation is based on both standard versions. It uses the *kiyomoto* text heard in present performances and the script and notes in Gunji Masakatsu's edition of kabuki dances in Vol. 25 of the *Kabuki On-Sutēji* series.

CHARACTERS

KASANE, *a beautiful young woman*
YOEMON, *a handsome young samurai*
POLICE OFFICERS
KIYOMOTO, *the musical ensemble that accompanies the action*

> *(A clack of the* ki *indicates the beginning of the play, and a light patter of drumbeats from the offstage music room* [geza] *suggests a rainstorm. To continuous clacks of the* ki, *the curtain is pulled open. The setting represents the riverbank of the Kine River. A high dike with a ramp leads up to it, right. At left is a pond spanned by a bridge of small logs covered with dirt. Behind the bridge is a sluice gate. At the center of the dike is a maple tree with green leaves. The rear of the dike is covered with thick clumps of grass. Toward the dike's right end is a wooden marker, "Kine River." Below the dike and around the pond are pink blossoms* [nadeshiko]. *Far left is an old mill, its roof lifted and its front wall dropped forward to reveal the* KIYOMOTO *ensemble, which begins with a fast, furious passage for shamisen—one of the most famous moments in* Kiyomoto *music—followed by the opening sung passage that sets the mood of the play.)*

KIYOMOTO:
> Loving thoughts and the human heart. / Passion soaks into mind and heart, / dying them a deep, rich color. / Then, truly this is what can be called love: /

White Evening Face blossoms. / The green summer grasses have all taken on
their hues, / but flourish only momentarily before withering, / vanishing like
the dew on the tips of the grasses; / drying away like the moisture by the roots
of the plants. / Thus is the way of the world. / Two roads separate, / one has
gone before, one goes after.

(A drum pattern represents a rain shower. To a fast, furious shamisen passage
KASANE and YOEMON enter quickly, she on the main hanamichi, he on the
secondary hanamichi, their steps emphasized by rapid tsuke beats. They stop at
shichisan. *KASANE carries a half-opened blue parasol covered with thin silk.*
Her hair is dressed in a tall, dignified bun, and her obi is tied diagonally, indicat-
ing that she is a lady-in-waiting in a samurai mansion. YOEMON is dressed in a
samurai's formal black silk kimono, the hem tucked up into his obi, revealing his
bare legs and feet and the white, hanging flap of his loincloth. A white cotton cloth is
wrapped around his sword hilt, and a straw mat around his shoulders protects him
from the rain. Posing, the pair looks warily around for pursuers.)

Even separated, they both are united / in their feelings of anxiety. / Around
them, a wild tangle of fresh green summer maple leaves. / The rain does not
stop / and the raindrops cling to the tips of the branches.

(The two are driven back by the rain. KASANE protects herself with the parasol,
and YOEMON wraps the straw mat around him. Then they turn around and pose
at the same instant, KASANE holding the parasol open on her shoulder, YOEMON
stretching the mat behind him.)

The showers are endless; / so is one forever lost in this dream of a floating
world, / suffering eternally without waking.

(KASANE half-closes the parasol and looks around her. Meanwhile, YOEMON
rolls up the straw mat and brushes the rain from his hair, looking very handsome
as he does so.)

She goes to meet her man, / catching him just in time, / carrying a delicate
silk parasol. / The rough road may rip the fragile silk / leaving nothing but
bones: / the bamboo framework of the parasol. / But even so, she does not
mind. / Her woman's heart can think of nothing / but the moment when
she will be united with her love.

(KASANE poses at shichisan with the parasol on her shoulder and her back to the
audience.)

Her devoted love gives her the strength / to travel even along this frightening
road, / and she has already come very far. / They both hide from pursuers. /
They look with fear even at the glistening of the dew / on the tangled grasses
on the fields, / and the floating lights of the fireflies. / They both wonder
if those are the lanterns / of pursuers and prepare themselves. Their hearts
are filled with anxiety, / but they have come far, / now here beyond the way

station of Sekiya, / there are no more barriers. They have arrived at the banks
of the Kine River.

(KASANE *takes the parasol and straw mat and places them right, just below the*
dike. KASANE *and* YOEMON *sit on the front of the stage below the dike and speak*
to one another, YOEMON *left, crouching with one knee up,* KASANE *sitting for-*
mally right. Slow shamisen music accompanies their dialogue.)

YOEMON: Kasane, this is certainly a shock meeting you in such a place. Why have you
come?

KASANE: Why? It is cruel of you to be so surprised. We promised one another to commit
love suicide together, yet you left a suicide note and departed by yourself. I
have followed you all this way. Please, let us die together.

YOEMON: It is only natural for you to be suffering, but recall that your adoptive father
lost the precious Nadeshiko tea caddie entrusted to him by his lord and is now
being punished. As long as your father is in such a position, it would be a grave
failure of filial piety for you to die. I beg of you, return home immediately.

KIYOMOTO:

As he utters these awful words, / she gazes at his face as he speaks.

(*With gestures* YOEMON *tries to persuade her to go home, but she shakes her head.*
They move closer to one another, and as KASANE *touches* YOEMON*'s arm, she*
looks at his face.)

She recalls that she reached this state / due to the strange fate that linked
them together. (*She weeps in shame.*) / "It may be very disrespectful to such
a holy man, / but at the Urabon ceremonies last year at the beginning of
autumn, / I participated in the funeral ceremonies of holy Yūnen."

(*She points into the distance several times, indicating that she is recalling the past.*
She bows respectfully to the holy man for the prayer ceremonies.)

"That was when I caught a glimpse of you. / I fell deeply in love at that
instant."

(KASANE *approaches* YOEMON, *from behind, and glances at him over his*
shoulder, then runs a few steps away and hides her face bashfully with her
sleeves.)

"Truly, it was not the god of marriage who brought us together. / Rather, we
spent our first night together in the garden of the Buddha, / in the land of
the dead. / From the very first, we were united / on the same lotus blossom
in paradise."

(*She embraces* YOEMON, *then takes the cloth that was wrapped around the hilt of*
his sword. She uses it like a hand towel [tenugui] *to express feelings of love.*)

"I prayed in my heart with a Buddhist spirit, / but instead of praying for the
salvation of those who have gone, / my faith turned to the man that I would
forever call my husband."

(She poses, showing her anguish by biting the cloth. Again YOEMON *tries to leave and she pushes him back, spreading the cloth between her hands. Finally, the two pose,* KASANE *sitting below, biting the cloth, pointing at the man she loves, while* YOEMON *stands, one hand on the hilt of his sword, the other resting on her shoulder.)*

"Now I serve in the spacious women's quarters of a samurai mansion."

(She folds the cloth like a napkin in a formal tea ceremony to suggest her mansion service, then the two dance gracefully together, holding the cloth between them.)

"When the women gossiped about their favorite actors, / I imagined that the kabuki actor Danjūrō must look just like my love."

(She uses the cloth to mime a woodblock print of a kabuki actor, suggesting that YOEMON *looks just like Danjūrō, the role's first actor, but he waves his hand modestly to deny this. Finally, they pose,* YOEMON *sitting right,* KASANE *standing left and modestly holding several layers of tissues and her mirror to her mouth.)*

"So did I entertain myself thinking of you. / At a party to mark the end of the year, / there was a lively song, full of percussion music."

(He puts the cloth away, and she takes out an elegant black-ribbed fan covered with silver paper on one side and gold paper on the other. She moves rhythmically as the music evokes a lively popular song punctuated by the beats of a fulling block [kinuta], *suggesting a country atmosphere.)*

"A name tattooed in love, a name tattooed in love."

(She delicately points at her forearm with her fan to suggest the tattoos that women wore to indicate their undying love.)

"Written oaths on holy paper may turn into worthless scraps of wastepaper."

(She mimes writing on her open fan.) / "But a baby carried for five, six months can't be thrown away so easily. No, no."

(She walks jauntily, holding her open fan in front of her belly, subtly suggesting a pregnant woman.)

"I never thought that this song would describe my own fate. / How ashamed I am." / She cannot speak any more, hoping that he will understand her feelings.

(She hesitantly approaches YOEMON *and places his hand on her belly to tell him that she is carrying his child.* YOEMON *is shocked and then saddened as he realizes what they must do.* KASANE *leans against him bashfully. They sit apart as* YOEMON *speaks sadly.)*

YOEMON: We have no other choice; now we must die together. How sad that I did not realize the depth of your love. I only lament that the unborn child in your womb must die as well. But alas, this, too, is the way of the world. How full of sadness this world is.

KIYOMOTO:

"I had not a hint of the true deepness of your heart."

(He holds his hands at his chest, suggesting his heart.)

"I did not realize how sincerely you were willing to sacrifice your dew-like life for the sake of such a one as I."

(He starts to go and **KASANE** *tries to stop him, but he gestures that he is not leaving and, pointing to the dike above the river, indicates that they should go there to commit suicide together.)*

"When I think of it, how pitiful it is." / They grasp each other's hands and lament.

(He helps her walk up onto the dike and assists her over the rough ground. They hold hands and gaze deeply at one another.)

"At least I wish I could say farewell to my adoptive parents / and even though they are now not related, / to the parents that gave me life. / This night we must say farewell forever. / How multifold are the sins against filial piety / that we commit with our deaths. / Please forgive us!" / Together they lament and weep / as they stand on the riverbank.

(They kneel and bow, begging forgiveness from those they leave behind, and then collapse in tears. Suddenly there is the sharp sound of the mysterious dorodoro *drum pattern from the* geza, *and the sluice gate opens by itself. Slowly, a long grave marker comes floating into the pond through the sluice gate, under the earthen bridge. On top of the marker is a skull with a rusty sickle thrust into one empty eye socket. A chill wind seems to blow, and* **YOEMON** *is pulled back as though by some ghost.)*

How strange! In the river, a skull comes floating. Joined are the spirit of Suke and a rusty sickle.

(With the final words of the preceding song, **YOEMON** *poses handsomely on top of the dike, bending over and looking intently at the strange object in the pond below. Meanwhile,* **KASANE** *cowers on top of the dike, holding up her sleeve to protect herself. The shamisen continues a tense, intermittent pattern.* **YOEMON** *tries to reach the object from the top of the dike, but it is too far away. He climbs down from the dike and tries again, but it is still too far away. Finally, he draws the object toward him with his sword. He brings it to shore, wipes his sword with the white cloth, and carries the object up onto the dike. He then wipes the mud from the grave marker and holds it up. He can just make out the name.)*

YOEMON: In life, his name was . . . Suke!! *(He is shocked to see the name of the man he killed.)*

KASANE *(Startled):* What?!

(YOEMON grunts as he breaks the marker in two and throws it away. KASANE screams in pain as her legs begin to hurt, followed by a burning feeling in her face.)

YOEMON *(Seeing what is happening to* KASANE *):* This must be the work of the ghost of . . .

(He pulls the sickle from the skull and throws the skull into the bushes. KASANE *cries out in fear and collapses in the bushes, right. A group of* POLICE OFFICERS [torite], *dressed in black, come running from left and try to capture* YOEMON.*)*

POLICE OFFICERS: Yoemon! You're under arrest!

KIYOMOTO:

As they fight briefly, a song can be heard faintly, / carried on the breeze.

(Two POLICE OFFICERS *fight with* YOEMON *and then pose to the sound of a temple bell. The music becomes slow and languid, accompanying a short "fight in the dark"* [danmari] *between* YOEMON *and the two* POLICE OFFICERS, *who grope through the dark. This love song is very famous, and the love letters in the lyrics are an ironic reflection of the letter for* YOEMON*'s arrest. The fight is punctuated by a series of striking poses accented by* tsuke *beats. The loneliness of this scene is emphasized by the occasional sound of the temple bell. In the course of the fight,* YOEMON *gains possession of the letter demanding his arrest.)*

"The night deepens. / Indeed, love letters are the only companions / that are always there in the bedchamber. / I burn the cap of my brush as a magic spell to call my lover, / but even that is of no use. / At the sandy shores of the beach, / the clouds grow faintly white as dawn approaches."

(Finally, YOEMON *hits the* POLICE OFFICERS, *and they run away. He unrolls the letter as the black curtain at the back of the stage drops to reveal empty fields and a thin crescent moon in the sky. He reads the letter and discovers that it is a warrant for his arrest. He starts to run away, but* KASANE *crawls out from the bushes with her back to the audience and calls out urgently.)*

KASANE: Ahh, wait . . . where are you going?

YOEMON *(Flustered):* I'm going to . . . I'm going . . . *(sees* KASANE*'s face and points in shock)* ahh! Your face!!

KASANE *(Calmly, unaware that her face has changed):* My face? What about my face?

YOEMON: How frightening it is.

KASANE: No, what is frightful is your cold, cold heart. Let me see that letter.

YOEMON: This letter? This letter is . . . is private.

KASANE: You can't let me see it! *(Certain that it is a love letter.)* Ah, I see, you can't let me see this letter. How cruel you are.

KIYOMOTO:

"You, you must have some other love. / That is where you are truly enjoying yourself."

(She slides toward YOEMON, *her back still to the audience, and grabs at the letter, tearing off the end of it. Clinging to* YOEMON, *she turns and the audience sees a ghastly purple wound obscuring her left eye, an external sign that the ghost of* SUKE

has possessed her. She bites on the letter to try to control her emotions and poses, berating YOEMON *for his faithlessness.*)

"That is why you deceived me."

(*She twirls her finger, accusing* YOEMON, *and moves with stylized dance movements of lamentation. As the singer draws out the words with rhythmical repeated syllables, she limps, adding a grotesque, syncopated touch to her normally smooth and graceful movements.*)

"How cruel you are."

(*She forces* YOEMON *to sit and listen to her, then poses, gazing into his eyes, but he turns away from the sight of her hideously disfigured face.*)

"I hoped that our love was true, / but in the end all is nothing but a floating world of sadness. / Oh, if only our love could have become a reality."

(KASANE *'s movements, in which she tries to express her feelings, are thrown off-balance by her limp. Finally, she poses with her back to the audience, emphasizing her large brocaded obi, tied diagonally across her back in the style of a samurai mansion lady-in-waiting.*)

"I would exchange my stiff, diagonally tied obi from the rear."

(*She mimes an obi tied in front.*)

"My formal hairstyle would change to a loose ponytail."

(*She indicates her hairstyle and, entreating* YOEMON, *holds out the tissues, which are inadvertently folded around her mirror. To prevent* KASANE *from seeing herself,* YOEMON *takes the mirror and conceals it in his sleeve. The shamisen music becomes lively and jaunty as* KASANE *imagines life as an ordinary housewife walking in common wooden clogs. Her limp adds a grotesque swing to her walk, but she is still unaware of how she has changed.*)

"If I could walk around like an ordinary wife in a commoner's clogs, / how happy I would have been."

(YOEMON *quietly reaches for his sword and tries to find an opportunity to kill her, but she pushes him back with her merry dance movements. Finally, the two pose, with* KASANE *clinging to him, holding the sword with her long kimono sleeves.*)

"To have dreamed so, only to find that all my hopes were false / makes me feel so ashamed." / How cruel, how terrible, she clings to him, / not knowing how her face has changed. / Her lamenting is a sad, but charming, sight.

(KASANE *takes the sword away from him and places it on the dike at right.* YOEMON *tries to get it back, but she refuses to let him have it. Gradually, she acquires a kind of power, since the sight of her face drives* YOEMON *back. Finally the two of them sit center, and she leans affectionately against him.*)

YOEMON: Yes, yes, you are absolutely right. I lied when I said that I was planning to die. I am actually returning to my home province. The journey will be very, very difficult, but let us go.

During the long, danced murder sequence, Kinegawa Yoemon (Kataoka Takao, later Kataoka Nizaemon XV) and Kasane (Bandō Tamasaburō V) strike a famous *mie*: he holds the murder weapon, a sickle, high overhead, while she bends away from him until her head nearly touches the floor. (Umemura Yutaka, Engeki Shuppansha)

KASANE *(Overjoyed):* We can go together?

YOEMON: Yes, let's go.

KASANE: Yes.

(YOEMON *motions for them to go. He is about to reach for his sword but realizes that he does not have it and that, even now,* KASANE *is going to fetch it. But the rusty sickle is in front of him; seizing it, he attacks her from behind, cutting deep into her shoulders. She grabs his arm and speaks desperately.)*

KIYOMOTO:

She staggers forward, but suddenly the cruel blade strikes her. / There is a spray of crimson autumn leaves. / It looks like the red brocade of the Tatsuta River in autumn. / Kasane clings to the hem of Yoemon's kimono.

KASANE: You've deceived me yet again!

YOEMON: No, I'm killing you! This is the reason.

(*He pushes her away and pulls out the mirror from his sleeve, holding it up for* KASANE *to see her face. With one glimpse she screams in terror and scrambles to escape. After a struggle,* YOEMON *holds her from behind, forcing her to look at the reflection.)*

KIYOMOTO:

> When she sees her reflection in the mirror . . .
>
> *(Again and again* KASANE *turns away. Finally,* YOEMON *holds back her arms so that she has no choice but to look at the mirror. She gazes deeply at her face, wondering desperately what has happened.)*

KASANE: Oh no! Why, why, why!? Why has my face changed like this? Oh, how it has changed. *(She collapses in tears.)*

YOEMON: Here, Kasane! Listen to the workings of fate. *(Crouches next to her, speaking quickly and firmly.)* I killed Suke, the husband of your real mother, Kiku. The punishment for that crime has gone around and around and now has destroyed your face. This is all determined by our karma from previous lives. I am your father's murderer. All this too is karma, so be resigned to your fate.

KIYOMOTO:

> He tells her to find salvation as he slashes out wildly at her. / But when he attacks, she fights back.
>
> *(Again* YOEMON *tries to kill her with the sickle, but* KASANE *pushes him back.* YOEMON *runs to* shichisan *and looks around to make sure that no one is watching. He pulls down the right shoulder of his kimono to free his hand for work, revealing a light-blue under kimono, while he holds the handle of the sickle with his teeth. The two pose to* tsuke *beats,* YOEMON *standing threateningly on the* hanamichi *and* KASANE *sitting on the dike center, her right hand held as though to push him back and her left hand on her right shoulder where* YOEMON *has wounded her.)*
>
> "How cruel! How hateful you are!"
>
> *(*YOEMON *approaches warily from the* hanamichi. KASANE *continues to gaze at her reflection in the mirror, shaking her head in anguish. She drops the right sleeve of her kimono to reveal a white under kimono decorated with a spray of crimson maple leaves, suggesting her shoulder wound.* YOEMON *comes and stands next to her, posing with the sickle held above his head, while she poses, sitting, below, gazing up at him, trying to contain her feelings of distress by biting on the sleeve of her under kimono.)*
>
> "I was entrapped by the thick cords of mortal passion. / I lost my way on the dark paths of love, / and fell in love with the murderer of my parents, / without knowing it." She screams with jealousy and hatred. / "I loved you, I loved you too much."
>
> *(Again and again* YOEMON *tries to attack, but the sight of her face keeps him from approaching her directly from the front. She stumbles down from the dike and the two pose to* tsuke *beats,* YOEMON *standing above her on the dike, holding the sickle threateningly, and* KASANE *sitting below, trying to push him back.)*
>
> She speaks all that is in her heart without concealment. / And this pain is all from a previous life.

(He pulls her up onto the dike. They pose, with KASANE *sitting on the edge of the dike looking down eerily at* YOEMON, *and then again looking up at him entreatingly. Horrified, he turns his face away even as he tries to stab her.)*

What hatred has gone cycling through cycles of rebirth.

(They struggle for the sickle, moving right until YOEMON *roughly pushes* KASANE *away and she rolls down the ramp of the dike. As* YOEMON *stands threateningly over her,* KASANE *reaches out and clings to his bare leg.)*

She weeps and pours out her feelings at him, / writhing in anguish.

(She tries to defend herself with YOEMON *'s straw mat when he circles around from on top of the dike and attacks her again.)*

"Will you be punished or not? / Now you will know heaven's judgment." / She suddenly stands straight and threatens him.

*(*KASANE *goes toward the dike, dragging the straw mat behind her. She stops at the edge of the dike, holds the straw mat in front of her, and slowly rises from a crouch to a standing position, one hand held limply in front of the mat like a ghost. As she rises, the mat gradually unrolls, hiding her legs and feet. She seems to be a ghost floating through the air. She poses, glaring at* YOEMON, *to mysterious* dorodoro *drumbeats.)*

As she violently flings her long black hair at him, / she looks like a living human being transformed into a demon from hell.

(The fight moves to the top of the dike. YOEMON *pulls at her obi and it falls loose, making a long train of brilliant, multicolored maple leaves that also suggests her loose hair, described in the lyrics.* KASANE *wrests the sickle from* YOEMON *and stands threateningly under the green maple tree at the center of the dike. She holds the sickle in her teeth and glares at* YOEMON, *who sits on the ground holding the end of the obi, which stretches between them. Seizing the sickle from her,* YOEMON *swings it again and again. The fight moves to the bridge, where they pose,* YOEMON *sitting on the edge of the bridge and* KASANE *glaring down at him.)*

He grabs the hair by the roots and plunges the blade deep into her body, / without a trace of pity or mercy. / Her life fades away like the frost melting in the morning sun, / a beautiful figure like a delicate blossom now dashed to pieces.

(Under the willow tree on the left end of the bridge, YOEMON *plunges the sickle deep into* KASANE *'s body, and she falls dead. He turns back, his gestures indicating he begs forgiveness. He puts his arm back into his sleeve and grabs his sword.)*

This, then, is the story of Kasane, told throughout the ages.

(The rain has started falling again, so YOEMON *grabs the straw mat, wraps it around his body, and runs off down the* hanamichi, *emphasized by the furious beating of the* tsuke. *Silence. Darkness. Suddenly, the dead* KASANE *'s hand begins*

to move and reaches out in YOEMON*'s direction. Alternating strokes of the shami-sen,* tsuke, *and eerie drums gradually become faster and faster.* KASANE *sits up and motions pulling* YOEMON *back. Suddenly,* YOEMON *appears on the* hana-michi, *running backward with the straw mat wrapped around him. He comes to the main stage, shakes off whatever force has pulled him back, and runs onto the* hanamichi *again.* KASANE*'s beckoning tugs him back again, forcing his arms open to reveal his panic-stricken face. He struggles back and forth on the* hanamichi *and is gradually pulled to the main stage. There he discards the straw mat and runs toward the* hanamichi *again, showing his unconscious concern for his appearance by automatically straightening his kimono collar as he goes. But he is stopped at* shichisan *by something pulling at his hand and holding him back by the shoulders. He tries running but can't move, his feet flying up vainly in the air. Gradually, he is pulled back to the main stage, spins around and around, and falls sitting center, his back to the audience.)*

A fearsome tale indeed.

(With one loud clack of the ki, *all the lights come up onstage and* YOEMON *poses center, hand on his sword, looking up at* KASANE *standing beneath the willow tree, hands limp like a ghost, the sickle sticking out of her body, obi trailing down the dike toward the river below. She gradually stands straight, making her look tall and thin, and she seems to rise slightly in the air. The singers and shamisen players end with the concluding* sanjū *pattern, and to a continuous* ki *pattern the curtain is pulled closed.)*

Two-panel woodblock print by Utagawa Kunisada I (later Utagawa Toyokuni III, 1786–1864). Ichimura-za, eighth month 1831. The right panel shows Oiwa's "ghost emerging from the lantern, Onoe Kikugorō [III], famous in the Three Cities." The inscription on the lantern reads: "A full house achieved for this autumn play: Oiwa, a stunning success." Oiwa's gangster husband, here called "Kamiya Niemon" ("Seki Sanjurō" II), stands, horrified, within a snow-covered bamboo grove as Oiwa's spirit materializes from the blazing lantern. (Tsubouchi Memorial Theatre Museum of Waseda University)

The Ghost Stories
at Yotsuya on the Tōkaidō
Tōkaidō Yotsuya Kaidan

Tsuruya Nanboku IV
TRANSLATED BY PAUL B. KENNELLY

ONBŌ CANAL
Juman Tsubo Onbōbori no Ba

THE DREAM
Yume no Ba

SNAKE MOUNTAIN HERMITAGE
Hebiyama Anjitsu no Ba

1825   NAKAMURA-ZA, EDO

The Ghost Stories
at Yotsuya on the Tōkaidō

INTRODUCTION

Tsuruya Nanboku IV's (1755–1829) *The Ghost Stories at Yotsuya on the Tōkaidō* was first produced at the Nakamura-za in Edo in the seventh lunar month of 1825 as a five-act summer play *(natsu kyōgen)*. An extraordinary production strategy was used whereby Acts III and V were presented on alternate days with 1748's classic revenge drama *The Treasury of Loyal Retainers* (Kanadehon Chūshingura), allowing audiences to contrast worlds of dark and light: the newer play's representations of ghosts and grim lower-class life were set against the aristocratic heroics of Japan's outstanding vendetta play. *Loyal Retainers* was performed with costumes and sets in period *(jidai-mono)* style, and *Ghost Stories at Yotsuya* was performed with those suited to the gritty raw-life *(kizewamono)* style of the Bunsei period (1818–1830). If *Loyal Retainers* epitomized feudal loyalty, *Ghost Stories at Yotsuya* treated this ethic as irrelevant, if not abhorrent. *Ghost Stories at Yotsuya* starred Ichikawa Danjūrō VII (1791–1859) and Onoe Kikugorō III (1784–1849), the former as Iemon, an archvillain *(katakiyaku)* in the newly developing subcategory of sexually appealing rogue *(iroaku)*, the latter in three roles: Oiwa, Iemon's wife, who becomes a vengeful ghost; Kohei, Iemon's servant, who becomes a ghost loyal to a feudal vendetta; and Oiwa's human avenger, Yomoshichi. Nanboku is renowned for writing plays in both the ghost play *(kaidan mono)* and the raw-life genres. *Ghost Stories at Yotsuya* is a masterful combination of those genres, a play providing spectacular moments of supernatural horror as well as depicting grinding poverty.

Nanboku drew on numerous and varied sources for *Ghost Stories at Yotsuya*, including contemporary novels *(gōkan)* (one actually written by Nanboku himself some twenty years earlier), historical records of an incident involving a mistreated wife and her jealous act of vengeance, the extremely popular (and frequently dramatized) tale of the Soga brothers' revenge against their father's murderer, and Nanboku's own plays.

Translated here are Acts III and V, the "Onbō Canal" "The Dream," and "Snake Mountain Hermitage" scenes. Act IV has no plot relevance to either act. Act I (trans. Oshima 1998) establishes the evil characters of Naosuke and Iemon, in particular Iemon's treachery toward his master, Enya Hangan—from the *Loyal Retainers'* world—and Iemon's murder of Oiwa's father. This sets in motion the play's main theme: Oiwa's vendetta against Iemon, which parodies the feudal revenge against the evil Kō no Moronao carried out by the forty-seven masterless samurai in *Loyal Retainers*. Act II embellishes Iemon's callousness. He is disgusted by Oiwa's unkempt appearance following childbirth and is impatient to rapidly restore his rank and stipend. With Iemon's consent, a neighbor poisons Oiwa, which results in horrible facial disfigurement. Iemon seizes all of Oiwa's belongings to pawn in exchange for some fine clothes to wear at his wedding to the neighbor's daughter. When Oiwa learns of the wedding, she prepares to confront Iemon at the neighbor's mansion. Overcome with jealousy and rage, her hair falls out as she combs it *(kamisuki)*, magnifying her ugliness. She dies accidentally—and grotesquely—before she can make the trip. Iemon blames her death on Kohei, his servant, and murders him. Then he orders his cronies to dispose of the two corpses by nailing them to either side of a raindoor *(toita)* and tossing it into Onbō Canal.

The first scene in this translation, "Onbō Canal," was probably performed at the close of day one of the original two-day performance and repeated as the first item on day two. The repetition would have served two purposes. First, it would have showcased the skill of Kikugorō, the star, in playing both male and female ghosts by means of quick changes *(hayagawari)*. In one of kabuki's most famous stage tricks, the raindoor switch *(toitagaeshi)*, a single actor plays the part of both Oiwa's and Kohei's corpses, which are nailed to either side of the raindoor. Both come briefly to life before turning into skeletons. The scene concludes with an elaborate nighttime mime scene *(danmari)* in which Iemon, Naosuke, and Yomoshichi struggle for a letter that is vital to the feudal vendetta in *Loyal Retainers*. The second purpose of the repetition relates to physical performance conditions. Theatres were lit by daylight through overhead windows and by candles when the windows were closed for scenes of darkness; audiences were thus accustomed to dim lighting. The performances at either end of the day would have occurred in intense gloom, emphasizing the shock value of the raindoor effect.

The next scene in the translation, "The Dream," is the first scene of Act V, an act that strongly resembles a *nō* play in structure. In the first half of a *nō* play a character encounters a ghost without realizing its true nature; in the second half, the ghost reveals itself and discloses an attachment to the living world. The revelation enables the ghost to break that attachment and find peace. "The Dream" scene occurs at the time of the Tanabata Festival (Festival for Separated Lovers) and the Bon Festival (Festival for the Pacification of the Dead), both held in midsummer. Iemon dreams of a future when he has been promoted to samurai status and of a past where he has met a young, beautiful woman who closely resembles

Oiwa. In fact, autumn flowers adorn Oiwa's cottage, and, at the present time, the young woman is a ghost. These seasonal and time discrepancies are typical of *nō* plays. The dream culminates with a highly erotic love scene *(nureba)* and the ghost's transformation into a monster.

The final scene in the translation, "Snake Mountain Hermitage," is the second scene of Act V. In it the immense beauty of the summer cottage is replaced by the ominous gloom of Snake Mountain Hermitage in winter. The contrast of light and dark settings and of dramatic moods is typical of Nanboku's writing. Iemon clings to a single hope: he intends to renounce his loyalty to Hangan to gain admission into Moronao's service. In a series of heart-stopping special effects, the ghost of Oiwa confounds Iemon's plan. The lantern-escape *(chōchin nuke)* episode in which Oiwa's ghost directly confronts Iemon was introduced in an 1831 production starring Kikugorō III. The episode has remained popular ever since and is included here. A series of murder scenes *(koroshiba)* follow, terrifying in their graphic cruelty but magnificent for their stylized, dreamlike quality. Particularly innovative is the Buddhist altar change *(butsudangaeshi)* episode in which the ghost of Oiwa, played by an actor attached to a wheel built into the scenery, appears and disappears from behind a Buddhist altar. The play ends with the demise of Iemon during a highly stylized combat scene *(tachimawari)*.

An annotated text is available in Gunji Masakatsu, ed., *Tōkaidō Yotsuya Kaidan: Shinchō Nihon Koten Shūsei*, Vol. 45. Videotapes used were of the Kokuritsu Gekijō (National Theatre of Japan) productions of 1971 and 1982 and of the 1983 Kabukiza production.

CHARACTERS

OIWA, *wife of* TAMIYA IEMON
TAMIYA IEMON, *a handsome* rōnin, *husband of* OIWA
OYUMI, *widow of* ITŌ *and grandmother of* OUME
OMAKI, *servant of* OYUMI
OKUMA, *mother of* IEMON
NAOSUKE GONBEI, *common-law husband of* OSODE
AKIYAMA CHŌBEI, *servant of* IEMON
KOBOTOKE KOHEI, *servant of* IEMON
SATŌ YOMOSHICHI, *a* rōnin, *brother-in-law of* OIWA
OMON, *servant girl*
SHINDŌ GENSHIRŌ, *former husband of* OKUMA
JŌNEN, *master of Snake Mountain Hermitage*

FOLLOWERS *of* JŌNEN

KOBAYASHI HEINAI, *a samurai in the household of* KŌ NO MORONAO

FOOTMEN *of* KOBAYASHI HEINAI

SEKIGUCHI KANZŌ, *a* rōnin, *former crony of* TAMIYA IEMON

BANSUKE, *servant of* SEKIGUCHI KANZŌ

STAGE ASSISTANTS, *black-garbed* kurogo

Onbō Canal

(To accelerating ki *clacks the curtain is slowly pushed open. The setting is a desolate, intensely gloomy graveyard by the side of the Onbō Canal, which flows beneath a high embankment—or dike—backed by a thick hedge of grass. At extreme right the* hana-michi *connects with an earthen ramp that ascends from the canal to a cluster of bushes atop the embankment. An upturned bucket sits on a small landing that adjoins the ramp. A sluice gate, the height of the embankment, is on the other side. At left, on top of the embankment, the branches of a massive pine tree dangle like fishing lines over wooden grave tablets and an upright barrel. Also at left, a flight of steps descends from the embankment to a large landing where two poverty-stricken women,* OYUMI *and her faithful servant* OMAKI, *sit. The fine quality of their dirty costumes hints at former occupations as mistress and servant in a large, prosperous household.* OYUMI, *her body crumpled and hair bedraggled, seems utterly crushed by woe, except for a single obsession.* OMAKI *massages her mistress' back and encourages her. At extreme left is a cooking pot suspended from a wooden tripod. Offstage, languid shamisen music completes the somber scene.)*

OMAKI: How are you feeling today, Oyumi?

OYUMI: Don't worry like that! I feel much better. *(Burning with a grudge.)* I just want to find Tamiya Iemon, who murdered my husband, Lord Itō, and my grand-daughter, Oume!

(She weeps, and OMAKI *retreats a short distance out of respect.)*

OMAKI: Now, now! I understand perfectly. You are all I have left in the world.

OYUMI *(Softening):* Yes, you have cared for me all through this trial. *(She draws a red brocade amulet from her bosom and holds it tenderly in front of her. She recalls the wedding night of* OUME *in horror.)* This amulet failed to protect Oume. Iemon displayed no fear of it at all. *(Overcome by grief, she lets her hands collapse into her lap.)*

OMAKI: Don't talk like that. *(She picks up a small bag of rice.)* I'll make dinner while you pray for Oume's repose.

(Offstage drum plays water pattern [mizu no oto] as OMAKI *turns her back to* OYUMI, *draws water from the river, and washes the rice.* OYUMI *wipes her eyes with a hand towel [tenugui] and starts to chant prayers, but, overcome with grief,*

she slumps forward holding the amulet. A black-garbed STAGE ASSISTANT [kurogo] *manipulates a pole* [sashigane] *to which a realistic rat prop is attached. The rat, which embodies the ghost of* OIWA, *pokes its nose out from the edge of the canal and waits for an opportunity to seize the amulet. It then grabs the amulet between its teeth.* Dorodoro *drum pattern as* OYUMI *and* OMAKI *recoil with a mixture of astonishment and terror.* OYUMI *flaps her towel at the rat.* OMAKI *waves her hands as the rat scuttles around and around the landing.* OMAKI *loses her footing and plunges into the canal. Triple* tsuke *beats.* Dorodoro. OYUMI *screams and reaches after* OMAKI. *Finally,* OYUMI *collapses sideways in a heap, her back to the audience. Double* tsuke *beats.* NAOSUKE GONBEI *appears on the* hanamichi *to offstage drums and flute* [narimono] *accompaniment. He has the air of a vagabond, eager to seize any opportunity that might come his way. He carries a bucket and long pole with a curved hook at one end and wears close-fitting pants that extend just below the knees in the manner of an eel fisherman.)*

NAOSUKE *(At* shichisan*):* Not a single measly fish for all my work! *(He stares into the canal.)* This spot looks promising, with all the water being thrashed about! *(Offstage shamisen music continues as* NAOSUKE *proceeds to the main stage. He walks partly up the ramp to the embankment and stops for a moment, crouching as if he has spied something in the canal. He puts down his bucket and lowers himself gingerly into the water, pole with curved hook at the ready. He dips the hook into the water three times.* Dorodoro *and* tsuke *beats accompany each attempt. The first two times turn up nothing but weeds. The third time, however, he feels an object on the hook. A clump of hair attached to it comes into sight.* NAOSUKE *tears the hair from the hook and spots the magnificent tortoiseshell comb handed down to* OIWA *by her mother. Triple* tsuke *beats. He holds the comb at arm's length and intently assesses its value. He ad-libs* [sutezerifu] *concerning the price it might fetch. He climbs back onto the landing at right center while a lively shamisen accompaniment announces the simultaneous entry on the embankment of the grey-haired old lady,* OKUMA, *at right, and the stylishly dressed* TAMIYA IEMON *from left.* OKUMA *carries a long, narrow wooden grave tablet held upright.* IEMON *wears the two swords of a samurai and a basket hat over his head as a disguise. He carries a long pole in his left hand and a box for fish bait in his right. Mother and son proceed at an identical pace toward the center. They counter-cross.* IEMON *places his right hand on the pole to defend himself. Tsuke beat. He recognizes* OKUMA *and relaxes. He invites her to sit on the barrel, and he sits on the ground slightly to her right.)*

IEMON *(Obviously relieved and delighted):* Hello, it's you, Ma! I sure am glad to see you!

OKUMA: Me too! I've come up with an idea to stop the manhunt for you. Do you remember that I worked as a cook in Moronao's household at the same time you were in Hangan's service? When I retired, Moronao gave me this letter in case I ever needed help. *(She produces a small cloth package from her bosom, unwraps the package, unfolds the letter it contains, and passes it to* IEMON. *He inspects the letter, refolds it, and places it inside his kimono.*) As soon as I heard that you had lost your position with Hangan's clan, I sent a message to Moronao to remind him of the letter. Later, I heard rumors that you'd been implicated in the deaths of Oiwa, Oume, and Lord Itō. So, I decided to come up with a deception. *(She holds out the wooden grave tablet.)* We'll spread our own rumor that you're dead by erecting this grave tablet! Aren't I the clever one?

IEMON *(With relish):* So that's what you're up to! A terrific plan! I've an idea as well. I'll shift the blame for the killings to my friend, Kanzō, and his servant, Bansuke. But let's try your plan first! Set the tablet up here!

OKUMA: Okay! This spot looks good*! (They both rise.* OKUMA *sets up the tablet slightly to her left. Then mother and son stand back to admire their handiwork. They pose to double* tsuke *beats.)* Well, I'll be off! Come visit any time!

IEMON: Good-bye, Ma! I'll be sure to visit!

(*Offstage* narimono *accompanies* OKUMA *lifting the left hem of her kimono and exiting left. Meanwhile,* NAOSUKE, *below and to their right, has listened attentively.* IEMON *sits down at center and, with his right hand, casts his fishing line into the water. Dorodoro. Holding another line in his left hand, he braces the fishing pole against the strong current while he sets the pole firmly in the embankment. He sits on a barrel and takes a pipe and tobacco pouch from his left sleeve, halting when he realizes that he has no light.* IEMON *catches sight of* NAOSUKE *out of the corner of his eye. He rises and approaches* NAOSUKE, *not yet recognizing him.)*

IEMON: Got a light?

NAOSUKE: Sure. *(He stands up, places his left foot on the upturned bucket, and leans upstage with the light. Tsuke beat.* IEMON *bends down to accept it.)* Well! Iemon! It's good to see you!

(IEMON *starts backward and is on guard immediately.)*

IEMON: Oh! Is that you, Naosuke?

(NAOSUKE *casually puts away the light, collects his bucket and pole, and ascends the few remaining steps to the embankment. He talks as he strides purposefully toward* IEMON, *now seated on the barrel at left center.* NAOSUKE *stops just beyond* IEMON*'s reach and puts down the bucket and pole. He crouches and then addresses* IEMON *in a challenging tone.)*

NAOSUKE: Naosuke? I'm "Gonbei the eel-catcher"! *(Menacingly, he states a common pseudonym for a gangster.)* You're the sworn enemy of Oiwa, my wife's sister!

IEMON *(Uneasily):* You're joking! What do you mean?

NAOSUKE *(Crouching):* Come on! You can't have forgotten! Oiwa's younger sister is Osode, my wife! *(Ironically.)* I could say, "On guard, Iemon!" but there's no need to fight. Instead, hand over that letter and I'll claim your position in Moronao's household. No one will know the difference!

IEMON (*Protesting*): This letter contains the seeds for my future!

NAOSUKE (*Taking up the words of a popular ditty*): "If you plant those seeds yourself, I'll dig them up right away" and turn you in to the cops!

IEMON (*Gratingly*): All right! There's no way out!

(*Dorodoro.* IEMON *'s fishing line begins to quiver violently. Both* NAOSUKE *and* IEMON *rise excitedly.* IEMON *bends down, picks up the pole, and heaves in his catch.* NAOSUKE *animatedly runs behind* IEMON, *uproots the tablet set up by* OKUMA, *and knocks the fish on the head. Tsuke beat.* NAOSUKE *thrusts the tablet away to the left and it plummets to the large landing below, where it strikes* OYUMI. *Tsuke beat. The shock revives* OYUMI, *who clutches her heart, props up the tablet, and stares at it in disbelief. The voice of* OYUMI *captures the attention of* NAOSUKE *and then* IEMON. *They lean toward her and listen carefully.*)

OYUMI (*Stunned*): Well! The name "Tamiya Iemon" is inscribed on this tablet! (*Her revenge reignites.*) Has he finally received his just reward?

(OYUMI *turns around, looks up, and spots* NAOSUKE *and* IEMON. IEMON *averts his face to avoid recognition. He pulls* NAOSUKE *'s sleeve and whispers to him to say, "He's dead."* NAOSUKE *nods his understanding.*)

OYUMI: Excuse me, sir! May I ask you a question?

NAOSUKE: Oh! What?

OYUMI (*Feigning nonchalance*): This tablet has the name "Tamiya Iemon" inscribed on it. Do you know how he died?

NAOSUKE (*Relishing* IEMON *'s discomfort*): What! Tamiya Iemon? He's here! (IEMON *tugs at* NAOSUKE *'s sleeve and again urges him to say, "He's dead."*) Just kidding! He's certainly dead! No doubt about it! A close relative erected that tablet after Iemon's death. No one would go to all that trouble if he were still alive! Would they? It's true! He's dead!

OYUMI (*With lingering doubts*): When did he die?

NAOSUKE (*Perplexed*): What do you mean? Certainly, today . . . (*almost at once he realizes his error and changes tack*) today is the forty-ninth day after his death and, thus, the end of the mourning period.

OYUMI (*Taken aback*): Eh? Is it the forty-ninth day? Oh! Oh! Oh!

(OYUMI *thinks of* OUME *and weeps piteously, head buried in her hand towel.* IEMON *rises and circles behind* NAOSUKE *to creep up on* OYUMI.)

NAOSUKE (*Watching* IEMON): There, there! (*Distracting* OYUMI.) Are you a sister of Iemon? Ah! That's it!

(OYUMI *lifts her head, by which time* IEMON *has descended the steps to the landing and is already behind her.*)

OYUMI: No, no! Iemon is my enemy. He murdered my husband and my only granddaughter! Since then my heart has burned with revenge! At last, my prayers are answered!

(IEMON *kicks* OYUMI *into the canal, where she disappears without trace. Loud* tsuke *beats accent the kick and the splash. A large temple bell tolls.* Dorodoro. IEMON *faces front, pushes his basket hat from his head until it hangs from his right shoulder, places his right foot on a short post at the edge of the landing, and, with his left foot well behind, strikes a* mie. *The bell tolls again together with a single loud* tsuke *beat.*)

NAOSUKE: Truly . . .

IEMON: Your actions . . .

NAOSUKE: Are incredible!

(*The bell tolls continuously as drums swell in volume.* NAOSUKE *collects his pole and bucket, rapid shamisen music plays, and he briskly marches off left. He completely forgets to collect the letter from* IEMON.)

IEMON (*Sneering at* OYUMI): That bitch popped up in one too many places for her own good! (*He ascends the steps, bends over to pull in his fishing line, and rises quickly in surprise.*) Damn! The bait's disappeared!

(*He replaces the bait and sits down at center. Drum plays water pattern [*mizu no oto*] with a shamisen accompaniment as* AKIYAMA CHŌBEI *enters right, on the embankment, with a confident spring in his step. He wears the single sword of a townsman and a pale hand towel covers his bedraggled hair. He removes the towel and folds it before he stops at the sluice gate.*)

CHŌBEI (*Pretending surprise*): Ah, Tamiya! I didn't expect to run into you!

IEMON (*Startled*): What? You!

(CHŌBEI *addresses* IEMON *in a menacing tone. Throughout the following episode the standing* CHŌBEI *harangues the seated* IEMON *with contemptuous hand gestures. Clearly he holds the whip hand and is determined that* IEMON *know it.*)

CHŌBEI: Well, well! You've killed Oiwa and Kohei and, on top of that, Itō and his granddaughter, too! Since you disappeared the police have been hunting Kanzō, Bansuke, and myself for the murders. Of course, we'll turn you in straightaway if we're caught!

IEMON (*Cowed*): Look here! Haven't we worked hand in hand until now? Surely we can make a deal?

CHŌBEI (*Triumphantly*): Now you're talking! We'll all disappear if you come up with enough hard cash!

(*The dialogue grows increasingly rapid.*)

IEMON: All right, but where can I find the money?

CHŌBEI (*Not taken in for a moment*): Then I'm off to the police now!

IEMON (*Beaten*): Wait!

CHŌBEI: The cash or the police?

IEMON (*To himself*): Mmm. What will I do for the money?

CHŌBEI: Well?

IEMON: Well . . .

CHŌBEI: Well . . .

BOTH: Well, well, well, well . . . well!

> *(The repeated "wells" rise to a climax [kuriage].)*

CHŌBEI: Well, where's the cash coming from?

> *(IEMON ponders and then fishes the letter out of his kimono.)*

IEMON *(Conspiratorially):* Look! This letter bears the personal seal and guarantee of my fortune by Lord Moronao. Take it!

> *(IEMON proffers the letter to CHŌBEI, who reads it with great deliberation.*
> *IEMON rises and stands a respectful distance from CHŌBEI.)*

CHŌBEI: I see. You'll give us the cash in return for this letter.

IEMON: That's right.

CHŌBEI: We have a deal, Tamiya, sir.

IEMON: That's agreed, Akiyama, sir.

CHŌBEI: Good-bye!

> *(To offstage shamisen and the tolling of the bell, a smug CHŌBEI puts the letter in his kimono, walks behind IEMON, and exits left. IEMON watches him depart, his left arm outstretched in despair. IEMON collects his fishing pole, basket hat, bait box, and tobacco pouch. To languid shamisen and light dorodoro he crosses from the earthen ramp to the hanamichi. Drumbeats accelerate. IEMON reaches shichisan as offstage flute and large drum play wind pattern [kaze no oto]. He halts and nervously looks around in all directions. A raindoor bearing the corpses of OIWA and KOBOTOKE KOHEI on opposite sides floats into view from stage left. IEMON is irresistibly drawn back to the embankment, where a STAGE ASSISTANT relieves him of his belongings, except for the fishing pole. IEMON peers down into the canal, spots the raindoor, and grimaces in horror. He recovers his nerve in an instant and strides quickly to the barrel. He faces front and, using the fishing pole, steers the raindoor to the bank, where it disappears. After a few moments, it reappears in a vertical position, immediately below IEMON. Fast and loud dorodoro as IEMON reaches with the pole and draws the raindoor halfway up the embankment. The lights dim, dorodoro softens, and eerie flute swells. IEMON places the pole on the ground to his right. He raises the cloth covering the raindoor and takes in the horrible sight. Thundering dorodoro. He throws the cloth into the canal, revealing the corpse of OIWA dressed only in a somber, flimsy kimono. Her arms hang down limply. Her hairline is set well back from the eyebrows and her hair dangles loosely to below the shoulders. The forehead and skin around the right eye are horribly disfigured as a result of the poison IEMON consented to give her. She begins to move her head and right arm listlessly.)*

IEMON: Oiwa, Oiwa! Forgive me! I'm sorry!

Standing on the embankment of Onbō Canal, Iemon (Kataoka Takao, later Kataoka Nizaemon XV) pulls from the water the disfigured corpse of his wife, Oiwa
(Bandō Tamasaburō V), which he had previously fastened to the raindoor. (Umemura Yutaka, Engeki Shuppansha)

146

(*OIWA straightens her left arm above her waist, with the extended hand clutching* OUME*'s amulet.*)

OIWA (*Weakly but eerily*): Let the leaves of the Tamiya and Itō family branches wither to exorcise my vengeance!

IEMON (*Still crouching directly over her*): Oh, Buddha! Save me! Save me! Save me!
(*The left arm gradually falls back to its side in apparent submission. Then the corpse collapses back onto the raindoor.*) Ha! So you're not ready to make your peace yet!
(IEMON *turns the raindoor over to hide the corpse, but this action reveals another somberly clothed figure attached to the reverse side of the door. A crown of waterweeds covers the head and shoulders.*)

IEMON: My God! On the other side, too!
(IEMON *grasps the waterweeds and holds them. The dramatic tension rises as deafening* dorodoro *accelerates.* IEMON *whips away the weeds and reveals* KOHEI*'s corpse. A wide bald strip runs through the center of his hair, and one side of his scalp bears a bloody wound. The same actor, concealed in a compartment in the embankment, plays both* OIWA *and* KOHEI. *He pokes his head through a hole to provide* OIWA*'s head and, after a quick makeup change,* KOHEI*'s head. He also thrusts his arms through separate holes.*)

KOHEI (*With a piercing stare*): My master has an incurable disease. Give me your family medicine!

IEMON: Is this the work of a ghost, too?
(IEMON *abruptly retreats, then recovers his nerve and replaces the weeds covering* KOHEI*'s head. When, after some moments, he releases his grip, the mask drops, and the cloth covering the corpse falls to reveal a skeleton. Its head moves as if trying to speak. In terror,* IEMON *bolts upright and the skeleton collapses into the canal. Booming* dorodoro. IEMON *raises both hands to fend off the ghosts. As a last resort, he kneels, head bowed and hands clasped in prayer. The ringing of a metal bell is heard. On its final ring the lights come up, revealing* SATŌ YOMOSHICHI *posing down right, below the embankment. On the embankment* IEMON *is at center and* NAOSUKE *at left, dressed in a light summer kimono [yukata] hitched up to reveal his legs and cradling a fishing pole in his left arm. They begin a mime struggle as if in the darkness [danmari] for a letter in* YOMOSHICHI*'s obi containing details of the vendetta against* KŌ NO MORONAO. *Shamisen music plays.* YOMOSHICHI *and* IEMON *reach for their swords and pose in a* mie *to double* tsuke *beats.* NAOSUKE, *holding his pole vertically, attacks* IEMON. *They pose in a* mie *to double* tsuke *beats.* IEMON *fingers his sword hilt, forcing* NAOSUKE *to retreat several steps twirling his pole.* NAOSUKE *creeps past* IEMON, *brushing his left shoulder.* IEMON *swats him with an upraised left arm, and* NAOSUKE *retreats left.* YOMOSHICHI *mounts the steps to the earthen ramp and counter-crosses with* IEMON, *brushing his arm. Double* tsuke *beats. All three*

strike a mie. YOMOSHICHI, *facing rear, and* IEMON, *facing front, grope toward each other. Drums.* NAOSUKE *slashes with his pole as* IEMON *moves toward the barrel.* IEMON *grasps the pole and raises his other hand high, then, in a single sinuous movement, drops it behind his back.* YOMOSHICHI *raises his left leg and poses with both hands resting on his hips. Fast* tsuke *beats fade and loud drums beat briefly. A single* tsuke *beat. The bell tolls.* IEMON *casts off* NAOSUKE *'s pole.* YOMOSHICHI *straightens, gropes, steps away from* IEMON, *and then counter-crosses, stopping by* IEMON *'s side.* NAOSUKE *retreats left. Offstage musicians sing as* OMON, *carrying an umbrella that obscures her upper body, enters left and stops.* NAOSUKE *darts past* OMON, *stopping by her side. Both pairs converge. Tsuke beat.* YOMOSHICHI *approaches* OMON, *touches her umbrella, momentarily starts backward, and then moves boldly past her, grasping* NAOSUKE *'s horizontal pole. He casts away the pole and grips* IEMON *'s left sleeve.* OMON *brushes* IEMON *and retreats left, passing* YOMOSHICHI. NAOSUKE *takes* OMON *'s left sleeve, and they all dance a single step right.* OMON *takes* YOMOSHICHI *'s left sleeve, forming an unbroken line, and all dance two steps left. Breaking the line,* OMON *releases* YOMOSHICHI *'s sleeve, and all dance two steps right before rejoining. The men strike a powerful* mie *with legs far apart.* IEMON *brings his right hand to his chest;* YOMOSHICHI *raises his left arm above his head;* NAOSUKE *holds his pole vertically under his left shoulder. Double* tsuke *beats.* OMON *counter-crosses with* YOMOSHICHI *and meets* IEMON *behind the umbrella. Double* tsuke *beats.* OMON, *the umbrella still hiding her face, runs to* shichisan *and kneels. Unbeknownst to* YOMOSHICHI, NAOSUKE *snatches the letter but drops it. He raises his pole horizontally, and the three men seize it. As they struggle, the pole moves rhythmically left, right, and again left. Releasing his grip,* IEMON *cuts the pole. Double* tsuke *beats.* YOMOSHICHI *retains one-quarter of the pole and charges right while* NAOSUKE, *moving left, keeps the remainder. Double* tsuke *beats.* NAOSUKE *cowers left.* YOMOSHICHI *poses martially;* IEMON *stands center, head high, slowly swinging his sword out to his right. The men strike a final powerful group* mie. *Very loud, repeated* tsuke *beats as* YOMOSHICHI *extends his left leg wide,* IEMON *shoulders the sword, and* NAOSUKE *studies the letter held high in his left hand. The curtain closes, leaving* OMON *alone on the* hana-michi, *revealing that she is* OIWA, *played by a stand-in actor. She adjusts her appearance to that of a lovely young lady and, fanning herself all the while, exits along the* hanamichi *to the clacking of the* ki.)

The Dream

(The curtain is pushed open to accelerating ki *clacks that gradually fade. A single loud* ki *clack. Eleven* FOLLOWERS *of* JŌNEN, *the master of Snake Mountain Hermitage, are seated in a row across the stage and facing the audience. To the accompaniment of loud* dorodoro, *a small banner is raised at extreme stage left*

bearing a large Chinese character meaning "spirit" [kokoro], *signifying the path to
Buddhist paradise. Dorodoro fades and then swells as the curtain is pulled aside
to reveal a summer cottage at left, raised on a low platform. Strips of gaily colored
paper on which poems are written for the summer Tanabata Festival drift in the air
from bamboo poles on either side of a fine bamboo screen, which conceals the cottage
veranda. Squash vines coil down from the roof to the eaves against an elegant background of plum and cherry trees. Vines also cling to a wicket of chestnut wood at
center, adjacent to the cottage, while bush clover grows in profusion beneath the
portal, providing the autumn semblance of a peasant's cottage. At right is a lattice
fence leaning under the burden of squash. Thunderous* dorodoro *announces the
presence of* OIWA*'s ghost. Then silence. A solo offstage singer accompanied by a
shamisen begins singing a plaintive song* [dokugin], *which accentuates the eerie
silence. A flute plays as a hawk flies into the cottage. A single loud* ki *clack. An
imperious* IEMON *appears on the* hanamichi *dressed ceremoniously in a dark
formal* haori *and the light-patterned* hakama *of a samurai. A pale blue silk braid in
the style of fireflies beating their wings adorns his topknot, and he wears garden
sandals. A hawk's tether dangles from one hand while a resplendent Bon Festival
lantern hangs from the other. Behind* IEMON *strolls* CHŌBEI, *now dressed in a
dandified manner and leading a dog played by an actor in a dog costume* [nuigu-
rumi]. CHŌBEI, *with pomaded hair, wears a white satin kimono and purple socks.
The bamboo screen rises, disclosing* OIWA. *She wears a brightly colored light silk
kimono with long, flowing sleeves and a black satin obi. The apron and towel, which
cover her hair, complete the image of a beautiful country maiden.* OIWA *sits at a
spinning wheel, weaving multicolored thread, with a pretty, paper-enclosed lamp by
her side. Her appearance is consistent with the legend that held that a woman could
improve her needlework on the day of the Tanabata Festival.* IEMON*'s hawk is
perched atop the lamp.* IEMON, *standing at* shichisan, *and* OIWA, *in the cottage,
catch sight of each other and strike a* Tanabata mie, *leaning toward each other like
lovers yearning to reunite, to plaintive shamisen music and triple* tsuke *beats. The
moment is symbolic, not literal, as* IEMON *is outside and* OIWA *inside, thus making it impossible to actually see each other. As the moon floats free from its veil of
clouds, both characters utter passionate ad-libs* [sutezerifu] *appropriate to long-
separated lovers. Then the music ceases. A sharp* ki *clack: fireflies manipulated with
long poles by several* STAGE ASSISTANTS *swarm onto the stage, bringing the
tableau to life.)*

IEMON: The late evening shoals and white-capped waves of the Milky Way . . .

OIWA: Are spanned by a magpie bridge of reproach. *(Reverting to normal prose.)*
Although this hawk is not a magpie, it has wandered in here to rest.

IEMON: I wondered where Kogasumi, my prize hawk, had disappeared to, so I went
searching and hoped to stumble upon a beauty!

CHŌBEI: Truly, this evening is the Tanabata Festival! With a name that means "love-struck," it's no wonder that Kogasumi went astray on the very day that lover-stars meet! *(He parodies* IEMON*'s yearning.)* Has he flown off to the Milky Way?

IEMON: Twaddle! My truant hawk is sure to be in the neighborhood. Come on! Search for him! Search for him!

> *(The offstage solo song resumes as* IEMON *and* CHŌBEI *approach the door of the cottage.* CHŌBEI *peeps inside, sees* OIWA*, and is astounded.)*

CHŌBEI: Master! Master! Look at that beauty spinning thread!

IEMON: What! A beauty?

CHŌBEI: Yes!

IEMON: Where? Where? *(Curiosity compels him to peek inside the cottage.)* I see! A rare country maid! Ask her about my hawk.

CHŌBEI: Yes sir! *(He enters.)* Hey, girl! My master's hunting hawk has disappeared. Has it popped in here?

OIWA: Yes. This hawk just flew in and perched itself next to me.

CHŌBEI: Terrific! I'll call my master. *(He returns to* IEMON *to tell him the good news.)* The hawk's here!

IEMON: Is that so? I'll go and collect it. Come with me!

> *(*IEMON *enters and is instantly smitten by* OIWA*'s loveliness. To a sharp triple tsuke beat he strikes a* mie*, legs far apart, eyes bulging, and head thrust forward.* IEMON *sits down cross-legged upstage, and* OIWA*, as the dutiful hostess, moves close.* CHŌBEI *sits behind his highly excited master.)*

IEMON: Well, well! You do have a stylish home! My hunting hawk strayed in this vicinity, and when I learned it was here, I came to retrieve it.

OIWA: How ceremonious you are! By all means, take your hawk.

IEMON: Too kind! I'd like to take it now, but *(striving for an excuse to remain)*, well, a return journey on foot this evening would certainly be more trouble than it's worth due to the darkness.

CHŌBEI *(Cantankerously):* What's that, Master? How can it be dark, Master? This evening is the Tanabata Festival. The moon is risen and it's just like day! Besides, you brought this lantern on purpose for the homeward journey. The darkness will vanish when I light the lantern. Come! Let's go home! *(He takes the lantern from* IEMON *and, oblivious to his master's wishes, hangs it from the eaves as* OIWA *goes inside.)*

IEMON: What? You presumptuous fool! It's only bright out front! I said I wouldn't return because of the darkness, but since you mentioned this evening's moon, you go! Set the hawk on your arm, take the dog, and go on ahead by yourself! Idiot!

CHŌBEI: Hey! Don't order me around! Now that I'm your servant I call you "Master," but before I was your comrade, Akiyama Chōbei, just like a dog is a sidekick and a hawk is a companion. *(His scorn turns to anger.)* You're the master so take them yourself, you wretch! *(He flings the dog's leash at* IEMON.*)*

IEMON: No! Damn you! Before was before! Now you're my servant, so take them home!

CHŌBEI: A mere servant! Don't get pompous with me! Now you've moved up in the world, but not so long ago, as Tamiya Iemon, you were dirt poor and a villain! And then there's the disappearance of Oiwa after you eloped with her! Take the dog home yourself!

IEMON: No! You take it!

(The dog is shoved aside by both IEMON *and* CHŌBEI *to sharp* tsuke *beats.)*

CHŌBEI: *(Baiting the dog):* Sic him, boy!

(The dog howls. OIWA *emerges from the cottage and halts the conflict.)*

OIWA: Oh, dear! What's happened? Please don't argue. I overheard you say that before you became master and servant you had been comrades. Let me attempt to reconcile the two of you.

IEMON: If you take charge, my heart will be in it!

CHŌBEI: As long as Tamiya understands I won't apologize, I'll agree!

OIWA: All right. I shall reunite the two of you!

CHŌBEI: You are amusing! *(His mood changes as he rummages through his clothing.)* Ah! Here's the sake that I brought! Shall we start? *(He holds out the sake flask.)* Pass me your cup, miss!

OIWA: Yes! Yes! *(She rises and extends her cup to* CHŌBEI.*)* Hmm. Well, there are a few skewered pieces of pickled mackerel left over from today's celebrations. Help yourselves, both of you! *(She delicately removes the skewers from the pieces and serves the food in a bowl.)*

IEMON *(Leaning back against* OIWA*):* Oh! How interesting, these skewered pieces are linked just like the two of us.

OIWA: Why would a splendid samurai like you fall in love with a country maid?

IEMON: Such words of gratitude! Right now I'm a bachelor. He's my guarantor, ah, servant.

CHŌBEI: Yes, yes! He had a wife, but she vanished. Well, as this is your home, you have to open formalities.

OIWA: Then, let's begin! *(*CHŌBEI *fills the cup that* OIWA *holds out to him. She casts a glance at* IEMON, *emphasized by a sharp* tsuke *beat, and then drinks. Flirting.)* I wonder to whom I should next pass this sake cup?

IEMON: Do me the honor!

CHŌBEI: Oh, yes! Marinate the skewered master first!

OIWA *(To* IEMON*):* Allow me.

IEMON: Let's drink together.

*(*IEMON *and* OIWA *both drink sake and snuggle together lasciviously.)*

CHŌBEI *(Scornfully):* Will Master Iemon allow his servant-comrade to drink, too?

IEMON: Of course! Serve yourself!

CHŌBEI: You're too kind! *(Clutching the portable sake flask, he gulps down a few cups and rises unsteadily.)*

IEMON: My reeling servant, pass the cup and dance!

OIWA *(Mischievously):* Yes! Dance!

CHŌBEI: No way! I'm not dancing for the two of you!

IEMON: It's a special request!

CHŌBEI: No! Who do you think you are?

IEMON *(To OIWA):* Come on! Help me!

OIWA: Yes! Yes! Please dance! Dance!

CHŌBEI: No. This is embarrassing!

> *(Offstage drums and flute music suggest a lively festival dance. OIWA cups her hands over CHŌBEI's eyes and IEMON turns him round and round. CHŌBEI whirls in a merry, erratic dance as the dog barks until, eventually, servant and dog depart to continuous tsuke beats. IEMON and OIWA are left alone.)*

IEMON: He's an utter fool! Well now, are you a farmer's daughter?

OIWA: I am a humble maid who was raised in a cottage near here.

IEMON: Oh, you were raised in a cottage, and my family name, Tamiya, sounds like "cottage!"

OIWA: Well then, I shall call you Tamiya.

IEMON: Indeed, that's my name!

OIWA *(Ominously):* Well, I have exactly the same name!

> *(Instantly, the mood transforms. To loud triple tsuke beats, OIWA strikes a mie, staring vindictively into IEMON's face. The large drum plays the wind pattern as one of the strips of paper tied to the bamboo poles flutters free, falls, and drifts toward OIWA. She deftly picks it up and presents it to IEMON.)*

OIWA: Here is my name.

IEMON *(Reading):* This is a verse in the *One Hundred Poems* collection that is offered at the Tanabata Festival. "A rock dams the rapids . . ."

OIWA: "And, after it divides the river, I know the two branches will meet again." Divided in the end. . . . *(Loud tsuke beats as OIWA strikes a mie. Her head thrust forward, she glares at IEMON.)* It is Tamiya whom I will meet! *(A single, sharp tsuke beat.)*

IEMON: Heavens! You sound like the lunatic Oiwa that everyone's gossiping about!

OIWA: I am called "Iwa," the same as the rock in the poem, and you must be the lover for whom I yearn! *(She leans against IEMON's knees and feigns a loving look at him.)*

IEMON *(Naively):* You're the exact image of my wife, Oiwa, long ago when she was just a country girl . . .

OIWA: Separated by a rock I am your lover. From today . . .

In "The Dream" scene, the young and beautiful ghost of Oiwa (Bandō Tamasa-burō V) flirts with Iemon (Kataoka Takao, later Kataoka Nizaemon XV). She is about to read the poem in her right hand alluding to the karma that brings them together: "[A] verse in the *One Hundred Poems* collection, . . . 'A rock dams the rapids and, after it divides the river, I know the two branches will meet again.' " (Umemura Yutaka, Engeki Shuppansha)

IEMON: I shall love you! Oh! I was blind to you before!

OIWA: You are fickle!

IEMON: As are the hearts of all men! *(He takes* OIWA *by the obi, lays down his sword, and leads her willingly into the cottage.)*

OIWA: No one can see except for your hawk.

IEMON: It's a nighthawk, just like a prostitute on the prowl!

OIWA: Am I such a nighthawk?

IEMON *(Embarrassed):* Not at all! The lamp! *(He extinguishes the lantern.)*

OIWA: Oh! Wait! There's no smudge fire for the mosquitoes!

IEMON: Indeed! I can see striped mosquitoes! *(Several* STAGE ASSISTANTS *manipulate* sashigane *poles to which are attached firefly props.* IEMON *pauses in a reflective* mie *to* tsuke *beats.)* Oh! It's the light of fireflies!

OIWA: In the gloom, even the fireflies fall in love with me. They resemble both the morning glories and the dew which, like a dream, vanish instantly in the blaze of day! *(She fixes her gaze on the lantern.)*

IEMON *(Beginning "divided" dialogue* [warizerifu]*):* Even the wilting flowers . . .

OIWA: Share the fate of dew.

IEMON: Oh! Blooming morning glories . . .

OIWA: Wilt in autumn's breeze.

IEMON: Alas!

OIWA: It is chilling!

> *(They pose to a single loud* tsuke *beat,* OIWA *resting against* IEMON *'s lap. The offstage solo song resumes to plaintive shamisen accompaniment as the bamboo screen is lowered to conceal the lovers. Then, to lively drums and flute music,* CHŌBEI *approaches the cottage, dragging the dog.)*

CHŌBEI: Hey! I'm so drunk! My eyes are spinning after all that sake and dancing! Lord Buddha! I feel horrible! I wonder where that wastrel Tamiya went with the girl? Even she gave me some awful looks. I'll bet they're in the cottage. That's it! Damn them! *(He embraces the dog, mocking the figures of* IEMON *and* OIWA, *which can be glimpsed through the bamboo screen. The dog howls and clamps its teeth down on* CHŌBEI*'s hair. He chases the dog away to continuous* tsuke *beats.)* Ouch! Ouch! That beast made a meal of my skull! How did Tamiya seduce her so easily? I'm green with envy! *(He is breathless with excitement.)* I'll just take a peep. *(He goes to one side of the bamboo screen and peeps through the crack. A loud* tsuke *beat. He recoils in terror.)* My God! What's this? The girl has a monster's face! I'm out of here! I'll grab the lantern, turn tail, and run! *(He pauses to inhale and summon his courage. Then he removes the lantern from the eaves. Ominous* dorodoro *as the lantern takes on the visage of* OIWA. *He screams, petrified with fright.)* What's happening? It's incredible! *(In terror he prances backward and forward.)* Master Tamiya! Master Tamiya! *(He glances once more at the eaves.*

A hanging squash basket begins to acquire the face of OIWA. *A sharp* tsuke *beat and it splits in two. Then, to continuous* tsuke *beats culminating in a deafening clack, the head of* OIWA *lunges out.* CHŌBEI *is paralyzed with terror.*) Dear Buddha! Dear Buddha! Let me out of here!

(*As light* dorodoro *plays, he flees, tumbling and in a cold sweat, toward the* hanamichi. *The bell tolls the hour and the offstage shamisen play a menacing tune* [sugomi] *as the bamboo screen rolls up.* IEMON *stands, perches the hawk on his arm, and puts on his sword.* OIWA *catches the hem of his kimono.*)

OIWA: Are you leaving, already?

IEMON: Yes. I'd better return home while the night remains young. I'll come again.

    (OIWA *takes his hand to detain him.*)

OIWA: Just a moment. You are a handsome man, and since you had a wife called Oiwa, you must be merely flirting with me!

IEMON: No! Why should I flirt? Although I had a wife called Oiwa, she was an evil woman. I left her because she was a damned nasty case!

    (*A sharp* tsuke *beat.*)

OIWA (*Anguished*): Have you eternally forsaken your former wife, of whom you speak so spitefully, Iemon? (*She fixes* IEMON *with a venomous stare.*)

IEMON (*Shuddering*): Somehow your expression and that of Oiwa . . .

OIWA: Resemble each other? The light of the moon should guide me to Buddha's paradise, but instead it chills like the vengeful face of Oiwa. The twin tides of the same moon pound the damming rock with pain from this world.

    (*A sharp* tsuke *beat.*)

IEMON: Heavens! What did you say?

OIWA: Vengeance on Iemon!

IEMON: My God!

    (IEMON *recoils from* OIWA, *and they cut a* mie *to continuous, furious* tsuke *pattern* [uchiage]. *The hawk changes into a rat and leaps at* IEMON. *Light* dorodoro *rumbling. A black curtain falls to cover the moon. A sharp* ki *clack. Suddenly* OIWA *reveals herself as a ghost to the reverberations of crashing* dorodoro. *Both* OIWA *and* IEMON *strike an aggressive* mie *to triple* tsuke *beats, the ghost with arms outstretched and* IEMON *with legs set apart and eyes glaring defiance.*)

IEMON: Has revenge completely possessed you?

OIWA: To hell you come, Tamiya!

IEMON: No way!

    (*Assailed by magical forces,* IEMON *attacks wildly. Powerful* dorodoro. *Several* STAGE ASSISTANTS *attack* IEMON *with flickering, phosphorescent green "soul fires" burning at the ends of* sashigane. IEMON *fights the fires to the brink of agonized exhaustion with sword slashes punctuated by double* tsuke *beats. He is sur-*

prised by flickering green fire that lights up the spinning wheel's frame. A sharp tsuke *beat. Now a four-wheeled cart, which has lost a wheel, catches fire and starts to charge around in circles.* IEMON, *terrified, and* OIWA *strike a* mie *to triple* tsuke *beats.* IEMON *attempts to escape from* OIWA's *extended arms until he collapses, exhausted. Joint* mie *to thunderous* tsuke *beats.* OIWA *and* IEMON *sink together on a trap* [seri] *into hell to deafening drums. The banner splits, and the* kokoro *character falls to a sharp* ki *clack.)*

Snake Mountain Hermitage

(A loud ki *clack. The bell tolls and the stage revolves. Another* ki *clack signals the scene to begin. The set darkens as large offstage drum plays snow pattern* [yuki no oto] *to indicate the arrival of winter; offstage shamisen play in the background. The interior of a hermitage is seen, with grey walls, a Buddhist altar at center, and a rear door to the left. Outside, snow lies piled up against a log gate, right, and covers four wooden grave tablets and a willow tree. Seated and talking together at center are* JŌNEN, *the black-robed master of the hermitage, who clasps a strand of rosary beads, and* SHINDŌ GENSHIRŌ, IEMON's *father, dressed in white pilgrim's attire.* JŌNEN's FOLLOWERS *sit in a row across the back of the stage. The shamisen abruptly ceases. In an adjoining room, left,* IEMON *lies in painful exhaustion under a paper mosquito net. With a rattling sound* IEMON, *scabbard in hand, rises and tears the net to pieces, each slash accompanied by double* tsuke *beats. He is dressed in a dirty black kimono and grey obi typical of a destitute* rōnin. *His face is pale and feverish, framed by bushy, unkempt hair that signifies illness bordering on madness.* JŌNEN's FOLLOWERS *mill around* IEMON *helplessly.* IEMON *bursts from the room to continuous* tsuke *beats.)*

IEMON: You bitch, Oiwa! Stand where I can see you! *(He is on the verge of drawing his sword again but is detained by* JŌNEN *and* GENSHIRŌ. IEMON *sees their faces and experiences a flash of recognition, and his anger subsides as he falls in a heap beside them.)* Oh, was it a dream? How terrifying! I saw fire carts from hell in the land of the living! *(He tears himself from his dream.)* Oh, Lord Buddha! Oh, Lord Buddha!

(Exhausted, IEMON *heaves a sigh of relief.* JŌNEN *faces rear and raises his arms to calm his* FOLLOWERS.*)*

GENSHIRŌ: Hello, son! Don't you know your father?

IEMON: Ah! Is it really you? Why are you here?

GENSHIRŌ: An old *rōnin* cannot serve two masters in a lifetime, so I'm in the middle of a pilgrimage to pray for salvation. *(Changing the subject.)* Your bout of illness . . .

IEMON: Is the result of a curse by a miserable ghost of a woman!

GENSHIRŌ: Well! Are you recovering?

IEMON: Yes, I feel all right, although occasionally I have bouts of fever. In fact, the master of the hermitage brought me here.

GENSHIRŌ: I didn't know that. *(To* JŌNEN.*)* I'm indebted to you.

JŌNEN: You're much too kind!

GENSHIRŌ: In that case, I'll stay a little while at the hermitage.

IEMON: Good! Then we shall be father and son until this snow lets up! We'll chat later.

(To an offstage musical accompaniment the temple bell tolls the lateness of the hour. The FOLLOWERS *rise and filter out through the back door followed by* JŌNEN *and* GENSHIRŌ. *The music increases in tempo. Ominous* dorodoro. *Alone,* IEMON *remains seated. His twisted face, unsteady hands, and limp arms all indicate physical torment by the ghost of* OIWA. *The sliding door opens and* OKUMA, *attired in a drab kimono, trots toward* IEMON.*)*

OKUMA *(Full of concern):* Oh, Iemon! My divorced husband, Genshirō, has unexpectedly dropped into the hermitage. Do you remember that after the divorce I entered the service of Lord Moronao? If I take the letter that I left with you to Moronao we'll have money to burn!

IEMON: In any event, I want out of this hermitage! The payoff will be a position of rank in Moronao's household in the near future if the letter does the trick!

OKUMA: Genshirō will go berserk when he learns of our deal with Moronao!

IEMON: No question! At any rate, I'll soon be strong again. By the way, have you had any trouble with rats lately?

OKUMA: Are you joking?! Today there have been hordes!

IEMON: Born in the Year of the Rat, so rat by nature, Oiwa by name! Her spite torments both mother and son!

(Quiet offstage shamisen and percussion accompaniment [mokugyō iri] *creates a melancholy mood. As the large drum softly plays snow patterns,* KOBAYASHI HEINAI *arrives at the door. He is dressed in a magnificent formal costume, wears the two swords of a samurai, and carries an umbrella with a bull's-eye design. One* FOOTMAN *lugs a heavy black box.* IEMON *hears the arrival and goes to his side of the door, where he waits, doubled over in pain.* OKUMA *follows and sits close behind him.)*

HEINAI *(Calling at the door):* I've come on business for Iemon, who is staying at this hermitage.

IEMON: Kobayashi Heinai! Come in out of the snowstorm!

*(*IEMON *slowly staggers away from the door.* HEINAI *folds his umbrella, passes it to the* FOOTMAN, *and enters.* IEMON *and* OKUMA *bow respectfully.* HEINAI *marches past them to take the seat of honor, left.)*

HEINAI: Good! After I examine the letter, which we discussed before, and ensure that the seal is authentic, I shall escort you to your investiture by Lord Moronao.

(To the FOOTMAN.*)* Display the clothes and swords of a retainer, which Lord Moronao has sent.

FOOTMAN: At once!

(*The* FOOTMAN *places the gifts on a purple cloth that covers a large wooden tray.* OKUMA *places the tray in front of* IEMON, *who bows deeply.*)

HEINAI *(Formally):* Accept these gifts from Lord Moronao.

IEMON *(Bowing):* Thank you. I shall entrust myself to you regarding the investiture.

HEINAI: Now show me the letter. It is time for the inspection.

IEMON *(Rattled):* Ah! Because of my illness, I have entrusted it to someone nearby. I shall reclaim it later and give it to you then.

OKUMA *(Suspiciously):* Hey, son! Why did you part with so precious a letter?

IEMON *(To* OKUMA*):* What? Don't worry, Mother! *(To* HEINAI.*)* In any event, please inspect it later.

(HEINAI *rises and marches imperiously to the door while* IEMON *and* OKUMA *bow deeply.*)

HEINAI *(Turning back):* I shall come again, and then I want to examine that letter without fail!

IEMON: Yes, sir! Please convey my best wishes to Lord Moronao.

HEINAI: I'll take my leave.

(HEINAI *exchanges bows with* IEMON *and* OKUMA. *Offstage* narimono *accompaniment as the* FOOTMAN *opens* HEINAI*'s umbrella and hands it to* HEINAI. *The bell tolls.* HEINAI *and the* FOOTMAN *depart.* OKUMA *rises and circles around to* IEMON*'s left.*)

OKUMA *(Anxiously):* Son! Where in the world did you put that precious letter?

IEMON: Chōbei blackmailed me! He said that he would turn me in to the police unless I loaned it to him as collateral.

OKUMA: Oh! So it was to hold him off for a while.

IEMON: I'll recover it. Don't worry!

OKUMA: Heavens! It's already dusk!

IEMON: Soon Oiwa will afflict both of us with fever. Don't go soft on me!

OKUMA: Let's stay on guard!

IEMON: I'll light the lamp. *(The bell tolls. Offstage shamisen and singing establish a peaceful mood.* IEMON *and* OKUMA *stand and strike a* mie *to double* tsuke *beats. They turn away from each other.* OKUMA *enters the room to prepare for sleep. Shamisen and song continue as* IEMON *lights a small lamp and opens the door. He picks up the water ladle and looks pensively at the winter scene.)* Ah! Mounds of snow, dazzlingly white! *(He catches sight of* CHŌBEI *asleep by the side of the snow-covered log gate.* IEMON *sneers unsympathetically, crosses outside, and sees the grave tablet of* OIWA. *He speaks in a trembling voice weakened by the curse of the ghost.)* It is inscribed with both her posthumous and worldly names. Even if I pray for her she'll never achieve rebirth. At summer's Bon Festival for the dead she'll be terrifying! *(Fearfully.)* Still, I'd better pray for the brat and her just in case. *(He pours the holy water from a bucket and then kneels near the grave tablet. Eerie flute music* [netori bue], *suggestive of wind blowing through crevices, signals the appearance of* OIWA*'s ghost. The bell tolls repeatedly and the stage plunges into darkness. A flame circles within the paper lantern. Loud* dorodoro *as the flame starts to burn a hole in the paper. Thunderous* dorodoro *and offstage* narimono *as the silhouette of* OIWA*'s face becomes visible. Finally, the lantern splits into two halves* [chōchin nuke], *and* OIWA*'s ghastly head thrusts through the gap. Netori bue music. Dorodoro resumes and the set is again plunged into darkness. A sharp* tsuke *beat as the light begins to return. The bloodstained body of the ghost has emerged from the lantern and stands, cradling* IEMON*'s infant son, to the left of* IEMON. IEMON *trudges a few steps forward and then discerns the shape of the ghost. Dorodoro.* IEMON *strikes a* mie *of horror in a half-standing position. Then he sits and speaks derisively.)* Vindictive ghost! Listen! You forced me to kill my father-in-law, Itō Kihei, and my new bride on our wedding night. Your curse also drowned my mother-in-law and her wet-nurse. To crown it all, you cursed your own family and killed our newborn son. What a loving mother! *(*OIWA *points twice at the infant and raises her hand to the scars on her face to remind* IEMON *of the abandonment of his son and of her own poisoning.* IEMON *kneels and prays. Sharp* tsuke *beats.* OIWA *clamps both hands over her ears. Then, trailing blood in the snow, she quickly circles* IEMON *and surrenders the infant. Dorodoro.* OIWA *exits right, one arm pointing at* IEMON. *He drops the infant. A sharp* ki *clack and the infant instantly turns into a stone statue of Jizō, the Bodhisattva of children. A sharp* tsuke *beat.* IEMON *hurriedly retreats inside the house.* CHŌBEI *enters right looking like a wild man from the country.* IEMON *is surrounded by scampering rats manipulated on the ends of* sashigane *by* STAGE ASSISTANTS.*)*

CHŌBEI *(Tremulous):* Beasts! *(He kicks the rats away and enters the house.)*

IEMON: What spite! *(He stares into space. Dorodoro resumes.)*

CHŌBEI *(Hearing* IEMON*'s voice, enters the hermitage):* Is that you, Master Iemon?

IEMON: Chōbei! Am I glad to see you! Listen! I've come by a stipend with the house of Moronao thanks to that letter I loaned you, so I want it back right away!

*(*CHŌBEI *sits in front of the Buddhist altar.)*

CHŌBEI: All right! I'll return it. When you entrusted it to me I took it home the same evening. However, I was overrun by a swarm of rats, which gnawed everything from my hair down to my fingernails. It was sheer hell! I'll return it! Anything to get rid of it!

IEMON: Did rats attack you, too? Oh! The ghost of Oiwa is here as well! *(He strikes a terrified* mie *to triple* tsuke *beats.)* Lord Buddha! Lord Buddha! Hurry up and bring me the letter!

CHŌBEI: You've killed a lot of people and already laid the blame on Kanzō, Bansuke, and myself. Look, Tamiya! Why do you want the letter so badly?

IEMON: My mother originally belonged to Moronao's clan, so it was easy for her to obtain my entry into his household. *(He abruptly stops.)* Do you hear anything? *(Crashing* dorodoro *as* IEMON *is distracted. The actor who plays* OIWA *is attached to a wheel hidden behind the altar. The wheel is rotated forward, and* OIWA *descends headfirst over* CHŌBEI*'s head. Taking a hand towel* [tenugui] *from around his neck, she slowly strangles him. He attempts to let out a scream, but* OIWA *slaps one hand over his mouth. He falls dead to one* tsuke *beat. The wheel is rotated backward, and* OIWA *drags the corpse into the compartment at the altar's rear.* IEMON, *ignorant of* OIWA*'s attack, suddenly detects the ghost and strikes a frightened* mie *to triple* tsuke *beats. He staggers. Blood begins to drip from the top of the altar. Each drop hits the floor to the accompaniment of a* tsuke *beat. Seeing the blood,* IEMON *summons all his willpower to look up.)*

IEMON: Is this the curse of Oiwa, too? *(A letter falls from the altar's crossbeam and* IEMON *grabs it.)* The letter I entrusted to Chōbei!
(Just then, HEINAI, *attended by four* FOOTMEN, *comes rushing along the* hanamichi *to continuous* tsuke *beats.)*

HEINAI *(From the door):* Iemon! Iemon! Show me that letter you promised a little while ago!

IEMON: Welcome! Yet, from the garb of your party, I have some doubts as to your purpose.

HEINAI: The reason for my appearance is that I have orders to apprehend one Seki-guchi Kanzō and his servant, Bansuke, for the murder of a retainer of Lord Moronao, one Itō Kihei, and of Itō's granddaughter. Now I need to see that letter, so get a move on!

IEMON: Verify it for yourself!
*(*IEMON *presents the letter to* HEINAI. *To a soft, menacing rumble of* dorodoro *drums* HEINAI *unrolls the letter. A sharp* tsuke *beat.)*

HEINAI *(Aghast):* My God! The seal and the crest have been gnawed away by rats! Now it's just a scrap of worthless paper! What's happened here?
*(*IEMON *takes it and, staring at it in disbelief, strikes a* mie.)*

IEMON: It was the work of Oiwa's damned rats! *(Despondently.)* There's no hope!

HEINAI: My visit has been a complete waste of time! I'll inform my master. *(To his* FOOTMEN.*)* Collect the gifts, footmen!

FOOTMEN: Yes, sir! *(They pick up the tray containing the gifts.)*

IEMON *(Despairingly):* All the gifts!

HEINAI: I shall return to Lord Moronao with my report. Fool, Tamiya! Fool!

(HEINAI *laughs in derision. Loud* dorodoro *as* HEINAI *and his* FOOTMEN *charge off along the* hanamichi. IEMON *strikes a* mie *to* tsuke *beats, staring blankly. At this moment,* GENSHIRŌ *peeks out.*)

IEMON: The curse of Oiwa's ghost and the deeds of the rats have confounded my mother's plans for my promotion. Erecting this grave tablet for Oiwa was futile!

(*As he starts toward the door,* GENSHIRŌ *restrains him.*)

GENSHIRŌ: Son! You're angry, but don't break that tablet!

IEMON: I had intended to hold a proper prayer service for Oiwa, but she won't listen.

(IEMON *marches toward the grave tablet, but again* GENSHIRŌ *stops him.*)

GENSHIRŌ: Wait! You haven't an ounce of compassion! You're just a traitorous *rōnin*! (*Rage wells up inside him.*) This is good! A restless ghost and a dissatisfied traitor! You even relied upon your mother, who had wheedled herself into the household of our archenemy, Moronao! Unprincipled son! You've tarred your own father with a traitor's brush! You despicable wretch!

(IEMON *thinks quickly and then hits on a deception.*)

IEMON: Father! I infiltrated our enemy's household in order to assist my loyal comrades!

GENSHIRŌ: Lies! All lies! Traitor, Tamiya! Die! (*Momentarily forgetting that he is an ascetic, he reaches for the sword he no longer carries. Chagrined, he strikes a* mie *to* tsuke *beats.*) I'm no longer a samurai because I've taken to the roads as a begging pilgrim. (*Then he picks up the T-shaped wooden hammer used to strike his bell and thrashes* IEMON, *each hit accompanied by a double* tsuke *beat.*) I disown you! We are no longer father and son!

IEMON: What! My own father disowning me!

GENSHIRŌ: I'm not your father! Do as you please!

(GENSHIRŌ *continues to beat* IEMON. *Shrill music is heard and a bell tolls the hour as* GENSHIRŌ *goes inside.*)

IEMON (*Angrily*): Obstinate antique! Now I'm disowned as well as cursed! Damn you!

(*Continuous* tsuke *beats as the sliding door opens to reveal* OKUMA *in pain.*)

OKUMA: Oh, no! Rats! Rats!

(*Menacing* dorodoro. *Rats, held on* sashigane *by* STAGE ASSISTANTS, *dart at* OKUMA *from all directions as she frenziedly tries to dodge them.*)

IEMON (*Dismayed*): Come on, Ma! Take heart! Chin up! Come on, Ma! (*Desperately.*) Come on! (*To the rats.*) Vermin! (*He picks up the wooden hammer and slashes left and right, each movement accompanied by a double* tsuke *beat. Eventually, he gets rid of the rats.*) Oh, the fever again! Pray for me!

(JŌNEN *and his* FOLLOWERS *enter through the back door in response to* IEMON*'s distress.*)

JŌNEN: Is it the sickness again? Quickly! Pray!

FOLLOWERS: We understand! *(They encircle* OKUMA *by linking hands while* IEMON *remains outside looking anguished.)* All together now! Pray!

JŌNEN: Help us, Buddha!

FOLLOWERS: Help us, Buddha!

*(*IEMON*, entering the rosary circle, joins in the chanting. Dorodoro continues, interspersed with double* tsuke *beats.* OIWA *revolves around the circle and stares vindictively at* OKUMA*, who is wracked with pain. No one apart from* OKUMA *and* IEMON *can see* OIWA*. Light, menacing* dorodoro. OIWA *seizes* OKUMA *by the collar and sends her body into massive contortions. Loud* tsuke *beats. The prayer circle disintegrates and the* FOLLOWERS *fall back.* IEMON *waves his sword above his head in a futile gesture. Loud* tsuke *beats.)*

IEMON: Come on! Pray! *(They all chant more loudly.* OIWA *strikes a* mie *to continuous* tsuke *beats while she stares at* IEMON*. Then she resumes tormenting* OKUMA*.)* I feel the eyes of the ghost again*! (Horrified,* IEMON *strikes a* mie *to triple* tsuke *beats.)* Pray! *(They chant repeatedly as* OIWA *seizes* OKUMA *and, to the accompaniment of a flute, rips out* OKUMA*'s throat with her teeth.* IEMON *watches his mother die with a gurgling sound. The chanters scream in terror and rush out the rear door.)* Lord Buddha! What a way for my dear mother to die! *(*IEMON *is at a loss for words. He approaches the corpse and inspects her bloodstained throat. He clasps the hilt of his sword.)* Ghost! *(He draws his sword and slashes. Dorodoro reaches a crescendo as* OIWA *afflicts* IEMON *with spasms of agony. She dangles upside down behind him and approaches the wall of the room.* IEMON *sees her, totters, and then strikes at the wall. It collapses, exposing the corpse of* GENSHIRŌ*, dangling by a rope.* IEMON *watches* OIWA *vanish into the wall.)* Lord Buddha! Father's hanged himself and I've lost both my parents in the blink of an eye! What heartbreaking corpses! All because of Oiwa! Oh! Oh!

(To continuous tsuke *beats* SEKIGUCHI KANZŌ *and* BANSUKE *run onto the stage from the* hanamichi*, apparently seeking refuge. They barge into the room, and* IEMON *recoils in fear. Urgent* tsuke *beats accompany* HEINAI *and* FOOTMEN *running onto the* hanamichi *searching for the two.* KANZŌ *and* BANSUKE *peep in at the door.)*

KANZŌ: Iemon! I confessed to all my past misdeeds, and both of us were arrested.

BANSUKE: However, he avoided implicating himself under cross-examination, and when the interrogators' vigilance lapsed, we ran for it and fled here.

KANZŌ: We're giving you time to run, too!

(They vigorously urge IEMON *to flee.)*

IEMON: So you came all the way here out of loyalty to me!

KANZŌ and BANSUKE: Hide yourself! Disappear!

IEMON: I get it. But what will I do for money?

(KANZŌ *and* BANSUKE *rise and exchange glances. A sharp* tsuke *beat.*)

KANZŌ and BANSUKE: Got you!

(*They seize* IEMON, *but he breaks free, draws his sword, and lunges at them. Each movement in the combat scene* [tachimawari] *is emphasized by a double* tsuke *beat, and each series of strikes and parries culminates in a* mie.)

IEMON: A trap? Just as I thought!

HEINAI: Catch him!

KANZŌ and BANSUKE: Got you!

(*Martial drum patterns accompany the* tachimawari. *They again try to seize* IEMON, *but he defeats* KANZŌ, BANSUKE, HEINAI, *and all the* FOOTMEN *one by one. Weary from his exertions,* IEMON *stands just outside the door.*)

IEMON: A murderer haunted by a ghost can't escape heaven's net, but I'll try anyway.

(*A sharp* ki *clack. The stage revolves to reveal a desolate, snow-covered scene partially obscured in a blizzard of falling snow. It appears to be far from the hermitage.* YOMOSHICHI *enters left wearing a light-grey outer kimono with his head covered in a basket hat. He knocks* IEMON *off-balance from behind and then discards the hat, which is removed by a* STAGE ASSISTANT. *He begins to take off his outer kimono, preparing to fight. The kimono half-removed,* YOMOSHICHI *strikes an aggressive* mie *with one arm and one leg thrust forward. Triple* tsuke *beats.*)

YOMOSHICHI (*Pausing*): Hold it right there, Tamiya Iemon!

IEMON: Oh! It's Satō Yomoshichi! Why attack me?

YOMOSHICHI: You are the enemy of Oiwa, the elder sister of my wife, Osode. I am her avenger!

IEMON (*Sarcastically*): Bravo, Satō! Don't get in my way!

YOMOSHICHI: On guard, Tamiya!

(*Martial drum patterns accompany their fight. They pose aggressively, slash, and pass each other several times.* YOMOSHICHI *pins* IEMON'*s sword under his own. Tsuke beat. They battle until* YOMOSHICHI *scores a hit.* YOMOSHICHI *glowers at* IEMON, *who holds his wounded right shoulder. They pose in a joint* mie *to double* tsuke *beats. Light* dorodoro. *Flames erupt at the end of poles held by* STAGE ASSISTANTS *to signal that* OIWA *is inflicting pain on* IEMON. *Tsuke beats accompany his agonized* mie. *Numerous rats on* sashigane *appear and swarm up* IEMON'*s sword, forcing him to drop it.* YOMOSHICHI, *on bended knee, runs the standing* IEMON *through. With* YOMOSHICHI *triumphant and* IEMON *stunned, they strike a joint* mie *to furious* tsuke *beats* [uchiage]. *Loud* dorodoro, *which swiftly fades.)*

YOMOSHICHI *(Addressing* OIWA *):* Find rebirth in Buddha's paradise!

IEMON: You wretch, Yomoshichi!

*(*YOMOSHICHI *and the dying* IEMON *pose. Accelerating* ki *clacks as the curtain is pushed closed on the final tableau. Loud double* ki *clacks end the performance.)*

One-panel woodblock print by Utagawa Toyokuni III (1786–1864). Morita-za, Edo, tenth month 1857. The artist has combined what were probably two separate scenes from the dance finale, *Bountiful Brushwork, Folk Pictures from Ōtsu* (Saishitsue no Ōtsu-e). The "Wisteria Maiden" (Nakamura Fukusuke I), trailing a sprig of flowers over her shoulder, is dressed in a sensuous, long-sleeved kimono decorated with wisteria vines and blossoms and a black obi into which are woven the actor's family crests (two small drums, reverse peony, and crossed scrolls). Beside her, an actor, possibly Bandō Mitsugorō VI, dressed and made up as a "monkey," clutches a "gourd" while riding on a "catfish," three images that were popular in Ōtsu-style folk paintings. (Tsubouchi Memorial Theatre Museum of Waseda University)

The Wisteria Maiden
Fuji Musume

Katsui Gonpachi (text); Kineya Rokusaburō IV (music)

TRANSLATED BY LEONARD C. PRONKO

1826   NAKAMURA-ZA, EDO

The Wisteria Maiden

INTRODUCTION

The Wisteria Maiden was originally one of five dances performed one after the other in rapid sequence by the same dancer who effected multiple quick changes of costume, wig, and makeup. These transformation dances *(hengemono)* were very popular in nineteenth-century kabuki and exhibited the virtuosity of the actor-dancers. The entire dance from which *Wisteria Maiden* derives was known as *Ōtsu of the Ever-Returning Farewells* (Kaesu Gaesu Nagori no Ōtsu). It featured characters that appeared in the popular, naive folk pictures known as *Ōtsu-e* (Ōtsu pictures), which were sold in the Ōtsu region to tourists visiting the area around Lake Biwa. In the original dance, Seki Sanjūrō II (1786–1839) performed as five different characters: the wisteria maiden, the god of calligraphy, a footman *(yakko),* a boatman, and a blind man. The only dance that has survived is the first, *Wisteria Maiden.*

The original dance is short and contains the traditional sections: "entrance dance" *(de),* "narrative" *(monogatari),* "lamentation" *(kudoki),* "rhythmic finale" *(odoriji),* and "ultimate finale" or "scattering" *(chirashi).* In 1854, the actor Naka-mura Nakazō III (1800–1886) introduced after the lamentation section a short, popular boatman's song known as "Itako Dejima" (a place name). It became tradi-tional to include this section, or at least portions of it, in the performance until 1937, when Onoe Kikugorō VI (1885–1949), known as "the god of the dance," changed the entire format of *Wisteria Maiden.* It is not known in exactly what set-ting the first dance was performed; perhaps it was in front of panels representing the five Ōtsu pictures, which came alive as the actor stepped out of the panels to dance. Kikugorō changed the decor to the brilliant one used today: the trunk of a pine tree from which bright purple wisteria blossoms fall in dazzling profusion. He also replaced the "Itako Dejima" section with a newly composed "Fuji Ondo" (Wisteria Dance), based on a folk song and dance. It stresses the more mature, experienced, womanly feelings of the wisteria maiden and is danced twice, the second time in slightly inebriated fashion, since during the first round the maiden has partaken of sake. The skill of the dancer is revealed in his ability to express drunkenness without vulgarity.

To dazzle the audience further, Kikugorō did not enter on the *hanamichi,* but was already onstage when the music began. The first bars of music are sung in a totally darkened auditorium, and just as the dancer is about to begin, the lights are suddenly turned on at full intensity. Kikugorō also introduced a number of costume changes that take place behind the broad tree trunk, the dancer emerging several times in different kimono or with the top pulled down *(hadanugi)* to reveal different colors beneath.

Among variations on this popular piece are those that attempt to return to the original dance, garbing the performer in a kimono copied from the original *Ōtsu-e*. The choreography differs from one dance school to another. Indeed, some schools have a number of variations on specific sections: one sees the *kudoki*, for example, performed holding a hand towel *(tenugui)*, or using the black lacquered hat as a prop, or empty-handed.

The lyrics of *Wisteria Maiden* are a tissue of allusions, esoteric references, and plays on words, thus making ready comprehension virtually impossible, even for the scholar. Because the meaning is somewhat tenuous, the movement patterns *(furi)* are often less realistic than those in more down-to-earth dances. Instead, they tend to suggest emotions, character, and attitudes in a general way. The lyrics pile meaning on meaning, referring, for example, to the "Eight Famous Views of Ōmi," since Ōtsu is in that region. All eight are named in the song, and each evokes for the classically trained observer a particular emotion: autumn moon at Ishiyama, for example, or night rain at Karasaki. But many of the names carry other meanings as well: Ishiyama (Rock Mountain) suggests the firmness of a vow; Awazu is the negative form of the verb *au,* to meet, and the word bell, associated with it, is a homonym for promise; Seta is also a word for deception. The place name Karasaki is an example of a *kakekotoba,* or pivot word, which has one meaning as the ending of one word cluster and a different meaning as the beginning of another: *utusu-semi no kara* means the sloughed-off shell of a cicada, but *kara* is also the first syllable of the place name Karasaki. In the "Fuji Ondo" section, the phrase "Return is a forbidden word" implies that one would not want the bride to return to her parents' home. In the final section, skirt *(tsuma)* can also mean husband. These intricacies are explained here in order to avoid interrupting the flow of the lyrics.

The "entrance dance," which might most logically be performed on the *hana-michi,* is today performed almost invariably at stage center. Whereas in nineteenth-century performances the maiden's kimono was black with a pattern of bright wisteria blossoms, today's basic costume color is likely to be more vivid. Across her shoulder, the maiden carries a long branch of wisteria, which she holds in various positions. A liberal use of graceful feminine movements adds charm to the dance: the slip-step *(suberiashi),* for example, or the characteristic three-part head movement *(mitsuburi).* During the entrance dance, the dancer must create a feeling of dignity and spirituality in keeping with the spirit of the wisteria vine—at least this was Kikugorō's interpretation. It is only in later parts of the dance that the performer begins to embody the more coquettish aspects of a woman.

In the entrance dance there occurs a good example of the tortured rhetoric of the lyrics. As the dancer gazes at the branch, or sometimes points or beckons to it, the singer describes the "wisteria that writes 'I love you.' " The word *"itoshii"* in the lyric means "sweetheart" or "beloved." But also, if one writes the Japanese syllabary symbol for *"i"* ten *("to")* times, each beneath the other, and then writes *"shi"* in a long, graceful swoop right down the middle, like a central vein, one has drawn a stylized wisteria vine.

The "narrative" actually contains no narrative characteristics, but it is so called in order to fill out all the requisite dance segments. The attenuated movement patterns may include looking off into the distance at the mountains, pointing with the branch, and hiding the face shyly. Frequently this segment is omitted.

The "lamentation" begins as the singer comments on man's fickleness. Using her hat, a towel, or her hands, the dancer may suggest looking into a mirror, the ringing of a bell (at the word "Miidera," a temple famous for its bell as well as for its associations with the classic ancient novel *The Tale of Genji* [Genji Monogatari]), the joining of lovers as she locks one finger to another or holds them side by side, and feelings of jealousy as she strikes at the absent lover. The reference to letters usually shows the maiden kneeling, mixing ink, wetting her brush (a finger or her hat ribbons), and writing, then offering the letter, often represented by the hat.

At this point either "Itako Dejima" or, more frequently today, "Fuji Ondo" is inserted. Either one strikes a nice balance between languor and strong rhythm and can be counted as part of the first "dance finale." Whichever one the dancer chooses, the usual prop is a fan. Some performers may opt for the original form, which includes neither of these sections and goes straight to the true *odoriji*, which is partly based on a folk song and, with its fast tempo and marked rhythms, offers a striking contrast to the sad and leisurely lamentation. Here, forgetting the faithlessness of the man, the lyrics sing erotically of the pleasure of being with one another. Needless to say, the lasciviousness of the lyrics is only vaguely suggested in the choreography; the most obvious moment represents sleep, with one hand curled near the ear as a pillow.

Finally, in the brief "scattering," which ends the performance, the maiden takes up her branch once more and gazes off into the twilight sky, attempting to follow the flight of the wild geese, symbolizing her sweetheart.

A dance appealing more to the connoisseur than to the uninitiated, *Wisteria*

Maiden is subtle, graceful, and full of exquisite traditional Japanese feminine feeling. One often hears audience remarks such as, "How pretty it was!" or "What a beautiful maiden he makes!" Beauty, however, is only the surface of such dances. To deserve masterwork status they must be performed with a depth of feeling expressing the underlying anguish of a woman's heart, dependent upon a man who, despite his protestations of love, is nonetheless faithless. This difficult dance calls for an understanding of life far beyond the experience of most young actors and requires a mingling of chastity with eroticism that tests the capabilities of even seasoned performers.

This translation is based on the text in Morisada Ichirō, *Nihon Buyō Kyokushūran*. Stage directions are based on a videotape with Onoe Kikugorō VII (b. 1942), choreography by Fujima Kanjūrō. I am indebted to Ogawa Shichirō and Tomono Takao for help in problematic areas of this translation.

CHARACTERS

WISTERIA MAIDEN, *sometimes conceived of as the spirit of the wisteria vine*
NAGAUTA, *musical ensemble of singers, shamisen, drums, flute, and small gongs*

(With the theatre in total darkness, the first line of the NAGAUTA *music is sung. This is the "introductory song" [okiuta].)*
NAGAUTA:

The light purple of the wisteria waves / resembles the ten-times / returning flower of the pine.
(The lights come up suddenly to total brightness, and we see the WISTERIA MAIDEN *standing at center, back to the audience, holding her wisteria branch over her shoulder. The stage is dominated by a huge pine tree from which hang purple wisteria blossoms. The singers and shamisen artists are seated downstage left, the percussionists and flute player downstage right. The* MAIDEN *begins her "entrance dance" [de].)*
A hat to hide from people's glances, / lacquered hat, and with / a branch held neatly across her shoulder. / Deep purple, happily dyed / in the water of the waterway, / her happy emotions. / Wisteria that writes "I love you." / It can't be helped. / Here, here, my skirt askew.
(She turns toward the audience and gazes off into the distance. She kneels, her branch sweeping the floor, and moves gracefully while still bent low, the blossoms representing the flowing water of the waterway. She briefly embraces the wisteria,

Wearing a black kimono decorated with lavender wisteria flowers, the Wisteria Maiden (Nakamura Tokizō V) appears at the beginning of the dance posed beneath huge, trailing bunches of wisteria blossoms while carrying a branch of the flowers over her shoulder. One of the several *nagauta* singers kneels behind the actor. (Umemura Yutaka, Engeki Shuppansha)

almost caressing it with her right hand, while moving sideways in a graceful slip-step. She beckons toward the blossoms, then frames her face with the wisteria branch, and finally retreats behind the tree. There follows the "narrative" section [mono-gatari], *usually omitted but included in this translation.)*

Mirror Mountain reflects, / instead of other peoples' / weaknesses, my own / mirrored in the saltless sea, / a maiden's reflection, / oh, how shameful!

(Here commences the "lamentation" section [kudoki]*.)*

What is hateful in a man's heart / is that, although / he promised by the gods never / to meet another woman, / he may be worshipping someone else. / Awazu and Miidera's bells / recall promises / firm as Rock Mountain, but in truth, / empty as the shell / of a cicada that has flown. / I pine, waiting in the evening, / but he is indifferent, / cold as the snows of Mount Hira, / although he melts when near. / Ah, I am so jealous! / He truly deceived me. / I have sent letters in vain. / My heart is turning to resentment.

(The MAIDEN *reappears from behind the tree, wearing the same kimono but holding the hat in her hand. She poses briefly among the low-hanging wisteria branches, then comes to center and beckons as though to her lover. She strokes the red ribbons of the hat, then holds them up to represent her and her lover, and ties them together. She makes a number of graceful hand movements, then cradles someone or something lovingly in her arms. She kneels and strokes gently the edge of her upright hat, rises and strikes provocatively at her lover with the ribbons, then dodges back and hides her face. She thinks of writing a letter, strikes her thigh resolutely, then kneels to rub the inkstone and, using the ribbon as a brush, writes a letter on the hat, which she proffers toward him as she rises. She hides her face behind the hat and poses, back to the audience, with the hat hanging by the ribbons over her right shoulder. Once again she goes behind the tree, and the instrumentalists play an extended interlude, beginning with the shamisen, then adding percussion. The "Fuji Ondo" described below, is performed to the following lyrics.)*

Wisteria blossoms in clusters, / lovely colored and long. / Intending to cherish him, / I bought sake / and offered it to him. / Embracing my be-loved, / just as the wisteria / twines round the pine. No matter what, / it's just like the name Togaeri: / return ten times. / "Return" is a forbidden word.

(A brief instrumental segment of ondo *music is performed.)*

Even though flowers aren't supposed / to talk, it's no good / pretending one doesn't know, / as they do in Nara. / Some like to hang from the pine, / some like to twine / round the pine. The relationship / of loving and being loved, / never apart, is evergreen. / Never leaving, always / together, you and I. / What joy! What joy!

(When the MAIDEN *emerges, she is clad in a pale lavender kimono with a wisteria pattern and a black obi also patterned with wisteria. She glances coquettishly from*

among the long hanging wisteria branches, then, accompanied by rapid shamisen music, goes to left and bows, repeats the bow at right, and finally does a slower bow at center, eliciting audience applause. She now performs the "Wisteria Dance." The first half is a hand dance, featuring, at first, graceful poses with the hands and the sleeves, all to languorous music of shamisen, flutes, and drums. At the mention of sake, she mimes pouring sake from a bottle made of her sleeve; then she begins to drink from her other sleeve as if it were a cup, but pours it out without drinking. She walks slowly, obviously reacting to her lover's grasp. She puts out her hands to keep him from leaving, weeps at his leaving, dries her eyes with her sleeves, and weeps again. Then she performs what can be considered the ondo *proper, a strongly rhythmed dance in which the accompaniment features a prominent use of bells. The movements are abstract and include a number of stamping and hand patterns of grace and complexity. Finally, as she turns upstage, she takes her fan into her right hand and begins the second "inebriated" part of the "Fuji Ondo." With the open fan, she mimes a window, opens it and glances out, nods to her lover, then closes the fan-window. She mimes lovers' quarrels and flirtations as he pulls her back by the sleeve. She fans herself, pours sake again from her sleeve, drinking it this time from a small cup symbolized by her partly opened fan. She raises the fan as though it were a knife and suggests she might cut off her raised little finger—a proof of love sometimes given in the pleasure quarters. Once again the true* ondo *music returns and she performs her abstract, rhythmic dance of stamps and hand patterns, but this time as though slightly drunk, since she has just taken a drink of sake. At the dance's end, she poses under the hanging wisteria, fanning herself coyly, then disappears once more behind the tree. The "rhythmic finale" [odoriji] begins.)*

"If you're going to plant a pine, please / plant it in Arima Village." / Vows unchanging, she tucks up her skirt. / However much we are intertwined / one with the other, / we never get to sleep enough together. / Although we come early / to bed, we never get / sufficient time to sleep. / "I want to sleep with wisteria twined about me." / Ah, what shall I do, / what shall I do? My tiny pillow / is the pillow of his arms.

(The MAIDEN *appears partly hidden by the tree trunk and poses, showing the red kimono that she now wears on top, having pulled down [hadanugi] the top part of her lavender kimono. She comes stage center and dances the* odoriji, *which is strongly rhythmed and rapid. The first line and the one about sleeping with wisteria twined about one are from folk songs. Some of the finale is made up of rhythmic slapping of the hands and stamping, and some of it is somewhat mimetic. The* MAIDEN *mimes, for example, putting on a bridal hat and gown and walking, then sleeping. She leans back and looks up at the pine tree; she lies down and beckons with her hand, then joins both hands in a gesture of entreaty or prayer. The "scattering" [chirashi] begins.)*

In the misty glow of the evening sky, / the wild geese fly off reluctantly.

(As a bell announces the coming of evening, the MAIDEN *goes to the base of the tree, where she retrieves the branch of wisteria with which she first appeared. She faces the audience and gracefully passes the branch behind her so that the blossoms fall over her left shoulder, and gazes up into the distance, thinking perhaps of her lover, symbolized by the wild geese. To the sound of the* ki, *the curtain slowly closes.)*

Three-panel woodblock print by Toyohara Kunichika (1835–1900). This triptych shows the six characters who appear in *Six Poet Immortals* and the actors who played these roles at the premier performance at the Nakamura-za in Edo, third month 1831. Inscriptions identify "Nakamura Shikan" II (later Nakamura Utaemon IV) as the actor of five roles: the courtier "Ariwara no Narihira," standing, "Priest Kisen," kneeling (left panel), the noble "Bunya Yasuhide," kneeling (center panel), the evil noble "Ōtomo Kuronishi," standing, and abbot "Sōjō Henjō," kneeling (right panel). Lady "Ono no Komachi," standing (center panel), is played by "Iwai Kumesaburō" II (later Iwai Hanshirō VI). (Tsubouchi Memorial Theatre Museum of Waseda University)

The Six Poet Immortals
Rokkasen

Matsui Kōji (text); Kineya Rokuzaemon X and Kiyomoto Saibei (music); Fujima
Kanjūrō II, Nishikawa Senzō, and Nakamura Katsugorō (choreography)

TRANSLATED BY PAUL M. GRIFFITH

HENJŌ

BUNYA

NARIHIRA

KISEN

KURONUSHI

1831   NAKAMURA-ZA, EDO

The Six Poet Immortals

INTRODUCTION

The Six Poet Immortals was first performed in the third month of 1831 at the Naka-mura-za in Edo by Nakamura Shikan II (later Nakamura Utaemon IV, 1796?–1852) under the formal title *Colorful Guises of the Six Poet Immortals* (Rokkasen Sugata no Irodori). The lyrics were by Matsui Kōji (later Fukumori Kyūsuke II, dates unknown), the music by Kineya Rokuzaemon X (1800–1858) and Kiyomoto Saibei (dates unknown), and the choreography by Nishikawa Senzō IV (1797–1845), Fujima Kan-jūrō II (1796–1840), and Nakamura Katsugorō (dates unknown). The play was a revised and enlarged version of an earlier dance called *The Six Poets in Gay Attire* (Yoso'oi Rokkasen) performed by Arashi Hinasuke I (1741–1796) to great acclaim in the eleventh lunar month of 1789 in Osaka, and later brought to Edo's Ichimura-za in the fourth month of 1800 by Hinasuke II (1774–1801). The latter was a great hit in Edo but was no longer performed after that one occasion due to Hinasuke II's early death. Shikan II's version was completely rechoreographed with new music, but he kept closely to Hinasuke I's overall structure and maintained the same order of characters. This is important because, although the "Bunya" and "Kisen" sections are most often seen as independent dances today, preserving each section's place within the framework of the whole brings out their true spirit and meaning.

Six Poet Immortals is a dance composed of five different parts connected by a unifying theme. As such, it belongs to the "transformation dance" *(hengemono)* category, which typically features a single actor dancing a series of contrasting roles in quick succession. Shikan II, the future Utaemon IV, was the successor to a still vibrant tradition of *hengemono*, in which the open and heated rivalry between his adoptive father Utaemon III (1778–1838) and Bandō Mitsugorō III (1773–1831) had pushed the development of this genre to its limits. The genre exercised enor-mous influence on the development of music and on such conventions as quick-change techniques *(hayagawari)*. *Yasuna* and *Wisteria Maiden*, two other dances translated in this volume, are, like a great many now independent dances in the kabuki repertoire, all that remain from such works. However, *Six Poet Immortals* is one of the very few still seen in what is close to its original entirety. Unfortunately, due to the shorter time available for modern performances, and perhaps also to the impatience of modern audiences, even this important work is never performed today without extensive cuts.

The essence of *hengemono* is the idea of transition within a given context. In earlier eighteenth-century examples, such as Hinasuke I's own version of *Six Poet Immortals,* this context was the story of the play, of which the dance was an integral part and to which it often provided a suitably lively and colorful finale. However, even when the emphasis shifted in the nineteenth century from dramatic content to dance for its own sake, *hengemono* still were never performed without some unifying concept, such as the four seasons or the five annual festivals, among others. Within this framework authors and actors tried to dazzle the audiences with ever more novel and unexpected transformations. The entire work became a series of related but contrasting variations on a theme, similar in spirit to the humorous linked verse *(renga)* of the day in which one idea would spark the next by means of association. It was for the audience to guess at the nature and reason for these links, but this was definitely part of the fun.

The eponymous theme of this dance concerns a number of medieval poets grouped together by Ki no Tsurayuki (883–946) in the preface to the *Collection of Ancient and Modern Poems* (Kokin Wakashū), since which time they have been hailed as among Japan's foremost literary geniuses. Though very little historical information is known about the individuals themselves, the solemn air of respect in which they have always been held and their near legendary status made them the perfect butt for kabuki's irreverent sense of humor when this dance was created. All were serious poets from the distant past, but kabuki's treatment of each character within the whole was very witty and did not necessarily conform to the established highbrow image. In *Minshi's Selection* (Minshisen, 1790), the personal critique of actor Arashi Hinasuke I—whose pen name was Minshi—the order and nature of each section of *Six Poet Immortals* is given as follows: "Henjō": *jidai* (historical); "Bunya": *sewa* (domestic); "Narihira": *jidai;* "Kisen": *sewa;* "Kuronushi": *jidai.* From this we can tell that while the overall character of the dance was historical and fell naturally into the *jidaimono* category, within it there were sections that seemed contemporary in feeling and had, at least in part, the flavor of domestic drama *(sewamono).* In fact, the dance is a perfect illustration of how famous characters from history, while never quite losing their original identities, can be reinvented in kabuki and brought up-to-date in a practice known as *mitate.* This will become clear if we look more closely at the individual characters.

There is little actual dancing in the brief introductory section, "Henjō," although what does exist is nevertheless quite moving. The section is basically a highly serious work portraying an old priest of great learning and position who must yet struggle to maintain dignity in the face of inner turmoil. If there is any real humor at all, it lies in the irony behind the fact that the lovely and sensuous Komachi herself must remind the priest of his sin. There is also an element of sarcasm during the two characters' religious discourse; the full lyrics, always cut in modern productions, are so pompous as to seem slightly ridiculous. The *takemoto* music engenders a suitably grave mood. In relation to the whole, "Henjō" functions importantly in establishing the overall historical context of the dance and the basic notion of a male poet who has come to woo Komachi, an idea that is repeated throughout the work.

Against this solemn background, the following section, "Bunya," seems to sparkle all the more brightly. In the *Collection of Ancient and Modern Poems*, the poet Bunya (or Funya) Yasuhide is described as a third-ranking official in Mikawa Province, which may have been a hint for his characterization here. As a provincial aristocrat, his access to women of higher rank would have been limited. Possibly for this reason, he is depicted as a rather comical courtier, even a touch vulgar, who is forever chasing after an impossible goal. Komachi does not even deign to appear in this section. In her place is a group of horrendous ladies-in-waiting, always played by comic actors *(sanmaime)*. Though the action may at times verge on slapstick, the humor is, in fact, very sophisticated. For example, as the women approach Bunya in an attempt to win him over for themselves, the lyrics suggest their bad breath by borrowing lines from Bunya's famous poem about a mountain storm that wilts the autumn grasses (*Collection of Ancient and Modern Poems*, no. 249). In this way, an ancient classic is given a fresh twist through humorous association. Such literary references are frequent throughout *Six Poet Immortals*. In "Bunya" and "Kisen" in particular, they are exploited for comic effect.

In "Bunya," the flavor of *sewamono* is most obvious at the mention of the soothsayer Hōin and his reputation among the courtesans of the licensed pleasure district. At this point, Bunya himself becomes one of the customers as we watch him on his homeward journey after a night on the town. Here, the contemporary world of the Tenpō period (1830–1844) is portrayed, and Bunya is clearly shown as a member of that society. This is pure *mitate*, for the humor in this situation lies in the transformation of a historical poet into a modern-day dandy of the merchant class. Furthermore, this modern feeling would have been increased by the musical accompaniment, for, while Hinasuke I's version of "Bunya" was written entirely for *nagauta* music, Shikan II changed this to *kiyomoto*. This is significant because *kiyomoto* was a relatively new style developed in Edo and still the height of fashion during the Tenpō period.

The lighthearted mood of "Bunya" contrasts strongly with the following section, "Narihira," where the music switches to *nagauta* and the atmosphere is serious once more. This section is the emotional center of the dance, arguably the most beautiful and moving part, and the section against which both "Bunya" and "Kisen" are set. While "Bunya" may be the most technically demanding of the five sections, it is commonly agreed that "Narihira" is the most difficult psychologically because the actor must project grace, dignity, and the pain of unrequited love all with relatively little movement. For the first time, too, the character of Komachi is given equal prominence with her male counterpart, and both she and Narihira are seen in the kabuki version of Heian-period costume. Yet despite the historical context, this is still very much the product of nineteenth-century sensibilities, for what we have here are two cultural icons portrayed as an ideal of ancient courtly romance.

In "Kisen," exactly the same thing happens as in "Bunya," although the *sewamono* spirit is even stronger. The music is represented by both *kiyomoto* and *nagauta* ensembles, a convention called *kakeai*. The lyrics say that the clergyman Kisen has become a priest of the modern floating world, the world of hedonistic pleasure that reached its height of cultural development in nineteenth-century Edo. In particular, the story-telling *(chobokure)* section of "Kisen" is an amusing parody, for this esteemed poet and hermit sage is seen performing as a common priest of the streets. The character of Okaji, too, is a fascinating example of *mitate,* for while the elegant court robe she holds over her head clearly hints at an aristocratic identity (Komachi herself), she is here portrayed as a smart and fashionable tea waitress. In fact, the name Gion no Okaji was taken from a real person, a waitress who worked within the confines of the Yasaka Shrine in Kyoto in the early eighteenth century and who was also a well-known poetess, even publishing her own collection of poems, *Kaji's Leaves* (Kaji no Ha). Needless to say, Okaji has no historical link with Ono no Komachi, but was merely used as a vehicle to bring together two of the six poets in an up-to-date guise. Furthermore, Okaji is linked to Kisen merely by a witty association based on tea: Kisen lived in Uji, known for its tea, while Okaji was a tea waitress.

With the final, very short section, "Kuronushi," the audience is again taken back to the world of historical fiction and to a scene that could not be more different from "Kisen." From the endearing and humorous priest, the same actor becomes one of kabuki's greatest villains as we watch his dastardly attempt to shame Komachi and place a curse upon the imperial house. (Although there is no known historical justification for treating him this way, Kuronushi is also shown as a maleficent would-be usurper in the dance-drama *The Barrier Gate,* translated in Volume

2.) The scene is based on the *nō* play *Komachi Washes the Anthology* (Sōshi Arai Komachi), but here it is treated with kabuki's typical dynamism and flamboyance as Kuronushi displays his prowess in magnificent *mie* poses and a *tachimawari* fight scene. Fittingly for the larger-than-life atmosphere of this section, the *nagauta* musicians begin their performance playing in the bravura *ōzatsuma* style. Of the five sections of the dance, the script for "Kuronushi" is the most likely to change from production to production, for there is practically no dancing at all, and the piece functions primarily as an exciting finale.

To experience the intended effect of *Six Poet Immortals*, it is necessary to see all the sections together, with one actor performing all five male roles and one other performing both principal women, for, like a visual exclamation mark, "Kuronushi" comes at the end of a series of contrasting sections, each seen in relation to what went before or came after, and each very much part of a greater whole.

This translation is based on the script of *Rokkasen Sugata no Irodori* used for the Kokuritsu Gekijō (National Theatre of Japan) production of October 1985, and on that found in Yoshida Yukiko et al., eds., *Nihon Buyō Zenshū*, Vols. 2, 5, and 8.

CHARACTERS

SŌJŌ HENJŌ, *an elderly abbot in love with* ONO NO KOMACHI, *whom he has come to woo; one of the Six Poets*

BUNYA YASUHIDE, *a court nobleman who lusts after* ONO NO KOMACHI; *one of the Six Poets*

ARIWARA NO NARIHIRA, *a court nobleman in love with* ONO NO KOMACHI; *famous as one of Japan's greatest and most handsome lovers; one of the Six Poets*

KISEN HŌSHI, *a soft-mannered, lascivious, but amiable priest of high rank; one of the Six Poets*

ŌTOMO NO KURONUSHI, *a wicked court noble who plans to take over the country; one of the Six Poets*

ONO NO KOMACHI, *a court lady famous for her beauty, intelligence, and reticence toward her many male suitors; one of the Six Poets*

GION NO OKAJI, *a beautiful tea waitress working at a stall close to Kyoto's Yasaka Shrine; a parody of* ONO NO KOMACHI

FIRST LADIES-IN-WAITING, *court ladies who attend* ONO NO KOMACHI

SECOND LADIES-IN-WAITING, *comical and ugly court ladies who obstruct* BUNYA YASUHIDE

PRIESTS, *acolytes from* KISEN HŌSHI's *temple who come to fetch him*

TAKEMOTO, *the chanter-shamisen player combination that accompanies certain sections of*
the performance
NAGAUTA, *musical ensemble that accompanies certain sections of the performance*
STAGE ASSISTANTS, *formally dressed* kōken *and black-garbed* kurogo
KIYOMOTO, *musical ensemble that accompanies certain sections of the performance*

Henjō

> *(Before the curtain opens, two* ki *clacks* [naoshi] *are the cue for offstage musicians*
> *of the stick drum, the large and small hand drums, and the* nō *flute to play* saga-
> riha, *and for the large drum and hand bell to play* ongaku, *creating an atmosphere*
> *of solemn majesty. The curtain opens to accelerating* ki *pattern revealing the interior*
> *of a palace with three rooms now hidden behind lowered blinds. Six* LADIES-IN-
> WAITING *are seated in conversation. They wear white kimono and long, crimson*
> *trailing trousers* [nagabakama] *typical of serving women at court.)*

FIRST LADY-IN-WAITING: Listen everyone, as an amusement to pass the time, a
poetry competition has been arranged, and a number of the ladies-in-waiting
have been chosen to participate.

SECOND LADY-IN-WAITING: The one requested was Lady Komachi, who excels in
both looks and intelligence and who descends from a house glorious as the
household cherry tree.

THIRD LADY: Indeed, surpassing in beauty China's Yōkihi cherry, she is the flower of
our native land . . . a spectacle of the stage!

FOURTH LADY: But whether it's the path of flowers or the path of poetry, we, on the
other hand . . .

FIFTH LADY: Who know nothing of characters or simple letters, to say nothing of
grammar, are as uncultivated as the wild mountain cherry . . .

SIXTH LADY: And are so ignorant that, no matter how lovely the cherries of Mount
Yoshino, we could never be moved by the sight.

SECOND LADY: We can't even put together a simple fish salad, let alone a thirty-one-
letter poem!

THIRD LADY: A collection of court women so witless is truly . . .

ALL: A ridiculous affair!

FIRST LADY: But really, we must be more circumspect in what we say. We had better get
on with preparations for the poetry contest.

ALL: Yes, let us do so at once.

> *(The blinds on the right lift to reveal the* TAKEMOTO *ensemble. The* LADIES-IN-
> WAITING *stand and retire to the back of the stage, seating themselves to the right*
> *and left. The large drum and bells play again to suggest an air of reverence as the*
> *great abbot* SŌJŌ HENJŌ *enters slowly through a door, stage right. Though old*

and somewhat frail, his appearance is still impressive. He wears a short, crimson kimono over pale blue pantaloon-like trousers [sashinuki]; *tied over one shoulder is a priest's surplice* [kesa] *of heavy gold brocade. His eyebrows and thin beard are white, and he clutches a Buddhist rosary in his hands.)*

TAKEMOTO:

Now before you comes abbot / Henjō, who / in the flower of his youth / was Yoshimine, / one who often trod the paths to / Saga's high palace. / Yet now, lost in thought, at the / foothills he arrives.

(He comes to a halt, right, to declare his identity.)

HENJŌ *(Solemnly):* I am the abbot Henjō, known to all as a learned priest. Yet that which wreathes about my person is a mantle of desire! For this, for all eternity, the Buddha's punishment . . .

(For the rest of the play, the name of a character in brackets [ ] preceding a passage of sung lyrics is meant to suggest that the words are spoken—or thought—by the character indicated.)

TAKEMOTO:

[HENJŌ] "I'll receive. But so be it! / Even should I fall / like the jewel-camellia / and end as dust, still, / I yearn to meet Komachi!"

(He glances down at his sleeves, their crimson color reflecting his sinful love, and turns toward the blinds behind which ONO NO KOMACHI *is seated.)*

Thus he approaches, / but his path is blocked by the / ladies of the house.

FIRST LADY: Why, who should it be but abbot Henjō!

SECOND LADY: Though you ask us to intercede on your behalf . . .

THIRD LADY: Lady Komachi is now within . . .

FOURTH LADY: Relieving the tedious hours with . . .

FIFTH LADY: A contest of poetry.

SIXTH LADY: If you wish to see her . . .

ALL: You must come another time.

TAKEMOTO:

[HENJŌ] "Even without this, / all my letters of love, piled / high upon my cart, / both by day and in my dreams, / are too much to bear. / Please understand the sorrow / that weighs on my heart . . . / now beyond words to express!"

(A voice is heard coming from behind the central blinds.)

Just at that moment . . .

KOMACHI *(Reading her own composition aloud):* "That which lacks color, / but as surely fades away / in this fickle world . . ."

HENJŌ *(Excited to recognize the voice):* She who speaks thus is the object of my love!

KOMACHI: "Is the blossoming flower / which we call the heart of man."

HENJŌ: How tender, this poet's heart! (*Turning front, he grasps his rosary, absorbed in thoughts of* KOMACHI.)

TAKEMOTO:

> With the cord of his abbot's / holy rosary, / he would bind fast his love. / Thus raising his arm, / "Come hither, come hither," he / beckons to her now. (HENJŌ *sits right. The large drum and* nō *flute play* midare, *joined by the drum and bells, creating an air of grandeur and suspense as two* LADIES-IN-WAITING *go to lift the central blinds. We see* KOMACHI *seated on a cushion, center, with a brush and poetry slip in her hands. She has a silver flower comb* [hanagushi], *and her hair is tied and looped over a drum-shaped ornament in the "blown-circle"* [fukiwa] *style associated with princesses or young ladies of high birth. Over a pink kimono she wears a dark purple over-robe* [hifu], *and on her feet are white* tabi. *Two more* LADIES-IN-WAITING *attend her on either side. In the background are panels of a sliding door painted with flower roundels on silver leaf.*)
>
> Most graceful is Komachi, / she whose very name / is of high repute at court, / high as the reed blinds / now lifting with her eyebrows / as she starts to smile.

KOMACHI (*Noticing* HENJŌ *and lowering her head modestly*): Why, your holiness, you're here again today.

> (*She looks back at her poem and begins to muse on the fleeting nature of time, perhaps reflecting on how all men, even priests, must grow old and pass away. She looks up at an imaginary scene of cherry trees and shades her eyes. Taking out her small fan* [onna ōgi], *she stands and comes forward, posing briefly on the step.*)

TAKEMOTO: "Flowers blossoming at their peak / in the trees of spring, / scatter, to leave nothing but / a sad, vacant shore."

> (*She glances at the young leaves sprouting in summer and raises her fan to shield herself from the autumn breeze. She uses the fan to mime the storms of winter.*)
>
> The greenery of summer, / in the autumn dies, / and the crying geese know well / how the leaves will fall. / There is no way to evade / the winter's cold blasts.
>
> (HENJŌ *points at his own crimson kimono and white under kimono as he and* KOMACHI *begin a moral discourse. He crosses his arms over his breast at the thought of sinful desire, while she poses in prayer. He pleads that she sympathize with him and relent.*)
>
> [HENJŌ] "We distinguish clearly the / color white from red, / and the choice of good or evil / is a matter of the heart. / We may lose ourselves to passion, / or attain enlightenment. / But for this, my sad condition, / please show sympathy."
>
> (*He stands and draws close to* KOMACHI, *but she forces him back with a gesture of reproach. She turns to go, but he tugs at her sleeve.*)

[KOMACHI] "If riled, even the Buddha / may turn a demon. / Dear abbot, you must choose the / path to salvation." / So saying, she makes to go, / but he pulls her back.

(*Two* LADIES-IN-WAITING *come forward to intervene. They seat themselves on either side of him, protesting.*)

FIRST LADY: It is pitiable indeed for one of your learning . . .

SECOND LADY: To suffer the tortures of love. How unbecoming!

THIRD LADY: Before you are seen by others . . .

FOURTH LADY: Quickly, quickly, back to the temple . . .

FIFTH LADY: You must return . . .

ALL: Abbot Henjō!

TAKEMOTO:

Those who now pull at his sleeves / he brushes aside . . . he brushes aside.

HENJŌ (*Sadly and somewhat resentfully*): Though flowers may bloom, what we cannot see from above are the sharp thorns beneath.

(*He looks hard at* KOMACHI *and turns to leave but cannot help looking back again. She lifts her fan to shield herself from his glare. At last, sad and dejected, he makes his way slowly to the door and exits stage right.*)

TAKEMOTO:

In Komachi's direction / he turns to look . . . he turns to look, / as, to the holy temple grounds, / he retraces his steps.

(KOMACHI *is obviously moved by the plight of her elderly admirer and looks in his direction through the ribs of her fan. She lifts it to her face to hide a tear. Then, gesturing to her* LADIES-IN-WAITING *right and left, she leads them back inside her room, and the blinds are lowered.*)

In his wake Komachi now / watches after him, / and the sadness that she feels / deep within her breast, / she conceals beneath the folds / of her kimono. / Now calling to her ladies, / they withdraw inside.

(*The blinds come down, left, hiding the* TAKEMOTO *musicians. The large drum, nō flute, and bells play again as the blinds, right, lift to reveal an ensemble of* KIYOMOTO *musicians. The mood suddenly becomes lighter.*)

Bunya

KIYOMOTO:

Dressed in formal cap, / restlessly he looks about, / hawk-like, wings folded, / and aiming at the little birds, / instantly he swoops! / In nature, too, tawdry and cheap / is Yasuhide, / frisking at the ladies' skirts / like a lovesick cat.

(*The large and small hand drums and nō flute play a fast pattern* [tsukkake] *together with the cymbals to create an excited and comical atmosphere as* BUNYA

YASUHIDE *rushes in through the door, right. He wears a black court cap* [eboshi] *and a pale mauve hunting coat* [kariginu] *over a kimono and pantaloon-like trousers* [sashinuki] *with white* tabi. *On the opposite side of the stage, a different group of eight* LADIES-IN-WAITING *also rush in, holding their arms outstretched to block his path. Though they wear the same court costumes as the previous group of* LADIES-IN-WAITING, *the women we see now are far uglier and more masculine, played by comic actors* [sanmaime] *who normally specialize in male roles.* BUNYA *makes his way past them, and when they pull him from behind, he kicks them to the floor, where they clutch desperately at his feet. The stick drum and* nō *flute play* kyōgen kakko, *producing a lighthearted air as two of the* LADIES-IN-WAITING *stand and trap him between them. When he pushes them away, one pinches his leg.*)

Though out of reach, still he comes, / sights set on his goal. / But then, "Hey, wait! Don't go on! . . ." / He is forced to halt. / "Oh, how odious to be / interrupted thus!"

(*The two* LADIES-IN-WAITING *are replaced by two others who stamp angrily on either side. Together with* BUNYA, *all three mime searching about in pitch-blackness as he recalls the appointment he made earlier with a woman whom he imagined beautiful. He rushes back to peek under the blinds, center, in the hopes that it was* KOMACHI *herself, but he is quickly forced to return by a* LADY-IN-WAITING *who pulls at his ear. Other women pull him this way and that, trying to whisper to him, but he waves them away with his opened fan and grimaces at their bad breath. With a* LADY-IN-WAITING *on either side, all three huddle close as though standing in a cold wind.* BUNYA *sneezes.*)

[BUNYA] "Beguiled by the darkness in / the palace kitchens, / a mouth whispered in my ear, / 'Meet me this evening!' / And with the force of mountain winds . . . / a dreaded night storm, / I was pierced to the core with / a rush of delight."

(*Anxious to win him over for themselves, the women continue to push and pull at him, eventually forcing him onto his back, where he lies helpless, like a top-heavy abalone shell. He breaks free and kicks them aside.*)

"But now, like autumn grasses, / I wither and go limp / to find I must sleep alone. / What shame for a man! / My letters still one-sided / as abalone shells. / 'It's just too cold-hearted for / you to treat me so!'"

(*The tempo picks up as stick drum and* nō *flute enter and* kyōgen kakko *resumes. Thinking of the hideous face and teeth of one of the* LADIES-IN-WAITING, BUNYA *points to his nose and shades his eyes to look down into a valley far below.*)

She advances, he pushes free, / "Good heavens! What's this?" / A nose low as plum blossoms / deep in the valleys, / and protruding just beneath / are frightening crags!

(He shakes his head in disbelief and mimes sprouting flowers as he wonders at these court ladies who are well past their prime. He lifts his hands to his eyes as though peering through spectacles and mimes a woman holding up a mirror, applying face powder to hide her age. He brings both hands to his heart, thinking of KOMACHI, *and turns back to face the blinds.)*

Blossoms of the deutzia / now out of season. / Squinting, I mistook them for / trees laden with snow, / piling like thoughts of my love / behind the reed blinds. / No longer will I bow to / feelings of restraint!

(He points into the distance as he recalls another of KOMACHI *'s suitors, the tragic courtier Fukakusa no Shōshō. As related in the* nō *play* Komachi and the Suitor [Kayoi Komachi], *she obliged him to visit her every night for one hundred nights. This he did faithfully, but he died one night before reaching his goal. Counting nine on his fingers,* BUNYA *mimes opening and holding up an umbrella, as Shōshō sets off to keep his promise through all kinds of inclement weather. He rests it on his shoulder, balancing unsteadily on a bridge suspended precariously above a deep ravine.)*

"Thinking thus, I'm reminded / of Shōshō, / who, consumed by his passion, / for ninety-nine nights / went bearing an umbrella / over high log bridges . . . / 'Whoops! How very dangerous, / for I almost fell!' "

(He mimes a broken clog and balances on one leg, at last placing one foot down gingerly in the freezing snow. Crouching low, he holds his hands together to keep warm.)

"His clog-thong had broken and / one-footed he went, / hob-hobbling and stomping . . . 'Oh! / How bitterly cold!' "

*(*BUNYA *glances down sadly at his own person, thinking how he, too, has come to visit* KOMACHI. *He rubs off the mud that spattered onto his sleeve while journeying along the open road. As he does so, some mud gets into his eyes, which he wipes away. He lifts a hand to shade himself from the glare of the morning sun and, his visit fruitless again, mimes walking slowly homeward.)*

"For your sake alone we tread / these pathways by night, / our robes soiled and dirty in / the new light of dawn, / when we return dejected / and with heavy hearts."

(He mimes writing a love letter but wipes away a tear, thinking how his love is un-requited. A LADY-IN-WAITING *approaches, but he pokes her in the cheek and tries to get away. She holds him back and both struggle, eventually shading themselves in embarrassment at their actions.)*

"Yet, even though my love prove / unattainable, / still would I be ashamed to / take one in her stead / with a nose as bright crimson / as the safflower!"

*(*BUNYA *retreats to the back of the stage, where a formally dressed* STAGE ASSISTANT [kōken] *helps to take off his coat. Coming forward, he holds his closed fan*

like a divining stick as he mimes a soothsayer telling fortunes. He points to the place where the famous soothsayer Hōin used to be found and mimes making a blessing as he sells another talisman. The one who bought the talisman was a customer on his way back from the pleasure district, and **BUNYA** *mimes the man snuggling up warmly beneath a blanket, the talisman tucked safely in his kimono, as he seats himself on the boat that will take him home. While on board, he yawns with exhaustion, looks out at the view, and settles down for a puff on his tobacco pipe.*)

Often talked of by girls in / the pleasure quarters / for ages in Tamachi, / by Imado Bridge, / Hōin has sold charms / which now nestle close, / as we wrap ourselves like rice cakes / aboard wooden punts, / our dreams of love awash in the / Sumida River.

(*Thinking again of his recalcitrant lover, he stamps angrily at her and mimes her rejecting a suitor. He points to his own mouth to represent her sweet lips that trick him into returning time after time and pulls a cart behind him as though he were no more than a dumb ox. Finally, he shakes his head, refusing anymore to put up with her treatment.*)

"Though it's men you'd avoid, still, / every time we meet, / from your mouth drip honeyed words / which keep me in tow. / No more will I permit you / to ride me for a fool!"

(*He begins to leave, but another* **LADY-IN-WAITING** *quickly stops him, hauling him backward. Turning around to face her, he kicks her away and gestures rudely by pulling down one eye with a finger.*)

As he attempts to escape, / "How heartless and cruel!" / They drag him from behind, though / he tears himself loose. / "Oh no, oh no, oh no!"

(*The* **LADY-IN-WAITING** *jumps into his arms, but he drops her. As she crawls away, he purposely steps on one leg of her long trousers, but, annoyed at him, she pulls it from beneath him, making him fall to the ground.*)

Love comes meeting, / love's kept waiting, / love remains concealed . . .

(*The lyrics here are a series of puns on the word* koi, *meaning both "love" and "come here." He mimes a palanquin bearer dashing along with a heavy load on his shoulders and opens his fan, raising it to call for a peddler of green mosquito nets to come by. Perhaps beneath a brand-new net he would lie with his lover. He gestures for all the* **LADIES-IN-WAITING** *to approach.*)

"Palanquin bearers say, 'Here we come,' / and mosquito net hawkers . . . / you can call them here!"

FIRST LADY: Well now, everyone. What do you say to embarrassing Bunya with a series of difficult questions?

SECOND LADY: Oh, but what a good idea!

THIRD LADY: Or else we could ask for a list of different kinds of love?

FOURTH LADY: Yes, a love list would be good.

FIFTH LADY: In that case, we'll ask Bunya right now.

ALL: We'll ask right now!

BUNYA: Yes, yes, whatever you like. Ask away! Ask away!

> (*They all start beating time with their fans as a single shamisen plays the rhythmic melody* gitchō *in the background. The tempo starts off very slowly but quickens later as the* LADIES-IN-WAITING *come up with an ever-increasing barrage of questions. The section is known as "koi-zukushi" and involves the rhythmical enumeration of a series of puns on the word "koi."*)

FIRST LADY: What kind of love's in a four-and-a-half-mat room?

BUNYA (*Miming a square-shaped mat*): Hmm. That'd be a mistress, a kept concubine.

SECOND LADY: How about a virgin, seven . . . eighteen years old?

BUNYA (*Covering his eyes*): Keeping it from neighbors, I'd have her come round!

THIRD LADY: A meal set before you by one other than the maid?

BUNYA (*Eating hurriedly and calling to his wife*): If untouched, a crying shame! Quickly
> bring it here.

FOURTH LADY: And what is that that's making a racket on the roof?

BUNYA (*Holding his hands out like paws*): A cat screaming out for love! Why, we all know
> that!

FIFTH LADY: What, floating in a bucket, looks gem-like and white?

BUNYA (*Shouldering a heavy load like a street peddler*): Rice dumplings in iced
> water. . . . My, how cold, how cold!

SIXTH LADY: Settling accounts on the last day of the year?

BUNYA (*Calculating on an abacus and waving the man away*): If the bill collector's come,
> he can call back later!

> (*The tempo speeds up.*)

SEVENTH LADY: As for a boat?

BUNYA (*Rowing*): It comes a-floating.

ALL: As for a kite?

BUNYA: It comes a-flying.

ALL: As for a crow?

BUNYA: It comes a-cawing.

ALL: And a mud hen?

BUNYA: Umm . . .

ALL: And a mud hen? And a mud hen? What about a mud hen?

BUNYA: Hmm! . . .

> (*Though at a loss for an answer,* BUNYA *folds his arms and stamps his feet defiantly, finally letting out a sigh of defeat. The* LADIES-IN-WAITING *all burst into laughter. Suggesting his frustration, he mimes blowing on a long tobacco pipe that's jammed with tar and points to his cheeks.*)

KIYOMOTO:

Blocked as a tobacco pipe / that's stuffed up with tar, / nothing but dimples emerge / however hard he blows. / "No, no. This will never do!" / says Yasuhide.

(The tempo slows and the flute [shinobue] *joins in, adding a soft, melancholic air.* BUNYA *mimes the sloping cone of Mount Fuji and, crouching, looks up at its summit. Balancing on first one, then the other, leg, he swerves about as his entire body becomes the smoke rising from the volcanoes. He sits on the ground like one of the palace guards keeping watch by a small fire and follows the line of smoke upward with his eyes. Suddenly noticing fireflies nearby, he stands and tries to catch them. Once more, he himself becomes smoke, now emitting from kilns on the beach where seaweed is burned to make salt, and he mimes the small incoming waves. Finally, raising a hand to his forehead in a gesture of despair, he walks like a man consumed by love.)*

[BUNYA] "From Fuji and Asama, / smoke curls into the air, while / the bonfires of night watchmen / glow bright as marsh fireflies. / On the strand, salt kindles, and / I, too, am ablaze! / Is that not so?"

(The tempo increases once more as, in a lighter mood, he points toward an imaginary lover. Kneeling down, he mimes holding her front collar and, tapping on the ground, entreats her to listen to him. His whole body then shakes with desire as he thinks of her lovely form.)

"How delicate the fate that / determines our ties. / Not even for a moment / are you out of my thoughts. / With all my mind and body / I have come to want you so! / Well, isn't that true?"

(He makes to dash off, but the LADIES-IN-WAITING *all gather on either side of him to stop him yet again. The cymbals, large and small hand drums, and* nō *flute begin, and* tsukkake *resumes as they drag at him from behind. He pushes them in a group to the floor and runs out stage left, but they quickly rise to their feet and chase after him.)*

Storms scattering the flowers / are bars to his love. / As they approach, he heads this way / through the sliding door, / toward the inner apartments.

Narihira

(The blinds right are lowered to mask the KIYOMOTO *musicians from view as the blinds left rise to reveal the* NAGAUTA *ensemble. Offstage, the large drum and bells playing* ongaku *combine with onstage stick drum, large and small hand drums, and* nō *flute playing* sagariha. *This creates a dignified, courtly atmosphere as the central blinds lift to reveal* KOMACHI *standing left and* ARIWARA NO NARIHIRA *kneeling right.* KOMACHI*'s long hair is decorated with a silver flower comb* [hanagushi]. *She wears the multilayered and multicolored costume* [jūnihitoe] *that was*

Ariwara no Narihira (Ichikawa Danjūrō XII) and Ono no Komachi (Nakamura Fukusuke IX) wear the elaborate and brilliantly colored dress of the imperial court. His left arm around the kneeling Komachi, Narihira gestures with the large, folded fan. Cherry blossoms on the sliding doors tell of springtime and sensuous pleasures. (Umemura Yutaka, Engeki Shuppansha)

the official court dress for ladies of rank, and she holds a cherry branch on which a wild pheasant perches, to symbolize the open country. NARIHIRA *wears a black formal cap decorated with flower sprigs, a large-sleeved hunting coat* [kariginu] *over wide, pleated trousers* [hakama], *and white* tabi *on his feet. He carries a bow and two arrows in his hands. Indicating their aristocracy, both have small black marks* [kuraiboshi] *above their eyebrows. Behind them are gold sliding doors painted with a cherry tree in full bloom. They come forward and begin to dance. As paragons of beauty and refinement, their movements are gentle, and they pose with all the elegance of their high status.)*

NAGAUTA:

[NARIHIRA] "Night draws in like the / ends of a catalpa bow, / and with its approach / springs forth all my heart's torment / on the paths of love. / My mind, like tangled ferns in / endless confusion . . . / mountains and plains all shrouded / in the mists of spring."

(Both retire to the back of the stage where formally dressed STAGE ASSISTANTS *take some of their props.* KOMACHI *is given a large fan to which long streamers are*

attached [hiōgi] *and which was considered a standard part of court costume. She comes forward as though speaking to* NARIHIRA, *who has come to woo her. He then approaches as though speaking his reply, entreating her to return his love, but she continues to turn away from him. He lowers his head despondently at the thought of his many visits and of the unhappiness she has caused him, while she tries to comfort him.*)

[KOMACHI] "Of gossip I care nothing, / yet, . . ." [NARIHIRA] "I beg you yield!" / In this way before / sacred-paper gods, / his heart laid bare as the shores / of Akashi Bay. / "How many nights I've traveled / to and fro like sea plovers that / shriek and cry and I am drenched / in the hard rain of my tears."

(*Again she turns from him and brings her open fan to her breast, insisting that her heart is unsullied by thoughts of love. She bemoans the transience of all things, physical beauty as well as man's emotions.*)

[KOMACHI] "But no. Like an unclouded moon, / my heart remains pure. / Ah! How the flowers' beauty, / your tenderness and love, have / faded and wasted away. / All to no avail!"

(*She glances at him reproachfully, and he comes forward to continue his pleas.*)

[NARIHIRA] "Enveloped in the shadows / of my heart's longing, / heedlessly I'd die and still / feel no repentance, / raise no objection, though it's / I myself who speak. / Do you hear? You who remain so sober there!"

(*The stick drum and flute begin, playing a sweet, seductive melody, as* NARIHIRA *begins a section telling of a young man's visit to the palace to meet his lover. He mimes composing a love letter, which he would take to her, and brings his own fan up behind his sleeve to represent a rising moon. He holds the fan up as we hear of moonlight filtering into the hallways, where the fragrance of court ladies pervades the air. At last,* NARIHIRA *goes to take* KOMACHI*'s hand and leads her forward, only to be rejected yet again.*)

"When this night spreads out like an / open fan, we swore to meet, / and harboring my love through / palace corridors, / now I see a fan-shaped moon / through reed blinds . . . seeping, / like the sweet perfume of fans, / seven-fold, eightfold, / ninefold, shielding palace ladies. / And which is the flower fan? / The fan of the bedchamber . . . / a love beyond dreams." (*He takes up his bow.*) "Ah, will it be so wretched, / your unrelenting heart?"

(*He continues to beg and entreat, but she will have none of him, finally retreating back into the room, center, and holding up her fan to cover her face from his view. The blinds are lowered, leaving* NARIHIRA *alone.*)

She brushes him aside, but / all the more he clings, / tugging at her sleeve until / she shakes off the poet's hand. / With his innermost thoughts / his heart is so full that he / can no longer speak.

(The STAGE ASSISTANT *helps him into black-lacquered clogs as* NARIHIRA, *bow in hand, makes his way slowly to the* hanamichi. *Stopping at* shichisan, *he glances back in* KOMACHI *'s direction and, wrapping his wide sleeve around one arm, lifts it to shade himself as he swings round to look full at her. Offstage large drum and bells join with onstage shamisen, stick drum, large and small hand drums, and* nō *flute* [sagariha] *to create an air of grave solemnity.* NARIHIRA *lifts a hand to his face, covering his tears, as he exits through the curtained* hana-michi *doorway* [agemaku].*)*

Knowing of none to read his verse, / he returns alone. / Knowing of none to read his verse, / he returns alone.

Kisen

(The mood shifts again as the large drum, two-headed lashed drum, and flute play a lively melody [daibyōshi] *suggesting a festive atmosphere. A single* ki *clack signals the central flats to lift, revealing a backdrop of distant mountains and cherry trees in full bloom and a high wall with a tiled roof, stage right.* NAGAUTA *musicians sit on two tiers covered in crimson cloth along the back of the stage, while* KIYOMOTO *musicians sit on a similarly covered rolling platform against the wall, right. Two rows of pink cherry branches* [tsurieda] *are suspended from above. The drums and flute stop, and another* ki *clack signals the singers to begin in chorus with a reference both to one of* KISEN *'s famous poems and to the actual address of the actor Naka-mura Shikan II.)*

KIYOMOTO:

[KISEN] "My hermitage lies / southeast of the theatre in / Tokiwachō. / Yet, far apart do I live / from the floating world."

(The shamisen, bells, flute, and stick drum create a buoyant, cheerful air [watari-byōshi] *as the priest* KISEN HŌSHI *shuffles in along the* hanamichi. *His head is shaved and he wears the white silk kimono, white obi, and translucent black apron* [koshi goromo] *typical of priests. On his feet are white* tabi *and straw sandals, while over one shoulder he bears a flowering cherry branch from which a gourd filled with sake is suspended. From his gait and other movements there seems something almost effeminate about this fun-loving holy man. He stops at* shichisan *and begins to dance. Straightening his collar, he briefly glances up at the cherry branch he holds. He shades his eyes to look, then points at the nearby trees in full bloom.)*

"Seduced by flattery and / the prospect of lechery, / never will I tire to gaze / at Komachi's cherry tree."

(He points again, indicating the lovely women he expects to meet soon, and licks his fingertips to smooth down his eyebrows, which, according to popular belief, is a precaution against being duped.)

"Unwary, I am mocked by her / to the hairs of my eyebrows."

(Putting down the cherry branch in front of him, he glances at his own priestly garb and mimes tying on a head scarf to disguise his features in case any should wonder why a holy man has come to the pleasure quarters. The large and small hand drums join in the music.)

NAGAUTA:

" 'Priest! Priest!' the woodpeckers cry, / peeking in shop fronts, / but how after just a look / can I return home?"

(He points down at the gourd tied to his branch of flowers. He picks it up, and his body begins to sway as he revolves in a circle like an object bobbing up and down on the water.)

"Carefree as a gourd am I / afloat upon a river."

(He mimes the long whiskers of a catfish.)

KIYOMOTO:

"Yet my love's like a catfish / too slipp'ry to hold. / Thus, drifting and wandering / once again today, / cheerfully and buoyantly / I've made my way here."

(He taps the front of his apron to straighten his appearance and proceeds onto the main stage. As he stands admiring the view, the tea waitress GION NO OKAJI *enters left. She wears a purple striped kimono and simple black obi with a bright red apron. On her feet are white* tabi *and black clogs. Her features are hidden beneath a pale silk embroidered kimono, which she holds over her head. From its elegant appearance, this robe suggests that there is something refined and aristocratic about her. The character of* OKAJI *is a parody of* KOMACHI *herself. Pausing briefly, she goes up to* KISEN *and tugs lightly at his sleeve. Both then turn to the back of the stage as two* STAGE ASSISTANTS *take away* KISEN*'s cherry branch and sandals and* OKAJI*'s clogs.* OKAJI *is given a porcelain teacup with lid. Both turn front, and* KISEN *tries to get a peek at* OKAJI*'s face. Hoping that she is indeed* KOMACHI, *he tiptoes up to her excitedly, lifts off the robe above her head, and inadvertently makes her drop the cup, spilling the tea down her apron. Taking her cloth, he wipes her down.)*

NAGAUTA:

"To one side, my heart is drawn for, / perchance, behind the blinds. . . . / Now the scent of 'Kisen' tea / heralds a tea maid."

KIYOMOTO:

"I attempt to soothe my breast . . . / a heaving ocean wave."

(OKAJI shields herself bashfully by raising a sleeve while KISEN wrings out the water from the cloth. The idea of being wet leads to the image of a boatman. KISEN tries to tie the cloth around his head as a headband [hachimaki], but because it is wet and his head is bald, it slips off twice. He then holds it straight and mimes the erotic image of a slippery boat pole plunging into water as he punts along a river. He

tosses the cloth back to OKAJI *and poses with a hand shading his eyes, gazing at her beauty.)*

"Though careless in appearance, / the band about my head / slips however I tie it . . . / a smooth boatman's pole."

(He takes her hand, but she rejects it. KISEN *mimes holding up a large umbrella while* OKAJI, *parodying the story of the* nō *play* Komachi Prays For Rain *[Amagoi Komachi], mimes writing a poem entreating for rain. He covers his head with both arms as a sudden downpour ensues, and both brush off the droplets of water from their sleeves.)*

NAGAUTA:

"Now I go to take her hand, / longing for wetness, / longing for the ties of love / beneath late autumn showers."

*(*OKAJI *sits and mimes a lady checking her appearance in a mirror as* KISEN *creeps up behind to spy on her. Standing, he points in astonishment at her lovely face and staggers backward, wobbling from side to side as he falls to the ground. They then pose, he with arms folded, looking up at her, she standing with her back to the audience, looking down at him.)*

KIYOMOTO:

"Arms folded at her window, / I watch her make up, / and, from whichever angle, / I quiver and shake."

(He stands and is about to go when she calls him back.)

OKAJI: Now, listen . . .

(Holding her arms outstretched, she prevents him from leaving as she begins her entreaty [kudoki]. She presses on his shoulder, forcing him to the floor. Untying her apron, she bites on it as she berates him for his inconstancy, then clutches it sadly to her breast. Passing a hand across her face, she glances up at the gathering clouds. When KISEN *stands and tries to take the apron away from her, she pulls it back and quickly covers his head and eyes with it, blocking out the light. Finally, she takes the apron back and poses, holding it above her own head as she stands over the crouching priest. Because she is a tea maid, the lyrics are now interspersed with the names of famous brands of tea.)*

NAGAUTA:

[OKAJI] "Today I'm pleased to meet you, / the 'First of Years Past,' / yet, hearing of your wickedness, / my mind clouds with doubts / like a 'Mist Shrouded Moon' or / the 'Shade beneath Pines.' "

(Walking up behind him, she nudges him gently and stamps, insisting that he listen to her words.)

KIYOMOTO:

"I am your sweet 'Lady Wife'! / Ah, if only some day / such fortune could be mine . . . / 'One Forest' of riches! / To be admired as your spouse / is my heart's desire."

Tea waitress Gion no Okaji (Onoe Baikō VII), a parody of Ono no Komachi, poses holding her apron overhead, dominating the priest Kisen (Onoe Shōroku II), who crouches comically before her. *Nagauta* musicians sit on two levels behind the actors. (Tsubouchi Memorial Theatre Museum of Waseda University)

NAGAUTA:

"Yet, how foolish to have fallen / so deeply in love . . ."

KIYOMOTO:

"When the depths of your heart are / difficult to know."

(Sitting before him, she clutches his front collar as though pleading. They play at having an argument, and to show her dominance, she stands behind him and causes him to revolve first to the right and then to the left. Eventually, he ends up flat on his

*stomach with his feet in the air and his head resting in his cupped hands as she
stands pointing at him and tittering.)*

NAGAUTA:

[OKAJI] "How very irritating / and vexing this is!"
(Picking himself up off the floor, KISEN *goes to take her hand.)*

KIYOMOTO:

[KISEN] "Then why did you fall for me, / my sweet little maid?"
*(She brushes him off, and, their playacting at an end, both smile with amusement as
they turn to the back of the stage.)*

NAGAUTA:

[OKAJI] "Why, how vain you have become! / Stop these heartless jokes!"
(The flute joins in to add a melancholic air as, dancing with a cloth [tenugui]
decorated with the actor's family crests, OKAJI *ties back her sleeves to mime a woman
at a spinning wheel. She looks up at an imaginary lover and flicks down
the cloth from her shoulder in vexation at his fickleness.)*

KIYOMOTO:

"In the hovels of the poor / women toil at spinning thread. / Yet, harder is
it by far . . . / oh my, oh my . . . to capture your heart. / Well, well, if that's
the case!"
*(Tucking the cloth in to her obi, she now sits and mimes the chores of a courtesan
entertaining a guest, bowing before him and pouring him sake.)*
"To humor others is my / familiar task, / and the treatment of patrons /
befuddled with wine / I can tell at a glance, for / so practiced I've become."
*(She mimes fighting with a customer who has had too much to drink and ends by
posing, seated on the floor with the cloth held proudly and defiantly over one
shoulder.)*
"Still, after all my efforts / there are always those / who will grumble and
complain."
*(She stands and, her dance at an end, brings the cloth to her face in embarrassment
as she retires to the back of the stage.)*
"Called elegant and chic, / what a merry pair we make!"
(The large drum and high-pitched nō *flute announce the start of the storytelling
section, called* chobokure. *The term originally referred to the rhythmic chanting of
Buddhist scriptures by itinerant priests wandering door-to-door requesting money in
return for prayers, but the practice soon degenerated into fake priests who would tell
lewd and amusing stories.* KISEN *now hurries to the front of the stage holding a
white fan opened like a prayer book and a short priest's stick decked with cherry
blossoms* [hana shakujō] *with which, as though chanting, he beats out the rhythm
of the music. The shamisen,* nō *flute, drums, and small cymbals play a cheerful
melody* [miya kagura].*)*

NAGAUTA:

[KISEN] "Dear me! It is in the world of love / that I have become a priest! / Dear me, oh dear! Dear me, oh dear! / My tale I'll tell for all to hear!"

(One shamisen and the large and small hand drums take over the accompaniment.)

KIYOMOTO:

"The abode of this foolish priest, / southeast of the capital, / on Mount Uji lies, which, folk say, / is where I grieve for the world."

(As Uji is famous for producing tea, KISEN *now mimes whisking green tea in a bowl and drinking it. The section has highly erotic undertones, for, in the courtesan critiques of the early Edo period, the word "tea" [cha] alluded to the female genitalia. The "Bridge Princess," therefore, refers not only to the goddess worshipped close to Uji Bridge, but also to a courtesan.)*

Chit-chatting in tea gardens, they / speak of love, strong as dark tea . . . / relations with the Bridge Princess.

(The following few lines are a comic allusion to the love between Ukifune and Prince Niou in the classic novel The Tale of Genji [Genji Monogatari], *here parodied as a secret tryst between workers from the tea plantations. In the original, Niou abducts Ukifune under false pretenses and takes her across the Uji River by boat.* KISEN *quickly mimes quarreling and then, sitting unsteadily, shades his eyes to see the view. He points into the distance at the thought of his wife finding out and mimes dashing homeward. Miming a woman's movements, he sticks two fingers in the air above his head to represent his wife's horns of jealousy and wipes away the saliva dripping at a cow's mouth. At last, he chases after fireflies, collects them into a cage, and poses diligently over his books.)*

"Last night's row, sweet murmurs of love, / linger like scent on your sleeve, / as we glide past this little isle / of orange blossoms; but now / with all speed I must away, / running back with all my might, / where, with horns of jealousy, / the wife awaits my return, / cowish, drooling at the mouth / like a river's gushing rapids / back to my house I dash, yet, / within my breast passion smolders / like the glow of fireflies / by which I feign a studious air."

(The large drum enters with the nō flute, and miya kagura *resumes.* KISEN *lifts one foot daintily into the air, as if about to embark on the road to the pleasure quarters, and briefly mimes a torrent of water with his stick. He sits with his back to the audience and looks up at towering Mount Asahi.)*

NAGAUTA:

"In every land, the paths of love / are kerria-blossom gold / spent in streams, glinting with the / morning sun on Mount Asahi, / like a courtesan at her peak."

(He mimes slicing off his little finger as a pledge and then poses as the Buddha in prayer.)

"Thus we vow eternal love / at Byōdō Temple / where all are equal. / Well now, I have said too much. / My tale has come to an end."

(He takes up his stick and open fan once more as though blessing those around him.)

KIYOMOTO:

"May we now receive your blessings, / oh profligate Buddha!"

(He goes to take OKAJI's hand again, but she rejects him and, covering his head with her apron and pushing him backward to the floor, laughs at him and exits stage left.)

NAGAUTA:

This is indeed the land of / ultimate delight!

(As OKAJI departs, KISEN is left struggling helplessly on the ground, but at the sound of voices calling out from the curtained doorway [agemaku] at the end of the hanamichi, *he picks himself up. A single shamisen and stick drum begin a lively melody [tsujiuchi] suggesting the bustling streets as a large group of PRIESTS, acolytes from KISEN's temple, dressed in similar white kimono and black aprons, enters on the* hanamichi, *the one in the lead carrying a large red umbrella.)*

ALL: Master, where are you? Master, where are you?

(They rush up to KISEN and stand in a long line.)

FIRST PRIEST: So, this is where you've got to, master! We have all come . . .

ALL: To get you!

KISEN: It isn't raining, so why have you brought that umbrella?

SECOND PRIEST: This is to admonish you.

KISEN: I see. Despising wetness, you'd stop me from getting soaked with love?

THIRD PRIEST: Well, yes. That's more or less . . .

ALL: What we meant.

KISEN: Be that as it may, let us now celebrate this happy reign, everlasting as Sumiyoshi's . . .

FIRST PRIEST: Evergreen pines . . .

ALL: With a dance.

(KISEN retires to the back of the stage as a group of ten PRIESTS form a line at the front. They have tucked up their kimono skirts, revealing bright yellow leggings, and have lowered part of their kimono tops, exposing their right shoulders and pink-and-grey under kimono. Shamisen and bamboo sticks [yotsudake] repeat a simple melody as all begin to dance with movements suggesting a strong wind. The follow-ing section of lyrics contains several phrases sung rhythmically and with no partic-ular meaning.)

KIYOMOTO:

[PRIESTS] "Reeds blown one-sided / in the Bay of Naniwa / begin to twist and tangle. / With a hey and a ho. Isn't this grand!"

(The large drum, stick drum, flute, and hand gong play shibai shōden *to increase the festive mood.)*

NAGAUTA:

"Yet, once loosened and unbound, / we will meet again. / It is well worth the waiting, / I say! . . . for the summer rains!"

KIYOMOTO:

"With a hey and a ho. Isn't this grand!"

NAGAUTA:

"I say, I say!"

KIYOMOTO:

"Well, and as for this . . ."

NAGAUTA:

"It's whatever that you please!"

(The group of PRIESTS *goes to the back of the stage, their places taken by a different group of five* PRIESTS. *They mime pointing at a tea stall and then the wooden tables at which they sit to smoke their pipes.)*

KIYOMOTO:

"Here at a teahouse / along Sumiyoshi's shore / we will stop to rest our legs. / With a hey and a ho. What d'you say to this!"

NAGAUTA:

"And with our pine tree branches / we will fish for clams! / How happy to meet beneath, / I say! . . . the bright summer moon!"

KIYOMOTO:

"With a hey and a ho. Isn't that grand!"

NAGAUTA:

"I say, I say!"

KIYOMOTO:

"Well, and as for this . . ."

NAGAUTA:

"It's whatever that you please!"

(The second group of PRIESTS *retires, and* KISEN *alone comes forward. He has also tucked up his kimono skirt to reveal pale yellow leggings, the top half of his kimono has been lowered to show a grey and bright yellow under kimono, and he now wears a crimson apron and oversized pink headscarf. He hurries forward with short, feminine steps. All his following movements are exaggerated as he begins to parody* [warumi] *a lowly maidservant trying to entice customers at a roadside inn. The large drum and rough-surfaced gong* [sōban] *are played at a slow tempo.)*

KIYOMOTO:

[KISEN] "Hey there, sister! Are you in earnest?"

(KISEN mimes the maid tidying her hair, arranged in the popular Shimada style, as a visual pun on the place of that name.)

"Shimada and Kanaya / between two rivers lie, / where it's established custom / to put up at inns."

(The tempo suddenly picks up as he mimes the maid tugging at the sleeves of passing travelers. He mimes a round bathtub and blows through a tube to heat up the fire beneath. He indicates the room's flat paper doors. Small bells [matsumushi] and the wooden xylophone [mokkin] help to suggest a comic atmosphere of exaggeration.)

NAGAUTA:

"If a rest is what you want! / then come to stay here! / There's plenty of hot water / boiling for your bath / and all the sliding panels are / newly repapered."

(He passes needle and thread up through new reed matting and mimes a masseuse hitting a guest's back.)

"The reed mats on the floors, too, / are recently changed, / and as for bedroom company, / just leave that to us!"

(He unties his sandals as though he were now the guest coming in from the open road. Eventually two PRIESTS join in, one on either side, as the large drum, stick drum, flute, and gong again play shibai shōden.)

KIYOMOTO:

"Your heart strings, like your sandals, / will soon come untied, / for new bonds of love you'll form with / a wife for the night!"

NAGAUTA:

"After all is said and done, / she wasn't that bad!"

KIYOMOTO:

"Oh my, yes indeed! Yes indeed! Oh, yes indeed!"

(A STAGE ASSISTANT takes KISEN's headscarf off, and KISEN retreats to the back of the stage. One PRIEST brings out and opens the red umbrella while the others begin to dance around it in a circle. The atmosphere of a crowded festival is created by flute, large drum and stick drum, hand gong, and shamisen playing shichōme.)

NAGAUTA:

"On the coast of Sumiyoshi . . . / pine saplings in abundance. / An auspicious sight!"

(At last, the PRIESTS stop and go to the back of the stage as KISEN comes forward again. His white kimono top has been replaced and the skirt lowered once more. One PRIEST helps him to put on his sandals as the umbrella is lifted above him. With a fan and rosary in his hands, he poses with a mock-pious air. All the other PRIESTS seat themselves in a line on either side of him with their hands together in prayer.)

KIYOMOTO:

"As a beast I'll be reborn / in the life to come, / but back to my hermitage / now I must return. / So, heading for my village, I / hurry
on my way."

Kuronushi

(*A single* ki *clack signals offstage large drum, two-headed lashed drum, and* nō *flute
to play quickly* [haya daibyōshi] *as a temporary curtain imitating a large wicker-
work fence is drawn closed. Immediately the large drum,* nō *flute, and bells play*
ongaku, *creating suspense and preparing us for the solemn and impressive scene to
follow. At a single* ki *clack, the curtain drops to reveal the inner garden of the palace,
with a view of trees and mountains in the distance.* NAGAUTA *musicians sit on
two tiers covered in crimson cloth, back of center, flanked on either side by cherry
trees in full bloom. The musicians perform the opening section in the flamboyant*
ōzatsuma *style.*)

NAGAUTA:

In this land of peace, / poetry has flourished since / the age of the gods, and
/ the names of Ōtomo no / Kuronushi and / Komachi have dazzled bright as
/ the Komachi cherry.

(*A* ki *clack is followed by large drum,* nō *flute, and shamisen playing* kagen *to
suggest that we are within the imposing confines of an imperial palace.*)

NAGAUTA:

And now, in this happy reign, / a poetry contest.

(*The two tiers on which the* NAGAUTA *musicians sit are pulled apart, and*
KOMACHI *and* ŌTOMO NO KURONUSHI *are pushed forward on a small rolling platform. The musicians' tiers close behind them.* KOMACHI *still wears the
multilayered* [jūnihitoe] *costume, but now without outer coat and without the silver
flower comb in her hair. She sits stage right, holding up a large anthology of poetry.
Seated by her side on a tall stool* [aibiki] *left,* KURONUSHI *wears a large-sleeved
silk outer gown* [nōshi] *over pantaloon-like trousers* [sashinuki] *and black lacquered clogs, all of which were typical daily apparel for court nobles. In this case,
however, the silk gown is jet-black, reflecting the sinister nature of this evil courtier
role* [kugeaku]. *On his head he wears a tall black cap of state* [kanmuri] *above a
voluminous wig* [ōji], *and above his eyebrows are the two black marks* [kuraiboshi]
*indicating nobility. In his right hand he holds a flat, wooden baton as a symbol of
his high rank.*)

NAGAUTA:

[KURONUSHI] "Though never sown, / from what seed does it sprout forth, /
this floating duckweed / that grows in such profusion? / Yet, reflecting clear,
/ to the very pond bed shines / the light of the moon."

Ōtomo no Kuronushi (Nakamura Kankurō V) stands alone, dressed in flowing black-and-red robes, before the *nagauta* musical ensemble. His formal dress, the small marks above the eyebrows, and the baton he holds forth in his right hand indicate his high rank, while his grey-white face marks him as an evil court noble (*kugeaku*). (Umemura Yutaka, Engeki Shuppansha)

(The two pose grandly to beats of the tsuke, *and offstage* kagen *resumes, continuing at a slow tempo in the background.)*

(Seething with feigned anger and disgust): You are a plagiarist, Ono no Komachi! Your poem, "From what seed does it sprout forth, this floating duckweed . . ." is certainly an ancient one!

KOMACHI: That I have no means to clear away such aspersions fills me with sadness. Yet by all the gods of heaven and earth, I would wash this anthology to manifest the truth!

(Having falsely accused her of copying a poem from the Collection of Ten Thousand Leaves [Manyōshū], KURONUSHI *is now nervous at her suggestion of washing the page, for it was indeed he himself who wrote in* KOMACHI *'s verse after overhearing her recite it to herself the previous evening. As ink takes a long time to dry completely, it is likely that the newly brushed writing will be erased, leaving only the original text.* KURONUSHI *'s treachery will thereby be exposed. Remaining seated on the platform, both sidle toward each other and glare in each other's faces. Holding the anthology between them, they stand and step down from the platform. After struggling for possession of the book,* KOMACHI *sits right, with the volume held high, while* KURONUSHI *stands, glowering at her. Both pose to beats of the* tsuke.*)*

NAGAUTA:

In Wakanoura Bay, / seaweed is washed clean / by the incoming waves that / beat upon the shore.

KOMACHI: I beg that Buddha and the holy god Tamatsushima grant me divine favor!

(She holds the anthology before her and bows reverently as a STAGE ASSISTANT *places a black-lacquered basin by her side. Holding the book over the basin, she takes a lacquered kettle and begins to pour water onto the open page. Music increases in tempo and, to fast* dorodoro *beats of the large drum, indicating a supernatural event, the newly written poem suddenly vanishes.)*

NAGAUTA:

In the stream of floating weeds, / traces of the brush / all disappear from sight like / the mists of evening.

*(KURONUSHI *is astounded, and both glare at each other once more before posing to beats of the* tsuke.*)*

KURONUSHI: What have we here?

KOMACHI *(Indignantly):* Though you thought to conceal it, the truth has shone out, clear as Mirror Mountain. Approaching its slopes, we can see that you intended your poem as a curse!

KURONUSHI *(Taken aback):* What are you saying?

KOMACHI: Now that you stand accused, do you dare refute it?

KURONUSHI *(Hesitantly):* As for that, well . . .

KOMACHI: Well?

KURONUSHI: Well . . .

BOTH: Well, well, well, well . . .

KOMACHI *(Holding the anthology out as irrefutable evidence):* What I say is surely true! *(Seeing that he is beaten,* KURONUSHI *can do nothing but own up to his wicked scheme and declare himself openly. As he does so, facing back, a* STAGE ASSISTANT *helps the actor out of the top half of his gown. Turning front, the gown falls from his shoulders, revealing a white kimono beneath, while his cap of state is thrown backward.)*

KURONUSHI: I expected no less from you, Komachi. You have found me out. Indeed, it is as you surmised, for I am the legitimate heir to Minister Yakamochi's designs to take over the realm. Approach closer and regard my face, for I am none other than Ōtomo no Kuronushi! *(He poses defiantly to strong* tsuke *beats.)*

KOMACHI: It's just as I thought.

KURONUSHI: Now you will receive just punishment for your deeds. Prepare to die!

KOMACHI *(Lifting a hand to call the guards):* Men. Come at once!

*(*KOMACHI *withdraws to the back as men* [hana yoten] *enter from either side of the stage. They wear crimson headbands and red-and-white kimono decorated with flowers and hold flower-decked spears in their hands. They challenge* KURONUSHI, *who stands center, brandishing a very long sword. All pose to* tsuke *beats. The* nō *flute and stick drum create a lively atmosphere as the opponents begin to fight* [tachimawari] *to frequent beats of the* tsuke.*)*

NAGAUTA:

Pillow words, too, twist and swirl / like leaves in a gale / that scatter, scatter, scatter . . . / a storm of petals!

(The men go to the back of the stage, and KOMACHI *comes forward. Still grasping the anthology, she continues to fight* KURONUSHI *until two black-clad* STAGE ASSISTANTS [kurogo] *carry forward a three-stepped platform* [sandan] *to place between them. Mounting the steps,* KURONUSHI *thrusts out his sword as a signal for the final* ki *clack and poses with sword held aloft as* KOMACHI *comes to kneel, right, holding up the anthology. The men gather on both sides for the final pose* [hippari no mie] *in which* KOMACHI *and* KURONUSHI *seem to pull away from each other unyieldingly, emphasized again by loud beats of the* tsuke.*)*

NAGAUTA:

Having passed, the clouds disperse / to leave a clear view / of the six immortal poets / in all their guises . . . / their works without equal in history.

(The shamisen, large drum, stick drum, and nō *flute play* sarashi *at an excited pace as the curtain closes to accelerating* ki *clacks.)*

Three-panel woodblock print by Utagawa Toyokuni III (1786–1864). Kawarasaki-za, Edo, eleventh month 1848. Kneeling on the steps of Masakado's ruined mansion, the Minamoto warrior "Ōya no Tarō Mitsukuni" (Ichikawa Kyūzō II) seizes one end of the dropped Heike clan banner. To the right of the steps, "Princess Takiyasha" (Bandō Shuka I) shines a bright light on the scene, while at her feet one of her minions, black cloth covering all but his eyes, holds fast to the other end of the banner. Posed on the crumbling veranda of his mansion, open fan held commandingly overhead, is the ghost of the "New Taira Emperor, Masakado." The print shows exceptional physical detail: costume construction (layering, mesh, fringes), woven and dyed textile patterns, sword and architectural fittings, plaiting of straw sandals, scattered grass, flying bats, and shattered wood. (Tsubouchi Memorial Theatre Museum of Waseda University)

Masakado

Takarada Jusuke (text); Kishizawa Shikisa V (music); Fujima Kanjūrō II,
Nishikawa Senzō II (choreography)

TRANSLATED BY LEONARD C. PRONKO

1836   ICHIMURA-ZA, EDO

Masakado

INTRODUCTION

Masakado is a striking representative of its time, for it focuses on dancing, which developed so richly in the first half of the nineteenth century, and it creates the strange and ghostly atmosphere greatly favored by audiences and playwrights of the period. Unlike the popular dance play *The Subscription List* (Kanjinchō, 1840, trans. Scott 1953 and Brandon and Niwa 1966), which dates from just a few years later, *Masakado* shows no influence from the *nō* theatre. It is an example of pure kabuki dance-drama *(buyōgeki)* and demands highly skilled performers. Although the actors for whom the piece was created—Ichimura Uzaemon XII (1812–1851), who played Mitsukuni, and Ichikawa Kuzō (later Ichikawa Danzō VI, 1800–1871), who played the witch princess Takiyasha—were not particularly distinguished, in the twentieth century *Masakado* became a favorite with the highly acclaimed Nakamura Utaemon VI (1917–2001), who brought to the role of Takiyasha all the feeling of ghostliness and weirdness of which he was a master.

Playwright Takarada Jusuke (1797–1838) took a popular novel, *The Legend of the Loyalty of the Hornbilled Puffin* (Utō Yasukata Chūgiden), by Santō Kyōden (1761–1816), and created a lengthy kabuki play from it—an increasingly common practice of the time—titled *Filial Love at the Abandoned Sōma Palace* (Yo ni Utō Sōma no Furugosho). All that remains, however, is the dance-drama from Act VI, formally known as "Thieving Night When Love is Blind" (Shinobi Yoru Koi wa Kusemono) but popularly referred to as *Masakado*. The official title, rarely used except on posters or in textbooks, is a complicated tissue of wordplay, some of which I have attempted to capture in my translation, but it is probably best to follow the Japanese usage and simply call the play *Masakado*. Actually, Masakado, the self-declared emperor of Japan who was slain by the true emperor's troops some time before the action of the play begins, never appears in the piece, but memories of him are everywhere. His bid for power was an early stage in the struggle that was to reach a dramatic climax in the plays based on the Heike-Genji wars of the end of the twelfth century, for Masakado is a member of the Taira (Heike) clan, while many, but not all, of his opponents were Minamoto (Genji).

The emperor has sent soldiers, including the handsome young Mitsukuni, to vanquish any remaining supporters of the traitor and destroy members of his family. Mitsukuni, coming upon a desolate palace in the mountains on a rainy evening, seeks shelter there, not realizing that Masakado's sorceress daughter, Taki-yasha, awaits him. She hopes to win him over to her side and so takes on the iden-tity of his sweetheart, Kisaragi, a high-ranking courtesan of the pleasure quarters in the capital. Mitsukuni is not deceived and recounts the story of Masakado's death in battle to see what the young woman's reaction will be. When she weeps, he is convinced of her true identity and confronts her. Taking advantage of her magical powers, Takiyasha fights with him and his warriors and finally causes the entire deserted palace to collapse, appearing finally atop the roof with her familiar, a gigantic toad. As in so many kabuki plays, there is no resolution to the conflict, but instead a beautiful pose at the end. We may assume that sooner or later, good will conquer evil. The scene with the giant toad's appearance and the spectacular destruction of the palace *(yatai kuzushi)* is strikingly reminiscent of a similar scene in *The Tale of Tokubei from India,* translated in this volume.

A full dance piece, whether short or long, usually exhibits certain traditional sections, and *Masakado* possesses them all to a stunning degree. They are per-formed to the sometimes tortured sounds of the *tokiwazu* music composed by Kishi-zawa Shikisa V (1806–1866). As the play opens, Takiyasha appears on the *hanamichi* elevator trap *(suppon),* an entry used only for supernatural creatures, and performs her "entrance dance" *(de).* To add to the gloomy, supernatural effect, the stage lights are turned off, and the ghostly apparition is lighted by two thick candles on the ends of slender sticks *(sashidashi)* held by black-clothed stage assistants *(kurogo)* kneeling at either side of the actor. The effect also creates an atmosphere of a bygone day in the theatre before electric lighting.

The entrance dance is particularly difficult for Takiyasha because she is wear-ing a heavy robe, foot-high black lacquered clogs, and a wig weighing close to thirty pounds. The choreography is slow and graceful, not demanding too much movement.

The second section is the "lamentation" *(kudoki),* in which Takiyasha shows her love, sorrow, and suffering. It opens here with the words "Saga and Omuro," names of two beauty spots near the old capital, as Takiyasha dances the description of her visit outside the pleasure quarters and mimes her meeting with Mitsukuni. It is gentle, graceful, and flirtatious.

The third section offers a dramatic contrast as Mitsukuni recounts the battle in which Masakado was slain. The "narrative" *(monogatari)* is considered the quint-essential male segment of any dance, just as the lamentation is the quintessential female segment. It is strong and highly mimetic, including depictions of horseback riding, fighting, and falling. Strongly rhythmed and virile, this narrative is one of two very beautiful battle narratives in kabuki dance scenes, the other appearing in the "travel dance" *(michiyuki)* of *Yoshitsune and the Thousand Cherry Trees* (Yoshitsune Senbon Zakura, 1747, trans. Jones 1995).

When a dance is not a solo, there is invariably a moment where the two main actors dance together. Mitsukuni joins Takiyasha in part of the slow dance beginning "Softly, gently" and in the "rapid finale" *(odoriji)* that begins with the "counting song" *(kazoe uta)*, the first lyric being "For one night of love," almost as soon as Takiyasha drops the banner revealing her family's brocade. The fight scene *(tachimawari)* between Takiyasha and Mitsukuni's soldiers, and Mitsukuni himself, constitutes the final "scattering"— the absolute finale *(chirashi)*—of the piece.

Masakado may be performed with an emphasis on either its dramatic or its dance qualities, and a number of variations have been created. As a dance, it may be done by two actors, without the soldiers, and without the palace collapse. In this case Takiyasha's rapid costume change *(bukkaeri)* may be performed by the actor himself, who pulls out the strings at his shoulders as he is speaking vengefully to Mitsukuni. In a full dramatic performance, a third character, one of Mitsukuni's lieutenants, may enter and report on a nearby battle, but this somewhat irrelevant section is usually excised in performance.

Masakado's *tokiwazu* music grew out of the dramatic puppet narrative music *(takemoto* or *gidayū)*, combined with the influence of the sensuous *bungobushi* musical style, which had been prohibited because of its perceived bad influence on society. The tone is lyrical and lighter than the puppet style, and it is usually performed by two singers and three shamisen players, whose instruments are heavier in construction and sound than those of kabuki's *nagauta* music.

The text translated here is an amalgamation of those found in Toita Yasuji et al., eds., *Meisaku Kabuki Zenshū*, Vol. 19, and Morisada Ichirō, *Nihon Buyō Kyokushūran*. For stage directions and choreography, I have drawn on a videotape featuring Utaemon VI and Kataoka Nizaemon XIII (1903–1994), as well as the choreography taught me by Fujima Kangōrō. For her great help with this translation, I am deeply indebted to Ms. Yoshiko Fujito.

CHARACTERS

ŌYA TARŌ MITSUKUNI, *an officer of the Minamoto clan, in the Imperial Army*
PRINCESS TAKIYASHA, *daughter of the Taira general Masakado; at first disguised as the courtesan Kisaragi*
SOLDIERS *in the army of* ŌYA TARŌ MITSUKUNI

SOLDIERS *and* SPEARMEN, *fighters in* ŌYA TARŌ MITSUKUNI'*s army*
STAGE ASSISTANTS, *black-garbed* kurogo
TOKIWAZU, *chanters and shamisen players who accompany most of the action*

(The curtain opens to the beating of the large drum [ōdaiko], indicating a scene deep in the mountains [yamaoroshi]. A dilapidated palace is seen. Up center is a noble pavilion whose walls are covered with gold decorated with flower blossoms. A wide, pointed, Chinese-style arch, hung with a silk curtain of colored vertical stripes, pierces the upstage wall. The black-lacquered railings and staircase leading up to the central platform suggest decaying grandeur, and a battered roof indicates abandonment. Large cypress trees add to the lonely, ghostly atmosphere, while a hanging border [tsurieda] of maple leaves running along the top of the proscenium brightens the autumnal feeling. The regular stage floor is covered with smooth dance platforming [shosabutai]. To right is a platform for the musicians.)

TOKIWAZU *(Singing gravely and dramatically)*:

It is told that in Gogyoshi, / in the fourteenth year of Shoko, / at Yosen in Rakuhei / Prefecture of China, / there long ago was a great lake, / filled plentifully with water / and covered with mists / that rose to the broad open sky, / then fell as rain upon / an old ruined palace, where grow / the flowers of regret.

(Sound of rain [ama oto] and the heavy drumbeats [dorodoro] that represent a supernatural atmosphere as PRINCESS TAKIYASHA *rises on the small* hanamichi *elevator [suppon]. She is dressed as a courtesan in gorgeous gold-colored robes, but a closer look reveals spider-web patterns that suggest something inhuman. Her large obi is tied in the front and hangs in two long bows before her. She is covered by a splendid embroidered robe [uchikake] and wears foot-high black-lacquered clogs used by courtesans in their grand processions. Her long hair hangs down her back, tied with heavy silver rope and decorated with ten ivory ornamental hairpins [kanzashi]. She carries an open, transparent silk umbrella over her shoulder and dances slowly, elegantly, and somewhat spookily to the words of the* TOKIWAZU *singers. To each side of her kneels a black-garbed* STAGE ASSISTANT *[kurogo] holding a slender stick [sashidashi] with a lighted candle attached to it, shedding a gentle, ghostly light on her in the darkened theatre.)*

Love is a thief in the lives of poor mortals, / struggling, oh, how pitifully, / in the deep gulf of confusion / as their lives follow the path / down from the mountain heights. / Perplexing, too, is the love of those / who sleep together in this floating world. / Wild ducks call out to each other, / "My beloved!" Our lives / are spent in writing tender words. / Even women of pleasure, / experts in the art of love, / cannot contain themselves / when they behold the man they love. / Pensively, in the spring rain, / falling like hidden tears, / she comes along under her umbrella.

(TAKIYASHA *dances slowly at* shichisan, *forming patterns with her umbrella and her sleeves. She takes a long letter scroll from her kimono, unfurls it gracefully, and reads it slowly. Finally, she rolls it up and returns it to her kimono. Drums join the singing and shamisen. Occasionally we see her glance fiercely and demonically at the stage, suddenly revealing her true nature. At last she comes onto the main stage, accompanied by the ghostly drumbeats representing the wind* [kaza oto]; *the stage lights come up revealing* ŌYA TARŌ MITSUKUNI, *kneeling at the center of the platform in a sleeping posture, his sword held vertically in his left hand. He is wearing a dark kimono with gold crests tucked into battle-style, knicker-like* hakama *of a dark color patterned in gold. His wig has a short ponytail suggesting a tea whisk* [chasen], *and hair has grown out over his forehead to indicate that he has been in the field for some time.* TAKIYASHA *advances toward* MITSUKUNI, *who awakens but appears to be unaware of her.*)

TAKIYASHA: Please, my Lord Mitsukuni!

(*While* MITSUKUNI *speaks, she crosses upstage right, to her* STAGE ASSISTANT, *who helps her remove the high clogs and takes her umbrella. She then crosses right center.*)

MITSUKUNI: Indeed! How strange! At this old palace deep in the mountains, Masakado set up his residence, and since his death his restless ghost has returned to haunt this place and is said to trouble those that venture near. Upon the command of Lord Yorinobu, I, Mitsukuni, have come to this desolate dwelling. During my brief slumber, there appeared a strange apparition in this room, doubtless the work of Masakado's ghost. And here, indeed, is the ghostly figure. Show now your true form! (*Crosses down the steps to center, holding his sword up.*)

TOKIWAZU (*Sung in part solo and in part in unison*):

He stands and draws near, / but the woman quickly repulses him.

TAKIYASHA (*Kneeling and holding up her hand to him as he leans toward her*): Oh, please! I cannot blame you for being suspicious, but I am in truth the courtesan Kisaragi, from the pleasure quarters of Shimabara, in the capital. Please, believe me.

MITSUKUNI: That is difficult to believe. There is no reason for a courtesan from the pleasure quarters of Shimabara to voyage to this distant land. You may indeed be a courtesan from the capital, but why do you, whom I have never seen, come seeking me here?

TAKIYASHA: Well . . . you need not ask, for the answer is in your heart. To dispel your doubts, then I shall tell you: it was in the spring of last year.

MITSUKUNI (*Still unconvinced; heroically*): What, then?

TAKIYASHA: Please, my lord, remember our first meeting.

TOKIWAZU *(Lamentation* [kudoki] *sung in delicate style):*

"In Saga and Omuro, / cherry blossoms in full bloom. / Coquettish butterflies, / colorful and flirtatious. / Accompanied by ladies / from the pleasure quarters, / we made a rare outing / to the hills of Arashiyama. / Do you remember? / My lord's *hakama* covered / with a spring-like pattern of shimmering mist. / But no mist in your countenance, / mirror-bright and clear. / It dazzled me at once, / and cast a red glow upon my face, / tremulously shy. / Deep in the woods, / wet by the morning dew. / Deep the love in my breast / as I first learned the name / of my lord, Mitsukuni. / From daybreak to nightfall, / a woman's unchanging love / has persisted to this very moment / of our happy reunion. / Please, oh, please, / cast aside your doubts," / she urgently repeats, / clinging to him and hiding / her blushing face behind / the screen of her sleeves.

(TAKIYASHA's lamentation is a graceful, seductive dance in which she attempts to beguile the warrior. She mimes many of the singers' words, raising her hand to her eyes as she gazes at the maple leaves in Arashiyama, using traditional gestures of wheedling and flirtation, and miming putting on hakama, *sleeping, and blushing. Finally, she clasps her hands in supplication and kneels as she hides her face shyly.* MITSUKUNI, *meanwhile, has removed his sandals and given his long sword to a* STAGE ASSISTANT.*)*

MITSUKUNI: You speak so convincingly that my suspicions are completely dispelled, and I have no wish to reject your love for me. But when I look upon the decaying splendor of this palace, my heart is overcome with sadness. When the magnificence of Masakado's eastern court of bygone days I call to mind, hm! what sorrow!

(He removes his short sword and hands it to a STAGE ASSISTANT, *who then hands him a fan as, moving to center, he begins his battle narrative* [monogatari].*)*

TOKIWAZU *(Strongly):*

"And it came to pass / that Sōma no Masakado, / pushing his power and fortune / to the extreme, conspired / against the Imperial House / and set up a rival court. / News of his extravagance / reached the capital. / And to quell the rebellious lord / they sent three . . . mighty generals! / In the second month, / when plovers abound, / they led the imperial troops / to the attack. / Many were the clashes / at Karashima. / The hastily gathered forces / of Masakado, / pitiful! / Driven by strong winds, / the deep snow fell in avalanches, / pushing back the rebel forces, / scattering and striking. / See now, see now / the final battle of Masakado, / prince of the Taira. / Bringing forth his fawn-colored horse, / known by the name of / Evening Moon, he mounts / and charges boldly into the mass of foot soldiers. / Seeing which,

Taira clan princess Takiyasha, in the guise of the courtesan Kisaragi (Bandō Tama-saburō V), attempts to seduce her Minamoto enemy, Ōya no Tarō Mitsukuni (Ichikawa Danjūrō XII). She leans seductively against him, her intertwined fingers suggesting her desire to be intimate with him. The spider-web design on the kimono indicates her true supernatural and evil nature. (Umemura Yutaka, Engeki Shuppansha)

the emperor's warrior, Joheida, / aimed an arrow at Masakado, / piercing him deep within the temple. / From his horse he fell / to his untimely death, / while the emperor's men / raised a joyful cry of victory." / Thus he narrates as though witness / to the very battle.

(*Using his fan and stamping the ground for emphasis,* MITSUKUNI *performs a dramatic, strongly rhythmed dance, miming in many instances the words that accompany him. The performance is accented at climactic points with strong* mie *accompanied by double* tsuke *beats: at* "three . . . mighty generals!"; *at the announcement of Masakado's final battle; as he leaps onto his horse; and during the description of the battle. Before the first* mie *he pulls down the top of his dark kimono, revealing a gold-patterned under kimono. With his fan he suggests wind, snow, swordplay, galloping, and, of course, Joheida's shooting of the arrow, its piercing of Masakado's forehead, his fall from the horse, and, finally, Masakado's beheading.*) As she recalls the death / of Masakado, / Kisaragi weeps bitter tears. / Seeing this, Mitsukuni / approaches and questions her.

(TAKIYASHA *rises and takes a step down left, gesturing in despair as though she saw her father dying, then slowly sinks to her knees, turns away from* MITSUKUNI, *takes the edge of her red inner kimono sleeve, and places it in her mouth in order to stifle her weeping.*)

MITSUKUNI: Hearing now the story of the battle, you wept. Tell me why you weep.

TAKIYASHA (*Laughing a dry, bitter laugh, at first slowly, then faster, stressing the rhythm*):
Ha-ha, ha-ha, ha-ha. Ha-ha-ha-ha-ha. Why indeed should I weep? . . . Such bitter tears as this . . . well, then. . . . When one bids farewell to one's beloved, in the graying hours of the dawn, the chirping morning sparrows are crying, too. And it was their sad song came to my mind, you see.

TOKIWAZU (*Sadly, as a melancholy flute joins the shamisen accompaniment*):
"Softly, gently, the sparrows / chirp in the ruined palace. / Watchmen extinguish / the torches of the night. / Beyond the screen, lovers, / whispering sweet nonsense, / can still be heard. / From our beautiful dream / I tore myself away, / for it is time to part, / to put on again my obi. / In a playful mood, / you've hidden it—how endearing! / Midst the fragrance of / your lingering perfume, / we share more lovers' cups / of sake. One more? / The shamisen has one string / broken, but let's see / if we can play it with but two. / Changing hearts on changing pillows, / we may never meet again. / If you insist on leaving / then leave me here alone, / singing a sad song."

(TAKIYASHA *begins the dance by letting her heavy over-garment fall from her shoulders, thus freeing her for easier movement. She takes the folded paper from the bosom of her kimono and dances, holding it in her hand. She beckons to* MITSU-KUNI, *who joins her in the dance. She is wooing, and he is reticent at first. The two of them mime serving and drinking sake, as in a marriage ceremony.* TAKIYASHA *poses enticingly with a hand towel* [tenugui], *then holds it extended across her body as though she were playing a shamisen. Finally, as she dances with* MITSUKUNI, *she drops from the bosom of her kimono a banner of the Taira clan, to which she belongs.* [*Actually, a* STAGE ASSISTANT *throws the banner from behind her at the appropriate moment.*])

MITSUKUNI *(Kneeling and seizing the banner):* Here now!

(TAKIYASHA *seizes it back and seems to hide it in her sleeve* [*she hands it to a* STAGE ASSISTANT *behind her*]. *They pose in a "pulling* mie*"* [hippari mie] *to double* tsuke *beats. The atmosphere has been broken, and the* TOKIWAZU *musicians now break into a rapid, rhythmic piece, the rapid finale* [odoriji], *which is based on the numbers from one to eight and is called a "counting song"* [kazoe uta]. *Augmented by stick drum* [taiko], *flute, and small gong, the music is dynamic and rapid.*)

TOKIWAZU:

For one night of love, / two pillows are too many. / For three or four moments / they hesitate. / But in less than five seconds / their obi are untied. / The room and their hearts / are at sixes and sevens, / when the eighth hour bell / puts an end to their play.

(*The two dance together briefly, but* MITSUKUNI *soon crosses upstage left to pull up the top of his kimono, which he had lowered during the battle narrative, and put his swords back into his obi. While he is doing this, two* SOLDIERS [yoten] *with spears enter and attack* TAKIYASHA, *who pushes them away, causes them to flip, and temporarily defeats them.* MITSUKUNI *engages her briefly, but* TAKIYASHA *pushes him right, and, held by her attackers, she goes up the stairs to the platform, where she strikes them to the ground and poses. As* MITSUKUNI *speaks, they rise and retreat upstage left.*)

MITSUKUNI *(Tensely, accusingly):* Now confess! Since you have in your possession the banner of the Sōma family brocade, you are without question the surviving daughter of Masakado. Princess Takiyasha is your name!

TAKIYASHA: I know not what you mean. I do not recognize that banner.

MITSUKUNI: Have you lost your courage? You are wise in the witchcraft of the giant toad, passed down many centuries from the great magician Nikushisen. The emperor himself has heard of your accomplishments. And now that he has learned you are in hiding in this crumbling palace, you cannot escape! So tell me your true name, and submit yourself!

(*He leans toward her. The intensity of the scene increases as they engage in a sequence of give-and-take* [kuriage], *which reaches a crescendo.*)

TAKIYASHA *(Hesitantly, drawing out the words):* Well, then . . .

MITSUKUNI *(In the same manner, with increasing intensity):* Well, then . . .

TAKIYASHA: Well, then . . .

BOTH: Well then, well then, well then!

> (*Silence.* TAKIYASHA *utters a fierce sound between a whine and a growl as her face lights up with hatred, her features working in anger. She extends her right hand toward* MITSUKUNI, *her left raised near her left breast, in a gesture that indicates enmity, both hands trembling with anger and held with fingers curved into claw-like fists.*)

TAKIYASHA (*Drawing out the syllables, with mounting fury and energy*): Ah! Damnation! Now that you have discovered my identity, why should I hide anything more from you? In truth, I am the daughter of Sōma no Masakado, Takiyasha of the Taira!

> (*As she speaks, she pulls down two long strands of hair from inside the sidelocks of her wig and removes the four ivory pins from her forelocks, thereby loosening her hair, which falls about her shoulders and gives her an eerie look. As she rises at the end of her speech, the two* SOLDIERS, *now revived, attack her once more, their actions accented by* tsuke *beats. She pushes them forward and over the edge of the platform onto the main stage floor and at the same time removes the large front bow of her obi and drops it behind her. Meanwhile, her* STAGE ASSISTANTS *are pulling the threads from the shoulders of her kimono, allowing the garment to fall open* [bukkaeri], *covering her former kimono on the bottom and revealing a new one on top. The white pattern with a gold-threaded design of maple leaves or curved lines shows her true identity as sorceress princess. With another gesture she forces the attackers to fall onto their backs with their feet up in the air.*)

TAKIYASHA (*Her voice strong, revealing her demonic powers and her anger*): Since you are a man of great capability, I had hoped to spare your life and make you an ally of our cause. But my efforts were in vain. Now that you have recognized me, I shall destroy you by my magic powers. Prepare yourself now!

MITSUKUNI (*Intensely*): Arrogant woman!

> (*She holds her sidelocks as she speaks from center of the platform. Two* SPEARMEN *enter and attack her, bringing her down to the main stage at center. She repulses them and they run off.*)

TOKIWAZU:

> Suddenly, her features are / transformed by fury. / Her eyebrows rise and fall. / Burning with anger, / her breath turns to flame. / Faced by such sorcery, / even a hero of great courage / is forced back. / The leaves on the trees / rustle in the wind. / The sorceress grasps him by the collar.

> (MITSUKUNI *attacks her at center.* TAKIYASHA, *however, makes a magical sign and becomes invisible to the warrior, who continues to strike blindly about him. We hear the mysterious drum sound* [dorodoro] *as* TAKIYASHA *pulls* MITSUKUNI *back and manipulates him magically.* MITSUKUNI *crosses right, calling his* SOLDIERS. *A group of six or eight gorgeously attired* SOLDIERS *run in and*

Minamoto warrior Ōya no Tarō Mitsukuni (Ichikawa Sadanji III) confronts Princess
Takiyasha (Nakamura Utaemon VI) in a final tableau (*hippari mie*). Using her
magic powers, Takiyasha has summoned a toad familiar who poses beside her
on the roof of her father's destroyed mansion. The banner identifying her as a
Taira enemy trails down from her shoulders to the ground. Below, Mitsukuni
opposes her with drawn sword. (Tsubouchi Memorial Theatre Museum of
Waseda University)

engage the witch princess in an elaborate fight [tachimawari]. *Accompanied by
clanging gongs, shamisen, and triple beats* [mitsu daiko] *of the large drum,* TAKI-
YASHA *pushes an attacker into the air and poses, "holding" him over her head.
There are slow, dance-like movements in which she parries and thrusts after grabbing
one of the spears of her attackers. She turns them, pushes them to the ground in
various patterns, flips them, and glares at them. One* SOLDIER *attacks her with
a maple branch. She seizes it, flips him to the ground, and poses with her foot on
his back, the branch over her head. Finally, she chases all the* SOLDIERS *off, and*
MITSUKUNI *engages her in one-on-one combat, he fighting with a sword, she with
the branch. They go to* shichisan, *pose there at length, and return to the stage, where
they fight on the platform, then pose on the steps.* TAKIYASHA *throws her branch at
him, makes a magical sign, and disappears through a secret door at upstage left on
the platform.* MITSUKUNI *thrusts blindly, then, enchanted, circles round and
round and falls unconscious to the floor as the bamboo curtain at the front of the*

platform descends, hiding him. The theatre is cast into darkness. To the sound of loud clanging and deep-voiced drums, the stage begins to transform: the old palace "collapses" by descending on the large stage elevator until the walls disappear and the roof becomes visible. The roof covers the entire space of the platform and has a large gable at center. As the lights come up, **TAKIYASHA**, *accompanied by her familiar, a gigantic, hideous toad, appears on the crest of the roof just left of center. The mysterious* dorodoro *of the large drum underlines her supernatural character. The panes of paper in the gable break apart and* **MITSUKUNI** *appears, entering through the window and onto the roof at center, below* **TAKIYASHA** *and to the right.)*

TOKIWAZU:

In midair they struggle, / caught up in the magic wind! / How strange! How frightful!

(As the actors assume their final pose, the **SOLDIERS** *run onto the stage, shout, and pose with their spears raised toward the roof, leaning in.* **MITSUKUNI** *passes his sword from his right hand to his left, points it at* **TAKIYASHA**, *raises his right hand, then pushes it out behind him, leaning toward the sorceress. She takes the banner that had dropped from her kimono earlier, unfurls it to her right so that it hangs down onto the roof, and raises the other end in the air with her left hand. Her* **STAGE ASSISTANTS** *increase her impressive appearance by raising the loose back-part of her kimono into the air to create a kind of frame for her. As tsuke beats rise to a furious crescendo* [uchiage], *the cast poses in an impressive "pulling tableau"* [hippari mie]. *The curtain closes to the sound of* ki *and loud drumbeats.)*

Three-panel woodblock print by Utagawa Kuniyoshi (1797–1861). This triptych shows the premier at the Nakamura-za in Edo, eighth month 1851. In the center, "Asakura Tōgo" (Ichikawa Kodanji IV) poses beneath an arched walkway on the Kanei Temple grounds that spans a small pond in which he and four attacking guards stand. Sōgo lifts high for the shogun's attention a petition for intervention that he has tied to a branch of maple leaves. Looking down from the walkway is the shogun, identified as "Lord Ashikaga Yoshimasa" (Bandō Hikosaburō IV), accompanied by a youthful sword bearer, ladies-in-waiting, and attendants. The title of this production, *The Higashiyama Story Book* (Higashiyama Sakura no Zōshi), safely sets this highly political story in the time of the eighth Ashikaga shogun, Yoshimasa, four centuries in the past. Higashiyama indicated the period of Yoshimasa's rule because the shogun's famous villa, the Silver Pavilion (Ginkakuji), is located in that area of Kyoto. (Tsubouchi Memorial Theatre Museum of Waseda University)

The Tale of the Martyr of Sakura
Sakura Giminden

Segawa Jokō III
TRANSLATED BY ANNE PHILLIPS

THE FERRYMAN'S HUT AT INBANUMA MARSH

Inbanuma Watashikoya no Ba

KIUCHI SŌGO'S HOUSE

Kiuchi Sōgo Uchi no Ba

MOUNT TŌEI: THE PETITION FOR MERCY

Tōeizan Jikiso no Ba

1851   NAKAMURA-ZA, EDO

The Tale of the Martyr of Sakura

INTRODUCTION

The Tale of the Martyr of Sakura concerns a popular historical figure known as Sakura Sōgorō or Kiuchi Sōgo, who is thought to have lived in the early to mid-seventeenth century. According to popular legend, peasants in the domain of Sakura in present-day Chiba Prefecture were being driven into famine because of harsh taxes imposed by the domain's ruler, Lord Hotta. Having unsuccessfully petitioned local officials for leniency, village representatives then aired their grievances at the lord's residence in Edo. This, too, was unsuccessful, and Sōgo, the mayor of one of the affected villages, decided to directly petition the shogun.

In the rigid social structure of the Edo period, ignoring convention and stepping outside the appropriate official channels was a serious crime in itself, but for a lowly peasant to appeal to the shogun directly was a crime punishable by death, regardless of whether his grievances were justified or not. Having presented his petition, Sōgo was executed together with his family. However, the play by Segawa Jokō III (1806–1881) translated here provides a more hopeful ending, broadly hinting that virtuous officials in the shogun's retinue will punish Lord Hotta and help the peasants after Sōgo is gone.

Despite the enduring nature of stories concerning Sōgo's martyrdom, historical evidence supporting his legend is scant. Even the name of Sōgo's village is unclear, and sources give several different names, possibly because the village of Kōzu was subdivided into five villages at about the time Sōgo was supposed to have died. In the kabuki play, Sōgo is the mayor of Kami Iwabashi Village.

As with other victims of violent and unnatural deaths, a shrine was established to pacify Sōgo's vengeful spirit. He is worshipped at Tōshō Temple in Narita, near the town of Sakura, as a part of the Sōgo religion *(Sōgo shinkō)*, which has been instrumental in disseminating details of his life. Because of this, it is often difficult to separate historical fact from elements that comply with ideas about what a religious figure should be. However, the significance of Sōgo's story lies less in the historical facts of his life and more in the remarkable power that his legend has exerted on the popular imagination. Indeed, later peasant protests were staged in the name of Sakura Sōgorō.

The kabuki version of the Sōgo legend began its life within the play *The Higashiyama Story Book* (Higashiyama Sakura no Zōshi), which opened in the eighth lunar month of 1851 at the Nakamura-za. It was a huge success, running for a striking 104 days straight. Within this seven-act, seventeen-scene drama, Jokō intertwined the legend of Sōgo with the plot of a contemporary popular novel, *The Rustic Genji* (Inaka Genji); this dramaturgical approach of combining well-known stories is called *naimaze*. Jokō likely chose the latter plot, a parody of the classic novel *The Tale of Genji* (Genji Monogatari) set in the last half of the fifteenth century (a period commonly known as Higashiyama), because this allowed him to circumvent contemporary laws prohibiting the depiction on stage of any politically sensitive Edo period figure. Moreover, for reasons of political expediency, Sakura Sōgo was called Asakura Tōgo, played by Ichikawa Kodanji IV (1812–1866). Later, Kawatake Mokuami (1816–1893)—who formed a famous collaboration with Kodanji —cut the acts concerning *The Rustic Genji* and set the play in the time of the fourth shogun, Tokugawa Ietsuna (1641–1680), to meet Kodanji's demands for an 1861 revival. Mokuami's revision forms the prototype for the version of *The Martyr of Sakura* that is performed today.

Since its premiere in 1851, this unusual kabuki play, with its country-born hero, has been produced more than 250 times, attesting to its widespread popularity. This is particularly evident in the period beginning in the late Meiji period (1868–1912) and extending through Taishō (1912–1926), during which *Martyr of Sakura* was performed at least several times each year. In this period, grass-roots democratic movements and, in particular, rural tenant unions flourished. Between 1905 and 1912 *The Martyr of Sakura* was performed an unprecedented fifty times. The play's ending, signifying that Sōgo's message was heeded and that his death was not in vain, may have provided inspiration or solace to the people of that time. Today, *Martyr of Sakura* is performed infrequently but remains extremely well known.

Martyr of Sakura is unusual for a number of reasons. First, the hero, Sōgo, is a peasant. Kabuki was predominantly an urban theatre form that reveled in depicting powerful samurai, swaggering townsmen, and even dashing thieves, but not dull and diligent farmers, at least not in leading—even heroic—roles. Furthermore, it was considered something of a production risk at the time of the first performance to stage a play in which the main character wore nothing but plain cotton costumes. Most important, *Martyr of Sakura* stands out as the only kabuki play with significant political content. The fact that a play showing a direct challenge to the political system was allowed on the stage at all is often cited as testimony to the declining authority of the Tokugawa regime during its turbulent final days.

Translated here are the three most popular and important acts demonstrating the theme of self-sacrifice that permeates the play. In "The Ferryman's Hut at Inbanuma Marsh," old Jinbei disobeys official orders and takes Sōgo across the marsh, knowing he will be severely punished or even executed. In "Kiuchi Sōgo's House," Sōgo returns home intending to present his wife with a petition for divorce. In Edo-period Japan a criminal's family was often punished along with him, and since directly petitioning the shogun was a capital offense, Sōgo decides that the only way to protect his family is to legally divorce them. His wife Osan, however, stubbornly insists that they must follow him even in death. Sōgo says good-bye to his children for the last time in a dramatic final parting between parent and child *(kowakare)*, a kabuki convention. This scene is particularly poignant because Sōgo not only parts from his children knowing he will never see them again, but he also knows (and they do not) that they will soon be executed for his crimes. Having torn up the letter of divorce at Osan's insistence, he has sealed their fate. To audiences of the day who were well acquainted with Sōgo's story and his family's execution, this scene was all the more tragic. The alternation of dramatic *takemoto* accompaniment with offstage *(geza)* shamisen in a musical pattern called *ueshita aikata* further heightens the intensely emotional tone of this scene.

Martyr of Sakura also treats the audience to an impressive display of kabuki scenery. In "The Ferryman's Hut at Inbanuma Marsh" and "Kiuchi Sōgo's House," a forbidding landscape heavily blanketed in snow emphasizes the straitened circumstances of the peasants. In contrast, in "Mount Tōei: The Petition for Mercy," Sōgo leaves this stark, snow-bleached environment for the opulent, red-lacquered buildings and dazzling autumn foliage of Kanei Temple. Here he will sacrifice his life by presenting his petition to the shogun, who has come on a regular visit to worship the spirits of his ancestors. Sōgo seems sorely out of place in this aristocratic setting, a small figure surrounded by the resplendent forms of the lords and the glorious red of the maple leaves. This image of Sōgo's heroic opposition to a seemingly invincible authority figure has ensured his popularity for well over one hundred years.

This translation is based on the text of the four-hour, full-length *(tōshi kyōgen)* production at the Kokuritsu Gekijō (National Theatre of Japan) in November 1998 and a videotape of that production.

CHARACTERS

JINBEI, *an elderly ferryman*
KIUCHI SŌGO, *mayor of Kami Iwabashi Village*

OSAN, *wife of* KIUCHI SŌGO

HIKOSHICHI, *their elder son*

OTŌ, *their daughter*

TOKUMATSU, *their younger son*

OMAKI, *a village woman*

OKIYO, *a village woman*

OKUWA, *a village woman*

OTANE, *a village woman*

CHŌKICHI, *a village ne'er-do-well*

TOKUGAWA IETSUNA, *the shogun*

MATSUDAIRA, LORD OF IZU, *retainer of the shogun*

KUZE, LORD OF YAMATO, *retainer of the shogun*

INOUE, LORD OF KAWACHI, *retainer of the shogun*

SAKAI, LORD OF WAKASA, *retainer of the shogun*

MIURA, LORD OF SHIMA, *retainer of the shogun*

AOYAMA, LORD OF HŌKI, *retainer of the shogun*

INABA, LORD OF TANGO, *retainer of the shogun*

MATSUDAIRA UKYŌDAIBU, *a high-ranking samurai official*

ITAMI, LORD OF HIZEN, *retainer of the shogun*

AKIMOTO, LORD OF TAJIMA, *retainer of the shogun*

CHISHŌ, *head priest of Kanei Temple*

GUARDS

PRIESTS

PAGE BOY

TAKEMOTO, *the narrator-shamisen player combination that accompanies the action*

The Ferryman's Hut at Inbanuma Marsh

(The curtain opens to offstage shamisen and ki *accompaniment. At center, a simple ferryman's hut sits on a riverbank. It has a low-pitched roof and a door at right leading outside. In front of this, a blue ground cloth [nami nuno] representing waves in the marsh covers the downstage area from stage left to stage right. Directly in front of the hut, a small ferryboat is chained and padlocked to a three-step landing leading from the riverbank down to the water. A slope extends up from the* hanamichi *to the riverbank, forming a pathway to the ferryman's hut. The pathway is covered by a white ground cloth [yuki nuno] representing snow. To the right of the ferryman's hut is a willow tree. The area behind the hut is filled with densely clumped river grasses. In the far distance we can see a range of snow-covered mountains. It is snowing, and the whole effect is of a frozen winter landscape. Inside the hut, a small screen at left shields a makeshift bed on which the ferryman,* JINBEI, *is sleeping unseen.)*

TAKEMOTO:

Wearing a sedge hat to ward off the cold / Kiuchi Sōgo trudges / through the incessant snow / into the ever-deepening night. He cuts a pitiful figure like a drenched heron / and the narrow path seems never-ending, / yet despite the snow he pauses / to survey his surroundings and to reflect.

(A loud, insistent drum pattern [yuki oroshi] *signifies a blizzard.* KIUCHI SŌGO *enters from the* hanamichi, *his face concealed by a muffler and a wide-brimmed sedge hat. He hugs a large cloak tightly to his body and picks his way laboriously through the snow, stopping at* shichisan *to look around. His actions are furtive, as if he is being followed. His speech is slow and deliberate, and it appears that his whole body is numbed with cold. As he begins to speak, offstage shamisen music and the forlorn melody of a flute waft through the air.)*

SŌGO *(To himself):* I went to Edo to present our demands to the fief elders. However, despite the promises of the senior official, Hayato, Lord Hotta refused to release my father and the others from prison. We have experienced fifty years of Tokugawa rule, and the fourth shogun, Ietsuna, is benevolent toward the common people, and so I have decided to present my petition directly to him in the hope that he will grant our demands. I have secretly returned home, but the fields are bare and there is no sign of life. Could it be that so many people have left? Everything looks so different. What miserable times these are.

TAKEMOTO:

Sōgo dwells on the road he has taken / and becomes despondent.

*(*SŌGO *turns around, facing the direction from which he came. He holds the brim of his hat with one hand and crouches slightly as if bracing himself against the wind and snow. He clasps his hands together in a gesture of misery.)*

SŌGO *(Quietly, as if numb with cold):* Light is coming from the ferryman's hut, so he must be inside. I'll ask him to take me across the marsh. *(He looks toward the hut.)*

TAKEMOTO:

Sōgo drags his frozen body through the snow / with determined steps / and lingers at the ferryman's hut.

*(*SŌGO *moves toward the hut, and a slow, soft drumbeat begins. He trudges up the slope leading to the hut. To loud, quick drumbeats and two double beats of the tsuke* [batan] *he trips halfway. He picks himself up and continues steadily on until he reaches the riverbank. He pauses to look around and then goes to the door.)*

SŌGO *(Urgently, afraid of being seen):* Ferryman! Please help me! *(Knocks intently at the door and looks around to see if anyone is following him.)*

TAKEMOTO:

Hearing a voice, Jinbei looks up.

(Hearing a knock at the door, JINBEI *removes the screen that has been shielding him and sits up on the end of the bed. His clothes are threadbare.)*

JINBEI *(To himself):* It's so cold that I can't sleep and I've only just got the fire going. Troublesome wretch! *(To* SŌGO*.)* I've strict orders not to take the ferry out after dark. Come back tomorrow!

TAKEMOTO:

The old man bluntly refuses.

SŌGO *(Trying to make himself heard through the door):* I'm sure that's the case, but I need to cross and come back tonight. I know I'm a nuisance for dragging you out in the cold, but please take me across.

JINBEI *(Irritated):* Why can't you listen to reason? I need to earn a living as much as the next person, but the magistrate gave me strict orders, and I can't break them.

SŌGO *(Frantically):* Isn't that Jinbei? Hey, Jinbei! *(He looks around as if he thinks someone is watching.)*

JINBEI: Who's that calling my name? Who is it?

TAKEMOTO:

Grumbling, he stands and goes to the door.

JINBEI *(Crossing to the door and opening it):* Who is it?

SŌGO *(Taking off his hat to reveal his face):* It's me, Sōgo.

JINBEI *(In disbelief):* Sōgo?

SŌGO: Jinbei?

TAKEMOTO *(Dramatically):*

Jinbei pulls Sōgo inside and bolts the door. / The smothered fire belches black smoke.

*(*JINBEI *quickly pulls* SŌGO *inside as the tone of the shamisen music intensifies. He is so forceful that* SŌGO *is accidentally thrown against the far side of the hut.* JINBEI *hurriedly shuts the door to two double beats of the* tsuke *[batan]. He smothers the fire so it won't attract attention, thus filling the hut with thick smoke and causing the two to cough violently.* SŌGO *covers his face with a cloth* [tenugui].*)*

TAKEMOTO:

Ensuring that their shadows won't be seen . . .

*(*JINBEI *covers the door with a raincoat made of rushes. He bends down to rekindle the fire, and the smoke finally clears. The two turn to face each other.)*

JINBEI *(Reaching out to clasp* SŌGO*'s hands):* Sōgo!

SŌGO *(Tearfully):* Jinbei! *(Weeping.)* You look well.

JINBEI: Sōgo, what are you doing here?

TAKEMOTO:

At this, Sōgo lowers his voice.

(SŌGO removes his cloak and sits on the bed. JINBEI kneels on the floor and adds kindling to the fire. The sound of a shrill, mournful flute continues through the following speeches, creating an atmosphere of despair.)

SŌGO: As you already know, my father journeyed to Edo with a petition asking for a reduction in unjust land taxes. Because of the evil schemes of senior officials like Kageyu, trouble broke out in the villages of Sakura. They blew our humble protests out of all proportion and ordered that my father and his companions be thrown into prison. I pleaded for their release with all my might, but my efforts came to nothing. While I was in Edo, I longed to see my family and the villagers who were left behind in Sakura. Now I have secretly come this far. . . . *(Wipes the snow from his clothes with the cloth.)*

JINBEI *(Hesitantly):* Have you heard news of what has happened since you left?

SŌGO: No, I haven't. What do you mean?

JINBEI: The officials imprisoned most of your friends. Villagers who could see their turn coming took their wives and children and ran for their lives. Others couldn't bring themselves to leave their fields and were hounded day and night by the bailiffs. Some stubbornly pleaded bankruptcy and were left to rot in stinking prisons awash with water. And people like you, Sōgo, who they said had disregarded the magistrate's orders, are being rounded up one by one and interrogated. The only reason your wife and children haven't been arrested is because the officials know that you'll come back to see them. And then they'll be waiting for you. They're watching like a hawk or a cormorant watches its prey. Be careful, Sōgo!

(SŌGO dries his clothes by the fire as he listens to JINBEI.)

TAKEMOTO:

Hearing this, Sōgo exhales sharply.

(SŌGO tucks the cloth into his kimono, and JINBEI wipes his eyes.)

SŌGO *(His grief-tinged voice dissolving into tears):* My poor, ruined village. In the short time that I have been away, villagers have left in droves. Before long we will be begging by the roadside. Starvation will soon be upon us, and it is all due to the house of Hotta and its despicable policies. *(He takes his pipe out of his tobacco pouch.)*

TAKEMOTO:

Seeing Sōgo's resentful tears, / Jinbei draws near.

JINBEI *(Tearfully, with head bowed):* A few years ago when I was ill, you and your father called the doctor and brought me medicine. Thanks to your kindness I survived, but now I'm doomed to live out the rest of my days in this frozen wasteland. My poor dead wife is fortunate not to suffer the same fate. Because of the unrest, I couldn't even find work during this autumn's harvest. *(Gesturing toward the boat.*) Now I can't make a living as a ferryman because officials chain up the ferry every night.

(SŌGO *fills his pipe and lights it. The flute stops.*)

TAKEMOTO:

His existence is as tenuous as that of the morning dew, / constrained like his boat, which is chained tightly outside.

(JINBEI *crosses both arms over his chest, then motions toward the boat.*)

JINBEI *(In utter misery):* Is there no hope for us?

TAKEMOTO:

They can but cry at this pitiful tale.

SŌGO: I don't see how peace can ever be restored to the 389 villages under Lord Hotta's rule.

JINBEI: Isn't there anything we can do?

SŌGO *(Hopefully):* So many thousands of people are in distress. What if one person could take on their suffering? What if I could make life in the villages happy and prosperous again? *(Smiling at* JINBEI *reassuringly.)* Don't worry yourself, Jinbei, I'll think of something.

JINBEI *(Happily):* Do you mean you would put yourself in their place?

SŌGO: Well, I've decided to sacrifice my life for the sake of the other villagers.

JINBEI *(Literally taken aback with surprise):* Ahh!

SŌGO: I haven't told a soul, but I can trust you, Jinbei. This is my idea.

TAKEMOTO:

And he whispers . . .

(JINBEI *crawls over to* SŌGO, *who whispers his plan to him.*)

JINBEI *(Loudly in surprise):* That means you . . .

SŌGO: Shh!

(*To intense* TAKEMOTO *shamisen accompaniment, both jump up and hurry to the door to see if anyone is listening.*)

JINBEI: Sōgo, if anyone can do it, you can. Your generosity ranks with that of the gods and Buddhas and puts mere humans like me to shame. *(He clenches his fists together in gratitude and weeps.)*

TAKEMOTO:

Seeing the old man's tears of happiness / Sōgo jumps to his feet.

(SŌGO *quickly rises and puts on his cloak.*)

JINBEI: Sōgo, where are you going?

SŌGO: When I think of the desperate plight of the villagers, I realize I haven't a moment to lose.

(SŌGO *picks up his hat, preparing to leave. Snow begins to fall to a soft, steady snow drum pattern [yuki no oto]. Snow continues to fall, gaining in intensity in the scene's climactic final moments.*)

230

Kikuchi Sōgo (Matsumoto Kōshirō VIII, later Matsumoto Hakuō) decides on the desperate strategy of personally confronting the shogun: "I've decided to sacrifice my life for the sake of the other villagers." He throws a straw cape over his shoulders and prepares to depart in the raging snowstorm. His old friend, the ferryman Jinbei (Ichikawa Chūsha VIII), struggles to hold him back. (Tsubouchi Memorial Theatre Museum of Waseda University)

SŌGO: I know what I must do. It's hardly the time to return home from Edo, but the others insisted that I come back to see my family once more. I just want to meet my beloved wife one last time to prepare her for the worst. I've come this far, but if the ferry is locked up, then there's no other way to get home. If I wait too long, I run the risk of being seen, and then all my plans will come to nothing. Yes, I'll just have to go back to Edo.

(SŌGO *moves toward the door, but* JINBEI *stops him.*)

JINBEI: Brave Sōgo! You've promised to save the other villagers by taking their sufferings upon your shoulders. Even though I've strict orders not to take the ferry out, how can I let you return to Edo without seeing your wife and children?

(JINBEI *tries to rush out, but he is stopped by* SŌGO.)

SŌGO (*Tensely*): How can you say that? The local constables have chained up the ferry and padlocked it to the pier. If you disobey them and take me across, who knows what punishment you'll receive? I couldn't let you do that. Tell my family what we've discussed tonight. Give these papers to my wife. Good-bye, Jinbei.

(SŌGO presses some documents, including a petition for divorce from his wife, OSAN, into JINBEI's hands and with great emotion bids him good-bye. SŌGO tries to open the door, but JINBEI holds him back once more.)

TAKEMOTO:

No sooner has he said good-bye than he moves toward the door.

JINBEI *(Weeping):* Wait! I don't care what becomes of me. I'm taking the ferry out.

SŌGO *(Weeping):* That's very kind of you, but I decided on my plan out of a desire to save people. If you break the chains and are punished, my efforts will have been futile. So you see . . . *(He wrenches himself free of JINBEI's grip.)*

JINBEI: Wait! Listen to me!

(The two struggle. JINBEI pushes SŌGO out of the way, throwing him to the other side of the room.)

TAKEMOTO:

Saying this, he outpaces Sōgo. / The aged Jinbei / summons all of his strength and breaks the chains.

(JINBEI rushes out and, as the offstage large drum loudly beats the snowstorm pattern [yuki oroshi], breaks the chains that secure the ferry to the pier. The drumbeats rise and fall.)

SŌGO *(Loudly):* The chains!

(SŌGO crawls to the door as JINBEI falls to the ground with the effort of breaking the chains. Both look around to see if anyone has seen what has just occurred.)

SŌGO *(In disbelief):* Jinbei, what have you done?

JINBEI *(Self-deprecatingly):* Climb aboard!

SŌGO *(Clasping his hands together in gratitude):* Oh, Jinbei. How can I thank you?

TAKEMOTO:

So saying, Sōgo looks around, / and despite the snow, Jinbei . . .

(JINBEI forces SŌGO to climb aboard the ferry. SŌGO slips at the first step, emphasized by two double beats of the tsuke *[batan]. To continued double beats of the* tsuke, *SŌGO boards the boat, covering his head with his hat. JINBEI returns to the hut, where he puts on his straw coat and hat and smothers the fire. He soon returns.)*

Jinbei hurries Sōgo on board and casts off the chains. / Swiftly, he guides the boat into the current.

(JINBEI frees the boat from the chains that bind it to the pier. With his back to the audience, he puts a pole in the water as if to push off from the riverbank. SŌGO once again clasps his hands together in a gesture of gratitude. They pose. A loud ki *clack [ki no kashira] signals the final sequence of the scene. At that sound, JINBEI pushes off from the riverbank. The boat heads left to a dramatic shamisen accompaniment [sanjū]. Widely spaced ki clacks [honmaku] increase in frequency as the curtain closes.)*

Kiuchi Sōgo's House

(Offstage music featuring drum, shamisen, and singing as the curtain opens. Large drum plays snow pattern. A large house on a raised platform is at center. The large central room, spare and slightly grimy, has tatami *matting. On the back wall right is a cupboard with sliding doors, and center is a large Buddhist altar. A large open hearth provides the only element of comfort in this cheerless room. To the right of this central room is a small kitchen, which also serves as an entrance hall leading to a gate. A set of steps leads down into the garden. To left is a small room in which a baby sleeps, sheltered by a screen. Sliding paper doors at the back of this room lead into an interior room. To the rear of the house is a bamboo thicket. It is snowing, and the area around the house is blanketed with deep snow.* OSAN *is sitting at the steps, and village women are gathered around her. The two younger children play at the hearth, and* HIKOSHICHI *reads at a small desk, stage right. All are dressed in simple, threadbare clothing.)*

OMAKI: I'm afraid we are intruding on your hospitality again tonight.

OKIYO: I see the children are playing happily.

OKUWA *(Tentatively):* Have you heard any news from Edo?

OSAN: No, I haven't. But as long as the present Lord Hotta is in control, we should feel uneasy. *(Sympathetically.)* I heard your parents are ill. How are they?

OKUWA: Thank you for asking, but they're old, and I'm afraid that they're not over the worst.

OSAN: I'm so sorry to hear that. *(Noticing* OKUWA*'s hunched posture.)* It seems that your back troubles you in the cold weather. And now it's snowing so heavily. How do you feel?

OKUWA: It hurts me a great deal.

OSAN: I'm sure it does. *(Concerned.)* But that thin kimono won't keep the cold out. Just wait a moment. *(She hurries to the cupboard and brings out the family's precious remaining clothing.)*

OSAN: These are the *hakama* Sōgo wears on official occasions. They may look a little odd on a woman, but it will certainly keep you warm. Okiyo, this is the kimono I wore at my wedding. There's a slight hole, but with a little mending no one will notice. Omaki, here's a padded jacket for you and an obi for Otane. *(She graciously hands out the articles of clothing.)*

OTANE *(Smiling):* Thank you . . .

ALL *(Bowing their heads in thanks):* So much.

OKUWA: Well, then, I'm going to try on my new *hakama* before I go home.

OSAN: Why don't you all try on your new clothes?

(The four women ad-lib [sutezerifu] *as they change.)*

OKIYO *(Girlishly):* Look at me! I feel like a princess. It reminds me of when I used to act in the village plays.

(All laugh, for the moment forgetting about their frozen limbs and empty stomachs.)

OSAN: It's been a long time since I last saw you all laughing like this.

OMAKI: Well, we should be going.

OKIYO: Yes, we should.

OTANE: Thank you so much.

OKUWA: Tomorrow we'll . . .

ALL: Come again.

> *(The four depart to offstage large drum and shamisen playing* yuki no aikata. *OSAN sees them to the door.)*

OSAN *(Her mood deflating):* No matter where I look, I see misery. What a wretched world!

> *(She locks the door after them. At OSAN's insistence, HIKOSHICHI puts away his desk and joins the other children sitting around the hearth. OSAN proceeds to fuss over them.)*

TAKEMOTO:

> Sōgo can barely distinguish his own house / in the relentless snow, / yet he trudges on, / step by determined step. / He knocks at the door, / disturbing the winter quiet.
>
> *(SŌGO enters from right and makes his way toward the door.)*

SŌGO *(In a loud whisper):* Osan! Osan! Open the door!

OSAN: Who could it be at this hour and in this snow?

HIKOSHICHI: I'll see who it is.

OSAN: It's probably one of the officials on his nightly rounds. Be quiet, children. I'm going to open the door.

> *(The children seem frightened. They hold hands and move back toward the cupboard. OSAN opens the door and SŌGO rushes in, his face still covered by his hat.)*

OSAN *(Worried):* What sort of guest doesn't take off his hat when he enters someone's house? Who is it?

SŌGO *(Takes off his hat):* Osan, it's me!

OSAN: Sōgo?

HIKOSHICHI and OTŌ: Father?

> *(The family excitedly greets SŌGO. He takes off his coat and gives it to OSAN, who puts it down on the* tatami. *He then sits on the step, and the children cluster around him. OSAN hangs back, standing slightly to his side.)*

TAKEMOTO:

> They can but cry tears of happiness.

OSAN: You're back!

SŌGO *(Quietly):* Quick. Shut the door!

OSAN *(Shutting the door and starting toward the kitchen):* I'll bring some water so that you can wash your feet.

234

Kiuchi Sōgo (Nakamura Kichiemon II) returns to his village from Edo, exhausted and cold from journeying through the snowstorm. His wife, Osan (Nakamura Matsue V), and their three young children excitedly welcome him at the steps of their poor home. (Umemura Yutaka, Engeki Shuppansha)

SŌGO: No, don't bother. It's snowing outside and my feet are quite clean.

    (SŌGO *removes his straw sandals and leggings as they ad-lib,* "I'm so glad you're back," "So am I.")

SŌGO *(Quietly):* Osan, make sure the children don't speak too loudly. We don't want to attract attention.

OSAN: Listen, children. Daddy's tired, so don't make too much noise.

    (OSAN *hangs up* SŌGO*'s cloak in the kitchen area, and* SŌGO *steps up into the central room. The younger children follow him, while* HIKOSHICHI *rests* SŌGO*'s hat against the outside of the house before joining the others.* OSAN *places the leggings near the fire to dry.*)

OSAN: Now, why don't you show your father how well you can bow?

    (*Kneeling, the children press their foreheads to the floor obediently.*)

SŌGO *(Touched):* Ah, that was very good.

OSAN: Sōgo, we've had a new addition to the family since you left for Edo.

    (OSAN *goes into the other room, gets the baby—a tightly wrapped doll—and shows it to* SŌGO.)

SŌGO *(Lovingly stroking the baby's head):* They've all grown so much. *(Shivering.)* But it's so cold in here!

OSAN: Your kimono is soaking wet. I've been sewing for you while you've been away. Luckily, I've just finished a kimono. You can change into that.

SŌGO: Yes, I think I will.

 (OSAN passes the baby to HIKOSHICHI and goes to the cupboard.)

TAKEMOTO:

 Osan jumps to her feet and with loving care / removes the basting threads from the freshly washed kimono. / More welcome than the comfort of the fresh cotton / is the tender attention of a loving wife.

 (The two younger children go back to their places behind the hearth, and HIKO-SHICHI stands near the cupboard. OSAN takes the kimono from the wardrobe and unwraps it. When she helps SŌGO to change into the kimono and a dry obi, she finds the letter of divorce in his wet kimono, but SŌGO quickly retrieves it. They look at each other and laugh nervously, uncertain how to diffuse this tense moment. Regaining her composure, OSAN hangs up the wet kimono to dry, then gently removes a loose thread from SŌGO's new kimono. They look at each other tenderly.)

OSAN: It's just been washed so it's a bit stiff. Put this on, too. *(She takes off her jacket and tries to put it on SŌGO.)*

SŌGO *(Gently stopping her):* Don't worry about me.

OSAN: I don't need it. I'm not cold. You wear it. Please.

 (OSAN insists that he wear it, and they share a moment of intimacy as she puts her arms around him when she places the jacket on his shoulders. She gathers the children around their father. SŌGO puts TOKUMATSU on his knee.)

OSAN *(Noticing the snow):* Tell me, how did you find your way home in this heavy snow?

SŌGO: Jinbei the ferryman owed me a favor. He ferried me across the marsh. *(Warmly, to all of them.)* And now I'm finally home.

OSAN: So it's thanks to Jinbei that you've come back to us.

SŌGO: Osan, I've been in Edo for less than six months, but everything has changed so much. Where are the servants?

OSAN *(Hesitantly):* Well, you were away, and the unrest started, so I let them go back to their families. *(She bows slightly as if in apology.)*

SŌGO: Is that so? People will regard you highly for that kindness. I'm proud of you.

OSAN *(Bowing again at SŌGO's compliment):* I heard that Father was arrested at Lord Hotta's mansion and imprisoned. Has he been pardoned yet?

SŌGO *(Lying to spare OSAN's feelings):* Yes. When news of the protests reached Edo, he was thrown into prison but was released the same day. We've discussed it and have decided to present another petition. Preparations are almost complete. *(Overly reassuring.)* There's nothing to worry about.

236

OSAN *(Doubtfully):* If that were the case, he would have written. Father might be getting on, but he always writes. I'm certain he would have sent news to us.

SŌGO *(Offhandedly):* In difficult times, who has time to write letters?

OSAN: Why have you returned home alone?

SŌGO *(Exasperated):* Osan, all of these questions! *(Faltering.)* He'll be home in two or three days, so don't worry. It's been so long since I've been home. Why don't we celebrate with some sake?

OSAN *(Teasingly):* So, you developed a taste for sake while you were in Edo!

SŌGO: No, of course not. But it's snowing, and dismal weather like this calls for a drink.

OSAN *(Apologetically):* If I'd known that you were coming home tonight I would have bought some especially, but it's far too late to go and get some now.

HIKOSHICHI: I'll go!

OSAN: In this weather? It's miles away!

SŌGO: But you don't need to go that far. The sake shop is just around the corner. *(To* HIKOSHICHI.*)* Go and buy some there.

OSAN *(Slowly, as if loath to tell him):* Oh, Sōgo, in the time that you've been away so many people have left.

SŌGO *(Surprised):* You mean you can't even buy sake here any more?

OSAN *(In a tear-filled voice):* It's like a different village now.

(*In shock,* SŌGO *almost lets* TOKUMATSU *slip from his knee.*)

SŌGO *(Composing himself):* Truly? Perhaps I don't need a drink after all.

HIKOSHICHI: I'll go and make some kindling for the fire.

OSAN *(Grateful for a change of subject):* You be careful now. I don't want you hurting yourself.

HIKOSHICHI: Yes, Mother.

(OSAN *takes the baby from* HIKOSHICHI. *He and* OTŌ *pick up the kindling box from near the fireplace and take it into the kitchen area.* SŌGO *looks lovingly at the baby.*)

SŌGO: The peaceful innocence of the young. *(Feeling a chill.)* It's cold in here. You'd better put him to bed so that he doesn't catch cold.

OSAN: Yes, that's a good idea.

TAKEMOTO:

The child nestles in her arms/ and she lulls it to sleep, / hovering over it like a bird protecting its young. / Soon it sleeps, and she stands / to pass the child to her husband, / who savors the delicate perfume of mother and child.

(SŌGO *sets* TOKUMATSU *down. At* SŌGO*'s insistence,* TOKUMATSU *takes the baby from* OSAN*'s arms and lays it down behind a small screen, right.* SŌGO *tenderly puts his coat over the baby. He looks around to make sure that* OSAN *is not watching him and, brushing away a tear, tucks some documents into the bedclothes.*

SŌGO *returns to the hearth, where he warms his hands.* OSAN *brings the tea things from the cupboard to the hearth. The children gather around their parents while* OSAN *makes tea.)*

OSAN: Sōgo, it's a such a long time since we've sat down to drink tea together. It's probably not very good, but it's all we have now.

SŌGO *(Happily drinking the tea* OSAN *has given him):* I wasn't aware of it while I was at home, but since I've been away I've noticed how quickly the children are growing up. *(Puzzled.)* But tell me, why are their clothes so shabby?

OSAN *(Temporizing):* Well, even though the children are quite grown up now, as soon as they put something on, they get it dirty.

SŌGO *(Displeased):* If I can see it, other people certainly will. What about the new clothes you made for them last spring? Where are they?

OSAN: During the time that you were away, many people in the village suffered great hardships. You're the village head, so they often came to me to ask if there was any news from Edo. I couldn't bear to see the way they had to live, so I gave the children's clothes to them.

SŌGO *(Surprised but pleased):* You gave the children's clothes away? You did well to help them. Good deeds are rewarded in paradise. Osan, your clothes are looking decidedly threadbare, too. *(*OSAN *backs away from him in shame.)* Why don't you change into something else?

OSAN *(Unhappily):* Well . . .

(A light ki *clack highlights the pause.)*

SŌGO: You gave yours away, too?

OSAN *(Crying):* Yes.

SŌGO *(Supressing tears):* I see. What can I say? In the whole six months that I was away I barely sent enough money to cover daily expenses. I've reduced my family to looking like beggars.

OSAN *(Tearfully):* I'm not the only one going without. We've all had to make sacrifices. So did you. *(Pausing to think about the future.)* You have to go away again, don't you?

TAKEMOTO:

She speaks out bravely, / yet Sōgo perceives her much reduced state / and is moved to tears.

*(*SŌGO *gulps down the tea to suppress his grief, but he chokes, and* HIKOSHICHI *dutifully pats him on the back.)*

SŌGO *(Pausing to dwell on his imminent death, then remembering his father):* Today is the anniversary of my father's death.

TAKEMOTO:

Sōgo stands at the Buddhist altar, / takes down the memorial tablet of his ancestor, / and turns to face his children.

(At OSAN*'s insistence, the children cluster around* SŌGO *while he takes down the memorial tablet.* OSAN *sits apart, slightly removed from the others.)*

SŌGO: Children, you know nothing of my life before I married your mother. Hiko-shichi, Otō, Tokumatsu, listen carefully. *(An offstage prayer bell sounds as* SŌGO *prepares to deliver a final lesson to his children. The bell continues to sound intermittently.)* The name inscribed on this tablet is Tekiryōgizan Eikankoji. It is the Buddhist name of my father, Tanigawa Sōemon. He came from a samurai family, but the house of his lord was reduced to nothing, and we fell on hard times. My father became a *rōnin,* and we wandered from place to place until we came to Shimōsa Province. After a little while, I married your mother and was adopted into her household. Not long after that my real father died. *(He puts both hands flat on the ground and bows forward in grief.)* Although I prayed earnestly for his soul's repose, I also honored my adoptive father, Osan's father, Rizaemon. I will never be able to repay one-hundredth of the kindness he has shown me. Now the village is in turmoil, and I have a duty as our village head to journey to Edo once more. *(*OSAN *looks up with a start as she realizes, for the first time, the implications of his visit.)* Death comes to old and young alike. When my time comes, take good care of your mother and follow the teachings of the priest. Be good to each other and everyone in the village, and don't forget your lessons.

*(*OSAN *cries quietly.)*

TAKEMOTO:

Hearing this, the children answer obediently.

(The children bow and speak bravely.)

HIKOSHICHI: The priest says that people who aren't kind to others are like rocks and trees. They have no hearts.

OTŌ: I will also . . .

OTŌ and TOKUMATSU: Remember this.

*(*SŌGO *and* OSAN *formally express their grief.)*

SŌGO: We can only despise the fate . . .

OSAN: That Sōgo must endure, and so we pray to the gods and Buddhas.

SŌGO: Our lot is to tread a dark and treacherous road . . .

OSAN: Through this world of illusion . . .

BOTH: Of this we can be sure.

*(*SŌGO *gathers the children in his arms.* OSAN*, sobbing, draws closer. Both parents cover their faces and weep. Suddenly, a mysterious figure appears at the window. It is* CHŌKICHI*, the local ne'er-do-well.* SŌGO *invites him in to see what he wants while* OSAN *quickly takes the children and the baby into an interior room. In doing this, she finds the documents concealed in the baby's bedclothes and takes them with her to read.* CHŌKICHI*, having seen* SŌGO *cross the Inbanuma Marsh*

illegally, tries to extort money from him in return for his silence. However, the local constables have been watching CHŌKICHI *closely, as he is a notorious thief. They come to the door, and* CHŌKICHI *flees. In their haste to apprehend him, they fail to register* SŌGO *'s presence. This close encounter greatly unnerves* SŌGO. OSAN *comes out to see who the visitor was.)*

OSAN: Sōgo, who was it?

SŌGO: No one important. There are some bad types about.

OSAN *(Relieved):* Then you should think about having some supper and getting to sleep.

SŌGO: Why, what time is it?

OSAN: It's already midnight.

SŌGO *(Grieved, realizing that they must part):* Midnight? *(Remembering his duty.)* Osan, take good care of the children.

> *(*SŌGO *prepares to leave.* OSAN *stops him and produces the documents from inside her kimono.)*

OSAN: Sōgo, what is this? What is the meaning of this? *(Hysterically.)* I will not accept this, Sōgo! *(Throws the documents to the ground.)* I won't! I won't! I won't! *(Both* SŌGO *and* OSAN *sink to their knees.* OSAN *unwraps the covering sheet and smoothes out the documents.)* This letter says that you are accepting the burden for the other villagers and are going to Edo again as their representative. It says that you don't know whether you will return and to take good care of the children. And this is a letter of divorce. It says that you're casting me off because of some wrongdoing. What have I done? You are so . . . cruel. You cold, heartless man!

> *(She trembles with rage and despair.* SŌGO *hides his face and weeps.)*

TAKEMOTO:

> So saying, she cries.

SŌGO *(Remorsefully):* You have a true and faithful heart. While I was in Edo, you not only ran the household, you also selflessly helped the other villagers. How could you be guilty of any wrongdoing? *(He sobs uncontrollably.)*

OSAN: Are you trying to prepare me for the worst? Could it be that the mission you are about to carry out in Edo will bring with it a dreadful punishment? Are you divorcing me so we will not be punished along with you?

SŌGO: Lord Hotta's cruelty forces me to do this. If I, a poor peasant, approach a man of rank, I will receive the severest punishment, even if my petition is granted.

TAKEMOTO:

> May they do with me what they will . . .

SŌGO: My only thought was to divorce you so you and the children would not share my cruel fate. *(Desperately begging.)* Osan, don't despise me. Please don't.

TAKEMOTO:

Hearing this, she cries tears of resentment.

OSAN *(Refusing to be convinced):* Why did you hide this from me? With this petition you will save the lives of many people, but you will give up your own. I am your wife, and if you must sacrifice your life, then so must I.

TAKEMOTO:

Without resenting her fate . . .

(OSAN crosses her arms over her chest and shakes her head, simultaneously refusing his divorce and showing that she will accompany him even in death.)

OSAN: I pity the poor children. They often asked me when their father was returning from Edo, and although I feared for your safety, I would tell them that Daddy was coming home soon. *(Looking pointedly at* SŌGO*.)* We never forgot you, Sōgo, not even while we slept.

TAKEMOTO:

Accepting that her life will disappear like the dew . . .

OSAN *(Moving to* SŌGO*'s side and placing her hand on his knee):* I would follow you to the depths of hell. *(Tearfully looking at him.)* Surely this is my duty as your wife.

TAKEMOTO:

Yet it is natural that she should grieve over their fate.

OSAN *(In disbelief):* Why must we endure this?

TAKEMOTO:

He tears the letter of divorce into a thousand pieces.

(SŌGO, acquiescing to OSAN*'s request, tears up the letter of divorce. They stare at the crumpled fragments.)*

OSAN: A sign that the bonds between a husband and wife . . .

SŌGO: Can never be severed. *(He throws the letter of divorce into the hearth and, with hunched shoulders, pauses to consider the implications of this action.)*

OSAN *(Bowing):* Sōgo, I'm so happy. Thank you. How happy I am! *(Pauses, realizing that her happiness will be short-lived.)* Poor Sōgo. Destined to perish . . .

SŌGO: And never see . . .

OSAN: His children grow and prosper.

SŌGO: Our short life together . . .

BOTH *(Agonized, through their tears):* As an ill-fated couple.

TAKEMOTO:

As they confront their pitiful fate, / Hikoshichi enters, holding the baby.

(OSAN moves to SŌGO*'s side, and he puts his arm round her. As they weep together, the baby cries in the interior room.* OSAN *picks up the remaining letter and hides it in her kimono.* HIKOSHICHI *enters, carrying the baby, followed by* TOKUMATSU *and* OTŌ*.)*

HIKOSHICHI: Mother, something has frightened the baby, and he's crying.

OSAN (*Wistfully*): He's probably seen our future in his dreams. Here. (*She stands, takes the baby, and shows him to* SŌGO.)

TAKEMOTO:

As Sōgo stands, unable to watch / the baby cradled in its mother's arms, / his older children cling to him.

(*As* SŌGO *moves toward the steps, the children block his way:* TOKUMATSU *on one side and* OTŌ *on the other, holding his arms, while* HIKOSHICHI *moves in front of him and seizes* SŌGO*'s obi.*)

HIKOSHICHI: Father, do you really have to go to Edo?

OTŌ: Can't you stay with us?

TOKUMATSU: Don't go . . .

OTŌ and TOKUMATSU: Away.

SŌGO: Oh, dear children. Hikoshichi, you're the eldest and you have to understand these things. When my petition is granted, I promise I'll bring back lots of presents for you. But until then you'll have to be a big boy and wait patiently. (HIKOSHICHI *stands back. The younger children still cling to their father.*) Tokumatsu. Otō. Let me go. (*Weeping.*) Osan, can't you do something with my stubborn children?

OSAN: Children. Do as your father says and let him go. (*Her voice dissolves into tears.*) Please let him go. Please.

(OSAN *gently pulls* TOKUMATSU *and* OTŌ *away from* SŌGO, *but they immediately cling to him again.*)

OSAN: Come away. (*Unable to convince the younger children to release their father, she moves away, weeping.*)

HIKOSHICHI: I had a wonderful dream that Father took us all to see the cherry blossoms. (*He mimes weeping, moving his hand vertically in front of his face.*)

SŌGO (*Weeping, struck by the impossibility of ever enjoying a family outing again*): You had a dream about the cherry blossom festival? You dreamt that we all went together? (*He sinks to his knees, the children doing the same*). Tokumatsu, Otō, listen to me. I'm going to bring Grandfather back with me, and when it's cherry blossom season I'll buy each of you a beautiful kimono. But until then, you'll have to be very brave, so please let me go. (*He tries to pull away, but the two younger children will not release his hands.* HIKOSHICHI *still kneels.* TOKUMATSU *and* OTŌ *shake their heads.*) Please . . . please . . . just let me go.

HIKOSHICHI (*Kneeling in front of* SŌGO): But Father, people say that dreams contradict reality and that if you have a good dream, the reverse will come true. You're not coming home, are you? (*He mimes crying.*)

TAKEMOTO:

Grieving as if this were the last time they would ever meet . . .

HIKOSHICHI *(Holding onto* SŌGO *'s obi imploringly):* Can't you please make Grandfather come back?

OTŌ and TOKUMATSU: Please!

TAKEMOTO:

Together they cling, / grasping at Sōgo's sleeves / and weeping tears of devotion / sufficient to swell the Tone River.

(TOKUMATSU *and* OTŌ *implore* SŌGO, *pulling him from left to right.* SŌGO *is wracked by tears and looks over to* OSAN *beseechingly. In desperation he pushes* HIKOSHICHI *away, but the child immediately takes hold again.* OSAN *draws near, and they huddle together as a group, crying.)*

The bell tolls.

(A bell [hontsurigane] *tolls the time.)*

SŌGO *(Standing):* It's already near morning. I must go quickly, before the dawn breaks.

OSAN: Are you leaving us already?

SŌGO *(Purposefully):* If I travel on the main road I'll attract attention. I had better go by the back road. *(Seized by sobs.)* But first, let me see the baby. *(He tucks the back of his kimono into his obi in preparation for the journey.* OSAN *shows him the baby once more.)* It sleeps in blissful ignorance. *(Ironically.)* It's dead to the world. *(SŌGO weeps.)*

TAKEMOTO:

As Sōgo prepares to depart, / the elder son stands in front / and the younger clings to his shoulders.

(SŌGO sits to put on his sandals with the help of HIKOSHICHI, *who then goes to get* SŌGO *'s hat from outside.* OSAN *gives the baby to* OTŌ.)

TOKUMATSU *(Clinging to* SŌGO *'s shoulders):* Daddy, if you have to go, then I want to go, too.

TAKEMOTO:

Hearing the child's tender entreaty, / Osan gently approaches him.

OSAN *(Tenderly):* Tokumatsu, Daddy is coming home again very soon, so you'll just have to be patient for a little while.

TOKUMATSU: Then I'll wait, but please bring me back a present from Edo.

SŌGO *(Taking money from his wallet):* Osan, we can't have the children going without. It's not much, but take this and buy something nice for them.

OSAN: I'll manage somehow. Sōgo, you take it. You'll need the money for the journey.

SŌGO: No, no. You take it. If I run out of money, I can always borrow from a friend.

OSAN *(Crying):* If you're sure you don't need it . . .

(SŌGO presses the money into OSAN *'s hand. She goes to her sewing basket and gets an herbal tonic for* SŌGO. *It starts to snow.)*

OSAN *(Giving the tonic to* SŌGO *):* Take these herbs with you just in case. And be careful.

SŌGO: This is for me? Thank you. *(He accepts the tonic.)* I can hardly bear to leave you. Take care, Osan. *(He closes his eyes, mustering the strength to leave them.)*

TAKEMOTO:

> Husband and wife part regretfully, / their falling tears beating a solemn percussion. / Sōgo attempts to leave but is forced to look back.
>
> *(Giving the baby to* OTŌ, OSAN *puts the cloak over* SŌGO, *who steps down from the house. He tries to take his hat, but* HIKOSHICHI *refuses to relinquish it. The other three look on from the house.* SŌGO *looks back toward them as he tries to pry the hat out of* HIKOSHICHI's *grasp. As the baby in* OSAN's *arms begins to cry, the large drum plays.* SŌGO *finally retrieves his hat, but* HIKOSHICHI *stands in front of him to prevent his departure.* SŌGO *pushes him out of the way and lunges forward, but* HIKOSHICHI *holds him back, and they pose.* SŌGO *pushes him away again and again. As* OSAN *holds out the baby,* SŌGO *looks back in grief.)*

TAKEMOTO:

> Advancing one step but retreating by three / he proceeds with the measured reluctance of a man walking to meet his death.
>
> *(SŌGO *tries to climb over a small fence extending from the right of the house. When he is halfway over,* HIKOSHICHI *pulls him back, and they pose. The drumbeat intensifies and* OSAN *cries out.* SŌGO *looks back toward the house. He pulls away from* HIKOSHICHI *and walks into the bamboo thicket at the back of the house, trying to get away, but* HIKOSHICHI *follows him. During this time, the stage begins to revolve.* HIKOSHICHI *cries out after* SŌGO. *The stage stops turning, showing the right side of the house. A small bridge must be crossed to reach a forest, which extends to the left. As* SŌGO *and* HIKOSHICHI *make their way across the bridge,* OSAN, *holding the baby, opens the window, through which she and the younger children call out to* SŌGO. SŌGO *poses on the bridge, held back by* HIKOSHICHI.)*

OSAN: The bond between a parent and a child lasts forever. Give them one last look at their father.

> *(SŌGO *looks back at his family. The highly emotive tones of the chanter and shamisen and furious beating of a snow pattern on the large drum, together with the pleading children and crying baby, create a clamorous scene.)*

TAKEMOTO *(Dramatically):*

> From the window . . .

TOKUMATSU: Daddy!

OTŌ: Daddy!

HIKOSHICHI: Father!

TAKEMOTO:

> The child she holds in her arms cries. / The distraught family is overcome by grief.

(SŌGO *takes a step, but* HIKOSHICHI *still holds fast to his cloak. Bracing himself against a sapling,* SŌGO *pushes* HIKOSHICHI *aside and turns his eyes away to avoid seeing the despairing expression on his son's face. This pose is emphasized by three double beats of the* tsuke [batan]. *Finally free of* HIKOSHICHI*'s grasp,* SŌGO *walks directly to the* hanamichi. *He falls at* shichisan, *picks himself up, and pauses. He holds the brim of his hat with one hand as one* ki *clack signals the concluding moments of the scene.*)

TAKEMOTO:

And they part.

(*Battling his feelings,* SŌGO *hurries away as* OSAN *cries out to him. Rapid* ki *pattern and a dramatic shamisen accompaniment* [sanjū] *play as the curtain closes.*)

Mount Tōei: The Petition for Mercy

(*The main curtain is drawn back to a* ki *accompaniment interspersed with the beats of a gong. The gong pattern* [terakane], *indicating a temple scene, sounds as the curtain opens to reveal a light-blue curtain* [asagimaku], *which screens off most of the stage. On either side of the curtain the extreme edges of a brilliant red stage set can be glimpsed. Offstage shamisen plays quietly. Two samurai* GUARDS *appear from left and two from right. They wear grey ceremonial robes* [kamishimo] *and swords. It is the Hour of the Tiger, about four in the morning, just prior to the Hour of the Bird, about six in the morning.*)

FIRST GUARD: I trust that your watch was without incident. It has indeed been a long night for you.

SECOND GUARD: And for you, my friend. What is the hour?

THIRD GUARD: The bell at Gōkoku Temple sounded not two moments ago. The Hour of the Tiger will soon be upon us.

FOURTH GUARD: The attendants are to assemble at the Hour of the Bird, and therefore his lordship will not be here for some hours.

FIRST GUARD: However, today's ceremony will be no ordinary event. Even the senior statesmen will be in attendance.

SECOND GUARD: That notwithstanding, we must keep strict watch until dawn.

THIRD GUARD: Well, gentlemen . . .

FOURTH GUARD: We shall meet . . .

ALL: At the appointed hour.

(*The* GUARDS *exit in the direction from which they entered. The high-pitched tones of the small shamisen used in offstage music change to the deeper tones of the large-bodied shamisen used for* TAKEMOTO *accompaniment.*)

TAKEMOTO:

On the eastern road / where the cockerel greets the dawn / lies Kanei Temple, mirror of Mount Hiei. / Of the lofty temple roofs / not the least splendid is that of this great hall.

(As the TAKEMOTO *accompaniment ends, a* ki *clack signals the curtain to fall, revealing Kanei Temple at Mount Tōei. Temple buildings at left and right are connected by a raised, arched walkway upstage, customary for important Buddhist temples. A plaque reads "Mount Tōei." Brilliant red maple leaves form a natural canopy over the roof of the bridge. The red-lacquered timber of the temple buildings complements the vivid colors of the maple leaves. Underneath the walkway to the rear are two white banners featuring two large crests of the reigning Tokugawa family. In the far distance, trees flank an imposing temple building. To slow drum, shamisen, flute, and dignified singing [kagen], the stately party enters. The military retainers and the shogun,* TOKUGAWA IETSUNA, *wear ceremonial robes [kamishimo]. The head* PRIEST *wears bright orange robes and a large gold hat. The retainers kneel in formal position, flanking the powerful standing figure of* IETSUNA. *The samurai speak in a very deliberate and formal manner, accompanied by an offstage shamisen melody [aikata].)*

SHOGUN: An ancient Chinese poet once wrote that, seeing the vivid hues of the maple trees blazing against a mist-enshrouded mountain, he felt compelled to capture their beauty and share it with his companions. The colors of the maple are fit to embellish the finest brocade. This is truly a splendid vista.

LORD OF IZU: Indeed, it is as you say. The poet Hakurakuten greatly favored the maple, and in *The Tale of Genji,* Murasaki Shikibu celebrated the maple-viewing season, praising it in words no less splendid than the vivid hues of the leaves that we see before us.

LORD OF YAMATO: Even the palace guards warm their wine on bonfires of flaming maple leaves.

LORD OF KAWACHI: All the dappled colors of the maple abound . . .

LORD OF WAKASA: At Tōshōgū Shrine, said to illuminate the east.

LORD OF SHIMA: At this time, the land is at peace . . .

LORD OF HŌKI: And your authority is as boundless as the wide horizon.

LORD OF TANGO: The bright maple shines resplendent . . .

MATSUDAIRA UKYŌDAIBU: Lit by the waters of Taki River.

LORD OF HIZEN: As the maple at Mama gleams in the evening light . . .

LORD OF TAJIMA: So shines your Momiji Mountain. It is true that there are many places fabled for their beauty, not the least of which is the splendid view at this temple.

HEAD PRIEST: Your lordship, the appointed time is drawing near. Shall we proceed?

IETSUNA: Certainly.

(A deep drumbeat resonates and ceremonial music [kagen] begins again as all exit left. The deeper sounds of the large shamisen used by the TAKEMOTO *signal a change in mood.)*

TAKEMOTO *(Chanting in the formal style of the* nō *theatre* [utaigakari]*):*
Like an orchid blooming among the briars / or gold dust found among the
sand . . . *(returning to normal* TAKEMOTO *style)* Sōgo, the martyr of Sakura, /
secretly hides, / determined to end the suffering of his fellow villagers.
(A gong sounds. The tone of the shamisen intensifies, and SŌGO *steps out from
behind the banner under the bridge at left. Kneeling, he pauses by one of the struts
under the walkway and looks up. The gong sounds again, and he moves to center.)*
Carefully looking around, / he takes out this heartfelt petition / and secures
it to a maple branch.
*(*SŌGO *unwraps a cloth that is tied around his waist and takes the petition from it.
He rehearses passing it to* IETSUNA *and then looks around as if he is being
watched. A single gong beat sounds again. He breaks a branch off a maple tree, left,
emphasized by four double beats* [batan] *of the* tsuke, *and ties the petition to the
branch.* SŌGO *is seen by two* GUARDS, *who creep up behind him from one side,
while a second pair of* GUARDS *do so from the other. All are dressed in ceremonial
robes. They try to seize him. To eerie flute, tsuke beats, and the occasional sound of a
small gong, a stylized fight scene* [tachimawari] *ensues. Through each sequence
SŌGO holds the maple branch with the petition out of their reach. He runs under
the bridge and then ducks out again. With his back to the audience and surrounded
by* GUARDS, *he holds the branch behind him, out of reach. He charges for the
bridge, petition outstretched, as if to present it to the shogun, but is pulled back.
He strikes a pose with the maple branch held high in his right hand, a* GUARD
posing on either side of him, and his left foot on the backs of two GUARDS *who
crouch at his feet. A large drum beats, and members of* IETSUNA*'s party cry from
offstage, "Ariya," signaling that they are returning from the ceremony.* SŌGO *lets
out a cry and pushes the* GUARDS *away. As* IETSUNA *and his party file onto
the bridge from left,* SŌGO *rushes forward but is dragged back and pushed to
his knees by the* GUARDS. *Haunting flute music and drumbeats accompany the
procession.* IETSUNA *stands in the center of the walkway, flanked by his feudal
lords.)*
LORD OF IZU *(Seated at* IETSUNA*'s left):* What have we here?
(Obediently, the GUARDS *pull back, leaving* SŌGO *prostrate on the ground.)*
LORD OF IZU: What is the meaning of this?
SŌGO: I, Kiuchi Sōgo, the head of Kami Iwabashi Village, Kōzu-Shinden, under the
dominion of Lord Hotta Kōzuke no Suke, humbly present this petition.
*(*SŌGO *thrusts out the branch in a fervent appeal. At a signal from the* LORD OF
IZU, *one of the* GUARDS *moves to take the petition from* SŌGO, *who removes it
from the maple branch. The* GUARD *takes the petition and, with a bow, presents
it to the* LORD OF IZU, *who proceeds to remove the cover sheet.* SŌGO *remains
prostrate as the petition is read out loud.)*

LORD OF IZU *(Reading):* "Fearfully, I present this written petition containing our earnest entreaty. The inhabitants of the 389 villages in the domain of Sakura from the province of Shimōsa, under the dominion of Lord Hotta Kōzuke no Suke, having been levied harsh taxes, and having found themselves unable to make a living, repeatedly appealed to the local officials. Not only did these appeals fall on deaf ears, the villagers were deemed to have disregarded their lord's orders, and the village representatives were, without exception, arrested. Being presented with no alternative, those left in the villages journeyed to Edo to present their petition at the residence of Lord Hotta, where here, too, their pleas were ignored. This being proof of Lord Hotta's misgovernment and having no other recourse for action, with great trepidation, and despite being a lowly peasant, I fearfully petition his lordship to consider this matter. Signed Kiuchi Sōgo, from Kami Iwabashi Village, Kōzu-Shinden, Inba District, Shimōsa Province, being the representative for the aforementioned villages."

SŌGO *(Fervently bowing his forehead to the ground):* I humbly plead with your excellency to consider the plight of the inhabitants of these 389 villages.

LORD OF IZU *(Quietly, to himself):* I never suspected Lord Hotta's misgovernment. *(With a start, he returns to protocol. Publicly.)* For a lowly peasant to petition the shogun directly is an act of gross insolence. Such a request cannot be granted. *(He makes a show of contemptuously throwing the cover sheet on the floor.)*

SŌGO *(Gratefully, because he realizes that the petition will be accepted):* Ah!

LORD OF IZU *(Emphatically):* Such a request will not be granted! *(He hides the petition in his sleeve, signaling that SŌGO's efforts have not been in vain and that he will present the petition to the shogun later, in private. In a stylized gesture, he transfers the petition to his right hand, pulling his right sleeve out stiffly across his chest with his left as he surreptitiously draws the petition into his right sleeve. For the benefit of those assembled, he glares at SŌGO, who bows in gratitude. It is a bittersweet moment for SŌGO: his relief that the petition will be accepted and his fellow villagers saved is tempered by the fact that he and his family will pay with their lives.)*

LORD OF IZU: It is time for his lordship's . . . *(Two GUARDS move forward to restrain SŌGO. They hold his arms out to each side in a dramatic pose. The GUARDS bind his arms to his sides to a single ki clack intended to signal the beginning of the scene's final sequence.)*

ALL: Departure. *(Offstage deep beats on the large drum, flute, and stick drums form a ceremonial melody [kagen], accompanied by dignified singing. To a soft, regular ki pattern [hyōshimaku] that intensifies and then tapers off, the curtain closes on this formal tableau.)*

Three-panel woodblock print by Utagawa Toyokuni III (1786–1864). Ichimura-za, Edo, first month 1860. Before the small "Kōshin Shrine" along a stone embankment of the Sumida River, "Oshō Kichisa" (Ichikawa Kodanji IV) poses center, standing on a straw mat while holding an offering sign taken from the shrine. He has interrupted a fight between "Ojō Kichisa" (Iwai Kumesaburō III, later Iwai Hanshirō VIII) and "Obō Kichisa" (Kawarasaki Gonjūrō I, later Ichikawa Danjūrō IX), who are kneeling with drawn swords, left and right. Designs on their kimono allude to characters' names or their nature: Oshō's religious status is suggested by the numerous offertory clay bells that decorate his kimono and the signboard; one crest on each sleeve of Obō's kimono consists of the ideograph for "kichi," which ironically means "fortunate"; and six-point "maple leaf" (momiji) patterns made of the same ideograph cover most of Ojō's kimono. (Tsubouchi Memorial Theatre Museum of Waseda University)

The Three Kichisas and the New Year's First Visit to the Pleasure Quarters

Sannin Kichisa Kuruwa no Hatsugai

Kawatake Mokuami

TRANSLATED BY KEI HIBINO AND ALAN CUMMINGS

KŌSHIN SHRINE BY THE SUMIDA RIVER

Ōkawa-bata Kōshin Zuka no Ba

KICHIJŌ TEMPLE AT SUGAMO

Sugamo Kichijōin no Ba

THE GRAVEYARD BEHIND KICHIJŌ TEMPLE

Kichijōin Urate no Ba

THE MAIN BUILDING OF THE TEMPLE

Moto no Hondō no Ba

THE FIRE WATCHTOWER AT HONGŌ

Hongō Hinomi Yagura no Ba

1860   ICHIMURA-ZA, EDO

The Three Kichisas and the New Year's First Visit to the Pleasure Quarters

INTRODUCTION

Surprisingly, *The Three Kichisas and the New Year's First Visit to the Pleasure Quarters*, Kawatake Mokuami's (1816–1893) self-acknowledged masterpiece, was not a hit at its premiere at the Ichimura-za in the first lunar month of 1860. The reason may be in part the play's complexity. Usually classified as a typical "bandit play" *(shiranami mono)*—a genre attributed to Mokuami—the play was written in eight acts and sixteen scenes and featured a double plot, as do many other nineteenth-century kabuki plays. The increasingly sophisticated tastes of late Tokugawa period audiences demanded that playwrights produce plays with highly complex dramatic structures. One of the plot lines, about three identically named thieves, would seem to be the invention of the playwright. The other—concerned with the love between a playboy merchant, Kiya Bunri, and the courtesan Hitoe—is based on Umebori Kokuga's (1750–1821) courtesan narrative *(sharebon) The Two Ways of Buying Courtesans* (Keisei Kai Futasuji Michi, 1798). This is the plot that is hinted at in the second part of the play's full title.

The pathetic story of Bunri and Hitoe's love was rather commonplace and in later productions was customarily cut entirely, as it is in this translation. (The abbreviated version of the play, which corresponds to current performance practice, only hints at the multiple layers, the sophisticated dramaturgy, and the wonderful intricacy of the original.) The other plot line, the picaresque romance of the rise and fall of the three Kichisas—Ojō, or "Little Miss" Kichisa; Obō, or "Young Master" Kichisa; and Oshō, or "Priest" Kichisa—has always fascinated audiences. The three Kichisas are villain-heroes who bravely challenge their predestined fate but are defeated in the end. As in his many other plays, Mokuami builds the plot around the popular belief in *inga*, originally the Buddhist concept of the universal principle of causality, but generally more narrowly interpreted as poetic justice. Most often *inga* is recognized through the punishment (rather than the reward) one receives as a result of actions committed before one's reincarnation in this world, hence a sense of an uncontrollable, external force affecting a person (since one cannot avoid *inga* by exercise of reason and caution). In *Three Kichisas*, although the three thieves are to die as a result of their own evildoing, and not that from their previous lives, the inevitability of their fate is underscored by their repeated references to *inga* as they gradually come to realize that they cannot escape its miraculous workings.

This recognition of their fate, together with their resultant tragic death, increases the thieves' heroic and sympathetic stature. On the other hand, it is also true that, in an age dominated by a highly moralistic concept of public probity, preaching *inga* was required so that the playwright and his audience could revel vicariously in the seductive appeal of evil in the assurance that censorship—whether imposed by the government or one's own sense of appropriateness—would not interfere.

Poetic justice and the appeal of evil suggest a useful parallel between kabuki plays and Western melodrama. Thriving roughly in the same period (from the late eighteenth through the nineteenth centuries) and attracting audiences from the general public rather than aristocrats or the wealthy bourgeoisie, both genres featured sensational stories focused on revealing evil while preaching moralistic improvement. *Three Kichisas* and contemporary Western melodramas such as Dion Boucicault's *The Poor of New York* (1857) and Augustin Daly's *Under the Gaslight* (1862) evoke the images of Babylonian vice-plagued cities full of excitement and terror. Separation and reunion are stock situations in both types of plays. In the final scene of *Three Kichisas*, we have the typical moment when Kyūbei, the father, encounters a young man and asks, "Why, is that you, my long-lost son?"

But while the plot may favor the sensational, the play's theatricality presents fascinating possibilities. Self-referentiality and self-consciousness are seen in the self-introductions of Obō and Ojō, who refer to their past roles, and Oshō, who mentions the popularity of the actors who played Ojō and Obō in the premier. One rarely produced scene, not translated here, provides an interesting example of the self-referential nature of kabuki plays in the nineteenth-century, when three old, ugly streetwalkers pretend to be the dashing thieves and parodistically reenact their first meeting. Taken together, these metatheatrical devices underline the closed nature of the dramatic world represented on stage, since the signs employed by the actors have no referents in the real world, only in the world of fiction. Late Tokugawa-period playwrights may well have believed that "There is nothing outside theatre."

The five scenes translated here deal with the first meeting of the three thieves, their reunion, and the denouement. These are the scenes that were performed in later decades following the 1860 premier.

Several elements in the play require explanation. First, since the opening scene is set at a Kōshin shrine, it should be understood that originally *kōshin*, or *kano-e saru*, was the fifty-seventh element of a classical Chinese calendrical system (itself called *etō* or *jikkan jūnishi*) widely adopted in premodern Japan. Within the *etō* system sixty patterns occur in a cycle, one cycle corresponding to either sixty years, sixty months, or sixty days. Hence there are *kōshin* years as well as *kōshin*

months and days. Like Western astrological signs, each *etō* element has a particular
implication that affects the fate of a person: thus a baby born on a *kōshin* day was
believed to be destined to become a thief. Mokuami integrates such *kōshin* beliefs
into the drama, which was premiered in 1860, a *kōshin* year.

The play was also loosely conceived within the framework of plays about
Oshichi and Kichisaburō *(Oshichi-Kichisa mono)*. As mentioned in Volumes 1 and 2,
when composing a play, it was customary for playwrights to first choose one of the
traditionally codified worlds *(sekai)*. Each had a set of characters, locations, and
actions associated with it, built up from dozens of previous plays and stories. The
sekai of Oshichi and her lover Kichisa(burō) was one of the most popular worlds in
Mokuami's time. In order to meet with her temple-page lover, the historical Oshichi set a fire—a capital offense in old Japan's fire-prone wooden cities. Although
she regretted her impulsive action immediately and climbed a fire watchtower at
Hongō to sound the alarm, it was too late. Oshichi was arrested and executed at
the age of seventeen in March 1683.

Ihara Saikaku (1642–1693) novelized Oshichi's story in his *Five Women Who
Loved Love* (Kōshoku Gonin Onna, 1686), and her fame was subsequently assured
through the many ballads based on broadsheets *(utazaimon)*, plays, and dances
written about her. When Mokuami wrote *Three Kichisas*, he borrowed Oshichi and
Kichisaburō's love story as his *sekai* and made one of the thieves, Ojō, dress himself
as Oshichi. Ojō's transvestism is explained as a robber's ruse, but his homosexuality
is also suggested. (Unlike in Christianized Western countries, homosexuality was
not regarded as a taboo subject in Japan, at least by the end of the Edo period, and
was often referred to subtly—and sometimes not so subtly—in art, literature, and
theatre.) Mokuami later created another transsexual thief, Benten Kozō, in the play
popularly known by his name (1862 trans. Ernst 1959 and Leiter 2000). The effects
of these devices are maximized in the Hongō watchtower scene (the fifth and final
scene of the translation), where the fugitive Ojō and Obō meet again. In this scene,
their reunion is not just enacted by the actors but also told through the songs
chanted by the *kiyomoto* and *takemoto* musicians, who depict their relationship as
that of lovers; thus the images of the tragic Oshichi and Kichisaburō were pro-
jected onto the thieves. This allusive use of *sekai* characterizes Mokuami's late
plays. *Sekai* no longer serves a dramaturgic purpose in terms of plot development,
as in his early plays. Instead, it suggests another world beyond the one represented
onstage, tapping audiences' memories to evoke various images associated with it.

The blurring of fiction and reality is commonplace in kabuki, as when the
streetwalker Otose blithely accepts Ojō as the real Oshichi (or possibly as an actor
playing the role of Oshichi) in the opening scene. Edo audiences enjoyed playing

with this double identity of character and actor. The aesthetics of kabuki and Tokugawa popular culture in general assumed that the boundary between reality and
fiction was always being blurred. As the great dramatist Chikamatsu Monzaemon
(1653–1725) formulated it, "Art should not reflect reality nor fiction but something in between them."

The present translation is based on the scripts and videotapes of productions
in 1972 and 1978 at the Kokuritsu Gekijō (National Theatre of Japan). Also consulted was the meticulously annotated Shinchōsha text, *Sannin Kichisa Kuruwa no
Hatsugai* (1984), edited by Imao Tetsuya, based on the 1888 *Yomiuri Shinbun* newspaper serialization version, presumed to be closest to the original script. We thank
Professor Valerie L. Durham of Tokyo University of Economy for her kind translation suggestions.

CHARACTERS

OJŌ KICHISA, *an itinerant actor posing as Oshichi, the greengrocer's daughter*

OSHŌ KICHISA, *a pickpocket, actually* BENCHŌ, *a priest at Kichijō Temple*

OBŌ KICHISA, *a* rōnin, *or masterless samurai, actually* YASUMORI KICHISABURŌ,
       heir to the Yasumori house

OTOSE, *a cheap streetwalker,* DENKICHI's *daughter*

JŪZABURŌ, *a shop clerk, lover of* OTOSE

KYŪBEI, *a greengrocer,* JŪZABURŌ's *father*

SAGINOKUBI TARŌEMON, *a moneylender*

GENJI, *sexton at the Kichijō Temple*

CHIEF, *the chief police officer*

TOKISUKE, *a gatekeeper in Hongō*

"SNAKE MOUNTAIN" CHŌJI, *a* rōnin

"EAGLE FOREST" KUMAZŌ, *a* rōnin

"RACCOON HOLE" KINTA, *a* rōnin

PALANQUIN BEARERS

POLICE OFFICERS

TAKEMOTO, *the chanter-shamisen player combination that comments on the action*

KIYOMOTO, *chanter and shamisen ensemble that comments on the action*

Kōshin Shrine by the Sumida River

    *(The curtain is run open to reveal the scene at the west end of the Ryōgoku Bridge,
on the north bank of Edo's Sumida River. Night. Offstage beats on the large drum
[mizu no oto] let us know that we are near running water. The downstage area is
covered with a huge blue cloth representing the river, and upstage a raised area,*

painted with masonry and waves, represents the riverbank. To the rear of the river-bank, on the upstage platform, is a white-painted stucco wall topped with heavy ornamental tiles. Also on the platform, to stage right and just off center, is a small shrine dedicated to the popular Kōshin figure of esoteric Buddhism. A board in-scribed with the words "Shōmen Kongō" [Blue Avatar] *hangs from its eaves: below is a collection box. Three stuffed monkeys* [the famous ones that neither hear, see, nor speak of human evil], *also associated with the Kōshin beliefs, hang from a second board. A bell tolls the hour. To an offstage shamisen and quiet percussion* [tsukuda bushi], *a streetwalker,* OTOSE, *appears from the rear of the* hanamichi. *She wears the typical outfit of an unlicensed prostitute—a black kimono and white headscarf—and carries the tool of her trade: a straw mat. Quiet* nami no oto *plays during the early part of the scene.)*

OTOSE: I'm searching for the customer who dropped his purse last night. Though it was dark, from his appearance he looked like a merchant's clerk. The money he dropped must belong to his master, so I want to return it as soon as I can. I thought that he might have come to see me again tonight at Yanagihara, so I brought the purse with me, but there was no sign of him. I hope that he hasn't done anything rash to make up for having lost his master's money. Though it was our first meeting, somehow I am unable to forget him. My heart tells me that something dreadful might have happened. Whatever shall I do?

(She lifts her hand over her eyes to see if he might be coming. Just then, OJŌ KICHISA *makes his entrance from the rear of the* hanamichi. *He is dressed in the theatrical costume of Oshichi, the greengrocer's daughter, a long-sleeved kimono* [furisode], *and the kind of hairstyle* [shimada] *typical of a well-brought-up young woman.)*

OJŌ *(Stopping at* shichisan*)*: Excuse me, miss, could you help me please?

OTOSE: Certainly. What is it?

OJŌ: Could you tell me how to get to Kameido?

OTOSE: To Kameido, you turn right here and go straight until you reach the end of the street. Then turn left . . . *(she takes note of the fact that* OJŌ *is dressed in the garb of a well-to-do young lady)* oh, I think I'm just getting you even more confused. I live along the way to Kameido, so I can take you as far as Warigesui.

OJŌ: I appreciate your kindness. I became separated from my servant and I've been wandering these strange streets all alone. I was so scared I didn't know what to do. I'd hate to put you to any trouble, but if you could come some of the way with me . . .

OTOSE: Not at all. It's on my route home anyway. It's nothing, really.

OJŌ: Well then, miss, lead on.

OTOSE: It's this way. *(She takes the lead.* OJŌ *goes to the main stage.)* Excuse me, miss, where do you live?

OJŌ: My father runs a greengrocer's in Hongō, in the second ward. My name is Oshichi.

OTOSE: So you're Oshichi, the greengrocer's daughter.

OJŌ: And where are you from, my dear?

OTOSE: Well, I live in Warigesui. My father's name is Denkichi, and mine is Otose.

OJŌ: And what do you do?

OTOSE *(At a loss about how to answer):* Me? Oh, I . . .

OJŌ: Do you sell something?

OTOSE: I do, on this mat—though I'm ashamed to say what.

OJŌ: Ah, so you're a . . .

OTOSE *(Embarrassed):* I am.

> *(As* OTOSE *lightly taps* OJŌ *on the back to suggest that his guess is right, she drops the purse.* OJŌ *quickly picks it up and surmises from its weight that it contains a large sum. He conceals his delight.)*

OJŌ: Excuse me, you dropped something. *(Handing the purse back to* OTOSE.*)*

OTOSE: Oh, thank you, I couldn't afford to lose this money.

OJŌ: Oh, was it money?

OTOSE: Yes, I have no less than one hundred gold pieces in this purse.

OJŌ: Business must be booming.

OTOSE: You must be kidding. *(Laughs.)*

OJŌ: Ahh! *(He suddenly clings to* OTOSE *in much exaggerated terror.)*

OTOSE: Whatever's the matter?

OJŌ: Something glittering just passed over the roof of that house.

OTOSE: Probably just a will-o'-the-wisp.

OJŌ: How awful!

OTOSE: What's there to be scared of? Since I work at night, I see them all the time, and now I'm used to them. I'll tell you what really frightens me though . . . *(a bell tolls the hour)* people, that's what.

OJŌ: You got that right, honey. *(He grabs the purse from* OTOSE's *kimono breast.)*

OTOSE *(Surprised):* What are you going to do with that money?

OJŌ *(His voice suddenly dropping an octave):* Nothing. Except take it.

OTOSE: What did you say? *(She is frightened.)* Then you're a . . .

OJŌ: That's right. A thief.

> *(A bell* [hontsurigane] *tolls once.)*

OTOSE: Oh, no.

OJŌ: Just like you say, people are frightening.

OTOSE: Let go of it!

> *(*OTOSE *tries to grab the purse back, but* OJŌ *shoves her away. She totters on the edge and falls into the river. A stick drum offstage provides the sound of a splash, and thin strips of paper represent the water splashing up.)*

OJŌ: Oh dear, she fell into the river. *(He looks down at the river.)* That was unfortunate! *(He pulls a wrapped package of money out of the purse.)* An unexpected bonus, these hundred gold pieces.

(OJŌ laughs coldly. Suddenly the moneylender SAGINOKUBI TARŌEMON *appears from behind and attacks* OJŌ*.)*

TARŌEMON: Those hundred gold pieces are mine!

(He attacks OJŌ *and tries to seize the purse, but* OJŌ *pushes him backward, making* TARŌEMON *spin.* OJŌ *then puts the money into the purse and slips the purse into his kimono breast.* TARŌEMON *comes at him again, but* OJŌ *skillfully fends off his clumsy blows and at the same time snatches away the short sword, Kōshinmaru, that his attacker is carrying. As* TARŌEMON *approaches again,* OJŌ *draws the sword and brandishes it. At the same time, two* PALANQUIN BEARERS *carrying a palanquin enter running from the rear of the* hanamichi *but, surprised at the fight, leave the palanquin and exit left, quickly followed by* TARŌEMON*.)*

OJŌ *(Seeing him run away):* Gutless wretch! *(He examines the sword by the light of the lantern hanging from the palanquin.)* This could come in handy on the way home. *(He thrusts the sword into his obi and looks up at the hazy moon. The musical lines he recites in distinctive seven-five meter rhythm* [shichigochō] *are among the most famous in kabuki, eagerly applauded by audiences.)* The misty moon floating / in the spring sky / blurs even the lights of / the whitebait fishers. / The chill wind refreshes / the drunkard staggering / home to roost, / a solitary crow. / Along the riverbank, / like water dripping from the oars, / an unexpected windfall. *(He produces the purse from his kimono breast and grins. From offstage right is heard the traditional call of an itinerant exorcist, who sells spells against bad luck:* "Banish your ill-luck! Spells against ill-luck!"*)* So tonight's the last day of winter. / I'd forgotten. / Out with the old, in with the new / and into the river with that whore. / Luckier than any beans / this bag of gold. / Looks like my luck has / changed with the coming of spring!

(OJŌ strikes a mie. *Suddenly, the curtain of the palanquin abandoned by its bearers at left is lifted from within, revealing* OBŌ KICHISA. *His gaze is fixed upon* OJŌ. OBŌ *wears a black kimono with distinctive diamond crests and the grown-out "fifty-day" wig* [gojūnichi] *of a hardened gambler. At his waist he carries two swords, indicating his original samurai status.* OJŌ *hurriedly slips the purse into his kimono breast and the sword into his sleeve and walks away toward right.)*

OBŌ: Excuse me, lady, wait a minute.

OJŌ *(Resuming his falsetto):* Why? Do you want something?

OBŌ: I wouldn't have stopped you if I didn't, now, would I?

OJŌ: I don't know what your business is, but I'm in a hurry. *(Making to leave.)*

OBŌ: I'm sure you are, but I won't take much of your time. *(Roughly.)* I asked you to wait, now I'm telling you. *(He now emerges from the palanquin holding his swords. They glare at each other.)*

OJŌ: You asked me to wait and so I will, but what do you want of me?

OBŌ: My request is just this. As you can see from my two swords I'm a samurai, though currently without a master. But I'm prepared to forget about my rank and beg you for a loan.

OJŌ: Whatever could a young girl loan to a samurai?

OBŌ: That golden windfall of yours.

OJŌ: What!

OBŌ: I saw you steal it.

OJŌ: Then you were watching me . . .

OBŌ: *(Delivers a passage of self-introduction* [tsurane]*):* Dozing in a / gently rolling palanquin / slightly drunk, / pleasant New Year's dreams. / Awakened by / the clink of gold on gold. / Thieves both, / our hearts the same. / Down on my luck / since last year, / no jobs that've / paid me over fifty pieces / and running short on / drinking money. / But I guess / that's the way of the world. / You with your / fine silks and long sleeves, / quite the / proper young lady. / No one'd take you / for a vicious thief. / Now, look at me, / forehead unshaven / rumpled kimono, long sword swinging. / One look and / they run a mile. / No wonder / business hasn't been good.

OJŌ: So that's your game—money with threats. *(He produces the purse from his kimono breast.)*

OBŌ: Just forget you ever stole the money and give it over to me.

OJŌ *(With a sardonic laugh):* You're making a big mistake. I thought you were maybe asking for my life because you wanted to check the edge on that new sword. I didn't realize it was only good for scaring off stray dogs! But since it's only a few coins you're after . . . I'm sure I'd love to lend it to you, but I never lend to those who threaten me. In a word, I politely decline your request. So sorry, I'm sure.

OBŌ: If you're not lending then I'm not borrowing. But why don't you act the part you're playing and beg me not to kill you? These swords are no mere show. A samurai learns to take what he wants with his sword, so just drop the cash and beat it.

OJŌ: Forget it. If you want the money, it's you who should be begging. That's a lot of gold for an average Joe, but I make my way in the world by robbing, and the money means nothing to me. But when someone tries it on with me like you've done, I'm no willow to bend to the breeze of your demands. If a samurai kills to get what he wants, you're going to have take my life before I give you this money.

OBŌ: You don't have to ask twice. I'll bet you've got quite a name for yourself as a thief. It would be a shame to put you in an unmarked grave. Tell me your name, and I'll offer a flower and incense before your tomb forty-nine days from today. *(He refers to the end of the traditional period of mourning, when the soul was believed to finally leave the body.)*

OJŌ: I'll tell you my name if that's what you want. But you'd better give me your name too, so I can write it on your seven tomb markers.

OBŌ: My mistake, I'm sure. Certainly it's only polite that I should give my name before asking yours. They call me Obō, the young master. Wet behind the ears to begin with, I've accumulated vices year after year, from blackmail through con games to robbery. *(The actor playing* OBŌ *is referring to the roles he has played.)* Now I've become the samurai outcast they call Obō Kichisa!

OJŌ: So you're the Obō Kichisa people have been talking about.

OBŌ: I am. And what's your name?

OJŌ: It seems conceited to announce myself on demand, but what the hell. From old hags to priests, many's the role I've played since last spring. I tried my hand at villains, but there's nothing more useless than chilies with no heat or crooks with no balls. So I came up with a new ruse and became Oshichi, the green-grocer's daughter. Because I work in a young girl's kimono, they call me Ojō—or "Little Miss"—Kichisa, the lowest of the low!

OBŌ: Since our names are so alike, I took note of the rumors I heard about you, Ojō, which will make it all the more satisfying to rob you.

OJŌ: To be robbed by you would dishonor my reputation . . .

OBŌ: But if I don't and I lose, my name will be mud.

OJŌ *("Divided dialogue"* [warizerifu]*)*: Reputation is all in our game. There can be no turning back . . .

OBŌ: Like a young frog transfixed by a snake, you'll not live to see the spring . . .

OJŌ: Wagering our lives . . .

OBŌ: I'll gulp you down, frog, even if it splits my belly . . .

OJŌ: This gold our stake. *(He puts the package of money in the middle of the stage.)*

OBŌ: Our sport no child's play . . .

BOTH: Let's settle it here and now!

*(*OJŌ *and* OBŌ *slip their kimono off their shoulders—the sleeves dangling from their waists—draw their swords, and begin to duel.* OSHŌ KICHISA *enters from the rear of the* hanamichi. *He wears a blue overall* [haragake], *leggings* [momo-hiki], *a down jacket* [dotera], *and a short, thin coat* [hanten], *his face wrapped in a headscarf.)*

OSHŌ: Stop it, both of you. *(He forces his way between them to stop the fight. Slipping off his jacket, he throws it over the crossed blades of their swords and holds them down with one foot. The three strike a tense* mie.*)* I don't know what you're fighting about, but I'm stopping you. Cool it! *(He whisks off his headscarf.)*

OBŌ: Who the hell are you? This is none of your business.

OJŌ: Beat it . . .

BOTH: Before you get hurt!

OSHŌ: I'm not leaving. *(Slipping into rhythmical seven-five meter dialogue.)* Too early / for spring thunderstorms, / yet the lightning / of steel on steel flashes / along the frozen bank. / We've never met / yet I know your faces, / the famous Kichisas. / Your blood may be up, / but this isn't the / time for street performances, / still too early for New Year / sword dances. / A shame if you were / to injure each other. / *(Refers to the actors' respective guild or family nicknames* [yagō].*)* Short Takashimaya / between two high peaks, / Fuji's Yamatoya and Tsukuba's Yamazakiya. / Your fans quake with fear; / thus I jumped in— / even my name / suggests peace, / the ex-priest Oshō Kichisa. / Tonight is winter's end, / so out with your quarrel / and in with the new, / a partnership of three Kichisas! / Let's drink a New Year's cup / of beans and salted plum, / and set aside your grudges. / Let my tiny pepper grains / expel this bad luck / and bind you two together!

OBŌ: So you're . . .

OJŌ: That notorious . . .

OBŌ: Ex-acolyte from Kichijō Temple . . .

BOTH: Oshō Kichisa?

OSHŌ *(Holding his head with his hands):* A compliment like that makes me blush. I'm far from notorious, just a cheap rogue. *(Again slipping into seven-five meter dialogue.)* I was the acolyte Benchō, / a mere kitchen hand / at the Kichijō Temple. / For robbing the collection / and filching donations, / I was kicked out on my ear. / More than once / I've traded my monk's gray / for prison-issue blue / and stinking gruel. / My crimes are not serious enough / for execution, / but I love this life. / To dance at the end of a rope / for theft / is a fair enough fate, / but to die in a fight / makes no sense at all. / You will tell me more later, / but for the moment / put aside your doubts / and lay down your swords.

OBŌ: I'm prepared to accept your offer, Oshō, as long as he is, too.

OJŌ: If he's agreeable, then I am, too.

OSHŌ: Then you two are convinced . . .

OBŌ: To let it go at that . . .

OJŌ: Entrust our swords to Oshō . . .

OSHŌ: And back down.

OBŌ: We are . . .

OJŌ: We are . . .

BOTH: Indeed.

(OSHŌ *removes his jacket from over* OBŌ *and* OJŌ *'s swords as they move away to right and left.*)

OSHŌ *(Nodding in gratification)*: So what were you fighting about?

OJŌ: Nothing of much importance. Just over these hundred gold pieces that I stole.

OBŌ: I asked him to lend them to me, we quarreled, and it turned into a sword fight.

OSHŌ: You were going to throw away your lives in a fight over a mere hundred gold pieces? I might sound like a drab Yuranosuke, but *(quotes a famous line from the play* The Treasury of Loyal Retainers [Kanadehon Chūshingura]*)* "You still lack in judgment." I'll settle your dispute, so swallow your objections and just say yes. First we'll split these hundred gold pieces into two, then each of you will give me half of your share for my work as a peacemaker. In return, I'll give you my two arms. You might think that's a lot to pay for someone's arm, but my judgment says that your swords can't be returned to their sheaths without first drawing blood. So lop off my arms and let them make up for the hundred gold pieces!

(*He tucks up his sleeves and thrusts his bare arms at them.* OBŌ *and* OJŌ *are impressed.*)

OBŌ: You'd sacrifice your own arms to settle our dispute? Well, you deserve your reputation, Oshō Kichisa.

OJŌ: We owe you too much to slice them off, but we will respect the feeling behind your offer . . .

OBŌ: And cut those arms . . .

OJŌ: You have offered.

OSHŌ: Don't hesitate. Go ahead and cut them off. (*He stretches his arms out in front of them.* OBŌ *and* OJŌ *exchange looks and nod determinedly. Together they nick* OSHŌ *'s arms and then their own.*) Why did you cut your own arms as well as mine?

OBŌ: As the proverb says, you'll never know till you try. We'd rather have that courage of yours on our side.

OJŌ: By drinking the blood that streams from these wounds . . .

OBŌ: Our one desire . . .

OJŌ: To become . . .

BOTH: Your sworn blood brothers.

OSHŌ: Just what I'd wanted to hear. In truth, I'd had the same idea, but I didn't want to sound arrogant, so I kept my peace. I'm overjoyed that you should ask me.

OBŌ: Then you'll grant our request . . .

OJŌ: And become our brother?

OSHŌ: How could I refuse? (*Refers to a competing production of a kabuki play based on a Chinese classic at the neighboring Nakamura-za.*) I hear that they're putting on

The Water Margin next door. There's no way we can match that cast of heroes, but *(referring to another Chinese classic)* let us stage our own *Romance of the Three Kingdoms* and vow brotherhood here under this plum tree by the wall, though it's a far cry from that famous peach orchard.

OBŌ: Fortunately, here's an offertory bowl . . .

OJŌ: Let's seal our bond of blood by drinking in turn.

    (OBŌ brings an earthenware bowl out of the Kōshin Shrine. The three drip blood from their arms into the bowl.)

OBŌ and OJŌ: After you, Brother.

OSHŌ: I accept the honor. *(OSHŌ, then OBŌ, and finally OJŌ drink in turn from the bowl. OJŌ returns the bowl to OSHŌ.)* Now, to seal our brotherhood. . . . *(He throws the bowl to the ground and breaks it into pieces.)* Until this bowl returns to clay . . .

OBŌ: Our bond unbreakable . . .

OJŌ: Brothers three.

OSHŌ: That we three should meet is indeed a strange twist of fate. Our appearances so different, but we share the same thief's heart.

OBŌ: They say a baby who is born in the Year of the Monkey will grow up to be a thief. This is the Year of the Monkey.

OJŌ: And as our bond was sealed by drinking from this bowl from the monkey shrine . . .

OSHŌ: Let these stuffed monkeys stand as proof of our brotherhood. *(He crosses to the shrine and takes down the board from which three stuffed monkeys hang. He removes them and gives one each to OBŌ and OJŌ.)*

OBŌ: Divided amongst us three . . .

OJŌ: Even were we to put them into our charm bags and go our separate ways . . .

OSHŌ: We three are chained to the very end . . .

OBŌ: Dragged on horseback to the execution ground, like monkeys still troubled by our uncontrolled desires . . .

OJŌ: People will talk of us . . .

OSHŌ: Saying, there were once three thieves . . .

OBŌ: Our names tainted, even after death . . .

OJŌ: A story to tell on Kōshin nights . . .

OSHŌ: How wretched and miserable . . .

ALL: Our fates are! *(They are filled with deep emotion.)*

OSHŌ: Well, we can't hang around here. *(He picks up the packet of money.)* Let's divide these hundred gold pieces now.

OBŌ: No, you saved our lives, lives that we were about to waste . . .

OJŌ: So not as a token of gratitude, but like the bone stolen while two dogs fight over it . . .

OBŌ: We offer you these hundred gold pieces.

OSHŌ: I can't take this. Please take half for yourselves.

> (OSHŌ *twists the package open, roughly divides the coins into two piles, and offers them to* OBŌ *and* OJŌ. *They exchange looks and seem to agree silently on something before accepting the money.*)

OBŌ: If you insist, we'll take it for now . . .

OJŌ: And then give it straight . . .

BOTH: Back to you. (*They return the money to* OSHŌ.)

OSHŌ (*Nods in understanding):* Since morning draws near, we'll work out who owes who later. I'll respect your wishes and take this money. (*He takes the money and wraps it in paper.*)

OBŌ: Now, we too . . .

OBŌ and OJŌ: Are satisfied.

OSHŌ: I'll return your favor some day.

OBŌ: A new partner for the New Year . . .

OJŌ: This calls for a celebration.

> (*They stand. Suddenly, the two* PALANQUIN BEARERS *from before reappear.*)

BEARERS: Thieves!

> (*They attack* OSHŌ *from both sides. He shoves them away.* OJŌ *and* OBŌ *seize them.*)

OSHŌ: All for one . . .

> (OJŌ *and* OBŌ *nod and fling the* BEARERS *away. They fall to the ground and struggle to get up.* OBŌ *holds one down with his foot while* OJŌ *sits on the other.* OSHŌ *whips his headscarf around the back of his neck, stretching it tight. Single* ki *clack.*)

THREE: And one for all!

> (*To a rising crescendo of* tsuke *beats the three thieves freeze into a tense tableau* [hippari no mie]. *Offstage, the large drum plays water pattern* [mizu no oto] *while offstage shamisen begin to play the lively boatman's melody* [fune no sawagi uta]. *The curtain is run closed to accelerating* ki *clacks.*)

Kichijō Temple at Sugamo

> (*To gloomy* zen no tsutome *offstage musical accompaniment the curtain is drawn open to reveal the interior of Kichijō Temple in the Sugamo District of Edo. A huge table upstage center holds the three articles used in Buddhist ritual: a censer, candles, and a vase. Behind the table and covered by a sheet stands a double-door altar containing a statue of Buddha. At left is a huge wooden column, its gold leaf now much faded. The space between the head jamb and the ceiling is covered with three huge carved panels, each with a relief of a goddess. The panel at left is detachable so one can enter through the hole into the space behind it.* GENJI, *the temple*

sexton, sits by the hearth center, burning some old tomb markers as firewood. He wears a grey cotton down jacket and grey cotton hood, which conceals his shaven head.)

GENJI: The first day of spring's come early this year, but it's still freezing out. They say that when there's snow on the New Year decorations, it'll fall another seven times before spring comes. I reckon we're in for some more again tonight. I'd better break up more tomb markers for the fire before it gets dark. Hope Oshō brings a big bottle of sake back with him. I can't stand this cold without a bellyful of drink. Brrr!

*(*GENJI *huddles closer to the fire. To the same gloomy* zen no tsutome *accompaniment* OBŌ *enters from the* hanamichi, *his face wrapped in a towel* [tenugui] *and the hem of his kimono tucked up and folded into his obi. He stops at* shichisan.*)*

OBŌ: Fugitives in plays are always saying, "No matter how clear the sky is, I must hide in the shade, and no matter how solid the earth is, I must tread lightly." How true those words are! I didn't know until I became a wanted man myself, but now I'm on the lam and they're closing in on me, even wide streets feel narrow. Rumor has it that my blood brother, Oshō, is living in this temple, so I thought I'd have a farewell drink with him before I scram to the provinces to try and find some action. *(He comes onto the main stage and spots* GENJI. *He calls out.)* Excuse me.

GENJI: Yeah, whaddya want?

OBŌ: Is this the temple of the priest Benchō?

GENJI: He's just gone to the bath, but you're welcome to wait for him here if you want.

OBŌ: Thank you. I'll wait here.

GENJI: It's so drafty there. Come and sit by the fire.

OBŌ: Thank you for your kindness. *(He takes off the towel with which he had been concealing his face and sits by the fire. Suddenly, he recognizes* GENJI.*)* Genji? Is that you? Genji the fisherman?

GENJI: Is that really you, Kichisa? I never thought I'd meet you here, of all places.

OBŌ: You've changed a lot.

GENJI *(Referring to an earlier play in which the characters of* OBŌ *and* GENJI *appeared)*: Since that ghost appeared and frightened Shichigorō and his daughter into a miserable death, I've been too scared to go fishing. And my health was never the best, so I packed it in. Look. *(He takes off his cap to show his shaved head.)* I shaved my head, and now I'm the sexton at this temple.

OBŌ: Shichigorō was always good to me. It was a crying shame what happened to him.

GENJI: I wish I could offer you a cup of sake or two, for old times' sake.

OBŌ: No, no, I should have brought a cask of sake with me for Oshō, but I don't know this part of town. Genji, would you mind going to buy us a couple of casks?

GENJI: You bet. I'm off like a shot as soon as I hear the word.

OBŌ: And get us something to eat, too, with this. *(He takes a silver coin out of his purse.)*

GENJI: A chicken hot pot would be just the thing in this cold. *(He stands up and fetches his clogs* [geta] *with grey strings.)* You don't mind staying here on your own?

OBŌ: The cops are on my tail, so I can't risk anyone seeing me.

GENJI: You could hide yourself under the altar there, if you don't want anyone spotting you before I get back.

OBŌ: Got it.

GENJI: I'll be back in a bit, then. *(Crosses to the* hanamichi.*)*

OBŌ *(Looking around):* I hear this used to be a rich temple, but there hasn't been a priest in residence for years, and now it's desolate and lonely. But it's a great hideout for foxes and raccoons—and for wanted men who can't show their faces during the day. *(Noticing someone coming onto the* hanamichi.*)* Damn! Someone's coming. I can't be seen here. I'll hide under the altar.
(He does so as the shaved-headed OSHŌ *runs onto the* hanamichi *wearing straw sandals and a quilted* hanten *over a pale indigo blue cotton-lined jacket tied with a grey obi. He is pursued by four* POLICE OFFICERS [torite] *holding metal truncheons* [jitte]. *They are followed by the* CHIEF, *whose quilted jacket with a deep cut in the back allows him to easily unsheathe his sword and dagger.)*

CHIEF: Arrest that man.

POLICE OFFICERS: Yes, sir.
(They charge at OSHŌ *with their truncheons. A battle* [tachimawari] *ensues.* OSHŌ *dodges and throws one to the right, another to the left. The other two continue to attack, but* OSHŌ *manages to come to the main stage, where they keep fighting until he throws them all and then sits down.)*

OSHŌ: What's your game, then?

CHIEF: Don't act the innocent. You're one of that infamous criminal gang, the three Kichisas. You were formerly Benchō, the acolyte at this temple; now you go by the name of Oshō Kichisa. You won't get away with all your crimes!

POLICE OFFICERS: Surrender! *(They surround* OSHŌ, *their truncheons raised.)*

OSHŌ: Officers, I'm a reformed man now. I won't resist if you insist on arresting me for my old crimes. Come, tie me up. *(He puts his arms behind him.)*

CHIEF: Your honesty is impressive. Since you haven't tried to lie to me, I won't tie you up. In fact, I think I'll let you go.

OSHŌ: What? Just like that you're going to let me off?

CHIEF: You don't get something for nothing. In return, I order you to hunt down your sworn brothers, Obō Kichisa, the son of Yasumori Genjibei and banished from the samurai class, and Ojō Kichisa, also known as Oshichi, the daughter of Kyūbei the greengrocer. The crimes these two have committed are many, and we've left no stone unturned to hunt them down, but they have vanished without a trace, and their faces are unknown to us. We'd prefer you to take them

alive, but if they are too much for you, we'll settle for their heads. Fulfill your
task well and we may pardon you for your old crimes and even give you a
reward. Hunt them down as though your life depended on it.

OSHŌ: So you mean to offer me a pardon in return for capturing them?

CHIEF: That is our offer.

OSHŌ *(Thinking):* There comes a time when a man's got to do what's right. No matter
where they've gone to ground, we were once thick as thieves. And as they say,
it takes a thief to catch a thief. You can rely on me to hunt them down and
deliver them over.

CHIEF: Should your old bonds prove too strong and you help them in their flight,
you'll be punished ten times over.

OSHŌ: Don't worry yourself on that score. You've offered to not only pardon me,
but give me a hefty reward as well. I am, after all, a villain, so why would I
bother to help them? *(Laughs.)* So, how much of a reward can I look
forward to?

CHIEF: Five gold pieces per head.

OSHŌ: Is that all?

CHIEF: That's not enough for you?

OSHŌ: Come on. You want me to betray my sworn brothers and have people sneering
at me. I've agreed to search for them only because I need the money. I'm not
a greedy man, so I'll tell you what—if you give me a hundred gold pieces, I'll
accept your offer.

CHIEF: You don't come cheap, but I suppose it can't be helped. You'll have your
reward, so hunt them down and deliver them.

OSHŌ: Since there's money involved, you won't have to wait till tomorrow. I'll hand
them over this very night.

CHIEF: So I can wait for . . .

OSHŌ: My good tidings.

CHIEF: Excellent. Men, move it out.

POLICE OFFICERS: Yes, sir.

> *(To the sound of the drum beating time, they return to the* hanamichi.*)*

OSHŌ *(Seeing them off):* The law would seem to be serious about tracking them down
this time. Neither Ojō nor Obō can remain in Edo.

OBŌ *(Emerging from his hiding place):* Brother, welcome home.

OSHŌ: Why, Obō, when did you get here?

OBŌ: Just now, but I hid under the altar so I wouldn't be spotted.

OSHŌ: I'm glad you made it safely. It's been weeks since we last met, and I've been
wanting to see you. Why not lie low here for a few days?

OBŌ: No, I can't afford to hang around. The cops are onto me and I can't stay in town
much longer. I thought I'd take a road trip, and so I came to say farewell. But

266

as I'll be caught some day, I'd rather it was you that captured me than some stranger. Tie me up and hand me over.

OSHŌ: What are you talking about?

OBŌ: I know you've been pardoned and you feel like earning some reward money.

OSHŌ: So you overheard us just now? Stop acting like a fool—don't you get it? Once we swore to be brothers, they'd have to kill me before I'd sell you out. Surely you don't take me for such a coward!

OBŌ: I know you aren't. But since we're all destined to die, and I've trusted you as a brother, I've decided to give my life to you so you can be pardoned.

OSHŌ: I appreciate the thought, but I'd never turn you in. I only said I'd hunt you down for a hundred gold pieces so that they'd think I was after the money. Then, when their guard was down, I was going to help you get away. If you're going to blow town for a while, make sure you go far enough away so you can sleep easy at night. That cop was saying that you came from a samurai family, the son of Yasumori Genjibei. Is that true?

OBŌ: Yeah, my dad was Yasumori Genjibei, a personal attendant to the shogun and as straight a man as they come. He was a sword assessor, and Lord Yoritomo entrusted him with a short sword called Kōshinmaru. But someone swiped it, and there was nothing he could do to make amends but cut his belly open. Our family was disinherited and I became a *rōnin*. Then my mother got sick, so my little sister sold herself to a brothel in the quarter to buy medicine for her. Anyway, the medicine didn't do her any good, and in the end she died. There was nothing I could do but hand my little brother Morinosuke over to the old family servant to look after. That was when I started down the slippery slope. But all the while I've never forgotten my dream of finding the sword and restoring my family. But I haven't a clue where it is, so I guess I'll just have to forget that dream.

OSHŌ *(With sudden realization):* Then . . . *you* are the son of Yasumori Genjibei? I had no idea . . .

OBŌ: What? You knew my father?

OSHŌ: It was my father who . . . I mean, I've heard my father talk about Kōshinmaru. I'd like to help you search for it. What does it look like?

OBŌ: It was made in Soshū and is unsigned, but there is a pattern of three monkeys forged into the blade. It's about this long. *(Draws and shows his own sword.)*

OSHŌ *(Taking it):* Umm . . . so it's about this long. *(Examining the sword, then surprised.)* Hold on, the other half of your crested hilt decoration is missing. What did you do with it?

OBŌ: Well, the other day, in front of the Governmental Bamboo Storehouse . . .

OSHŌ: Yeah?

OBŌ: A dog started barking and went after me. I must have dropped it while I was running away. But since it's on the back of the hilt, I let it go.

OSHŌ: What a loss!

OBŌ: Well, be that as it may, I feel like having a cup of sake—I wonder where Genji has got to.

OSHŌ: You and Genji seem to go back a long way. Did you ask him to go and buy something?

OBŌ: We were so cold that I asked him to go and get some sake.

OSHŌ: Damn, but you asked the wrong man. You'll be lucky if he gets back without having run his mouth off. Anyway, we'll talk more after night falls. Until then, you better hide yourself in there again. It'll be cramped, but you'll have to put up with it.

OBŌ: Then I'll take a nap to pass the time.

OSHŌ: Keep yourself warm with these.

> (OSHŌ *gives him the altar cloth and a handwarmer. A brief shamisen interlude in syncopation with the beating of the wooden temple gong* [mokugyō] *is heard.* OBŌ *hides himself under the altar. Carrying a gallon cask of sake, a chicken, and some leeks,* GENJI *enters from the rear of the* hanamichi. *He is followed by* JŪZABURŌ *and* OTOSE.)

GENJI: That's Kichijō Temple over there.

JŪZABURŌ: Thank you for your kindness. Is Master Benchō around?

GENJI: He said he was going to the bath, but he should be back by now.

OTOSE: Would you mind telling him that his sister is here?

GENJI: By all means.

> (*They come to the main stage.* JŪZABURŌ *and* OTOSE *remain at right while* GENJI *approaches the hearth.*)

GENJI: I'm back.

OSHŌ: Ah, Genji. What's that you've got there?

GENJI: While you were at the bath, Obō Kichisa . . .

OSHŌ (*Afraid of someone eavesdropping*): Shhh!

GENJI: He asked me to buy some sake, and I thought a chicken and leek hot pot might warm us up.

OSHŌ: Good thinking.

GENJI: Oops, I nearly forgot. Just now I ran into someone who said she was your sister, so I've brought her around.

OSHŌ: What, my sister? Here?

OTOSE: Brother, it's me.

OSHŌ: Otose, it's good to see you again. Come in, come in.

JŪZABURŌ: You're most kind.

> (OTOSE *and* JŪZABURŌ *enter and kneel at right.*)

GENJI: Oops, there's me nearly forgetting again. I'll just go and cook that chicken.

OSHŌ: You know how to cook?

GENJI: Bet your life I do. *(He takes the sake and chicken.)* I'll show you what a real chicken hot pot should be! *(Exits to rear.)*

OSHŌ: Come, Sister, make yourself comfortable.

OTOSE: Thank you, Brother. Jūza, come and sit beside me.

JŪZABURŌ *(Coming closer):* I'm honored to make your acquaintance. My name is Jūza.

OSHŌ: There's no need to introduce yourself. I've already heard from a friend about the strange twist of fate that brought you and my sister together. *(He seems struck by a painful thought.)* She's my only sister, so I hope you'll treat her well.

JŪZABURŌ: As a matter of fact, I, too, have no other relatives. Now that we're in-laws, thanks to Otose, I hope that you'll look kindly upon me.

OSHŌ: How I could I fail to do otherwise, since we're brothers now?

JŪZABURŌ: Thank you.

OSHŌ: Sister, how is Father?

OTOSE: What? You mean you haven't heard?

OSHŌ: I haven't heard what?

JŪZABURŌ: Your father was cut down several weeks ago, and he died a pitiful death.

OSHŌ: What! Where?

OTOSE: On the evening of the third day of last month, in front of the Governmental Bamboo Storehouse, he was cruelly murdered.

OSHŌ *(In shock):* So the old man's gone. And to be murdered—what an awful way to go. . . . *(Glancing at* OTOSE *and* JŪZABURŌ.*)* Still, at least he's at peace now. Do you know who killed him?

OTOSE: We don't know who he was, but by the body . . .

JŪZABURŌ: They found half of this crested hilt decoration. This is our only clue to the villain. *(From his purse* JŪZABURŌ *produces the hilt decoration.* OSHŌ *examines it.)*

OSHŌ *(Shocked):* Why, this is . . . *(he glances toward the altar where* OBŌ *is hidden)* this is a wonderful clue. *(He gives the decoration back to* JŪZABURŌ.*)* I hadn't heard anything about it. I'd heard rumors that the old man was hard up for cash, so just like in the old days, I . . . I mean, no, unlike in my old days, I'm a priest now. I've caused the old man nothing but trouble since I was a kid. I'll make up for it all by praying for his happiness in the next life. *(He wipes at his eyes.)* And then on top of everything, there's all that trouble you two are in. I won't press you, but tell me briefly why you need the hundred gold pieces.

JŪZABURŌ: Even if you hadn't asked, we were planning to tell you . . .

OTOSE: Our miserable story from beginning to end, and why we need the money.

JŪZABURŌ: Listen to our tale . . .

BOTH: We beg you.

JŪZABURŌ: I was in service to the merchant Kiya Bunzō. The other day we sold a sword to a samurai customer called Ebina Gunzō. I went to pick up the money, but on my way back to the shop Otose's pluck on my sleeves made me forget all about my errand. I was enticed into her hut, but before we could consummate our passion a fight broke out. I panicked and ran off and dropped the hundred gold pieces.

OTOSE: I picked it up. I thought he'd visit me again, so I went to the hut the next evening. But he didn't come, so I wandered home, totally depressed. Along the way, on Ryōgoku Bridge, I met a respectable young lady of seventeen or eighteen, wearing a long-sleeved crested kimono. Her crests were of a sealed letter in a circle. By the time I realized I shouldn't let my guard down, it was too late. She was a thief, and she stole the money and pushed me into the river. I almost drowned, but fate must have been on my side because Jūza's father, Kyūbei the greengrocer, pulled me out. He saved my life.

JŪZABURŌ: I didn't know about any of this, and I was about to throw myself into the river when Denkichi stopped me. You can imagine my joy when he told me that his daughter had found the money and he invited me home. But then I heard what had happened to her. Denkichi was kind enough to suggest that I should stay there until he raised the money. His kind offer was what brought us together, and now we're promised to be married, without a matchmaker, though.

OTOSE: Father went all over town trying to raise the money for us. But a hundred gold pieces is a lot of money, and all his efforts came to nothing. Then he was cruelly murdered in front of the Bamboo Storehouse. Even now, talking with you, I can still see the way he looked in death. What an awful, awful fate!

JŪZABURŌ: And on top of everything else, my master started visiting a courtesan called Hitoe at the Chōjiya house. He got more and more involved, but his pride wouldn't let him back down. And as is always the way in the licensed quarter, he started to run out of money. His business went from bad to worse, and now he's living in poverty in Imado. That's why I so want to repay the money, but there's nothing I can do to raise that amount.

OTOSE: Ever since Father died, we've had no one else to turn to. We've wept away more than two months, but now the forty-ninth day since his death has passed, so . . .

JŪZABURŌ: We've decided to hunt down his murderer and take revenge. But as you can see, I'm not a strong man. Please agree to join us in our quest . . .

OTOSE: And also help us find the money to help Master Bunri in his distress.

JŪZABURŌ: We realize our requests are irksome, but you're the only person we can turn to.

OTOSE: Agree to help us, we beg you . . .

JŪZABURŌ: In avenging Father's murder . . .

OTOSE: And in raising the money . . .

JŪZABURŌ: On our knees . . .

BOTH: We beg for your help.

OSHŌ *(Moved):* To avenge my father's death, even if you had not asked me, I am
duty bound. How could I do otherwise? And since you are married to my only
sister, I will undertake to find the money for you. You need concern yourself
no more on that matter.

JŪZABURŌ: Then you will answer . . .

OTOSE: Our prayers?

BOTH *(Delighted):* We thank you with all our hearts.

OSHŌ *(He looks at them gloomily. Under his breath):* That joy will be the last they
know . . .

JŪZABURŌ and OTOSE: What did you say?

OSHŌ: Nothing. There is much we must talk about, but since that old sexton's in
there, let us walk around to the graveyard where we can talk without being
overheard.

JŪZABURŌ: I cannot thank you enough. Your father will surely be rejoicing in heaven.

OTOSE: Come, let's hurry to the graveyard.

OSHŌ: I'll be right behind you. You two go on ahead.

JŪZABURŌ and OTOSE: We will wait for your coming.

OSHŌ: Wait for me in the corpse-washing hut. *(To* zen no tsutome *accompaniment*
JŪZABURŌ *and* OTOSE *exit right.* OSHŌ *sees them off.)* Look at them, so
happy and so innocent of what fate has brought them! This, too, must be
heaven's retribution for my father's crimes. Ah, truly one cannot do
wrong . . .

GENJI *(Appearing from the building carrying a large bowl with a knife on top):* Who says
you can't?

OSHŌ *(Startled):* What?

GENJI *(Shows the chicken hot pot):* Look. I'm done.

OSHŌ: It looks good.

GENJI: The trick's in using a sharp knife. You've no idea how much I sweated over
sharpening it.

OSHŌ: Well, it certainly looks sharp enough.

GENJI: I bet you could even kill a person with it.

OSHŌ *(He takes the knife and suddenly thinks of something):* Oh, I completely forgot it,
Genji, but could you go on an errand to Komagome for me?

GENJI: What? Now?

OSHŌ: I'd like you to go before it gets dark.

GENJI: If you insist, but I want some of that chicken first.

OSHŌ: Eat it on the way. *(He gives* GENJI *a silver coin.)* Here, you can get yourself two chicken hot pots and five flasks of sake with this. And you can keep the change.

GENJI: You're going to give me all that? Why, thank you. What do you want me to do, then?

OSHŌ: Go to the coffin makers at Komagome and buy two sets of coffins and shrouds. *(He gives* GENJI *another coin.)*

GENJI: What do you want them for?

OSHŌ: I've got a funeral to perform.

GENJI: I'll be off, then.

OSHŌ: Take your time.

GENJI: I'll have a drink somewhere first. I won't be hurrying anywhere for a while. *(To* zen no tsutome *accompaniment* GENJI *puts on his clogs and heads off down the* hanamichi. OSHŌ *examines the blade of the knife, nods pensively, and then wraps it up in a towel.)*

OSHŌ: Ah, I have no stomach for it, but I must commit a murder . . .

GENJI *(Turning back):* What was that?

OSHŌ: Are you still here?

GENJI: You said there was no hurry.

OSHŌ: Get going.

GENJI: All right, all right. I don't know what to make of it, though. *(He exits.)*

OSHŌ: There's a pair of chickens waiting for the slaughter. *(He exits right to* zen no tsutome *accompaniment.)*

OBŌ *(Crawling out from under the altar):* I didn't think that guy I did in at the Bamboo Storehouse was just some old codger, but I had no idea that he was Oshō's father. The hundred gold pieces I stole that night I thought to give to Master Bunri as thanks for taking good care of my sister. Denkichi kept asking me to lend it to him because he, too, wanted to give it to Master Bunri to repay the hundred that Jūza lost. If only we had talked, his life needn't have been wasted. But talking about what is done won't change fate. What makes it worse, once Master Bunri heard that the money was from the hand of the infamous Obō, he refused to touch it. So I've still got it here, and it seems to weigh me down. Is what I overheard here some omen telling me to kill myself? Now he's seen the hilt decoration from my sword, Oshō knows for sure that I killed his father. If I hadn't overheard, I might act differently. But now that I know, there's no point in trying to hide any longer. And besides, the cops are on my trail and I won't live much longer. Since I'm going to die anyway, I might as well give this money back to Oshō and then kill myself in apology for murdering his father. That's the only way I can repay my debt to him.

(He strikes a determined mie. *Suddenly, the carved panel on the ceiling is slid aside from within.* OJŌ, *still wearing his long-sleeved kimono but with his previously proper* shimada *hairstyle now disheveled, is seen lying in the space behind.)*

OJŌ *(Sticking his head out):* Hey, Kichisa, Kichisa.

OBŌ *(Looking around in astonishment):* That sounded like someone calling my name.

OJŌ: Hey, Kichisa, Kichisa.

OBŌ: There it is again. Where's it coming from?

OJŌ: Hey, up here.

OBŌ *(Looking up at* OJŌ. *Then, loudly):* Is that you up there, Ojō?

OJŌ: Shhh!

OBŌ *(He checks that the coast is clear, then in a whisper):* Then you, too . . .

OJŌ: Yes, I arrived a few days ago and have been hiding up here ever since.

OBŌ: How I've wanted to see you!

OJŌ: And I, you.

OBŌ: Anyway, get yourself out of there.

OJŌ: I'll be right down. *(He slides down the banner that hangs from his hiding place.)*

OBŌ: When was it when last we met . . .

OJŌ: I think of it day and night . . .

OBŌ: But then we became fugitives . . .

OJŌ: And I knew not where you were . . .

OBŌ: Or how you were . . .

BOTH: Ah, how I've missed you!

OBŌ: Since you were hidden above, you heard? . . .

OJŌ: I heard everything, and it chilled my heart. I can no longer go on living. Let us die together!

OBŌ: What? Why do you have to kill yourself?

OJŌ: I'll tell you why. The woman who stole the hundred gold pieces from Oshō's sister was none other than this Kichisa, disguised as a girl. With the evidence of the sealed letter in a circle—my crest—Oshō will surely have guessed that it was my work. As I was lying there I thought to myself, if only I hadn't stolen the money, it would be returned to Jūza, who dropped it in the first place, and that would have been the end of it. But because of my theft, Oshō's father died a miserable death, my father, Kyūbei, suffers in poverty, and Bunri, my brother-in-law's master, was put to no end of trouble. And all of this because of me. Just when I was consumed by remorse, you said that since we cannot but die on the execution ground, we might as well kill ourselves here. By way of apology for all the trouble I have caused, let me die here together with you.

OBŌ: Your explanation does carry some truth, but since you yourself didn't cause anyone's death, there's no reason for you to kill yourself now. The money you stole has gone around and come to me. This I'm going to return to Oshō.

You must live on so you can tell him everything that happened. Every year on this day think of me and offer water before my tomb as a token of our brotherhood.

OJŌ: But you're not the one who's to blame. Even if I myself didn't kill anyone, it amounts to the same thing because what I did started everything. It's a disgrace not to die at the appropriate time. How can you tell me to live on? Why don't you ask me to die together with you?

OBŌ: I get what you're saying now. You've made up your mind, and I'm not going to stand in your way. Come then, let us die together here.

OJŌ: That's the sprit of real brotherhood. Much better than you trying to stop me killing myself.

OBŌ: Ah, now I think on it, how I've wasted my life! I was mollycoddled from the day I was born, all because I was the eldest son who would carry on the Yasumori family name. I was even told that I needn't take the ancestral forename of Genjibei until I turned forty, because it wasn't a suitable name for a young man. They must have expected me to live to be a hundred, but now I'm barely twenty-five, and because of my crimes, I must go to hell. How my parents will resent me!

OJŌ: How different from my upbringing! When I was five I was kidnapped and brought up by strangers to be a traveling player. One day when I was walking, still wearing my girl's makeup and costume, a man mistook me for the real thing and tried to make love to me. Before I knew it, I'd blackmailed him. Evil habits form easily, and since that day I've treated other people's money as my own, and my crimes have piled up thick. I know who my real father is, but if I announced myself as his son, he might have to take the blame for my crimes. That's why I've kept away from him, but if he hears afterward, how he will weep.

OBŌ: But since our destinies are fixed, there's nothing to be gained by complaining. Many may blame us, asking why we steal when we have such insight, but no one will praise us.

OJŌ: How true your words. If I'd sacrificed my life for my master or parents, they would pity me because of my youth. But now I'll be blamed for my untimely death.

OBŌ: And if it were up to those we've robbed of their cash, we'd be crucified upside down.

OJŌ: How cheated they'll feel when they hear that we've died like men, making amends for our crimes.

OBŌ *(The images in the following interweave the traditional vision of Buddhist hell with terms used for various tortures and types of execution):* We haven't suffered in this world, but in the next we'll plummet to hell . . .

OJŌ *(Indicating a hanging scroll in which Buddhist hell is depicted):* Then, as that scroll shows, our crimes will be revealed for all to see in mirrors of crystal . . .

OBŌ: Coughing up gore, we'll be tied to rocks and thrown into the bottomless Lake of Blood . . .

OJŌ: Bound to the Scales of Karmic Justice, to weigh up our good and evil . . .

OBŌ: Red horse-headed demons from the hell of beasts will drag us through the hell of eternal war and the hell of hunger . . .

OJŌ: Turned from ice in the eight freezing hells to rust on the Mountain of Swords . . .

OBŌ: And at last, our severed heads arrayed on spikes on the King of Hell's table.

OJŌ: For another hour or two . . .

OBŌ: While we still have breath left in our bodies, we'll know heaven . . .

OJŌ: How miserable indeed . . .

BOTH: Our lives are!

> *(They sigh over their fates. The temple bell tolls once.)*

OBŌ: However, if we were to kill ourselves here and now, no one would know . . .

OJŌ: The reason for our deaths . . .

OBŌ: Happily, here's a white banner . . .

OJŌ: On which, with a stroke of the brush . . .

BOTH: We'll inscribe our stories.

> *(A bell tolls the hour, followed by a plaintive offstage shamisen melody* [dokugin no aikata]. *When* OBŌ *picks up the white satin banner and* OJŌ *produces a brush box and begins to rub an ink stick against an ink slab, they freeze into a* mie. *The stage revolves.)*

The Graveyard behind Kichijō Temple

> *(At the graveyard behind the main building of Kichijō Temple. Tombstones can be seen here and there, bathed in the hazy light of a cloud-streaked moon. At stage left is a tumbledown shack, where corpses were once washed to prepare them for burial. At stage right is an equally decrepit old well with a broken pulley, and beside it is a willow tree. Several clumps of thick bamboo to rear form the background. The stage swings around to reveal a frozen tableau:* OSHŌ *standing with the knife raised high and the wounded* JŪZABURŌ *and* OTOSE *at left. To the ominous beating of the large offstage drum suggesting the sound of wind* [kaze no oto] *the stage stops revolving and* OSHŌ *resumes his attack on them.* JŪZABURŌ *pulls an old tomb marker from the ground and clumsily tries to fend him off, but the rotten wood shatters with a single blow from the knife. Finally,* JŪZABURŌ *trips over a tombstone, loses his balance, and falls.* OSHŌ *holds down the two lovers with his foot.)*

OTOSE: Brother, have you gone mad!

JŪZABURŌ: Whyever . . .

OTOSE: Are you trying to kill . . .

Early in the murder scene *(koroshiba)*, set in the graveyard of Kichijō Temple,
Oshō Kichisa (Matsumoto Koshirō IX) poses with a kitchen knife behind his
back. Oshō's head is shaved like a priest's, and his grey clerical robe is pulled off
one shoulder to reveal underworld tattoos. His mortally wounded sister, Otose
(Nakamura Fukusuke IX), and her husband, Jūzaburō (Ichimura Manjirō II), cling to
Oshō's legs as they plead for their lives. (Umemura Yutaka, Engeki Shuppansha)

BOTH: The two of us!

OSHŌ: No, I'm not crazy, but there's a good reason why I can't let you live. I know your
wounds must pain you, but please, bear your hurt a while and listen to my tale.
(He sits on a toppled tombstone.) Listening to your stories just now, every element struck a chord in my memory. That thief disguised as a young girl in the
five-crested kimono who stole your money, Otose, is a young queer called Ojō
Kichisa. The man who murdered father and dropped half of his hilt decoration is from the same gang, a *rōnin* named Obō Kichisa. Since last spring,
these men have been my sworn brothers. What's more, they came asking for
my help, so I'm hiding them in the ceiling and the altar at this very temple.
They're sure to have overheard your stories, and that is why, unfortunately,
I've got to kill you. Things work differently in our world. For us on the wrong
side of the law, keeping the faith is what counts. You're trying to kill them, so
I've got to kill you first to square my bond to them. I'll kill Ojō and Obō later
in revenge for what they've done to you. Think of it this way—it's our parents'
fault that you wound up with a bad brother, and now you're going to have to

die for no good reason. I know this must be hard, but you've got to let me kill you. Look, I've got my hands together and I'm begging you.

JŪZABURŌ: If that's the truth, why should I begrudge you my life? In one sense, my life is already yours, since it was Denkichi who pulled me out of the river more dead than alive.

OTOSE: I, too, should have died then. But because I've lived this long, I was able to become man and wife with Jūza. How happy I am that we can even go hand in hand into the next world!

OSHŌ: If only you'd died then, this wouldn't be so painful for us all.

JŪZABURŌ: But such is our fate from our previous lives.

OTOSE: What a pitiful end . . .

ALL THREE: We must face!

(*Jizō sutra, an intoned solo, is heard.* OSHŌ *fetches a pail and two cups, draws water from the well, and tries to give some to* JŪZABURŌ *and* OTOSE. *Their wounds are too painful for them to stand, so they crawl forward and lap at the water like dogs.* OSHŌ, *seeing this, feels miserable and sorry.*)

JŪZABURŌ (*Resolved*): My only wish is for you to return the money I lost to Master Bunri, who has taken good care of me since I was ten.

OSHŌ: You needn't concern yourself about that. I'll get that money to him even if it means my life.

JŪZABURŌ: Thank you. Now I can die in peace.

OSHŌ: Sister, I'll avenge your death. You, too, can travel to the next world with no regrets.

OTOSE: Since Jūza will be with me, what regrets could I have . . .

JŪZABURŌ: On the one lotus leaf, we'll spend a second lifetime as man and wife.

OSHŌ (*Half to himself*): But they won't go to paradise.

JŪZABURŌ and OTOSE: Whatever do you mean?

OSHŌ (*To himself*): The parent's crimes have been visited on the children, and in the next world they'll be destined for the hell of beasts.

JŪZABURŌ and OTOSE: What?

OSHŌ: Nothing. I mean that I, who am worse than any beast, worse than a dog, have decided to turn over a new leaf. I will become a living Buddha and will lead you to the next world.

JŪZABURŌ: With the power of your piety, guide . . .

OTOSE: Our journey together to paradise . . .

OSHŌ: Once departed, you can never return. This, our last farewell.

(*Tenderly,* OSHŌ *lifts their faces so he can gaze into their eyes. He is obviously distraught.* JŪZABURŌ *and* OTOSE *writhe in agony.*)

JŪZABURŌ: The end draws near . . .

OTOSE: Please, spare us from this pain . . .

BOTH: Let us die quickly.

OSHŌ: You need only ask once. (*Offstage shamisen play plaintive melody* [dokugin no aikata]. *Swinging the knife upward,* OSHŌ *pulls* JŪZABURŌ *close to deliver the coup de grace to his throat. His hand trembles, and he cannot do it. At last he finds the strength and stabs the knife into his throat.*) Hail to Amida Buddha . . . (OSHŌ *twists the knife and* JŪZABURŌ *writhes in agony.* OTOSE *loses consciousness and collapses.* OSHŌ *brushes away his tears and strikes a* mie. *The temple bell tolls once, and the stage begins to revolve back to the previous scene.*)

The Main Building of the Temple

(*The stage revolves, and we return again to the interior of the temple.* OBŌ *and* OJŌ *have just finished writing their suicide note to* OSHŌ.)

OBŌ: There, I've explained why I murdered his father. Now he'll understand why we killed ourselves.

OJŌ: With this note, Oshō will have nothing on his chest . . .

OBŌ: And having repaid our obligation in an unexpected way . . .

OJŌ: On these *tatami* mats . . .

BOTH: We can die peacefully.

OJŌ: Obō, you're the son of a samurai family. You must know how to slit your belly open.

OBŌ: Well, I've heard people talk about it enough, so I shouldn't make a mess of it.

OJŌ: I don't know how to do it, and it wouldn't be pretty to mess it up and leave myself wriggling all over the floor. Obō, before you kill yourself, wouldn't you do me first?

OBŌ: All right, since you don't know how. It'll be the work of a minute.

OJŌ: Then before Oshō comes back . . .

OBŌ: The sooner the better . . .

(*They gaze into each other's eyes. The plaintive melody* dokugin *is sung offstage to shamisen accompaniment.* OBŌ *takes a red cotton cloth from the altar and spreads it out on the floor to prepare an appropriate place for* seppuku. *They straighten their clothes in preparation.*)

OBŌ: Are you ready?

OJŌ: I have no regrets.

OBŌ: Then, once and for all . . .

(*As the offstage accompaniment ends,* OBŌ *draws his dagger and grabs the collar of* OJŌ*'s kimono. They look at each other emotionally. Just as* OBŌ *is about to thrust his dagger into* OJŌ*'s breast,* OSHŌ *rushes in from the right to a flurry of clattering* tsuke *beats. He carries two bundles wrapped in white cloths soaked red with blood. They obviously contain* OTOSE *and* JŪZABURŌ*'s freshly severed heads.* OSHŌ *grasps* OBŌ*'s upraised hand.*)

OSHŌ: Wait! Don't be so rash. You don't need to kill yourselves.

OBŌ and OJŌ: What? What are you talking about?

OSHŌ: I'll explain everything. Listen. *(Offstage accompaniment begins.)* The money Ojō Kichisa stole from my sister was given to me when first we three met. As it was an unforeseen gift, I decided to give it to my father. If he had returned it to Jūza's master, that would have been the end of it. But he said it was dirty money and refused to take it—that was my father's mistake. Since it was his fault, then Ojō wasn't to blame. And when Obō Kichisa killed my father in front of the Bamboo Storehouse, he was merely avenging his own father.

OBŌ: What do you mean?

OSHŌ: It all goes back ten years. The man who broke into the Yasumori mansion and stole the Kōshinmaru sword was my father, Denkichi. As a penalty for losing the sword, the Yasumori family was disinherited and your father killed himself. In a way, my father Denkichi was responsible for your family's difficulties, and his humiliating death was thus just retribution for his crime. I bear no grudge against you two. So there's no need for you to kill yourselves.

OBŌ *(Suddenly understanding):* So . . . it was your father who stole Kōshinmaru? And if you were once my enemy, I am now become yours.

OJŌ: And I gave the money to you, but the crime lies with me who first stole it.

OBŌ: What's more, our crimes of all hue have piled up . . .

OJŌ: And our pursuers will soon run us to ground . . .

OBŌ: Rather than the shame of being bound . . .

OJŌ: And, as our apology to you, Brother . . .

BOTH: We yearn for nothing but death!

OSHŌ: But I have found a way that you can escape the punishment that pursues you and walk the world with your heads held high. *(He produces the severed heads of* JŪZABURŌ *and* OTOSE *wrapped in cloth.)*

OBŌ and OJŌ: How?

OSHŌ: The chief police officer told me that if you were too much to capture alive then I could take just your heads. Look, these two will take your place.
(OSHŌ unwraps the cloth and shows them the heads. OBŌ *and* OJŌ *recoil in shock.)*

OBŌ: But that is the head of your only sister . . .

OJŌ: And that, your brother-in-law . . .

OBŌ: They were guiltless. How could you sacrifice them for our sakes?

OJŌ: How cruel of you to behead them!

OSHŌ: No, you're wrong. I killed them not out of cruelty, but out of a brother's love.

OBŌ and OJŌ: What do you mean?

OSHŌ: I mean they were committing incest.

Oshō Kichisa (Onoe Shōroku II), revealing his gangster's tattoos by dropping his priest's robe off one shoulder, displays the severed heads of his sister, Otose, and her husband, Jūzaburō: "I killed them not out of cruelty, but out of a brother's love. . . . I mean they were committing incest." Ojō Kichisa (Onoe Baikō VII), left, and Obō Kichisa (Nakamura Kanzaburō XVII), right, look at the heads in shock and horror. (Tsubouchi Memorial Theatre Museum of Waseda University)

OBŌ and OJŌ: What?

OSHŌ *(Dolefully):* I will tell you everything. They were twins, both born of my father. Jūza was abandoned soon after his birth, but still fate led him to meet and copulate with his sister like beasts. On that night we talked about, a dog barked at my father after he stole Kōshinmaru and was escaping over a wall. Thinking to silence it, he killed it but was cursed by the dead dog's spirit. My father confessed this to me. Otose and Jūza knew nothing of the dog's curse, but they would soon have found out. Upon that day, there would be nothing for them but to weep ceaselessly over how dreadful their fate was and, in the end, to kill themselves. The pain that they would surely feel tormented my heart, and so I asked for their lives, lying and saying that it was for the sake of our parents. Though it was an act of compassion, imagine the anguish I felt in my heart having to kill my own dear sister and brother. *(He wipes away his tears.)* So that their deaths not be in vain, I struck on the idea of cutting off their heads and letting them stand as substitutes for those of you two wanted criminals. Happily, in this last testament in your own hands, you admit to regretting your past wickedness and killing yourselves. If I take this to the authorities, the hunt for you will be called off, and you'll be free to go where you please. To think that all this misery was heaven's retribution for my father's crimes! Since I've decided to renounce my past wickedness, you two as well should change your ways and go straight as though you've been born again. No matter where you wind up, if one day you remember the fate of these two, then make that their memorial day and offer up a glass of water and a prayer to their memory.

OBŌ: We had no idea that they were brother and sister. And though we can well see your compassion in killing them before they learnt the truth . . .

OJŌ: We cannot allow you to use them to save us, as we are the cause of your pain.

OBŌ: We are determined . . .

OJŌ: To accompany them to the next world!

(OBŌ *and* OJŌ *draw their swords.*)

OSHŌ *(Holding them back):* So you're going to let their deaths be for nothing?

OBŌ: If you feel that way . . .

OSHŌ: You'd throw my kindness back in my face?

OJŌ: No, that's not so . . .

OSHŌ: Isn't it?

OBŌ *(Giving way):* Your kindness overwhelms us, Brother.

OJŌ: We'll do what you say, and make good our escape.

OSHŌ: So these heads won't go to waste after all? Thank you, Brothers.

OBŌ *(Producing the package of money):* I almost forgot these hundred gold pieces. It'll make up for the money that was lost, and be my offering to the spirits of your sister and brother.

OJŌ: As a symbol of my resolve to go straight, take this sword—I won't be needing it again. Think of it as a keepsake, Brother.

(OBŌ *puts the package of money in front of* OSHŌ, *and* OJŌ *does likewise with the sword.*)

OSHŌ: I accept this sword and hundred gold pieces.

(OSHŌ *unsheathes and examines the sword.* OBŌ *looks at it, too.*)

OBŌ: Why, that sword . . . the size is similar, the workmanship superlative . . .

OSHŌ: And here, forged into the blade as clear as day . . . the three monkeys!

OBŌ: It can only be Kōshinmaru. *(To* OJŌ.) Where did you get it?

OJŌ: I found the sword when I stole the hundred gold pieces.

OSHŌ: Unexpectedly, here they are . . .

OJŌ: The lost money . . .

OBŌ: And the missing sword!

OSHŌ: Now we have them both, here, Ojō, take the money to Kyūbei. *(He hands the money to* OJŌ.) *And Obō, deliver the sword to your home right away. (He gives the sword to* OBŌ.)

OBŌ and OJŌ: We'll be off, then. *(Suddenly the muffled beatings of the search party's drums are heard offstage.)* That sound . . .

OSHŌ: It can only be the police—and in force!

OBŌ: Then, for now . . .

OJŌ: Let us part by separate roads . . .

OSHŌ: As swiftly as we can . . .

OBŌ and OSHŌ: You said it, Brother!

> *(To rapid offstage drumbeats* OBŌ *and* OSHŌ *rush off down the* hanamichi. OSHŌ *watches them leave, then puts the two heads on the stage. He gazes at them and dabs at his eyes before retiring into the back room.* GENJI *enters from the rear of the* hanamichi *with two cheap, barrel-shaped coffins strapped to his back and the coffin poles in his hands. Hearing the low beating of the search party's drums,* GENJI *stops to look around and then comes to the main stage.)*

GENJI *(Calling out):* Hey, I'm back. Ah, I can't make out anything in this darkness. Is there anyone there? Hey! *(He clumsily gropes around until he stumbles over one of the heads and falls. The coffins come loose and roll across the floor, the funeral shrouds falling out from within. He begins to grope around again, and he finds one of the severed heads. He lifts it close to his face to take a better look.)* Ugh, a human head. *(Comically, he shivers with fear.* OSHŌ *appears behind him and snatches the head out of his hands.* GENJI *jumps with surprise and then gropes around again, finally lifting the other head.)* Ugh, not another one! *(At last he makes out* OSHŌ.) Is that you, Oshō?

> *(*OSHŌ *snatches the severed head from* GENJI*'s hands and pushes him away.* GENJI *stumbles backward and tumbles into one of the coffins. Ki clacks.* OSHŌ, *carrying the two heads, runs off toward the* hanamichi. *At* shichisan *he freezes into an anxious* mie. *The* ki *clacks* [kizami] *rise to crescendo, and the curtain is run shut.)*

The Fire Watchtower at Hongō

> *(A fire watchtower in Hongō. Night. In the background, flats represent a row of townspeople's houses, their roofs covered with a thin layer of snow. A snow-covered fire watchtower dominates up center. In front of the watchtower is a tall wooden fence with a gate, the kind that controlled passage between the city districts on either side and that were closed at dusk, acting as a kind of checkpoint. Three suspicious looking* rōnin, "SNAKE MOUNTAIN" CHŌJI, "EAGLE FOREST" KUMAZŌ, *and* "RACCOON HOLE" KINTA, *are standing around the gate. Their faces are*

*concealed by headscarves, and they carry swords at their waist. They are clearly up
to no good.)*

CHŌJI *(Calling out to the gatekeeper):* Hello! Is there anyone there?

(*Enter* TOKISUKE, *the gatekeeper, from left.)*

TOKISUKE: Who goes there?

CHŌJI: I live in the neighborhood. My wife has just gone into labor, and I need to fetch
a midwife. Please allow me to pass through the gate.

TOKISUKE: I see your trouble, but I can't allow anyone through the gate. Maybe you
should call a midhusband instead. *(He exits left.)*

CHŌJI: Who does he think he's talking to!

KUMAZŌ: Here, let me try this time. *(Knocking on the gate.)* Hey! Hello in there!

TOKISUKE *(Reappearing):* What a racket! What is it now?

KUMAZŌ: Excuse me, sir, but my mother's on her deathbed and I have to fetch the
doctor for her. Please let me through.

TOKISUKE: Ah, that's a crying shame, isn't it? But I can't let anyone through. Maybe
you should forget the doctor and go call a priest instead.

KUMAZŌ: This one thinks he's a real comedian!

KINTA: I wonder why they're being so strict. Excuse me, how come you've shut the gate
and won't let anyone through?

TOKISUKE: See that poster up there? The authorities are searching for those notorious criminals, the Three Kichisas. They promised a pardon to Oshō Kichisa
if he'd turn in Ojō and Obō. However, he took advantage of the authorities'
benevolence, but luckily the heads were recognized as fakes. They arrested
Oshō then and there, and to catch the other two all the gates in Edo were
ordered shut. When the others have been caught, the drums on the watch-
towers will be sounded, and that'll be the signal for all the gates to be
opened again so people can go through. So you see, no matter what your
reason is, I can't allow you to go through until I hear the drum being
beaten.

(He exits. Hearing this, CHŌJI, KUMAZŌ, *and* KINTA *panic.)*

CHŌJI: What? They've already nabbed Oshō of the Three Kichisas?

KUMAZŌ: If they arrest Obō, then he might blab about us. We can't hang around
here!

KINTA: We've got to get through this gate, whatever it costs. *(He thinks for a moment.)*
Excuse me, sir, if we were to treat you to a bottle of sake, would you allow us
through the gate in secret? *(He holds out one hundred coppers through the wooden
slats.)*

TOKISUKE *(Taking the money):* Well, I'm not supposed to allow anyone through. But if
you say so, I can let you through the wicket one by one. Just don't tell anyone.

ALL: Thank you, sir.

(CHŌJI *goes through the wicket. Just then the* CHIEF *enters with two* POLICE
OFFICERS.*)*

CHIEF: What's all this then? Arrest that man!

POLICE OFFICERS: Yes, sir. *(They hit* CHŌJI *with their* jitte. CHŌJI, *taken by surprise,
tries to run away, but they seize and bind him.)* We've got him!

CHŌJI: Curse it!

KUMAZŌ: Uh oh.

KINTA: Let's get out of here.

(They scurry off to right.)

POLICE OFFICERS *(Entering from right):* No, you don't.

(After a brief scuffle, KUMAZŌ *and* KINTA *are bound.)*

KUMAZŌ and KINTA: Shit, they got us.

CHŌJI, KUMAZŌ, and KINTA *(As they are dragged away):* Get your hands off!

(The sound of a bell tolling the time. Exit CHIEF, *the* POLICE OFFICERS, *the
three scoundrels, and* TOKISUKE *to left. At the signal of a single* ki *clack, a white
curtain at left is dropped to reveal a group of* TAKEMOTO *musicians sitting on a
raised dais. A flat at right folds upward to reveal a group of* KIYOMOTO *musicians. The two groups take turns singing* [kakeai], *the heavily ornate* TAKEMOTO
style contrasting with the lighter, more nasal KIYOMOTO.*)*

KIYOMOTO:

On a spring night / soft snow falling lightly, / but their crimes weigh heavy /
upon Obō and Ojō. / Now they lie low, their colors faded . . .

TAKEMOTO:

As last year's camellias / their heads soon to fall. / Nowhere to flee, / falling
white . . .

KIYOMOTO:

Six-blossomed flakes / falling on the four roads to the grave.

(A deep bell sounds [hontsurigane]. OBŌ, *wearing two swords, enters from the
rear of the main* hanamichi. *His head is wrapped in a scarf, the hem of his kimono
is tucked up and folded into his obi, and he is swathed in a straw mat to keep out
the cold. Simultaneously,* OJŌ *appears from the rear of the secondary* [kari] *hanamichi. He, too, wears a headscarf and has tucked up the hem of his kimono into his
obi, but he is swathed in a straw and hemp mat like that carried by streetwalkers.
Both stop at* shichisan.*)*

OBŌ *("Divided dialogue"* [warizerifu] *follows, the characters being in separate locations, their words gradually coinciding):* Looking back, more than ten years
have passed since Kōshinmaru was stolen. Tonight, by chance, I got it
back . . .

OJŌ: By chance the hundred gold pieces that my brother-in-law lost came into my
possession . . .

284

OBŌ: As I must hide from prying eyes by day, I hope to deliver this sword under cover of darkness . . .

OJŌ: But things never go according to plan, and our ploy with the severed heads failed . . .

OBŌ: Bursting like soap bubbles, our plot was revealed, and poor Oshō was taken prisoner . . .

OJŌ: I so want to help release him, but . . .

OBŌ: In order to capture the two of us . . .

OJŌ: Every gate has been sealed . . .

OBŌ: All our intentions foiled, all roads blocked . . .

BOTH: Such is how we stand tonight.

TAKEMOTO:

Fugitives looking over their shoulder, / trembling at the cold glint of icicles / hanging from the eaves . . .

KIYOMOTO:

Checking they are not hostile blades, / the spring winds blow chill / upon their necks.

TAKEMOTO:

Whether the chill gales of Mount Tsukuba to the north . . .

KIYOMOTO:

Or those from southern Fuji . . .

TAKEMOTO:

Dodging the winter blizzards . . .

KIYOMOTO:

They travel onward.

(OJŌ and OBŌ reach the main stage and see the wooden gate, center.)

OBŌ: When I managed to get past the last gate, I was so glad . . .

OJŌ: But here is another shut against me.

KIYOMOTO:

Their hearts as clouded / as the sky above, / not a star to be seen, / but by the snow-pale light / dimly they recognize each other.

(OJŌ and OBŌ are at a loss as to what to do. Then, through the timbers of the gate, they see each other, move closer, and gaze into each other's eyes.)

Drawing nearer / their faces alight.

OBŌ: Is that really you, Ojō?

OJŌ *(Joyfully):* And that voice—it can only be Obō!

OBŌ: Shhh!

(They look around to see if they have been overheard.)

KIYOMOTO:

"I missed you so much," / through the gate timbers / even his grasping hand trembles . . .

"Is that really you, Ojō?" "And that voice—it can only be Obō!" Fleeing from
the police, Obō Kichisa (Ichikawa Ebizō X, later Ichikawa Danjūrō XII), wearing
a samurai's plain black kimono, and Ojō Kichisa (Onoe Baikō VII), dressed as
the greengrocer's daughter Oshichi, pose in the snow, separated by a closed city
gate. To the right, a ladder goes up to a signal tower, where, by beating a drum,
the city gates can be opened. (Tsubouchi Memorial Theatre Museum of Waseda
University)

TAKEMOTO:

> From the spring cold, / but now, safe and warm / like a chick under its
> mother's wing, / unwilling to part. / To a passerby . . .

KIYOMOTO:

> They'd look to be lovebirds / paired for life.
>
> *(OJŌ grasps OBŌ's hands, trembling with the cold.)*

OBŌ *(Offstage shamisen accompaniment begins):* I decided to take Oshō's advice and start
over, just as one reels off a new white thread yet to be tainted with evildoing.
After returning the sword, I intended to leave Edo and wash clean the stain on
my family's name.

OJŌ: I, too, intended to give the hundred gold pieces to my parents and to dress again
as a man. As though reborn, I would do only good and pray for the souls of
poor Otose and Jūza.

OBŌ: But heaven won't allow us to do so, and we've been hunted down to this crossroads dead-end.

OJŌ: I'd thought to escape, but surely this night we'll be taken . . .

OBŌ: Our preordained fate, the disgrace of binding ropes and death.

286 OJŌ: Though it is too late to change anything . . .

KIYOMOTO:

> Kidnapped at the age of five, / leaving his hometown behind / for gloomy
> years on the road. / From the Echigo shore to wretched Shinano, / then
> suddenly to Michinoku, / straying far on the roads of greed . . .

TAKEMOTO:

> Knowing not his reputation / as a bandit, / white waves erasing his traces /
> along the road to Edo. / There, swearing brotherhood to two Kichisas, / their
> bond as thin as ice . . .

KIYOMOTO:

> Now splintered and / flung to the same wind / that brought these hundred
> gold pieces. / What fate conspires / that he may not deliver them?

TAKEMOTO:

> Sunk in their own sorrow, / suddenly they notice the tower's drum.
> *(Muffled drumbeats suggest the sound of snow falling thick and fast* [yuki oroshi].
> *A bell tolls the hour.* OBŌ *and* OJŌ *look up at the watchtower.)*

OBŌ: Hmm, it says on that notice there that when we've been arrested, a drum will be
beaten as a signal to open all the gates.

OJŌ: It also says that if anyone beats it without permission they'll be put to death.
But since we can't possibly escape, what matter if we add another crime to
our tally?

OBŌ: Once we've got them to open the gates, we can deliver the sword and the
money . . .

OJŌ: Then we must sacrifice our lives to help Oshō . . .

OBŌ: Or we'll not be worthy of our bonds of brotherhood.

OJŌ: Luckily there's a ladder . . .

OBŌ: And the drum lies waiting for us to beat it . . .

OJŌ: What else can we do?

KIYOMOTO:

> Looking up at the sky, / the evening wind whipping his sleeves, / so he folds
> them into his sash / and tucks up the hem of his kimono . . .

TAKEMOTO:

> While the police officers watch him climb.
> *(Looking up at the tower,* OJŌ*'s face assumes a stern expression. He folds his long,
> flapping sleeves into his obi, tucks up the hem of his kimono, and begins to scale the
> ladder. Four black-clad* POLICE OFFICERS *appear from both the left and right.)*

POLICE OFFICER: You criminals there, hold it!

> *(To repeated triple drumbeats* [mitsudaiko] *the four* POLICE OFFICERS *sur-
> round* OJŌ *and* OBŌ. *After a brief choreographed fight* [tachimawari], OJŌ
> *and* OBŌ *manage to drive them off to right and then exit, following them. A*

single ki *clack signals the upstage part of the stage to begin to sink, to give the*
impression that we have climbed the tower. Now only the snow-covered roofs of
the surrounding houses can be seen. OBŌ *enters again, fighting over the roof-*
tops with two POLICE OFFICERS. *As they come fighting downstage, the upstage*
part rises.)

TAKEMOTO:

Drifting snow / turns roofs into white peaks, / where Obō slashes at the
officers / so that they cannot impede Ojō. / Flurries of snow blossoms scattered / by brandished blades . . . / Warding off attacks / Obō grabs their
arms / and tumbles them down / to right and left, / rolling like dogs wallow-
ing in snow.

KIYOMOTO:

Sleeves fluttering, / Ojō scales the bamboo ladder, / his numbed feet slipping
/ on ice-slick rungs. / Shouts echo left and right, / a flock of startled geese.

TAKEMOTO:

Unable to climb, / a helping hand from Obō below, / and at last he reaches
the platform, / takes the drumsticks, / and beats the drum.
(While OBŌ *battles with the* POLICE OFFICERS, OJŌ *reaches the platform of the*
watchtower and beats the drum. Finally driving the POLICE OFFICERS *offstage,*
OBŌ *grasps one of the watchtower's pillars and strikes a victorious* mie *with his left*
foot wrapped around it [hashiramaki no mie]. *Low beatings of the pursuers' drums*
are heard at the rear of the hanamichi, *and* OSHŌ *rushes into sight.)*

OBŌ: Hey, that looks like . . .

BOTH: Oshō Kichisa!

OSHŌ: And those voices can only be Obō and Ojō's.

OBŌ: To save your life . . .

OJŌ: We've beaten the drum on this watchtower.

OSHŌ: So it was thanks to you that the gates were open?

TAKEMOTO:

Just then, Kyūbei the greengrocer appears.
(To a clattering of tsuke *beats,* KYŪBEI *rushes on from the left, carrying a lantern*
marked with the name of his shop.)

KYŪBEI *(Looking at* OJŌ *):* Why, is that you, my long-lost son?

OJŌ: Father, is that really you?

KYŪBEI *(Surprised):* And isn't that young Master Yasumori, and Denkichi's son
with you?

OBŌ: Then, Ojō's father was our family greengrocer.

OBŌ: A strange twist of fate has tied Kyūbei to all three of us.

OSHŌ: I found the hundred gold pieces that my brother lost, so please give them to
Master Bunri. *(Removes the money from his kimono breast and gives it to* KYŪBEI.)

288

OBŌ: And to Yajibei this sword, which was stolen from our house. *(Takes the sword from his kimono breast and gives it to* KYŪBEI.*)*

KYŪBEI: So you managed to find the fabled Kōshinmaru and the hundred gold pieces. How can I ever thank you?

OSHŌ: Hurry, before the cops return.

KYŪBEI: With these, the Yasumori family will be restored to its former glory, and Master Bunri will prosper again. I would like to stay longer, but something tells me it would be imprudent. *(Slips the money into his kimono breast and thrusts the sword into his obi.)*

OSHŌ, OBŌ, and OJŌ: You must leave here immediately.

KYŪBEI: You don't need to tell me twice.

TAKEMOTO:
With that gallant answer / and clutching the two items / Kyūbei runs as though he had wings.
(To a flurry of tsuke *beats and offstage "snowstorm"* [yuki oroshi] *music,* KYŪBEI *crosses to the* hanamichi, *stops to blow out the lantern, and hurries off down the* hanamichi.)

KIYOMOTO:
Recognizing their end is near / the three grasp each other's hands . . .

OSHŌ: Nothing left to repent . . .

OBŌ: Amends made for all our crimes . . .

OJŌ: Now we'll take our own lives . . .

ALL: Together, hand in hand.
(Six POLICE OFFICERS *enter again and try to seize the thieves. They fight briefly. Finally,* OSHŌ, OBŌ, *and* OJŌ *throw them to the ground. Holding them down with their feet, the three thieves together strike a triumphant* mie, *with* OSHŌ *center,* OJŌ *right, and* OBŌ *left.)*

OSHŌ *(To the audience):* And this is where we must end today's performance.
(All the characters throw small souvenir packets of coins to the audience. The curtain is drawn shut to accelerating ki *clacks and beats on the large offstage drum* [uchidashi].*)*

Two-panel woodblock print by Utagawa Chikashige (active 1869–1882). Nakamura-za, Tokyo, March 1870. "Gorozō the Gallant" ("Onoe Kikugorō" V), left, and "Starlight Doemon" ("Ōtani Hiroji" V), right, both former samurai, strike a challenging pose beneath hanging cherry blossoms (tsurieda). Their ferocious opposition is shown by their coiled body stance, crossed eyes (nirami), and readiness to draw their swords. Each is flamboyantly dressed: Gorozō flaunts a white kimono decorated with bold pine clusters and curling, fire-breathing dragons; Doemon wears a sophisticated lavender kimono patterned with spring symbols of falling cherry petals and darting swallows. (Tsubouchi Memorial Theatre Museum of Waseda University)

Gorozō the Gallant
Gosho no Gorozō

Kawatake Mokuami

TRANSLATED BY ALAN CUMMINGS

THE NAKANOCHŌ LICENSED QUARTER
Nakanochō Deai no Ba

THE INNER ROOM AT THE KABUTOYA
Kabutoya Okuzashiki no Ba

LATE NIGHT IN THE LICENSED QUARTER
Kuruwa uchi Yofuke no Ba

1864   ICHIMURA-ZA, EDO

Gorozō the Gallant

INTRODUCTION

Gorozō the Gallant, its formal title *The Soga Design and the Gallant's Dyed Kimono* (Soga Moyō Tateshi no Goshozome), premiered at the Ichimura-za in Edo in the second lunar month of 1864. The play was written for the leading actor of the day, Ichikawa Kodanji IV (1812–1866), by the last great kabuki playwright of the traditional school, Kawatake Mokuami (1816–1893). A contemporary performance record, *Kabuki Chronology Supplementary* (Zokuzoku Kabuki Nendaiki), contains the following note about the genesis of the play:

> One day, Kodanji turned to Kawatake and asked him to write a difficult new play
> that would put Kodanji's acting abilities to the test. [He] wracked his brains and
> came up with this unusual play in which [the hero] plays his flute after cutting
> open his belly. When [Mokuami] showed it to him, Kodanji displayed not the
> slightest sign of being perplexed and urged that the play be performed. When it
> was, the reception was most favorable, and the play was a great hit.[1]

Following Kodanji's death two years after the first performance, the role of Gorozō was revived on four separate occasions by the brilliant star of the Meiji era, Onoe Kikugorō V (1844–1903). Continuing this acting tradition, Kikugorō's adopted nephew, Ichimura Uzaemon XV (1874–1945), excelled in the part before World War II. In the postwar period, the enormously popular Ichikawa Danjūrō XI (1909–1965), Nakamura Kanzaburō XVII (1909–1988), and Onoe Shōroku II (1913–1989) all played Gorozō to acclaim, and the play remains a popular part of the repertory.

Gorozō the Gallant was very closely based on the novel *Picture Book Memories of Mount Asama* (Asamagatake Omokage Zōshi) by the popular novelist Ryūtei Tanehiko (1783–1842), first published in parts between 1809 and 1812. The novel itself drew upon the love story of Tomoenojō and the courtesan Ōshū, a story that had been a perennial theme for kabuki dance pieces since the end of the seventeenth century.

Translated here is the whole of Act V, written in domestic play *(sewamono)* style; this is the only part of the original six-act play still regularly performed. Act V focuses on the rivalry between the evil Hoshikage Doemon, possessor of magical

---

1 Tamura Nariyoshi, *Zokuzoku Kabuki Nendaiki* (Kabuki Chronology Supplementary) (Tokyo: Ichimura-za, 1922), 49–50.

ninja powers, and Gosho no Gorozō. Both men had previously been in the service of Lord Asama Tomoenojō. The first four acts, rarely performed since the 1890s, focus on Doemon's scheming to seize power from his master; Tomoenojō's growing infatuation with Ōshū, who closely resembles his murdered mistress; and Gorozō's dismissal because of an illicit affair with a lady-in-waiting, Tsuji. In current performance practice the final curtain closes as Gorozō and Doemon fight. However, the original ending to the scene in Mokuami's text is quite fascinating: in the midst of their fight, Doemon suddenly disappears through the stage lift *(suppon)* on the *hanamichi*. The curtain is drawn on a bewildered Gorozō, and then, to the accompaniment of supernatural offstage drum music, Doemon reemerges on the elevator. The moon appears and Doemon gazes at it and laughs coldly before leisurely exiting down the *hanamichi*.

Mokuami's sixth and final act, in which the various strands from the first half are drawn together and which ends with Gorozō and Satsuki being reunited in a double suicide during which they play a duet for flute and Chinese fiddle, is intensely dramatic, but it is rarely performed today and is not translated here.

One reason for the continuing popularity of *Gorozō the Gallant* is the play's evocative portrayal of life in the declining pleasure quarters during the last years of the feudal Tokugawa regime. The political and economic turmoil of the time and the rise of the fashionable (and frequently unlicensed) geisha had sounded the death knell for the official licensed quarters. Against this somewhat shabby background, Mokuami moves his thieves, murderers, pimps, and other lowlife. Mokuami was so closely identified with such characters that one of his nicknames was the "bandit playwright" *(shiranami sakusha)*. While he never shied away from painting contemporary life in all its grimness and squalor, his true talent lay in the creation of romantic panoramas, where desperadoes or their prostitute lovers suddenly break into verse. The opening scene in the current translation is Mokuami par excellence: two opposing gangs of thugs—dressed in eye-catching garments—line up on the two *hanamichi* against a breathtaking vista of cherry trees shining in the lantern light to duel in the distinctively musical seven-five verse form *(shichigochō)* with their words traveling back and forth above the heads of the audience. Regrettably, this effect has been abandoned in recent production; only one *hanamichi* is used, and the second gang appears on the stage proper. Their words refer to the major locations passed on a journey by palanquin or boat to the Yoshiwara licensed quarters. Without these colorful living tableaus (it is often said that they are like woodblock prints given flesh), Mokuami's plays would seem grim indeed, leading, as they inevitably do, to tragedy and death.

An extra frisson of interest for the theatre connoisseur is provided by the knowledge that this colorful opening scene, the subsequent abortive confrontation between Gorozō and Doemon, and the situation of Satsuki being "bought" by Doemon all echo well-known events of the earlier *The Scabbard Crossing* (Saya-ate) plot line. (See the introduction to *The Execution Ground at Suzugamori*, translated in this volume.) The writing of theatrical pastiches (whose endless self-referential recycling presages contemporary postmodern methodologies) is such a marked feature of Mokuami's style that he was referred to by the important early critic Tsubouchi Shōyō (1859–1935) as the "great wholesaler of Edo theatre."

Two other highlights of the play are the beautifully stylized murder of Ōshū and the "breaking off" scene *(enkiri)* between Gorozō and Satsuki (the name Tsuji took following her forced descent into prostitution). In the latter, we witness Gorozō's gripping transformation from incomprehension to rage as he is taunted by Doemon's henchmen.

A brief word is in order about Gorozō's position as a "chivalrous commoner" *(otokodate)*. These men saw themselves as self-appointed defenders of the townsmen class against the deprivations of the samurai, and numerous popular legends sprang up around their sense of justice, honor, and style. In reality, they were probably little more than flashily dressed hoodlums and gamblers, the precursor of today's urban gangsters, the *yakuza*, but from the late seventeenth century on they began to be idealized as dashing and gallant kabuki heroes. The most famous Edo theatrical *otokodate* was Sukeroku—fearless, quick to anger, and with an insouciant style that no samurai could match. Originally, Mokuami underlined the link between Gorozō and Sukeroku by having Gorozō and his gang carry large paper umbrellas in the opening scene, echoing the chic umbrella flourished by Sukeroku during his famous danced entrance in the play *Sukeroku: The Flower of Edo* (Sukeroku Yukari no Edo Zakura, 1713, trans. Bowers 1952 and Brandon 1976), though recent productions of *Gorozō the Gallant* have omitted them. Noting that the two plays clearly reflect their different eras, kabuki scholar Kawatake Toshio points out that Gorozō is a much more three-dimensional, darker character than Sukeroku. Gorozō's poverty is continually emphasized, and there is a sense that he is trapped in a value system, however noble, that has had its day. As Doemon's henchmen observe, now it is money, not honor, that makes the world go round.

For the present translation, the main text consulted was in Toita Yasuji et al., eds., *Meisaku Kabuki Zenshū*, Vol. 11. For stage directions, I viewed videotapes of the September 1974 production at the Kabuki-za, starring Shōroku II as Gorozō, Matsumoto Kōshirō VIII (later Hakuō I, 1910–1982) as Doemon, and Nakamura

Jakuemon IV (b. 1920) as Satsuki; and the December 1987 production at the
Minami-za in Kyoto, with Kataoka Takao (currently Kataoka Nizaemon XV, b. 1944)
as Gorozō, Nakamura Tomijūrō V (b. 1929) as Doemon, and Onoe Kikugorō VII
(b. 1942) as Satsuki. I would like to offer my thanks to Professor Iwai Masami for
his assistance.

CHARACTERS

GOSHO NO GOROZŌ, *disgraced samurai, now a "chivalrous commoner"* (otokodate)
HOSHIKAGE DOEMON, rōnin *and sworn enemy of* GOSHO NO GOROZŌ, *now a*
        fencing instructor
GOSHO NO GOROZŌ's GANG MEMBERS
HOSHIKAGE DOEMON's HENCHMEN
KABUTOYA YOGORŌ, *owner of the Kabutoya house of assignation*
YOSUKE, *owner of the Hanagataya brothel*
ŌSHŪ, *high-ranking courtesan, beloved of Tomoenojō,* GOSHO NO GOROZŌ's *former*
        master
SATSUKI, *high-ranking courtesan, wife of* GOSHO NO GOROZŌ
MAIDS
ATTENDANTS
STAGE ASSISTANT, *black-garbed* kurogo

The Nakanochō Licensed Quarter

(*Lively offstage shamisen, drum, and vocal music* [ryōgin]. *The curtain is run*
open to the sound of accelerating ki *clacks. The scene is Nakanochō, the bustling*
main street of the Yoshiwara licensed quarter in Edo. A mass of cherry trees in full
bloom, surrounded by a low lattice fence of green bamboo, occupies the center of the
stage. Chinese roses and distinctive standing lanterns bearing the names of various
brothels and houses of assignation are visible among the trees. Two benches covered
in red cloth have been placed in front. It is the third lunar month, the time of Yoshi-
wara's annual cherry festival, when blossoming cherry trees were transplanted in
Nakanochō. To left is the entrance to the Kabutoya house of assignation, identified
by a large shop curtain. To right, the latticed facades of a row of similar establish-
ments stretch off in the distance. They are gaily decorated with rows of red lanterns
above the first and second stories, and colorful shop curtains. The one nearest the
audience bears the name of one of Yoshiwara's most famous brothels, the Matsubaya.
A border of hanging cherry blossoms [tsurieda] *frames the set overhead. A secondary*
[kari] hanamichi *has been added to join the stage at left. Simultaneously, the cur-*

tains at the rear of both hanamichi *open, their clattering rings drawing our attention.* HOSHIKAGE DOEMON *and four* HENCHMEN *appear on the main* hanamichi, *while* GOSHO NO GOROZŌ *and four* GANG MEMBERS *appear on the secondary* hanamichi. DOEMON *wears a respectable black crested kimono with a restrained willow pattern at the hem and tied with a gold obi. He carries two white-handled swords and wears the bushy "fifty days" wig* [gojūnichi], *symbolizing that he has not shaved his pate for some time. On his feet he wears high wooden clogs* [geta]. *His* HENCHMEN *wear brown kimono and striped formal* hakama. *All wear single swords and carry fans.* GOROZŌ *is the picture of fashionable gallantry, wearing a bulky white kimono with a bold ink-painted dragon pattern and wooden* geta. *His obi is checkered blue, and his pate is carefully shaven. He carries a single sword, and a large flute, symbol of the* otokodate, *is thrust into the back of his obi. His* GANG MEMBERS *are fashionably dressed in thin black kimono with a pattern of vertical blue stripes and gold circles. They carry folded white towels* [tenugui] *over their shoulders. The two parties line up along their respective* hanamichi *and express themselves in "passed-along dialogue"* [watarizerifu], *which is woven in and out of the early part of the scene.)*

DOEMON *(In Edo dialect, deep and sonorous, but with a hint of arrogance):* The winds that blow back the Tsukuba gales / chill the skin south of Fuji. / Before whipping past the village of Minowa / where rain clouds over / the tolling bells of Ueno, / and cries of wild geese / fall upon the paddy waters . . .

GOROZŌ *(Equally sonorous and in Edo dialect):* Mount Matsuchi, standing abreast / the clouded sky / as if painted in grey ink. / Yearning for blossoms, / whitebait and double-oared screened boats / swimming with the evening tide / toward Yoshiwara . . .

DOEMON: In a three-man palanquin / matching step at Primping Hill, / looking back on the fields / around the Willow Street, the Village of Flowers . . .

GOROZŌ: Ducking under the famed Great Gate / and into the nightless town. / The cackling of dandified crows / fretting over where to roost tonight.

FIRST HENCHMAN: Drawn by the whores' melodies . . .

FIRST GANG MEMBER: Swaggering to the pimps' bells . . .

SECOND HENCHMAN: The Hoshikage gang ringing the changes . . .

SECOND GANG MEMBER: The Goshō lads throwing our weight around . . .

THIRD HENCHMAN: Birds of a feather flocking together . . .

THIRD GANG MEMBER: Even the flimflam men and quarter punks . . .

FOURTH HENCHMAN: The brands on our rented wicker hats . . .

FOURTH GANG MEMBER: Give these men of honor a wide berth!

DOEMON: Ringing of angry hearts, / soothed by women and wine, and / the sight of the quarters in spring.

GOROZŌ: Now plum blossom has given way to cherry, / how much more gorgeous looks Nakanochō!

DOEMON: This meeting foretold by crossroads' fortune / and Boys' Day fateful iris.

GOROZŌ *(Referring to the traditional autumn festival, when Yoshiwara's prostitutes parade in white kimono):* In the light from the eaves-lanterns, / the chrysanthemum beds dazzle August-white.

ALL HENCHMEN: Amongst the blossoms of every season . . .

ALL GANG MEMBERS: By pretty flowers in full bloom . . .

DOEMON: We're drawn to sport in the quarter.

GOROZŌ: A most delightful . . .

ALL: View indeed!

> *(Offstage shamisen, drum, and vocal music. Both parties casually approach the stage and pass by each other at center.* DOEMON *appears to recognize* GOROZŌ *and pauses by the bench to left. He turns slightly.)*

DOEMON: Stay a moment, sir.

GOROZŌ *(Stops near the* hanamichi *but does not turn around):* You address yourself to me?

DOEMON: Indeed it is you, sir, to whom I spoke.

GOROZŌ: Then, have you some business of me?

FIRST HENCHMAN: If he didn't have business, he wouldn't have stopped you, would he?

SECOND HENCHMAN: Don't be afraid now . . .

THIRD HENCHMAN: We won't lay a finger on you . . .

FOURTH HENCHMAN: So quit your trembling . . .

ALL HENCHMEN: And get over here now!

FIRST GANG MEMBER: We don't know what the hell you want . . .

SECOND GANG MEMBER: But we're not going over there.

THIRD GANG MEMBER: You got something to say?

FOURTH GANG MEMBER: Then crawl over here on your knees . . .

ALL GANG MEMBERS: And tell us all about it!

FIRST HENCHMAN *(Angrily):* Who do you think you are? An ignorant townsman, ordering a samurai around!

FIRST GANG MEMBER: Who're you calling ignorant? If you've got something you wanna say, then you're the one who should come over here.

SECOND HENCHMAN *(Shouting):* There's no way we're going over there!

SECOND GANG MEMBER: And there's no way you're making us go over there!

ALL HENCHMEN: That's what you think! *(They turn in unison, hands to sword hilts.)*

ALL GANG MEMBERS: Come on, then! *(They, too, turn, hands to swords.)*

DOEMON *(To his* HENCHMEN *):* Hold your clamoring!

GOROZŌ *(To his* GANG MEMBERS *):* Be silent!

DOEMON *(Turning to front):* It was impolite of me to command you, but equally, you cannot expect me to come to you.

GOROZŌ: Well then, let us meet each other halfway . . .

DOEMON: Both stepping out at once . . .

BOTH: Come, let us talk.

> *(Offstage shamisen and bell accompaniment. Proudly, the two men slowly approach each other. They stop, leaving about ten feet between them, and glare at each other.)*

DOEMON: Your appearance may have changed, but I still recognize that face *(referring to GOROZO's former name)*—Sugaki Kakuya . . .

GOROZŌ: Still carrying your two swords of old, you are much the same as then— Hoshikage Doemon . . .

DOEMON: What a most unexpected . . .

BOTH *(They turn to face front and pose briefly):* Meeting this is!

> *(They sit down deliberately on the benches.* HENCHMEN *and* GANG MEMBERS *also seat themselves on benches on opposite sides of the stage.)*

GOROZŌ: So, Doemon, did you have some reason for stopping me?

DOEMON: Although this is the first time we have met in years, and I do not wish to cause offense so soon, nonetheless there is something I must say. My students here tell me that you viciously set upon them the last time they were in the quarter.

FIRST HENCHMAN: What had we done to deserve such abuse?

SECOND HENCHMAN: You thrashed us like a piece of jelly until we were black and blue.

THIRD HENCHMAN: We were too scared of you to make reply . . .

FOURTH HENCHMAN: But today we're with the boss . . .

ALL HENCHMEN: And now you're going to catch it!

GOROZŌ *(Unapologetic):* Hmm. So you're saying that we started the trouble then?

DOEMON: Indeed, it was you.

GOROZŌ: And you're out to settle that score . . .

FIRST GANG MEMBER: Boss, don't you worry. We'll take care of them . . .

SECOND GANG MEMBER: They've long been spoiling for a fight . . .

THIRD GANG MEMBER: And now's the time to settle it. They're backing up their boss . . .

FOURTH GANG MEMBER: And we'll back up ours . . .

ALL GANG MEMBERS *(Standing, hands to sword hilts):* To the death!

GOROZŌ: Stop butting in. I can handle this myself without your help.

ALL GANG MEMBERS: You mean . . .

GOROZŌ: Yeah. Sit down and shut up.

> *(They go to take a step forward, but* GOROZŌ *holds them back with an angry glance. He then nods to them to sit down.)*

Seated on benches before lushly blooming cherry trees in the Yoshiwara licensed quarter, "Gorozō the Gallant" (Nakamura Kankurō V), left, challenges "Starlight Doemon" (Ichikawa Sadanji IV), right: "You've harbored your grudge against me for seven years—let's settle it now!" Both arrogantly face front, too proud to deign looking at their opponent. (Umemura Yutaka, Engeki Shuppansha)

ALL GANG MEMBERS: Right you are, Boss.

GOROZŌ *(To offstage shamisen music):* Now, Doemon. My boys didn't know that those were your students, but the pleasure quarters are for love, and all should give way. Your ignorant shrimps were walking four abreast down the street, so it was only natural that we should teach them a lesson. They brought it on themselves. And you won't see Gosho no Gorozō backing down just because they wheeled on a big lobster like you. You've harbored your grudge against me for seven years—let's settle it now!

DOEMON: Come, come. You've got the wrong end of the stick. I didn't stop you to start a fight—I wanted to thank you.

GOROZŌ *(Mystified):* Thank me?

DOEMON: Many's the time I have warned them against quarreling or fighting in the quarter, but, as you say, they are ignorant shrimps and do not heed my words. Since they were born with claws, they are naturally prone to be belligerent. They can count themselves lucky you taught them such a lesson. I want to thank you.

GOROZŌ *(Skeptical):* Hmm. I sense some irony in your thanks. Your students have been handed a whipping, but you as their boss really want to thank me?

DOEMON: And if you catch them doing it again, please make an example of them.

GOROZŌ: Even if they had done something wrong, as their boss you are duty bound to defend them. But still you say nothing. . . . You must be hiding something.

(Shamisen accompaniment ceases.)

DOEMON *(Gloating at* GOROZŌ*'s puzzlement):* Well, you deserve your reputation, Gorozō. I have indeed something to hide.

GOROZŌ *(Emphatically):* Then what is it you hide?

(Shamisen resumes.)

DOEMON: You remember the lady-in-waiting Satsuki from the Asama household? The one who would meet you in secret and who was expelled from service for her infidelity? Now she works in the quarter, the jewel of the Hanagataya house. As a prostitute her bedpartner changes nightly, and she cannot refuse a customer. *(With relish.)* Since, as they say in the quarter, you are her jealous pimp, I thought I should tell you that from tonight I intend to make her mine.

GOROZŌ *(Reveling in this chance to get one up on his rival):* We agreed that my wife Satsuki should take customers to save us from poverty, and she contracted herself to a brothel. Call for her if you like, but the rules of the quarter say that since she is already mine, you cannot buy her time. I'm sorry to have to tell you that you'll have to make do with her maid.

DOEMON: I know all about her situation. But there'd be nothing you could do if I were to produce a thousand gold pieces, buy out her contract, and take her home with me.

GOROZŌ: True, since she's for sale, there's nothing I could do to stop you buying out her contract. But since my seal is on her contract as her husband, if you do buy her out, you cannot marry her without my consent.

DOEMON *(Confidently):* I will just have to get you to give her to me, then.

GOROZŌ: Well, if I was a potato picker or a hole digger I might just give her to you. But I'm not—they call me Gosho no Gorozō after the famous battle of the Soga brothers, Jūrō and Gorō. I, too, fought on the same night as they did, the twenty-eighth of the fifth month, a night when the Soga brothers' swords flashed in the dark and the tears of their lovers rained down in torrents across the land. People look up to me as a man of honor, and I cannot back down.

(He strikes a forceful mie, *with his hands in his sleeves.)*

DOEMON: So you will not give me what I want because of your reputation?

GOROZŌ: If word got around that I gave away my wife because I was scared that you might take revenge on me for giving your students a thrashing, I'd never be able to live it down. If you want her, you're going to have to settle that score right now.

DOEMON: For the sake of Satsuki, and out of the kindness of my heart, I had
thought to let you off lightly. But since you say I won't get her without a
fight . . .

GOROZŌ *(Angered):* Let the winner take her, along with the loser's life as a wedding
gift. Come on, let's get down to it.

DOEMON: Fighting words indeed! If that's what you wish, come . . .

GOROZŌ: We'll hack our fans down to their ribs . . .

DOEMON: Tearing each other to pieces . . .

GOROZŌ: Or else meekly present . . .

DOEMON: A willow barrel of wedding sake, and part.

GOROZŌ: Good and evil divided . . .

DOEMON: Butterfly or moth?

ALL HENCHMEN *(Standing, eager for a fight):* Our boss'll turn yours into flaked fish!

ALL GANG MEMBERS *(Standing, equally aggressive):* We'll snap your legs like dried
cuttlefish!

GOROZŌ *(To his* GANG MEMBERS *):* This is just between the two of us . . .

DOEMON: All of you stay where you are and observe.

GANG MEMBERS and HENCHMEN: You mean to say . . .

GOROZŌ and DOEMON: Yes, sit down and shut up!
(They hesitate for a moment, but GOROZŌ *'s powerful stare defeats them, and as
commanded, they sit down again on the benches.)*

GOROZŌ: That puts them out of the way . . .

DOEMON: Now let's settle this score . . .

BOTH *(Rising to a climax* [kuriage]*):* Right now!
*(The two men jump to their feet and turn to face each other. Just as they are about
to draw their swords,* KABUTOYA YOGORŌ, *the master of the Kabutoya house
of assignation, suddenly appears to the sound of* tsuke *beats and throws himself
between them, his arms raised to hold them back. His dress is that of a stylish and
prosperous merchant—a pale-green* haori *and darker green* hakama *over a pale-
green kimono.)*

YOGORŌ: Wait! Please, I beg you.

DOEMON: Who dares to interrupt us?

GOROZŌ *(Surprised):* It's the young master from the Kabutoya.

YOGORŌ: My name is Yogorō, of the Kabutoya teahouse. *(He bows briefly. Offstage
shamisen music.)* I overheard everything. In the past you worked side by side
in the same mansion, as close as a fish and water. Then came the crime of an
imprudent love affair, whose punishment has been escaped these seven years.
Now the river of life has brought you together again here in the Yoshiwara
quarter. Though this may be your first meeting, the roots of your past are
deeply entwined. You both know that while one of you may triumph in your

302 quarrel, you cannot triumph against the law. What's more, all of us worry that you may injure yourselves. Please, allow me to settle this quarrel amicably.

DOEMON: Your words are wise, and if Gorozō is of a mind to settle . . .

GOROZŌ: Then I, too, shall make no objection.

YOGORŌ: So you will . . .

DOEMON: My resentment remains . . .

GOROZŌ *(Removing his hand from his sword):* But since it is spring . . .

YOGORŌ: Permit me to settle the matter?

DOEMON: Since this is our first meeting . . .

GOROZŌ: We will allow you the honor . . .

(Slowly they turn and face front, their sleeves held wide to create a powerful silhouette.)

BOTH: Of settling this quarrel.

YOGORŌ: For which honor, I thank you.

FIRST HENCHMAN: Just when we were looking forward to a scrap . . .

FIRST GANG MEMBER: An unexpected end to the spat . . .

SECOND HENCHMAN: No fight to the death, thanks to the Kabutoya's young master . . .

SECOND GANG MEMBER: Their lives saved for another day.

YOGORŌ *(To* DOEMON *):* Why don't you come in for a drink to celebrate?

DOEMON: Even tripping over a stone may be the work of fate. I will accept your offer.

YOGORŌ: I would be honored. Master Gorozō, will you join us?

GOROZŌ: I thank you for your offer, but unfortunately I have a prior appointment I cannot break.

YOGORŌ: But surely you have time for just one . . .

GOROZŌ: I will let you settle our quarrel for the moment.

DOEMON: If you will not drink with me . . .

(Suddenly DOEMON *raises his right hand and mimes hurling a fan at* GOR-OZŌ, *who "catches" it. One* tsuke *beat.)*

GOROZŌ: What's this?

DOEMON: Let us celebrate our prosperity / with an exchange of cups on opened fans.

*(*GOROZŌ *turns front, opens the fan, twirls it upside down, and holds it aloft.)*

GOROZŌ *(Punning on a place name):* Turn it upside down / and we can drink sake below Mount Fuji. / Now I return your cup . . .

*(*GOROZŌ *turns suddenly toward* DOEMON, *closes the fan, and mimes hurling it back. One* tsuke *beat.* DOEMON *"catches" the fan.)*

DOEMON: And I accept it. *(Tucks the fan into his obi.)*

YOGORŌ: And so you two are reconciled.

GOROZŌ: Then, Doemon . . .

DOEMON: Then, Gorozō . . .

(Both swivel to face front as YOGORŌ *again spreads his arms to hold them apart. A single, echoing* ki *clack. They freeze into a tense* mie *to loud* tsuke *beats.)*

BOTH: We shall meet again!

(Lively offstage vocal, shamisen, and drum music. GOROZŌ *and* DOEMON *turn toward their men, nodding. As the two turn their backs on each other, the curtain is drawn closed to rapidly accelerating* ki *clacks.)*

The Inner Room at the Kabutoya

(The curtain opens to rapid ki *clacks. Revealed is an elegant reception room at the Kabutoya house of assignation. A picture of a cherry tree in bloom is painted on the sliding doors at the rear of the room. The alcove to the left of the doors contains a hanging picture and a small vase. To left is a circular window looking out on a small garden. In a corner of the room is a pile of cushions. To right is an entrance to the room from outside. The only furnishings are a small, elaborately decorated lacquer tray holding various smoking implements, and a small standing screen. The high-ranking courtesan* SATSUKI *sits in the center of the room, talking to a* MAID. SATSUKI *is dressed in all the finery of her professional rank: an elaborate hairstyle supported by a porcupine profusion of large hairpins, a vast and gorgeously embroidered obi tied in front, and many layers of rich, heavy kimono that spread out around her. Large multicolored flowers decorate her outer robe* [uchikake]. *Her face is heavily powdered white. The* MAID *wears a simple black kimono with a silver obi tied in front. Languid offstage shamisen music.)*

SATSUKI *(Concerned and gentle):* What was Gorozō's reply?

MAID: He said that he has promised to return the two hundred gold pieces he owes tonight. He begs that you make the money ready.

SATSUKI: I know that he said tonight, but I had hoped that he would be able to gain an extension. So, he needs the money by tonight . . .

MAID: He also said that he has written everything down in this letter.

(She stands and passes a rolled up letter to SATSUKI, *who delicately unfurls it and begins to read.)*

SATSUKI *(Deeply worried):* If he does not return the two hundred pieces of gold to the master of the Hanagataya brothel by tonight, he says there is no way he can go on living. Whatever am I to do?

MAID: Shall I mention your predicament to the master?

SATSUKI: Would you?

MAID: Very well, mistress. I will report back presently. *(Exits through rear sliding doors.)*

SATSUKI *(Facing front, at a loss):* I must find some way to obtain two hundred gold pieces. Gorozō borrowed that amount from the master of the Hanagataya, in order that his former lord could meet with his beloved, Ōshū. If I were a normal working girl, I could doubtless tap some customer for a hundred or

304

even two hundred gold pieces. But as I am a working wife, my heartstrings tied to my husband, I have no such customers. Though it is spring and the world flourishes anew, I alone wither, bereft of blossoms.

(She rises to her knees, her voice quivering with emotion as she shakes her head slightly from side to side. Suddenly, the rear doors are flung open and DOEMON *enters. He is dressed in an informal maroon kimono with a design of various diamond-shaped crests. He still carries his swords.)*

DOEMON: I shall lend you the money. *(Kneels beside her.)*

SATSUKI *(Startled):* Ah, it is you Doemon. Then, you heard . . .

DOEMON: I overheard everything from the next room.

SATSUKI: So you will lend . . .

DOEMON *(Magnaminously):* You need not ask twice. I will lend you the money.

SATSUKI *(Puzzled, she hides her hands beneath her obi):* But why would you want to help me, after I have refused to entertain you in the past?

DOEMON *(Grandly):* It is only natural that your shallow woman's heart should have such doubts. Here, take these two hundred gold pieces and use them to save your husband, Gorozō, from the trouble he faces this night. *(He reaches into his sleeve, pulls out a small parcel of coins wrapped in a piece of purple cloth, and places it beside* SATSUKI. *He then takes out his pipe and begins to fill it.)*

SATSUKI: So you were unable to look coldly upon my plight and will truly lend me this money?

DOEMON: I am a samurai—my word is my bond.

SATSUKI *(Overjoyed):* If you speak the truth, then . . .

(She reaches for the packet of money, but DOEMON *seizes her hand.)*

DOEMON: Satsuki, to twist the old saying, if your falling leaves have a yearning, then these flowing waters of mine will not flow on regardless. *(He pauses.)* If you truly desire this money, then all you have to do is write a brief letter in your own hand. *(He gestures with his pipe.)*

SATSUKI *(Hopefully):* Is it a promise to repay you wish me write?

DOEMON: I said that I will lend you the money. I need no written promise.

SATSUKI: What then is it you wish me to write . . .

DOEMON *(Emphatically):* I wish you to write . . . a letter of divorce to your husband, Gorozō.

*(*SATSUKI *recoils in shock. Quickly she stands, as though to leave, but* DOEMON *holds down the hem of her kimono, preventing her flight.)*

DOEMON: Satsuki, wait. Since you wish to storm out of here with nary a word in reply to my proposal, am I to assume that you do not need my money? Don't you need these two hundred gold pieces this very night in order to repay your debt of gratitude to the Asama family? Gorozō stands on his bond as a man of honor, so without this money he cannot live on. Whether he is to live or die, the choice is yours to make. Show some grit and make your reply!

(With each phrase of DOEMON*'s,* SATSUKI *shivers with a sharp intake of breath, recognizing the truth of what he says. Her face betrays her confusion: her heart tells her to refuse his offer, her head tells her to save her husband. Finally, in a bid to hold back her tears, she painfully closes her eyes and sinks to the floor beside* DOEMON*.)*

SATSUKI *(Drained):* I will write your letter.

(Slow offstage shamisen music.)

DOEMON: Once you have written the letter, you will submit to me?

SATSUKI *(Weakly):* I am sure you will despise me for being a calculating woman for saying this, but I fell out of love with Gorozō long ago.

DOEMON: What?

SATSUKI: Thanks to him, I have to sell my body in this wretched place. I had resigned myself to our ill fortune, but every year he keeps extending my original five-year contract. I cannot bear it that the man to whom I had dedicated my life should make me work here until I am old and wrinkled. I had long thought to transfer my affections to some new customer, but until now there was no such man. Please give me that money so that I may at last be free of Gorozō.

DOEMON: If you will break off with him, this money shall be yours.

SATSUKI: My heart is overjoyed. *(She joins her hands together and bows to him before taking the packet of money. Her expression changes, and she turns away from* DOEMON *softly.)* With this, my beloved . . .

DOEMON: What's that?

SATSUKI: I mean, beloved Doemon, I will now write my letter of divorce, a symbol of my affection for you.

(The rear doors slide open and DOEMON*'s* HENCHMEN *enter.)*

HENCHMEN: Our congratulations, Boss.

DOEMON: Rejoice for me, lads. This burning love that I have nurtured these past seven years has now come to fruition.

HENCHMEN: Let's call for some sake and celebrate in style!

(They call for refreshments, and three MAIDS *appear with trays containing sake flasks and cups. They set out cushions to sit on and begin to serve the men.*

SATSUKI *kneels before her tobacco tray, conceals the packet of money, then takes out paper and a brush and begins to write. The party is soon in full swing.)*

DOEMON: Have you not finished yet?

SATSUKI: I didn't know what to write. Do you think this will suffice?

(She passes the letter to DOEMON *for his inspection. He studies it carefully.)*

DOEMON: It will do well enough. At last my heart is at peace. *(To his* HENCHMEN*.)* Here, one of you take this to Gorozō.

FIRST HENCHMAN *(Taking the letter):* You want one of us to take this letter of divorce to Gorozō? *(He hurriedly passes it on to the man beside him.)*

SECOND HENCHMAN: You won't catch me taking it. When Gorozō reads this, he's going to blow his top. . . . *(He passes on the letter.)*

THIRD HENCHMAN: And he's bound to take it out on the bearer of the bad news. . . . *(Shoving the letter in the direction of the final* HENCHMAN.*)*

FOURTH HENCHMAN: Let's not fight about it. Why don't we all go together.

ALL HENCHMEN: That's what we'll do!

DOEMON *(Laughing):* You cowardly rogues.

FOURTH HENCHMAN *(Pointing):* There's no need for us to go after all. Here comes Gorozō himself.

SATSUKI *(Agitated, rising to her knees):* Gorozō? Here . . .

DOEMON: Even better. You can break off with him here in front of me.

SATSUKI: Here? Now?

DOEMON *(Staring at her, speaking forcefully):* Think of it as a token of your affection.

SATSUKI *(Trying to hold back her emotions, weakly):* Very . . . well.

FIRST HENCHMAN: This should be . . .

ALL HENCHMEN: Something to see!

> *(They resume drinking. Elegant offstage shamisen music* [hayari uta]. GOROZŌ *appears at the rear of the* hanamichi *wearing a lightweight, dark-blue kimono with an entwined plant pattern in white and an obi of horizontal green stripes. Sword and flute are tucked into the obi, and his hands are hidden in his sleeves. He is followed by* YOSUKE, *the master of the Hanagataya brothel, whom he is studiously ignoring.* YOSUKE *wears a brown kimono and* haori *appropriate to a prosperous merchant.)*

YOSUKE: Listen, Gorozō. You promised to pay up by tonight, and if you won't, I'll just have to go to Lord Asama's lodgings and ask him personally to return my money.

> *(*GOROZŌ *stops at* shichisan *and turns around.)*

GOROZŌ *(Irritated):* You really are lacking in style, aren't you? If I wanted you to go to Lord Asama about this, I wouldn't be standing here begging you.

YOSUKE: That's all very well for you to say. Our understanding was that you'd return the money today, and since you're a man who stands by his honor, I believed you. You're not getting any special treatment from me.

GOROZŌ: Couldn't you wait until tomorrow?

YOSUKE: Why should I? Forget about tomorrow, I'm not even going to wait another hour for my money.

GOROZŌ: Whad'ya mean by that? We agreed on tonight, so I've got until dawn.

YOSUKE: That's where you're wrong. Today ends at midnight.

GOROZŌ: Don't be such a petty old miser.

(Out of patience, he turns his back on YOSUKE *and walks away. As he approaches the main stage, the* HENCHMEN *call out.)*

FIRST HENCHMAN: Ah, Gorozō. Just the man. We were just about to . . .

ALL HENCHMEN: Go looking for you.

GOROZŌ: You got some business with me?

SECOND HENCHMAN: Business, you could say. Very important business.

GOROZŌ: Some message from Doemon, then?

THIRD HENCHMAN: Not from the boss . . . from your wife.

GOROZŌ: What do you mean, from my wife?

HENCHMAN *(Holding out the letter):* Read this and you'll get the picture.

GOROZŌ *(He quickly reads it and is shocked):* What's this! A letter of divorce from Satsuki . . .

FIRST HENCHMAN *(Rubbing it in):* She might have been your wife, but she's tired of you and your penny-pinching ways . . .

SECOND HENCHMAN: She's traded her old cow in for a new horse. From today, she's the boss' girl . . .

THIRD HENCHMAN: And once he's bought out her contract, she'll be his wife . . .

FOURTH HENCHMAN: And that's why . . .

ALL HENCHMEN: She's divorcing you.

GOROZŌ *(Disbelieving):* She has tired of me, and really wishes to break off? *(Feverishly, he rereads the letter in search of some explanation.)*

FIRST HENCHMAN: Hey, Gorozō. She's breaking off with you and trading you in for a better mount. If she stuck with you her whole life, there's no way she'll ever get ahead. You don't know the first thing about making money. You call yourself a chivalrous commoner and say that your honor is everything, but you're nothing but a penniless tramp!

SECOND HENCHMAN: In and out of the pawnbroker's every month and still only able to buy a handful of rice and a cup of sake. With her charms, she could have married into money, but if she sticks with you, she'll end up an old crone flogging glue on the streets.

THIRD HENCHMAN: On the other hand, if she marries the boss, there'll be no more scrimping and saving on the household accounts. Buying kimono or going to the theatre, she can have whatever she desires.

FOURTH HENCHMAN: Ninety-nine out of a hundred know greed. Trading your husband in for a better one is the way of the world today. Angry you may be, but you're going to have to bite your tongue because . . .

ALL HENCHMEN: Nowadays, it's money makes the world go round!

GOROZŌ *(Looking again at the letter and struggling to comprehend):* There was no hint of this the last time I saw her. How could Satsuki's feelings have changed so suddenly?

FIRST HENCHMAN: Because you're a . . .

ALL HENCHMEN: Spineless tramp!

> *(Enraged by their words,* GOROZŌ *suddenly rips the letter to pieces.)*

YOSUKE: Hmm. That Satsuki's got more brains than I credited her for, breaking up with you. I thought she might have been able to raise some money for you, but now there's no hope of that. There's nothing else for it. I'm off to Lord Asama's mansion to get my money. *(He prepares to leave.)*

GOROZŌ: Come on, give me a break.

YOSUKE: Are you going to pay me?

GOROZŌ *(Kuriage):* Well . . .

YOSUKE: Are you?

GOROZŌ: Well . . .

YOSUKE: Are you?

GOROZŌ: Well . . .

YOSUKE: Pay me now, or I'm gone.

SATSUKI *(Suddenly pushing aside the standing screen that has obscured her presence):* Yosuke, I have your money.

GOROZŌ: Satsuki, you were there all along?

SATSUKI *(Eagerly holding out the packet of money):* I have the money that you. . . . *(She catches hold of herself but turns her head away, unable to look* GOROZŌ *in the face.)* I mean, from this day forth we are strangers, so let this money break the bond between us. *(Sharply, she lays the money on the floor.)*

GOROZŌ *(Stuttering):* What do you mean, break the bond between us?

> *(Slow offstage shamisen accompaniment begins.)*

SATSUKI *(Still looking away):* Please, don't say any more. Just take the money. I have grown tired of your constant poverty, and since there is no sign of it improving I have made up my mind to break off with you.

GOROZŌ *(Distraught):* Then you truly mean to . . .

SATSUKI *(Leaning upon her long-stemmed pipe and trying to sound callous):* Let this money be proof of my resolve. Accept it as a gift of fate.

> *(*GOROZŌ *sits on a bench near the edge of the veranda, trying to control his resentment.* YOSUKE *sits beside him.)*

GOROZŌ: I don't know what's brought this on. Maybe you've fallen for one of your customers and that has driven us apart. But while our love began as an affair, over these seven years haven't we come to know everything about one another? Are we not husband and wife? I can't accept this.

SATSUKI *(Holding her emotions in check):* Whether you accept it or not is of no consequence. The fact is that if I remain faithful to you, my life will be one of hardship. By entrusting myself to Doemon, I can live a long life of ease. People will doubtless think me a wanton, faithless woman, but that is the only option left

to me. Without money, life isn't worth living. From this day forth I can see you
no more. Just as the Asuka River runs both deep and shallow, love is not forever. That is the wisdom of life, and of the licensed quarter.

MAID: And so, the mistress really means to . . .

GOROZŌ: To break off with me? *(He slaps his knees in disbelief and then glares angrily at*
SATSUKI.*)*

SATSUKI: Would I lie to you? *(Finally she gives way to tears.)*

DOEMON *(Nastily):* Just look at him, lads. He thinks that because he's eating rice cakes
it must be New Year. Fawning over some woman like a lovesick fool, believing
her flattery to be the truth. What sort of an idiot gets deceived like that!

ALL HENCHMEN: The longer we see his face, the stupider it looks!

(They all laugh cruelly. GOROZŌ*'s control snaps and he leaps to his feet. Unbal-*
anced, the bench tips up and throws YOSUKE *to the floor. To the sound of sharp*
tsuke *beats,* GOROZŌ *plants one foot on the bench and strikes an enraged* mie,
glaring toward SATSUKI *and* DOEMON, *his right hand gripping his left sleeve.*
He throws himself back down on the bench, legs spread wide.)

GOROZŌ *(Shouting):* Satsuki, I tried to tell myself it wasn't true, but I can hold back
no longer. Has even your heart become so stained with the dirty water of the
quarter that you'd throw me aside? I stuck by you all these years after we
were thrown out by our lord, and now you're going go off with Doemon, of all
people! Words fail me, you inhuman bitch!

FIRST HENCHMAN: Calm down. No matter how worked up you get, you can't change
the fact that your darling wife's run off with another man.

SECOND HENCHMAN: There's nothing you can do when your wench cuts you dead.
Just be grateful, take your two hundred gold pieces . . .

THIRD HENCHMAN: Bow and scrape to your betters . . .

FOURTH HENCHMAN: And beat it.

GOROZŌ: I don't want it. I need that money, but as a farewell gift, you can stuff it!

YOSUKE: Come now, Gorozō, don't let your pride get in the way. Take the money and
pay off what you owe me.

GOROZŌ *(A pained gesture of rejection):* I can't. Heaven knows I need that money, but if
people gossiped that Gorozō had taken a farewell gift from his wife, I could
never show my face again. *(Folds his arms, hands tucked into sleeves.)*

SATSUKI: So you will not . . .

(Melancholy offstage shamisen and flute accompaniment.)

GOROZŌ *(Slowly and gravely):* I cannot. The rules of honor of our world say we must
repay whatever we have borrowed. But to think of them will only cause me
pain and suffering. *(Turning quickly toward* SATSUKI, *his voice rising.)* But that
is as nothing compared to the pain I feel now that the thread of love that
unraveled in my heart has snapped like a one-penny kite. A love that you felt

as keenly as I. *(Again gravely.)* From today I will turn over a new leaf. What need have I of honor? Why should I repay the thanks I owe to my lord? *(To* YOSUKE.*)* And you won't see a penny that I owe you.

YOSUKE: So you're going to welsh on your loan, you . . .

GOROZŌ: Who cares whether I do?

YOSUKE: You're not getting away with this. . . . *(Tries to grab* GOROZŌ *'s kimono.)*

GOROZŌ: Honor's out of fashion these days! *(Rising to his feet, he seizes* YOSUKE*'s hand, twists it violently, and thrusts him away.)*

YOSUKE *(Rubbing his hand in pain):* Ow, ow. I don't like this new fashion.

GOROZŌ *(Pulling the flute from his obi):* And since I don't believe in honor any more, I'll take pleasure in breaking this flute into pieces over your head.

(He advances on SATSUKI *and* DOEMON *with the flute raised high above his head. The courtesan* ŌSHŪ *suddenly appears from the rear and rushes to throw herself before* GOROZŌ*, raising her hand to stop him. Her robes and hairstyle are as elaborate and beautiful as those of* SATSUKI.*)*

ŌSHŪ: Master Gorozō, wait please.

GOROZŌ *(Still bent on revenge):* Ōshū, get out of my way!

ŌSHŪ *(Pleading):* It is only natural that you should be angry, but there must be some explanation. This isn't the time to be hasty. Please wait.

GOROZŌ: I might agree if she were human, but she's worse than a dog or a cat. At least they know the meaning of gratitude. Don't try to stop me.

ŌSHŪ: Whatever you say, I know that there must be some reason she is unable to speak of. It avails me nothing to try and stop you. If not for my sake, then for the sake of my lover, your master, Lord Tomoenojō, please restrain yourself. Though it must be difficult for you now, I am sure that you will come to understand in time.

(GOROZŌ takes another step forward, and she clings to the front of his kimono, her back to the audience. They pause in an impressive tableau: GOROZŌ *with his flute raised high and anger on his face, the severe blue of his kimono melting into the rich silks of* ŌSHŪ*'s robes. At last, he looks down at her face, reflects for a moment, and then weakly relaxes his arm. Quiet offstage shamisen and flute music begins.)*

GOROZŌ *(Pained):* I would not have held back for anyone else. But I cannot go against the benevolence that Lord Tomoenojō has shown me. Your gentle words carry his authority. I will force myself to hold back, and today I will say no more. *(He lowers the flute and steps away.)*

ŌSHŪ: So you will listen to my words . . .

GOROZŌ: And suppress my naturally hot temper. I will endure this pain.

(A black-clad STAGE ASSISTANT *[kurogo] tucks* GOROZŌ*'s flute back into his obi.* ŌSHŪ *steps up into the room and sits behind* DOEMON.*)*

ŌSHŪ: Then I, too, am relieved.

Interceding on her fellow courtesan's behalf, Ōshū (Nakamura Tokizō V) urges Gorozō (Ichikawa Danjūrō XII) to control his rage over the presumed infidelity of his wife, Satsuki. As Gorozō raises his heavy wooden flute to strike Satsuki, Ōshū kneels before him, pleading, "Master Gorozō, wait please. . . . It is only natural that you should be angry, but there must be some explanation." (Umemura Yutaka, Engeki Shuppansha)

SATSUKI: I know not how to thank you.

ŌSHŪ: There is no need. It is for both our sakes.

GOROZŌ *(Now in control of himself):* Doemon, when we served close by our lord on the Asama estates in the north, we both fell for Satsuki and fought over her. Now she has changed for the worse, and though it still rankles with me, I am a man, and I thus give her to you with no hard feelings.

SATSUKI: How could you, my . . .

DOEMON *(Glaring at her):* What do you mean by that?

SATSUKI: I mean, how could we have foreseen such a happy parting.

DOEMON: You say you are over her, but you have been thrown over by a woman whom you trusted these seven years. Your heart is doubtless filled with resentment against me. Come to me whenever you please and vent your anger.

GOROZŌ *(Recovering his poise):* I am sure we will laugh about it one day. I will come soon with a barrel of sake and thus repay my debt to you and toast your success.

SATSUKI: Gorozō. The depths of my. . . . I mean, our relationship was deep, but now it has ended. I know you do not want to, but please take this money as my parting gift to you. *(She holds out the packet of coins to him.)*

ŌSHŪ: Please accept the money as a sign of her feelings for you.

GOROZŌ *(Coldly):* I don't want your money. You're nothing to me now. *(Turning toward* SATSUKI *angrily.)* I wouldn't take three bent coppers from you. *(Swiftly he turns and is about to walk away.)*

FIRST HENCHMAN: Don't be such a big boor, Gorozō. This isn't just a few coppers, we're talking about two hundred gold pieces.

SECOND HENCHMAN: They're not made of dirt. Two hundred freshly minted and stamped pieces of shining gold. You'll never see such money again in your life.

THIRD HENCHMAN: Stop taking pride in being a starving beggar. Take the money, that's what anyone would do nowadays.

FOURTH HENCHMAN: If you don't want it, then fine. But first . . .

ALL HENCHMEN: Take a good look at it!

GOROZŌ: Stop your chattering, you worthless pieces of trash. I'm not like you. Even if you were to pile up a thousand, ten thousand, gold pieces, I wouldn't take them from some creature who'd just thrown me over. If you want those coppers, try drawing some steel. *(He taps the hilt of his sword.)* Take them all! *(The* HENCHMEN *flinch.* GOROZŌ *stalks off toward the* hanamichi. YOSUKE *runs after him and clings to his kimono from behind.)*

YOSUKE: What about my money?

GOROZŌ *(At* shichisan, *tensing):* Hey, Doemon. On some moonlit night in the quarter, darkness awaits you. . . . *(He quickly turns, breaks* YOSUKE *'s hold, and shoves him backward. Then, hiking the loose flap of his kimono up to his knee, he strikes a powerful* mie, *right hand clenched at his breast, left leg thrust out, and glares at* DOEMON.) Remember my words!

(*Offstage shamisen, vocal, and hand-drum music.* GOROZŌ *hikes up the other side of his kimono and then stamps slowly and deliberately off down the* hanamichi, *his* geta *echoing loudly in time with accelerating* tsuke *beats.*)

YOSUKE (*Calling after him from* shichisan): Hey, Gorozō. (*He drops his* haori *on the ground. Then, humorously.*) Darkness awaits you . . . remember my words!

(*Comically, he imitates* GOROZŌ*'s* mie, *screwing up his face, fists clenched, and hiking up his kimono to reveal wrinkled blue underwear. He takes a couple of steps down the* hanamichi *before he realizes he has forgotten his* haori. *He runs back to pick it up, then scurries off after* GOROZŌ, *shouting, "Gorozō! Gorozō!" to drum and* tsuke *beats.*)

ALL HENCHMEN: Well, Boss, that's all cleared up, then.

DOEMON: Clear indeed, like the sun breaking out all over Japan. Let us repair now to the Hanagataya with Satsuki.

SATSUKI: I will follow you later. Please go on ahead.

DOEMON: Why can you not come with me now?

SATSUKI (*Her hand to her chest*): I have a sudden pain . . .

DOEMON: Strange that there was no sign of it until now. Does this sudden pain mean you are trying to avoid me?

(SATSUKI *bows her head, rubbing her chest.*)

ŌSHŪ: Excuse me, Master Doemon. I recognize your suspicions, but I remember Satsuki having such sudden pains before. She cannot possibly go with you now, but once the pains have subsided, she will immediately follow. Please allow her some time alone.

DOEMON: To show she has broken off with Gorozō, she must appear in public with me. If she does not, what is the point of having her?

ŌSHŪ: Then, won't you settle for my bronze in place of her silver? I will go upstairs with you.

DOEMON: Your offer honors me, but I will not be fobbed off.

ŌSHŪ: Then how about this? I will wear Satsuki's over robe and have my attendant carry her crested lantern. Anyone who sees us will think that I am her. I realize that this is presumptuous on our first meeting, but please grant my request.

DOEMON (*He considers the request for a moment, then nods*): Your reputation in the quarter is fully justified. I will not let you lose face.

ALL HENCHMEN: We will see you off, Boss.

(*The two* MAIDS *help* SATSUKI *and* ŌSHŪ *exchange over robes.*)

ŌSHŪ: Now I have become Satsuki.

DOEMON: And I will gladly accompany you.

FIRST HENCHMAN: Then let us quickly . . .

ALL HENCHMEN: Repair to the Hanagataya.

SATSUKI: Ōshū, I know not . . .

ŌSHŪ: Satsuki. I hope you feel better presently.

SATSUKI: I will soon follow you.

DOEMON *(Leering):* And I anxiously await your arrival.

> *(SATSUKI bows weakly to him. Offstage shamisen, percussion, and vocal music. The MAID opens the rear doors and DOEMON exits, followed by his HENCHMEN. The two courtesans bow to each other, and ŌSHŪ exits. The doors are slid shut behind her. SATSUKI takes up the packet of money. She kneels center, holding out the money and looking toward the hanamichi.)*

SATSUKI: Gorozō, how angry you must be. Please forgive me. I was unable to tell you the real reason for my actions. I only agreed to submit to your enemy Doemon so I could get these two hundred gold pieces and save you from dishonor. I so wanted for you to have this money, but you refused to take it from my hand. I should have asked Ōshū to deliver it to you. I will follow her. *(As she is about to rise, a crow caws twice offstage.)* The sound of a crow, although the moon is not full. I feel uneasy. Perhaps it is a sign that my troubles have not yet ceased.

> *(SATSUKI rises and then stumbles at the edge of the veranda. One sharp ki clack. She poses, one foot on the stepping stone, the packet of money held out, anxiously looking after GOROZŌ, her head shaking from side to side. To rapid shamisen music and ki clacks, the curtain is run closed.)*

Late Night in the Licensed Quarter

> *(The curtain is run open to slow and melancholy shamisen music. The stage is in semidarkness. Visible through the gloom across the back is the heavy, wooden, latticed outer wall of a brothel, painted a deep red, topped with a roof, and with a large gateway to left. To left of the gateway hangs a single lantern near a huge barrel of water, used to extinguish fires. In a sudden clatter of tsuke beats, GOROZŌ stealthily runs in from the rear of the hanamichi. He wears a dark-blue kimono with a zigzag white pattern, tucked up into his obi to reveal his red under kimono. Reaching the stage, he strikes a mie, folding both arms behind his back.)*

GOROZŌ *(With determination):* Clouds cover the moon / but the crest on her lanterns / I would recognize anywhere. / Her robe's water streams and chrysanthemums, / a pretty shroud for the next world. / Though it is spring / thrown over by her, / autumn reigns in my heart, / and tonight / a late frost will surely fall. / When her life's dews fade away, / her corpse will remain / a warning to travelers / at this crossroads of all six worlds.

> *(Offstage drumbeats. GOROZŌ hurries toward the gateway, where he extinguishes the lantern with a thrust of his sword. A bell tolls once offstage. Slow shamisen and vocal music as GOROZŌ gingerly feels his way toward the water barrel and con-*

ceals himself behind it. From the rear of the hanamichi *appears an* ATTENDANT *carrying a crested lantern. He is followed by* ŌSHŪ, *wearing* SATSUKI *'s robe. Shod in the high clogs* [takageta] *favored by courtesans on public appearances, she steadies herself by resting a hand on the shoulder of an* ATTENDANT. *Their pace is slow and deliberate. They are followed by* DOEMON *and his* HENCHMEN. MAID *and lower-ranking prostitutes bring up the rear.* ŌSHŪ *stops at* shichisan.)

ŌSHŪ: Late nights in the quarter are so different from early evening. It truly is peaceful.

FIRST HENCHMAN: Peaceful is fine, but it's so quiet here my knees are knocking together and I can hardly walk.

SECOND HENCHMAN: And it feels like we're walking slower than the festival floats with their pipes and flutes.

THIRD HENCHMAN: At this rate, by the time we reach the Hanagataya . . .

FOURTH HENCHMAN: Dawn will be breaking and cocks will be crowing.

FIRST MAID: Indeed, as you gentlemen say . . .

SECOND MAID: It is late . . .

THIRD MAID: And we must . . .

MAID and HENCHMEN: Make haste.

ŌSHŪ: Don't be in such a hurry. I am going as fast as I can.

(*Offstage shamisen and vocal music, underlain with tense beats on the large drum* [dorodoro]. *As the party approaches the gateway,* GOROZŌ *suddenly appears from behind the barrel. He has shrugged his kimono off both shoulders so it dangles from his obi, revealing the scarlet under kimono. As the drumbeats suddenly increase, he strikes out the lantern with his sword.* ŌSHŪ *takes refuge in the gateway as the* HENCHMEN *attack.* GOROZŌ *easily fends them off, then strikes a tense* mie *brandishing his sword above his head, two* HENCHMEN *on either side of him. In a brief fight scene* [tachimawari] *to offstage shamisen,* tsuke, *and drum accompaniment,* GOROZŌ *skillfully drives them off right.* ŌSHŪ *tries to flee, but in the darkness she bumps into* GOROZŌ. *He thrusts her back and slices viciously at her shoulder with his sword. She cries out and collapses in the gateway.* GOROZŌ *strikes a* mie *with the sword concealed behind him. Slow offstage vocal, large drum, and shamisen music as he searches for the attackers.* ŌSHŪ *staggers toward him from behind, and they confront each other in languid and erotic slow motion. He slices at her repeatedly; she collapses to the ground, hurling tissue paper into the air to distract him. It flutters down slowly, forcing him backward. They strike a* mie, ŌSHŪ *lying on the ground, one hand held out protectively,* GOROZŌ *with the sword poised to strike. A bell tolls once. Back to the audience, she grabs his kimono from the front, imploring him to stop, but he shakes her off. She moves to embrace him from behind, slipping out of her over robe as he takes one end of it. They strike a* mie, *the robe stretched out between them and his sword arm raised threateningly. She pulls*

In one version of *Gorozō the Gallant,* Gorozō kills his enemy Doemon. In the finale, Gorozō (Ichikawa Ennosuke III), with his kimono top dropped to reveal his red under kimono, kneels beside the corpse of Doemon (Ichikawa Danshirō IV). Expressing his gratitude, he raises his sword respectfully to his forehead. (Umemura Yutaka, Engeki Shuppansha)

the robe from under his feet, sending him tumbling to the ground. Sitting, bodies touching, their mie *is a grotesque parody of a love scene. When she stands, he stabs at her again and again, missing in the darkness. At last he pulls her toward him and runs his sword deeply into her breast. Screaming, she falls behind the water barrel. He goes to check, then staggers backward and falls to his knees in anguished contrition.)*

GOROZŌ: Ōshū? How can it be? Forgive me, please. Having killed my master's love, how can I live on? I will soon follow you in death. Do not cling to resentment. . . . *(He clasps his hands in prayer for her soul. Then, wiping his eyes, he stands.)* But before I die, I will slaughter Doemon and send his soul to hell.

DOEMON *(From offstage):* Hey, Gorozō. I'm over here. What's the matter? Can't you see me?

GOROZŌ *(Looking all around, mystified):* I can hear your voice, but where are you? *(Sudden beating of the large drum signaling the supernatural* [usudorodoro]. DOEMON *appears from within the shadows of the gateway, his hands crossed over his face in a magical mudra. He wears a brown kimono, which he has slipped off both shoulders to show a grey under kimono trimmed in black. The two strike a* mie, GOROZŌ *with his sword out, ready to strike.)* Doemon, I'll have your life. Prepare yourself.

DOEMON *(Contemptuous):* You dare to draw your sword on me? As foolhardy an act as trying to count a tiger's whiskers. Stop now, while you still can.

GOROZŌ: Tiger's whiskers? I'd steal a dragon's jeweled scales, and I'll take your life while I'm at it!

DOEMON: You think you can?

GOROZŌ: I'll show you.

DOEMON: Sniveling wretch!

(The two fight fiercely to tsuke *and offstage shamisen and percussion accompaniment. They seem equally matched until* GOROZŌ *knocks* DOEMON *on the forehead with the hilt of his sword. As* DOEMON *falls to his knees, the lights instantly come up. He gets back on his feet, and the fight resumes as the curtain is drawn closed to accelerating* ki *clacks.)*

Three-panel woodblock print by Toyohara Kunichika (1835–
1900). Morita-za, Edo, fourth month 1864. "Scarface Otomi"
("Sawamura Tanosuke" III) raises a kitchen knife to kill "Bat
Yasu" ("Ichikawa Kuzō" III, later Ichikawa Danzō VII), who
has fallen to the ground before a huge statue of Buddha.
He holds out a hand defensively. Watching carefully from
the left, "Izutsu Yoemon" ("Sawamura Tosshō" II, later
Sawamura Sōjūrō VI) joins Otomi and Yasu in a powerful
group *mie*. (Tsubouchi Memorial Theatre Museum of
Waseda University)

Scarface Otomi
Kirare Otomi

Kawatake Mokuami
TRANSLATED BY VALERIE L. DURHAM

THE COTTAGE AT SATTA PASS
Satta Tōge Hitotsuya no Ba

OUTSIDE THE AKAMAYA BROTHEL
Akamaya Misesaki no Ba

INSIDE GENZAEMON'S QUARTERS
Dō Okuzashiki no Ba

THE CHIKUSHŌZUKA AT KITSUNEGASAKI
Kitsunegasaki Chikushōzuka no Ba

1864   MORITA-ZA, EDO

Scarface Otomi

INTRODUCTION

Scarface Otomi was written by Kawatake Mokuami (1816–1893) in 1864. Mokuami, then writing under the name of Kawatake Shinshichi II, was forty-eight and at the height of his power, fresh from his successes with *The Three Kichisas and the New Year's First Visit to the Pleasure Quarters* (Sannin Kichisa Kuruwa no Hatsugai, 1860), translated in this volume, and *Benten the Thief* (Aoto Zōshi Hana no Nishikie, 1862, trans. Ernst 1959 and Leiter 2000). *Scarface Otomi* originally opened in the fourth lunar month of 1864 under the title *Wakaba no Ume Ukina no Yokogushi*, but the production was halted on the second day of the run (some accounts say before the play's formal opening) when a fire destroyed the Morita-za. The play reopened in the seventh month of the same year under the title *Musume Gonomi Ukina no Yokogushi*. This title, like most of Mokuami's works, resists translation into a semantic whole. *Musume gonomi* can be roughly translated as "the maiden's preference," *ukina* refers to a lovers' scandal, and *yokogushi* is an ornamental boxwood comb worn to the side of the head in the chic manner affected by the play's heroine. As a phrase, *"ukina no yokogushi"* refers to Segawa Jokō III's (1806–1881) 1853 masterpiece popularly known as *Scarface Yosa* (Kirare Yosa; full title Yowa Nasake Ukina no Yokogushi, trans. Scott 1953), of which this play is a rewrite, with Yosaburō's lover, Otomi, taking over as the scar-faced main character. The *"musume"* in the title is also a reference to the fact that the role of the hero in this play has been rewritten as a female part.

In *Scarface Yosa*, Yosaburō (Yosa for short) is a merchant's son who falls in love with Otomi, the mistress of the gangster boss Genzaemon. When Yosa and Otomi's illicit relationship is discovered, Otomi's patron has Yosa tortured with knife cuts, resulting in horrible scars over his entire body. Later, Yosa teams up with a second-rate hood, Kōmori ("Bat") Yasu, to extort money from Otomi, whom he believes to have betrayed him. In *Scarface Otomi*, Yosaburō is the young heir of a samurai clan and is searching for an heirloom sword, the loss of which cost his father his life. Otomi is still the mistress of Genzaemon, but in this version it is Otomi who is tortured and mutilated when her love affair with Yosaburō is discovered. As in *Scarface Yosa*, this play's highlight is the extortion scene; here, the scarred Otomi, accompanied by her common-law husband "Bat" Yasu, goes to extort money from her old patron Genzaemon.

Just as Jokō's earlier play is commonly called *Scarface Yosa*, this work is usually referred to as *Scarface Otomi* and is classified as a "rewritten play" *(kakikae kyōgen)*. Plays in which the role of the hero was recast as a female character were particularly popular in the late Tokugawa period, when the breakdown of the traditional role system made possible the creation of somewhat androgynous heroines like Otomi. But this play is significant not merely as a rewrite: it both stands on its own dramatic merits and typifies the popular aesthetic of its age. Although *Scarface Otomi* is relatively short, it is tightly constructed, with each of its acts highlighted by the kind of scene enjoyed by late Tokugawa-period kabuki audiences, including a love scene *(nureba)*, torture scene *(semeba)*, extortion scene *(yusuriba)*, and murder scene *(koroshiba)*. The first two, however, are not included in this translation. The play as a whole is classified as a "domestic piece" *(sewamono)*, while the scenes translated here fall into the subcategory of "raw domestic piece" *(kizewamono)*, which depict in a realistic if somewhat stylized fashion the doings of thieves, extortionists, gamblers, prostitutes, and other denizens of the underworld.

Scarface Otomi is also a well-known example of an *akuba mono*, a play featuring a type of female villain called *"akuba."* Such roles were first popularized by playwright Tsuruya Nanboku IV (1755–1829) in *The Scandalous Love of Osome and Hisamatsu* (Osome Hisamatsu Ukina no Yomiuri, 1813), translated in this volume. As is typical of *akuba mono*, the climax of *Scarface Otomi's* extortion scene is the *akuba's* stylized speech of defiance in rhythmic lines of seven and five syllables *(shichigochō)*. Mokuami's scene borrows the pattern set by Nanboku in *Osome and Hisamatsu* of having the *akuba* team up with her husband, the wife motivated by feudal loyalty, the husband by hope of personal gain. Needless to say, the scene in *Scarface Otomi* also parodies the famous extortion scene in *Scarface Yosa*. Here, as in Jokō's original, "Bat" Yasu is by turns obsequious and bullying. Current versions of the play even include lines such as "When I leave here, I mean to take not only these hundred gold pieces, but everything in this household, down to the very ashes in the hearth!" which echo dialogue from the earlier work. An even subtler reference to Jokō's play is the use of the offstage "Bat Song" *(Kōmori no Aikata)* in Act II, scene 1, which recalls the performance by Ichikawa Danjūrō VIII (1823–1854) in the 1853 premiere of *Scarface Yosa*. Such touches are intended to delight audiences familiar with the older play.

Also representative of the *akuba* genre is the deadly confrontation between Otomi and Yasu that concludes the version translated here. The sadistically beautiful choreography of the fight scene's poses, Otomi's boldly checked black-and-white kimono, and her choice of kitchen knife as weapon are all touches that can be seen in any number of similar works in kabuki, as well as in woodblock prints and popular fiction.

Mokuami's original play contained nine scenes in three acts; this translation is of the four scenes that are performed in modern productions. Present-day productions eliminate several earlier scenes depicting a lovely, unscarred Otomi that counter her later disfigured appearance, and it can be argued that their absence today robs her role of much of its perverse eroticism. This seems especially true when we consider that *Scarface Otomi* was written for Sawamura Tanosuke III (1845–1878), then only nineteen. In the twentieth century, Otomi has been performed by more mature actors, losing much of the aesthetic focus of the original production on the contrast between Tanosuke's youth and physical beauty and Otomi's ugly scars.

Further, this translation reflects current production practice in that it ends with Otomi's murder of Yasu, thus eliminating the original's final scenes in which Otomi discovers that not only are she and Yosaburō long-lost siblings, but that the murdered Yasu, switched with Yosaburō at birth, is in fact her feudal lord. Although the heirloom sword is indeed retrieved and the Izutsu clan restored, incest and the murder of her lord are sins for which Otomi must pay with her life. The incestuous love between a sister and brother ignorant of their true relationship is a thematic device that had been used by Mokuami earlier in *Three Kichisas;* the word used to describe such relationships, *chikushōdō,* refers to the belief that incestuous sinners would be reborn as beasts in their next life. Hence the fatal confrontation between Otomi and Yasu is set in a place named Chikushōzuka, literally "Beast Grave Mound."

Scarface Otomi was the first of a number of works written by Mokuami for Tanosuke, a gifted and popular actor who excelled at *akuba* roles. His interpretation is said to live on in such touches as the elongation of the last two words in Otomi's line, "Boss, it's been quite a while . . . *hasn't it,*" in the Akamaya scene. Tragically, only a year after the premiere of *Scarface Otomi,* Tanosuke developed gangrene, which would rob him of each of his limbs, his sanity, and, finally, his life. Other actors in the original production included his older brother Sawamura Tosshō II (later Suketakaya Takasuke IV 1838–1886) as Yosaburō, Ichikawa Kuzō III (later Ichikawa Danzō VII 1836–1911) as "Bat" Yasu, and Nakamura Shikan IV (1830-1899) as Genzaemon.

The somewhat peculiar aesthetic of this work, while typical of late Tokugawa-period kabuki, ran counter to the dramatic ideals soon to be espoused by Meiji dramatic reformers, leading this play to fall into disfavor with mainstream troupes.

But Otomi was too choice a role to be lost to the repertoire entirely. One actor instrumental in preserving the play was Sawamura Gennosuke IV (1859–1936), well known for his portrayal of *akuba*. Beginning in 1888, he performed Otomi in more than twenty productions; his legacy has been preserved in such details as the melody "Ōtsu pictures" *(Ōtsu-e aikata)*, which accompanies the extortion scene. Other actors who have excelled as Otomi include Kawarasaki Kunitarō V (1909– 1990), Onoe Baikō VI (1870–1934), Nakamura Tokizō III (1895–1959), and, in more recent years, Sawamura Sōjūrō IX (b. 1933) and Ichikawa Ennosuke III (b. 1939).

This translation is based on the script for the January 1992 production at the Kokuritsu Gekijō (National Theatre of Japan) and a videotape of the same production. Offstage music *(geza)* notations are taken from the video, the script, and the musicians' score *(tsukechō)*. Versions of the play that are more faithful to Moku-ami's original may be found in Kawatake Itojo and Kawatake Shigetoshi, eds., *Moku-ami Zenshū*, Vol. 7, and Toita Yasuji et al., eds., *Meisaku Kabuki Zenshū*, Vol. 23.

CHARACTERS

"SCARFACE" OTOMI, *wife of* "BAT" YASU, *lover of* IZUTSU YOSABURŌ, *and former mistress of* AKAMAYA GENZAEMON

IZUTSU YOSABURŌ, rōnin *searching for the Hokutomaru sword; lover of* OTOMI

"BAT" YASU, *husband of* OTOMI *and former henchman of* AKAMAYA GENZAEMON

AKAMAYA GENZAEMON, *former patron of* OTOMI; *proprietor of the Akamaya brothel, but really a thief named* KANNON ("GODDESS OF MERCY") KYŪJI

OTAKI, *wife of* AKAMAYA GENZAEMON

IWA, *palanquin bearer*

MATSU, *palanquin bearer*

KISUKE, *employee of Akamaya brothel*

TASUKE, *employee of Akamaya brothel*

HOZUMI KŌJŪRŌ, *police officer posing as a traveling merchant*

SANKICHI, *restaurant delivery boy*

FUKUYAMA, *prostitute at Akamaya brothel*

CHIDORI, *prostitute at Akamaya brothel*

KOCHŌ, *prostitute at Akamaya brothel*

KOKONOE, *prostitute at Akamaya brothel*

DEKOICHI, *blind masseur*

OKIN, *child maid at Akamaya brothel*

THREE TRAVELERS

POLICE OFFICERS

The Cottage at Satta Pass

(While the curtain is still closed, we hear two sharp clacks of the ki *followed by two preliminary beats of the large offstage drum* [ōdaiko]. *Then we hear the low drum-beat that represents the sound of waves* [nami no oto] *and a sprightly packhorse drivers' song* [mago uta] *titled* "Kasa o Te ni Mochi" ["With My Reed Hat in Hand"] *accompanied by shamisen. Both this song and the offstage bells* [ekiro] *representing the sound of packhorse harness bells indicate a scene along a thorough-fare. The curtain opens to accelerating* ki *clacks, music, and drum wave pattern, with one final loud clack of the* ki *signaling the dialogue to begin. The setting is an isolated cottage at Satta Pass along the East Sea Highway* [Tōkaidō], *in what is now Shizuoka Prefecture. This is the home of* "SCARFACE" OTOMI, *who runs a wayside teahouse for travelers. It is a humble dwelling with a thatched roof. Center is a small* tatami *room with a divided curtain* [noren] *leading inside. Right is a dirt-floored entrance area. In the distance are craggy mountain peaks and the sea and, beyond them, Mount Fuji. It is twilight, and* THREE TRAVELERS, *all women, are taking a rest. They are dressed for the road, with raised kimono hems and leggings, their reed hats beside them on the ground as they sit drinking tea.)*

FIRST TRAVELER: Even though I left my inn around three this morning, I'm from Edo, and I didn't realize how soon night falls in these mountain passes.

SECOND TRAVELER: Too bad it's dark now, but they say that during the daytime you can see all the way to the plains at the foot of Mount Fuji from this pass.

THIRD TRAVELER: That's right. I've heard that in the old days they used to call this pass the "Mountain from Which You Can See Mount Fuji."

FIRST TRAVELER: Well, we've rested enough. We'd better get going.

(Standing up, the TRAVELERS *take up their hats and put their payment on the veranda.)*

SECOND TRAVELER: Yes, let's go. *(To the proprietress inside.)* Missus!

ALL: We're leaving the money here. We're off!

(Offstage shamisen play the packhorse drivers' song as two TRAVELERS *exit right and one exits left. A temple bell* [toki no kane] *tolls the time in the distance. To drum wave pattern and sea chantey* [hama uta] *titled* "Oki no Susaki Uta" ["Shoals in the Offing"] *sung to shamisen accompaniment,* IZUTSU YOSABURŌ *enters along the* hanamichi. *The temple bell tolls again.* YOSA-BURŌ *is dressed for travel in a blue polka-dot kimono hitched to midcalf length over dark-blue leggings. He wears a dark-blue* haori *and straw sandals and carries a small cylindrical paper lantern in his hand. His white makeup and stylish costume indicate he is a young romantic lead* [nimaime]. *Although he wears the two swords of a samurai at his waist, the grown-out hair on his crown indicates that he is now a* rōnin. YOSABURŌ *stops at* shichisan, *and the song ceases. Shamisen accompaniment continues in the background.)*

YOSABURŌ *(Speaking in the formal manner of a samurai):* That must be the vespers bell. I am going to need a light once I am in the mountains. Luckily, there is a cottage over there where I can get a light for my lantern. *(Sea chantey and wave pattern resume as he crosses left to the veranda.)* Excuse me!

OTOMI *(From inside):* Yes, yes. Who is it?

> *(Song resumes as* OTOMI *comes out from inside the hut through the flower-patterned divided curtain. She is carrying a standing lantern* [andon], *which she places on the floor next to the curtain. She is dressed in a dark blue-and-white striped kimono with trailing hems, a white underskirt, and no under-collar. Her obi is of black satin with a lining of yellow-and-black plaid* [kihachijō] *and is tied in front in a flat, tab-like bow. A plain white cotton hand towel* [tenugui], *wrapped about* OTOMI*'s head in the manner of a housewife, partially conceals the scars on her face. The song stops, with the shamisen accompaniment for the sea chantey and wave pattern continuing.)*

YOSABURŌ *(Holding up his lantern for her to see):* If it would not be too much trouble, I would greatly appreciate your giving me a light for my lantern. *(Puts the lantern on the edge of the veranda.)*

OTOMI *(Looking outside at the sky):* With this rain we've been having, the tinder's too damp to be of any use. Hand me the candle from your lantern and I'll light it for you. *(She picks up the standing lantern and brings it closer to the veranda, where* YOSABURŌ *still stands.)*

YOSABURŌ: I am most grateful.

> *(He takes the candle for his lantern out of his sleeve and sets it on the veranda next to the lantern.* OTOMI *picks up the lantern and candle. As she does so, she and* YOSABURŌ *catch sight of one another's faces, illuminated in the light of the standing lantern. They are shocked to recognize each other. The music stops.)*

OTOMI *(In her surprise, she drops the unlit candle and lantern):* Is that you . . . Yosaburō?

YOSABURŌ: And you're . . . Otomi?

OTOMI: You mustn't . . .

> *(Still kneeling, she pulls away, trying to escape, but* YOSABURŌ *holds her back by her sleeve.* OTOMI *averts her face and covers her cheek with her hand in an attempt to hide her scars.)*

YOSABURŌ: Are you ashamed to have me see you in your present humble state, so different from when I first knew you?

OTOMI *(With her face still averted and the hand hiding her face trembling):* No, but . . .

YOSABURŌ: If that is not the case, then why do you try to escape?

OTOMI: It's . . .

YOSABURŌ: Have you grown tired of this Yosaburō?

OTOMI *(Face still averted):* How can you say such a thing!

YOSABURŌ *(Lets go of her sleeve):* Otomi, have your feelings changed?

OTOMI *(Slowly letting down the hand hiding her face):* No, my feelings have not changed. But, Yosaburō, my face has . . . look!

(She removes the towel from her head, revealing ugly scars: a crescent-shaped mark on her forehead, an X-shaped one on her left cheek, and a long slash on her right. Another scar is visible on her chest just above the kimono collar. Her hair is in the "horsetail" [uma no shippo] *style, a simple ponytail that has been looped over itself. Her sole hair ornament is a boxwood comb worn in the hair on the right side of her head.)*

YOSABURŌ: What are those marks on your forehead, your face?

OTOMI: Yosaburō, please listen as I tell the tale of how I got these scars. *(She remains kneeling inside the house;* YOSABURŌ *seats himself on the edge of the veranda left. A soft and slow shamisen accompaniment, "Yamanba"* ["Mountain Witch"], *begins.* OTOMI *gestures with her hand towel as she speaks.)* That day after we parted after our meeting at the shrine at the crossroads, I returned home, only to have a scoundrel named "Clamshell Matsu" tell my master of our tryst. Make excuses though I might, there was no hiding the fact that I had cut off a finger with your dagger as a pledge of love to you. My master was posing as a rich silk merchant from Jōshū named Akama, but in truth he was a gambling boss notorious in the regions of Dewa and Ōshū. He said, "No one shames me like this and lives! Tell me the name of your lover!" and ordered his henchmen to torture me with knife cuts. But as I had reconciled myself to death, I was somehow able to withstand the pain without revealing your name. To my great fortune, I lost consciousness, and they took me for dead. I was put into a wicker box, but as I was being carried off, I revived. It was Yasuzō who had been given the task of disposing of my corpse, but instead he nursed me back to health. After that, we went to live secretly in the countryside at Atsugi. There, I made a living by going from inn to inn performing the ballads that were my specialty. Meanwhile, Yasuzō demanded repayment for having saved my life, and I had no choice but to submit to his desires. Yet even in my changed state, there has never once been a moment when I have forgotten you and our love.

*(*OTOMI *weeps, pressing her face against her towel.* YOSABURŌ *also dabs at his eyes with his own hand towel.)*

YOSABURŌ: Looking back, it seems that it was an unlucky bond that we forged, that first night we spent together on the pleasure boat at Kisarazu. And then if we had not met again in Kamakura, you would not have been transformed into the pitiful figure I see before me now. Doubtless your parents must hold me responsible for your misfortune. But speaking of your parents . . . whence hails your father, and what might be his station in life?

OTOMI: My father is now a masseur who goes by the name of Jōga. But he was once a retainer of the Chiba clan of Shimōsa, where he served the samurai Izutsu Yozaemon *(bows her head briefly in respect)* and went by the name of Chūsuke.

YOSABURŌ *(Reacts with surprise. Shamisen accompaniment stops):* Your father was Chūsuke, in service to the Izutsu clan?

OTOMI: Do you know of him?

YOSABURŌ: Know of him? Your father's master, Izutsu Yozaemon, was my father! *(OTOMI is shocked. At this moment Yasuzō, who now goes by the name "BAT" YASU because of the bat tattooed on his cheek, returns home, entering right. He wears a light-blue jacket [happi] belted like a kimono, with only a bellyband and loincloth beneath. His bare feet are thrust into cheap straw sandals. The blue of his pate is shaded to suggest that it has not been shaved too recently, hinting at his seedy nature. Overhearing the conversation inside, he hides by the side of the cottage, where he continues to eavesdrop.)*

OTOMI: Out of my ignorance of the fact that you are my liege lord, I have committed the deepest disrespect! To have received your kind favor, not once but twice, was divine providence. Surely Father would be overjoyed to learn of this!

YOSABURŌ: If I still retained my former status, I would be able to rescue both you and your father from your present troubles. But now the only thing I still possess from my former life is my name; I do not have even a fixed abode.

OTOMI: The Izutsu clan was once famous as a great family. How come you, then, to be in your present state?

YOSABURŌ: Allow me to tell you my tale. *(Shamisen accompaniment resumes, and* YASU *goes to hide behind the cottage.* YOSABURŌ *gestures with his hand towel as he speaks.)* Five years ago, the Hokutomaru sword, a clan treasure with which my father had been entrusted, was stolen. In expiation for the sword's loss, my father committed suicide by ritual disembowelment. Afterward, I wandered here and there in search of the lost sword and finally succeeded in finding what is unquestionably the lost Hokutomaru in a curio shop in Fuchū. I could barely contain my joy when I found it, but the price for redeeming the sword is two hundred pieces of gold. Without that money I will be unable to gain possession of the sword. If I cannot come up with the necessary sum, I, too, shall have to cut open my belly in atonement. Because I am so determined, this is the last time we shall meet in this life. If, in the future, you should have occasion to remember me, please offer up a cup of water in my memory. *(Joins hands and bows his head in supplication. Shamisen accompaniment stops.)* Otomi, I bid you farewell.

(YOSABURŌ stands to leave, but OTOMI takes his hand and holds him back.)

OTOMI: Please, wait just a moment, I beg you!

YOSABURŌ: No, I must hurry. Farewell until we meet again.

OTOMI: I understand your position well, but what if, before the night is over, I am somehow able to obtain the two hundred gold pieces you need to gain possession of the lost sword? I understand your hurry, but young lord, I beg you to wait. *(She forces* YOSABURŌ *to sit down again on the edge of the veranda.)*

YOSABURŌ: I am most grateful for your concern, but in your present circumstances, so changed from the past, how could you ever hope to obtain two hundred gold pieces?

OTOMI: Getting such a sum is beyond any ordinary means. *(Her heretofore soft and feminine way of speaking suddenly becomes louder and more declamatory.)* But a woman who loves truly will think nothing of extortion and blackmail.

YOSABURŌ *(Startled)*: What's that?

OTOMI: Oh, nothing! In any event, I have a sure source for the money. I shall get it to you without fail, no later than tomorrow evening.

YOSABURŌ: So you will raise the money for me?

OTOMI: Surely.

YOSABURŌ: I have no words with which to express my gratitude. *(He joins his hands and bows his head in thanks. The metallic clang of a prayer bell* [darani no kane] *is heard.)*

OTOMI: That will be the prayer bell at Seigan Temple. *(She turns to light* YOSABURŌ*'s candle with the flame of the standing lantern.)*

YOSABURŌ: It would be awkward if Yasuzō were to find me here like this. *(Stands.)* I ask only that you somehow raise the money.

OTOMI: You need not worry. *(Hands the lighted lantern to* YOSABURŌ.*)* And where is it that you are staying?

YOSABURŌ: Near the entrance to the post town of Fuchū. You will find me by the back gate of Jōnen Temple, at the house with the willow tree at the corner.

OTOMI: It is most convenient that you are staying in Fuchū, for I can call on you on my way back from getting the money. Please wait there until I come. *(Bows slightly.)*

YOSABURŌ: Until then . . . Otomi.

OTOMI: Lord Yosaburō.

YOSABURŌ: I wait in expectation of good tidings.

(To wave pattern and the sea chantey with song YOSABURŌ *exits left.* OTOMI *picks up the hems of her kimono and steps down from the hut to see him off, ad-libbing good-bye. As she stands looking after him, the accompaniment ceases. A temple bell tolls in the distance.)*

OTOMI: The Yosaburō to whom I gave myself at Kisarazu with all the heedless passion of a young girl was, in fact, the son of my feudal lord. *(Lowers her head slightly in respect.)* Now is my opportunity to repay my obligation to him. *(The temple bell sounds once more. As* OTOMI *continues speaking, her voice gradually lowers in pitch.*) The two hundred gold pieces I promised to get by tomorrow is a small fortune. But I have a sure source for the money in the new brothel I have heard about of late, the Akamaya in Miroku. Is its owner indeed the Genzaemon I know? There must be some way to find out.

(To wave pattern on the large drum the palanquin bearers IWA *and* MATSU *enter from right, carrying an empty palanquin on their shoulders. They wear their kimono hitched up very short in back and are barefoot.)*

IWA: Hey, Sis!

OTOMI *(Startled at first, then cordial when she recognizes them):* Well, if it isn't Iwa and Matsu!

(Shamisen accompaniment reverts to the packhorse drivers' song. OTOMI *steps back into the cottage, and* IWA *and* MATSU *set down the palanquin, right.)*

MATSU: Sorry not to have been by to see you for a while!

OTOMI: And when are you going to return that money I lent you the other day?

MATSU *(Gets a packet from the palanquin and bows to* OTOMI *):* Awfully sorry, ma'am. Would you please take these as a pledge and wait a few more days? *(Standing next to the veranda at right, he hands* OTOMI *a bundle of folded garments.)*

OTOMI: So, you want me to take these until you can pay me back, eh?

*(*MATSU *bows again politely.* OTOMI *takes the bundle and looks at its contents: a kimono in a bold black-and-white check and a dark-green jacket with velvet trimming of a type worn by procurers who sell women to brothels. She sits in the center of the room, placing the clothes on the floor beside her.)*

IWA: In return, we promise to bring the money in two or three days.

OTOMI: Well, if that's the case, I'll wait. Anyway, why don't you have some tea before you go? *(*IWA *and* MATSU *ad-lib as they carry teacups and the teapot outside and go to a wooden bench right of the hut, where they sit and begin to drink their tea. Meanwhile,* OTOMI *sits inside the cottage, smoking a long-stemmed pipe.)* You two always seem to be barely getting by, but recently the post town is doing a good business, and I hear that palanquin bearers there are making a lot of money.

IWA: What? Nothing of the sort! What about you, Matsu? You said the other day that you'd gotten a good job.

MATSU: That? *(Takes the towel from his neck and gestures with it.)* It wasn't anything special. Three of us were hired to carry a palanquin to Miroku, and each of us got a tip of one silver coin. But Miroku is sure doing good business.

IWA: Are things really that good in Miroku?

MATSU: They sure are. And the busiest place of them all is the Akamaya, they say.

*(*OTOMI *stops smoking and knocks the tobacco out of her pipe with a sharp rap.)*

OTOMI: Matsu, wait a minute. The Akamaya . . . isn't that the new brothel I've been hearing about? And do you know anything about the owner?

330

MATSU: I don't know the details, but they say he used to be a gambling boss from Ōshū known as Kannon Kyūji.

OTOMI *(Her suspicions are confirmed):* What? Kannon Kyūji? So, he really *is* . . . *(she collects herself)* oh, you don't say.

MATSU: Rumor has it that he's always got two or three hundred gold pieces just lying around his private quarters.

IWA: Makes a man jealous to hear a story like that.

OTOMI: You guys—I've got something to ask you. *(Accompaniment stops.)* Will you do me a favor?

IWA: What is it?

OTOMI: Well, in fact, I'd like to go right now to that Akamaya you've been talking about. Will you take me there?

MATSU *(Eager at the prospect of work):* Sure, nothing could be simpler.

IWA: Just wait a bit while we catch a quick bite of some noodles.

OTOMI: All right. But be back as quickly as you can.

BOTH: Sure, we'll be back in a jiffy.

OTOMI: Don't forget, now. I'm depending on you. *(To the packhorse drivers' song and wave pattern beat on the large drum the two shoulder the palanquin and exit right. OTOMI rises to see them off. The accompaniment ceases. Still standing, she begins to speak in low, almost masculine, tones.)* Well, there can be no doubt that it is Genzaemon they were talking about just now. The time has come at long last for me to pay him back for these scars. *(She pulls up her kimono sleeve and briefly looks at a scar on the underside of her forearm.)* If I threaten to expose Genzaemon's past, he'll cough up two hundred gold pieces readily enough. And I'll trick "Bat" Yasu into going along as my partner. *(In a loud and declamatory fashion.)* For if it is for the sake of love, or loyalty to my lord, I'll make myself hateful, and subject myself to the insults of others. . . . *(Stretches and yawns.)* Yes, that's just what I'll have to do.

(During this speech, YASU comes out of hiding, right. Folding his arms, he addresses OTOMI.)

YASU: Otomi!

OTOMI *(Jumps):* Oh! You startled me!

YASU: I'm home. *(Unfolding his arms and pushing up the sleeves of his jacket, he crosses stage to center, to a slow and sinister shamisen accompaniment.)*

OTOMI: What, you're back? You're awfully late. Where have you been all this time? *(OTOMI sits in the middle of the room and begins to smoke. YASU seats himself on the edge of the veranda, left, in the same spot where YOSABURŌ sat earlier.)*

YASU: Well, just listen to this. I went gambling, see, and all I wanted was to break even so I could go home. But instead, I ended up owing *them* money.

OTOMI *(Ironically):* Quite an accomplishment!

YASU: You make me feel even worse when you say that. *(Laughing self-consciously, he briefly touches his pate with an embarrassed gesture.)* By the way, do we have any sake?

OTOMI *(Gestures with her pipe):* There's enough for a nightcap, but nothing to eat with it. Let me warm it up a bit for you. *(She stands up.)*

YASU: No, don't bother. Cold will be fine.

OTOMI: Really? You don't mind?

> *(She goes to get an earthenware sake jug and a towel-covered tray that are resting on the floor next to the standing screen, left, and sets them down on the floor, center. Meanwhile,* YASU *steps up into the room and briefly squats over a small charcoal brazier to warm himself between his legs. Then he goes to sit cross-legged on the floor, center, next to the sake bottle and tray.* OTOMI *sits down next to* YASU *and pours sake for him into an earthenware cup. He drinks with evident thirst.)*

YASU: My, this is tasty. It was nice of you to have bought such good sake for me. *(Drains his cup.)* Ah, that hits the spot!

OTOMI: How about some more? *(She pours again.)*

YASU *(Recalling his gambling losses):* I win, then lose, win and lose . . . my luck's just no good these days.

OTOMI: You're just like a human bamboo shoot—as soon as you show your head above-ground, you get cut down.

YASU: That's exactly right. *(Looks around him before speaking in confidential tones.)* By the way, Otomi, do you have any good ideas for making some money? *(His manner makes it obvious to the audience, but not to* OTOMI, *that he knows what the answer will be.)*

OTOMI *(Rubbing the palms of her hands together as if thinking):* Yes, in fact, I've got a plan in mind that's a sure thing. *(She gives him a sideways glance.)* Want to go along?

YASU *(As if he has no idea what she is about to say):* Sounds tempting, but what kind of job is it?

OTOMI: You know that new brothel called the Akamaya? They say it's run by Genzaemon!

YASU *(Pretending to be surprised, he puts down his sake cup with a clatter):* What! When you say Genzaemon, do you mean Kannon Kyūji, the guy who cut you up?

OTOMI: That's right, Kannon Kyūji. He's gone straight and now runs a brothel. They say he always has two or three hundred gold pieces just lying around his quarters!

YASU *(Sitting up):* Where'd you hear this?

OTOMI: From Iwa and Matsu, the palanquin bearers. They're going to come back in a minute, so you can ask them yourself.

> *(Shamisen accompaniment stops.)*

YASU: Well, well. It's a good thing for us he's gone straight. *(Voice darkens.)* All we'll have to do is hint about his past . . .

OTOMI: And blackmail him for the sake of my lord.

YASU *(Startled):* What?

OTOMI *(She laughs self-consciously and puts her hand on his shoulder):* I said, I'll do anything for *your* sake, dear.

YASU *(Chuckling good-naturedly):* You sure know how to flatter a fellow! Anyway, what's our strategy going to be for our little "visit" to the Akamaya?

OTOMI: Lend me your ear a minute, Yasu.

(*He cleans his ear with his finger, and she hides her mouth with her sleeve as she prepares to whisper into his ear. Before she can say anything, however, from offstage is heard a loud voice singing a packhorse bearers' song* [kumosuke uta]. *The two jump backward in surprise, and a sharp clack of the* ki [ki no kashira] *sounds, setting up the conclusion of the scene.*)

OTOMI *(In loud, masculine tones):* You startled me!

OFFSTAGE SINGERS:

The distance between us . . . / the greater it grows, / the weaker grow the ties that bind us . . .

(*As the curtain begins to close,* OTOMI *shows* YASU *the bundle of clothes left by* MATSU *and pantomimes her plan. Accompanying the curtain are the lyrics and shamisen music of the packhorse drivers' song* [mago(no) uta], *joined by the wave pattern on the large drum, packhorse bells, and rapidly accelerating* ki *clacks* [kizami]. *After the curtain has closed, the big drum plays the pattern for wind* [kazaoto] *that acts as a link* [tsunagi] *to the next act.*)

Outside the Akamaya Brothel

(*Wind pattern on the large drum reaches a climax, and two sharp clacks of the* ki *signal the start of* "Omae Sono Yō Ni" ["When You Drink Like That"], *sung to shamisen, stick drum* [taiko], *and metal gong* [dorabuchi] *accompaniment. This lively music evokes the bustling atmosphere of a post town. The curtain opens to slowly accelerating* ki *beats. The setting is the street outside the Akamaya brothel in Miroku, the licensed prostitution quarter of Fuchū in present-day Shizuoka City. It is a prosperous-looking establishment, with latticed windows flanking a raised portico. The divided curtain leading inside is dyed in the terra-cotta color associated with brothels, with large white characters reading* "Akamaya." *A square wooden water tank stands on the ground, left.* KISUKE *and* TASUKE, *two young employees of the Akamaya, are sweeping the street and sprinkling water to keep down the dust. They wear dark kimono hitched up over light-blue pants. Three ladies of the establishment,* FUKUYAMA, CHIDORI, *and* KOCHŌ, *are sitting in the entranceway waiting for customers. They are dressed in the manner of cheap prostitutes, in red under kimono and striped outer robes* [uchikake]. SANKICHI, *a delivery boy for a catering shop, enters right. He wears a livery coat* [happi] *over a hitched-up kimono and*) *light-blue pants and is carrying a tray on his shoulder. The song stops, with the shamisen accompaniment continuing.)*

SANKICHI: Sorry to have kept you waiting! *(Removes the towel tied around his head.)*

KISUKE: Dinner's ready, is it? Much obliged. *(Takes the tray and goes inside.)*

SANKICHI: Fuku and Chidori . . . busy as ever, I see.

FUKUYAMA: Please show some sympathy for us, Sankichi. It's no fun, always being the last chosen. *(She is playing a fortune-telling game in which twisted paper cords are tied together in order to predict whether someone for whom one waits will come or not.)*

CHIDORI: Ah, it doesn't matter who it is, let somebody, anybody, buy me . . .

KOCHŌ: Fukuyama, Chidori—despite what you say, everyone knows you have sweethearts you're waiting for.

FUKUYAMA: My, don't you talk big, Little Chō. Everything looks rosy to *you* because *you've* got a customer tonight.

TASUKE: Anyway, Fukuyama, what do you have to worry about? Your boyfriend Yoshi is sure to come any moment now.

SANKICHI: If you really mean it when you say that anyone will do, let me find you a customer.

CHIDORI: Really? Oh, please, please! *(Joins her hands in a praying gesture and bows prettily.)*

SANKICHI: All right, then. Let's see, there must be someone. . . . *(We hear the whistle of an approaching masseur advertising for customers. This gives* SANKICHI *an idea.)* Aha, a good customer is on his way now. Perfect, just perfect!

CHIDORI: Where?

SANKICHI: From over there. You'd better pretty yourself up for him!

(SANKICHI gestures for CHIDORI to come. Straightening her hair and holding up the sides of her outer robe so as not to trip, she stands and moves upstage to the entrance of the shop. DEKOICHI, a blind masseur with a shaved head, his kimono hitched up to midcalf length over light-blue pants, enters right, tapping with his cane.)

CHIDORI: Oh, I'm so happy. Where did you say he is? *(Looking around her, she sees no one who seems like a potential customer.)* There's no one there.

SANKICHI: Just you wait. *(He takes DEKOICHI by the hand and leads him over to CHIDORI. He calls out in the loud voice of a brothel servant announcing the arrival of a customer.)* Your customer has arrived!

CHIDORI *(Startled): That's* a customer? Sankichi, stop making fun of me. It's bad luck.

SANKICHI: But you said any customer would do.

DEKOICHI: Did you say "customer"? Please lead me to the customer's room. Who might it be?

CHIDORI: You're no customer of mine!

DEKOICHI: But didn't someone just say "customer"?

(He takes CHIDORI*'s hand, and she flings it from her angrily. He falls away, stumbling, as she stamps her foot in rage.)*

CHIDORI: You're disgusting! Leave me alone!

(Gathering her robe around her angrily, CHIDORI *goes inside.* TASUKE *has been watching the proceedings with amusement. He and* SANKICHI *laugh.)*

DEKOICHI *(Screaming):* Rotten hussy! Hmph! *(He exits left to the clatter of his wooden clogs and the furious tapping of his cane.)*

TASUKE: Hey, Sankichi. Chidori's awfully mad. It looks like you'll have to be her customer for tonight.

SANKICHI: You can't be serious!

TASUKE: And surely you can spring a little for the masseur, too.

SANKICHI: All right, I guess I don't have any choice. Have her wait until I come back.

TASUKE: Certainly. *(Shouting inside.)* A customer!

*(*SANKICHI *exits.* FUKUYAMA *continues playing the fortune-telling game. From inside the brothel* KOKONOE*, another prostitute, comes out and sits down.)*

KOKONOE: Kochō! Your customer's been making quite a fuss, looking for you. Please hurry up and go back to him.

KOCHŌ: Leave me alone, Kokonoe. I'm just trying to make him jealous.

KOKONOE: Well, well, you two must be pretty close, if you're having a lover's quarrel. You owe me one for this. Come on, now! *(She takes* KOCHŌ*'s hand. Ad-libbing, the two go inside.)*

TASUKE: It's a rare night that finds you alone like this. Where's that customer who always comes to visit you?

FUKUYAMA *(Unhappily):* I keep on playing the waiting game, but no matter how many times I do it, the knots just slip out. *(She shows him how the paper knot comes undone.)*

TASUKE *(Brightly):* Maybe it means he'll "slip out" from wherever he is and come to meet you. It's probably a good sign.

FUKUYAMA: Oh, I hope that's what it means!

TASUKE: "Slip out" . . . that's a good one. Yes, I'm sure someone's going to come very soon.

(Offstage singers resume "When You Drink Like That" to shamisen, stick drum, and gong accompaniment as HOZUMI KŌJŪRŌ*, a police officer on the trail of* AKAMAYA GENZAEMON*, enters along the* hanamichi*. Dressed as a traveling merchant, he wears a grey kimono tucked up behind for ease of movement and over it, a dark jacket and brown cloak with polka-dot lining. He has on light-colored leggings and lace-up straw sandals. He is carrying a sedge hat and wears a single sword in his obi. The song gives way to shamisen accompaniment as he stops at* shichisan.*)*

KŌJŪRŌ *(Looking around him):* I'd heard that Fuchū was a bustling town, but I hadn't expected Miroku to be this lively.

(Song resumes as he crosses to the stage. KISUKE *comes out.)*

KISUKE: Hey, mister! I'll give you a good deal. How about it?

KŌJŪRŌ: Well, I've got to stay somewhere. This must be the Akamaya that everyone's talking about.

KISUKE: That's right.

KŌJŪRŌ: In that case, I'll stay here tonight. *(Hands* KISUKE *his hat.)*

TASUKE: We still have a lot of girls who haven't been spoken for yet. Come inside and take your pick.

KŌJŪRŌ *(Removing his cloak and handing it to* TASUKE *):* That won't be necessary. I'll just take the girl here. *(He lets down his kimono and sits down on the raised ledge of the shop entrance to untie his sandals.)*

KISUKE: Certainly, sir. *(To* FUKUYAMA.*)* You've got a customer.

FUKUYAMA: Really? Oh, thank goodness!

(KŌJŪRŌ rises to go inside. Shamisen accompaniment stops.)

KISUKE: We'll be keeping your sword for you, sir.

(KISUKE and TASUKE bow respectfully to KŌJŪRŌ.)

KŌJŪRŌ *(Suspicious):* What? I have to check my sword?

KISUKE *(Deferentially):* Yes, that's the rule in Miroku.

KŌJŪRŌ *(To himself):* If I have to check my sword *(looking around him),* then this must indeed be the house of . . .

KISUKE and TASUKE: What?

KŌJŪRŌ: I said, I'll be glad to stay in this house.

(Shamisen accompaniment resumes as he hands KISUKE *his sword.)*

KISUKE *(Calling inside):* We have a customer!

(Shamisen accompaniment ceases as KISUKE *and* FUKUYAMA *accompany* KŌJŪRŌ *inside.* TASUKE *takes* KŌJŪRŌ *'s sandals and puts them away. He then takes a bunch of wooden tags on cords and hits them against the floor. Next, holding one tag, he taps it in a rhythmic pattern against the doorpost. This ritual, called "the squeaking of a rat"* [nezumi naki], *signals the beginning of the night's business for the brothel.* TASUKE *then carries the tag and shoes inside.* GENZAEMON, *the proprietor, comes out through the divided curtain, center. He wears a beige kimono with a black under-collar and over it, like a coat, a striped padded kimono* [dotera]. *The heavy black makeup around his eyes hints at his true character.)*

GENZAEMON: Kisuke! Come here!

(KISUKE, reentering, kneels to address his employer.)

KISUKE: Is there something you wish, Master?

GENZAEMON: That merchant who just came in . . . he's a samurai.

KISUKE: How do you know that?

GENZAEMON: It's the way he wears his sword. Come here a minute. *(KISUKE stands up and goes over to* GENZAEMON, *who whispers in his ear.)* So watch out for him.

KISUKE: I see.

> *(The offstage singers sing* "Komori no Aikata" ["Bat Song"] *to lively and rhythmic accompaniment of shamisen and stick drum.* IWA *and* MATSU *enter on the* hanamichi, *carrying a palanquin.* YASU, *now wearing a respectable dark kimono, black leggings, white socks, and clogs, follows behind. A blue-and-white hand towel with a design of pine needles is wrapped around his head. Over his kimono he wears the procurer's dark-green* haori *that* OTOMI *gave him. They all stop at* shichisan, *and the song gives way to shamisen accompaniment.)*

IWA: Hey, brother, that's the Akamaya over there.

MATSU: Do you want us to pull up to the front?

YASU: No, I have some business with the boss. Just pull up to the side.

IWA and MATSU: Will do.

> *(Song and drum accompaniment resumes as they proceed to the main stage, where* IWA *and* MATSU *set the palanquin beside the main entrance.)*

IWA: We've brought a customer!

> *(Song and drum accompaniment cease, with only shamisen accompaniment continuing.)*

KISUKE *(Coming to greet them at the side door)*: Bearers, take your passenger over there. *(Gestures to the front, where a customer would ordinarily be dropped off.)*

IWA and MATSU: But this customer has some business with the boss.

> *(KISUKE hurriedly puts on sandals and comes out. Meanwhile,* GENZAEMON *has recognized* YASU *and senses trouble. He stands up and attempts to slip inside before he is noticed by the newcomers.)*

YASU *(Letting down the hems of his kimono)*: Pardon the intrusion. *(To* GENZAEMON.*)* Ah, sir, if you'll just wait a moment.

> *(GENZAEMON stops.)*

GENZAEMON: Who's that calling me?

YASU *(Removing the towel from his head and bowing)*: It's me, Yasuzō.

GENZAEMON: Yasuzō, is it? *(Seeing he has no choice.)* Well, well, why don't you just step up here?

YASU: Don't mind if I do. *(Steps up onto the raised platform and sits on the lower level, right.)* It's been quite a while, but *(looking around him)* you seem to be doing well, as always.

GENZAEMON: Passably well, I suppose. My wife's family is in this line of work, so I just ended up going into the business, too. But thank you, we're making a profit.

YASU: Well, that's all that matters.

GENZAEMON *(Accompaniment ceases momentarily as he peers closely at* YASU *):* Be that as it may, Yasu, you've gone and gotten yourself an unusual tattoo on your face.

YASU *(Touching the bat tattoo on his cheek somewhat self-consciously):* Let me tell you how I got it. *(Shamisen accompaniment of "Komori no Aikata" resumes.)* After I left your service, I joined the fire brigade. Everybody was getting tattoos of butterflies and dragonflies and things, and, on a whim, I got a tattoo of a bat. Now I wish I hadn't.

GENZAEMON: Well, well. And what are you doing now, Yasuzō?

YASU: You know, it's a strange coincidence. You, Boss, are running a brothel, and I've become a procurer.

GENZAEMON: What? A procurer? That's perfect. If you come across any likely girls, bring them on over.

YASU: Don't worry, you can rely on me. In fact, since it's been so long since I've seen you, I've brought you a woman as a little gift. She's a real find.

GENZAEMON: You never were one to let the grass grow under your feet!

KISUKE *(Still standing outside the door):* And—what was your name, Yasuzō?—exactly what kind of woman do you consider a "find"?

YASU: What kind of woman? Why, one exactly suited to this establishment!

GENZAEMON: Hurry up, then, and show us what you've got.

YASU: If you wish. Hey, Iwa! Bring the palanquin over here!

IWA and MATSU: Right!

> *(They bring the palanquin to the front of the shop, its occupant invisible behind the closed flaps. Shamisen accompaniment stops.)*

YASU *(Addressing the palanquin's passenger):* Why don't you come join us over here?

OTOMI *(From inside the palanquin):* Yasu, is it really all right for me to come out now?

YASU: It sure is! Come on out, right over here!

> *(*GENZAEMON*'s curiosity has been piqued, and he cranes his neck to see who is inside. The reed flap of the palanquin is raised, revealing* OTOMI. GENZAEMON *is shocked to recognize her.)*

GENZAEMON *(Loudly):* Oh! You're . . .

OTOMI: Otomi!

GENZAEMON: Oh, no! How can this be!

OTOMI *(Steps out of the palanquin):* Boss, it's been quite a while . . . hasn't it? *(Shamisen begin* "Tana no Daruma" ["Daruma on a Shelf"].*)* Well, if you'll just pardon me. *(*OTOMI *now wears a navy-and-white checked kimono with a black satin collar, and over it, a short blue-and-white striped* hanten. *Her obi is black satin with a lining in large brown-and-green plaid on a white background. Removing her sandals at the entrance, she steps into the shop.)*

GENZAEMON: But I thought you were dead. How is it that you're here today?

The extortion scene *(yusuriba)* at the Akamaya brothel. Scarface Otomi (Sawa-mura Tosshō V, later Sawamura Sōjūrō IX) reminds her former lover, Akamaya Genzaemon (Bandō Kōtarō), seated inside, of how he had her disfigured and left for dead: "With cuts all over my body that required seventy-five stitches, there seemed no hope I would survive. Yet I did, and now we meet again, here in this world of the living." Otomi's current husband, "Bat" Yasu (Bandō Tsurunosuke IV, later Nakamura Tomijūrō V), insolently fans himself as he leaves the blackmailing to his wife. (Tsubouchi Memorial Theatre Museum of Waseda University)

(OTOMI and YASU sit on the lower level of the shop, OTOMI to YASU's left. KISUKE sits outside the entrance to the shop, right. GENZAEMON takes the place of honor farthest left. All face forward as they speak. Shamisen continues throughout.)

OTOMI: With cuts all over my body that required seventy-five stitches, there seemed no hope I would survive. *(Glances in GENZAEMON's direction.)* Yet I did, and now we meet again, here in this world of the living.

(As she speaks, GENZAEMON puts his hands in his sleeves and folds his arms.)

YASU: Boss! You'll have to agree that she's a real fine bit of goods.

KISUKE: You're right, she's a woman of *startling* looks. But beautiful though she may be, with those scars she's worthless.

YASU: She may be worthless at another brothel. But here . . . *here* she's worth something.

OTOMI *(Plaintively):* Please be so kind as to buy my services.

GENZAEMON: Well, if you're selling, I can't say that I won't buy. *(Not wanting the dealings to be overheard.)* But this is the front entrance. We'd better go inside.

OTOMI: I'm sorry if it inconveniences you, but I prefer it here.

GENZAEMON: Don't be difficult. Just come inside.

IWA *(Approaching the entrance):* Sis, what about us . . .

IWA and MATSU: What should we do?

YASU: Negotiations are going to take a while, so why don't you two go on home before us?

IWA and MATSU: Certainly, sir.

(YASU takes some coins out of his sleeve and hands them to IWA.)

YASU: It's not much, but take it and go home.

IWA and MATSU *(Ad-libbing):* Thank you, sir.

OTOMI: Just a moment! Please take that cotton kimono that's in the palanquin and deliver it to All-Night Kuma's.

IWA and MATSU: Sure thing, ma'am.

(The two exit right, carrying the empty palanquin. GENZAEMON stands up. Shamisen stops.)

OTOMI: Well, then. Let us follow Genzaemon's bidding . . .

YASU: And conduct our negotiations inside.

GENZAEMON *(Standing):* Enough of this small talk. Come with me.

(Komori no Aikata resumes as he exits through the divided curtain.)

OTOMI *(Ad-libbing):* Well, then, so we shall. *(Looking around her briefly.)* My, what a nice place you've got here!

(OTOMI and YASU follow GENZAEMON inside, YASU removing his jacket as he does so. KISUKE brings up the rear. "Komori no Aikata" ends, and the sinister sound of wind rattling the wooden frame of the building [kazaoto] signals a change in mood. KŌJŪRŌ comes back out. He looks around, then blows a whistle to summon his men. Two POLICE OFFICERS [torite] enter right, wearing headbands and black leggings over light-colored trousers, their kimono hitched up in back. KŌJŪRŌ whispers in the ear of one, who then bows in acknowledgment. The POLICE OFFICERS bow again to KŌJŪRŌ and disappear right. As KŌJŪRŌ takes a rope from the breast of his kimono, a sharp clack of the ki [ki no kashira] sounds, signaling the final sequence of the scene. KŌJŪRŌ flings out the rope and then reels it in, wrapping it around his arm, in anticipation of subduing his prisoner. The lively "When You Drink Like That" resumes. KŌJŪRŌ takes out a short metal truncheon [jitte] and then disappears through the divided curtain. The ki sounds again. The lights dim and the stage begins to revolve, and the song and shamisen give way to the percussive beats of the stick drum and gong. Then these stop as well, and when the stage has revolved halfway, showing the setting for the next scene, offstage shamisen play "Ōtsu-e Aikata" ["Ōtsu Pictures"], its dark atmosphere setting the mood for the new scene.)

Inside Genzaemon's Quarters

(A tatami-*floored room inside the Akamaya, the private quarters of* GENZAEMON. *Center are sliding doors* [fusuma] *leading to inner rooms. Against the back wall left is an imposing chest with locked drawers, which serves as a safe, and a small good-luck altar. Far left,* shōji *doors lead to a small room. Right is a hallway leading to the rest of the house. As the scene opens,* GENZAEMON *is sitting left, next to a long charcoal brazier.* OTOMI *and* YASU *sit right, with* OTOMI *closer to center. She sits in an insolently casual manner, her legs tucked up under her sideways. Her right hand holds a hand towel against her knee.* YASU *is smoking a pipe. A sharp clack of the* ki *signals the beginning of the act, and the lights go up.)*

GENZAEMON: As I said, I'd thought you were dead. So, how is it you're still alive?

OTOMI *(Ironically):* How is it I'm still alive? Because I'm not dead, that's why.

GENZAEMON: Stop beating around the bush. Seeing as you went to the effort to hire a palanquin and come all the way here, you must want something. Come out and tell me what it is.

YASU *(Smoking):* We don't want anything particular. Except . . . since I did bring Otomi here today, won't you be so kind as to buy her services for a year?

GENZAEMON: Rather than suffer a term of employment in this harsh world of prosti-tution, if what you're after is money, why don't you just come by quietly when you need it and let me lend it to you?

OTOMI: I appreciate your kindness. But if I borrow money, I'll be obligated to return it. As for the hardships of this profession, if I just sleep them off and live as I like, they won't be so bad. Yes, I really must insist that you buy me.

GENZAEMON: How could you think that this Genzaemon would be so cheap as to dun you for any money I might lend you? No, you'd best do as I say.

(GENZAEMON gets up and goes to the chest of drawers. The extortionists chat glee-fully behind his back.)

OTOMI *(To* YASU*):* The boss sure is generous.

YASU: It's only natural, considering all that money he's raking in.

OTOMI: Even the Buddha himself would never have guessed that the boss would set himself up in a brothel like this.

(GENZAEMON, having taken money from the chest of drawers, turns back to them.)

GENZAEMON: I advise the two of you to take this and leave without any further complaints.

(He unceremoniously tosses a paper-wrapped packet of money on the floor in front of OTOMI *and then sits down again at the brazier.* OTOMI *sits up and goes to take the money, ad-libbing,* "Why, thank you, Boss! Well, we'll just take this and be on our . . ." *but she stops when she sees it is only a single packet.)*

OTOMI *(In a low voice, as if at the end of her patience):* Boss. How much is this?

GENZAEMON: Certainly you don't think I'm so cheap I'd break a packet of one hundred gold pieces. Take it and leave.

(YASU *has been silently smoking his pipe as he leaves negotiations up to* OTOMI. *Now he hurriedly taps the tobacco out of his pipe and scoots along the floor on his hands and knees to pick up the money before* GENZAEMON *has second thoughts.*)

YASU: Thank you very much indeed.

OTOMI: What are you doing? Wait a minute there, greedy! *(She slaps* YASU*'s hand away.)*

YASU *(Incredulously):* What do you mean, wait? He's given us a whole hundred gold pieces!

OTOMI: Do you really think he can get me to leave for such a paltry sum?

YASU *(Uncomprehending):* What do you mean? Isn't a hundred gold pieces enough for you?

OTOMI *(Disdainfully):* When I leave here, I mean to take not only these one hundred gold pieces, but everything in this household, *(strongly)* down to the very ashes in the hearth!

YASU: Watch what you say, Otomi!

OTOMI: Just leave the negotiations to me.

YASU *(Dubiously):* All right, if you say so. But don't do anything so stupid you lose us these hundred pieces of gold.

OTOMI: Don't worry, just leave things up to me. (YASU *reluctantly goes back to where he had been sitting.* OTOMI *turns to* GENZAEMON.) Boss, we appreciate your kindness, but I'll return this money to you. *(She slides the money over the floor back to* GENZAEMON.) Instead, I ask that you purchase my services for a year.

GENZAEMON: Whether I kept you here for one year or until your hair turns white, I'll never be able to sell a woman who looks like you to my customers. You're not worth fifty, much less a hundred, gold pieces.

(KISUKE *and* TASUKE *appear in the hallway outside the room and eavesdrop on the conversation within.*)

OTOMI: Well, if you can't sell me to customers, we're old lovers, after all. I'll while away those nighttime hours for you, if you'll agree to purchase my services *(shamisen accompaniment ceases)* for two hundred pieces of gold.

GENZAEMON *(Shocked and angered, he takes his hands out of the sleeves of his kimono):* What? Buy you for two hundred pieces of gold?

OTOMI *(As if taken aback by his obvious lack of enthusiasm.):* What's wrong, Boss? Certainly it's not necessary for you to get that look of horror on your face. Remember the old days *(loudly)* and show me a little smile.

(She half-reclines in a provocative pose with one knee raised. Shamisen accompaniment resumes as GENZAEMON*'s wife,* OTAKI, *enters through the sliding door center, accompanied by the child maid* OKIN. OTAKI*'s dark striped kimono, shaved*

342

eyebrows, and blackened teeth identify her as a respectable married woman, but something in the chic way she wears her hair and obi hint of the world of the licensed quarter. OKIN *wears a checked kimono, a flowered obi, and a reddish flowered apron.* KISUKE *and* TASUKE *enter from the hallway right.)*

OTAKI *(Standing behind* OTOMI *):* Okin, who's this woman?

OKIN: That's a lady who's come to work here. She's got lots of scars on her face.

OTAKI: What? She's come to work here? You must be joking. Tasuke! Throw her out of here immediately! *(She sits at the brazier across from* GENZAEMON *and begins to smoke a long pipe.)*

TASUKE: Yes, ma'am.

*(*KISUKE *and* TASUKE *stand to* YASU*'s right. Unconcerned, he goes on smoking.)*

KISUKE *(Speaking politely, bowing first):* What's your name . . . Yasuzō? I'd like to have a little talk with you back in the shop.

YASU *(Unperturbed):* I don't know what you want to talk about, but seeing as I've brought Otomi here today as a kind of gift after not having seen you for so long, it shouldn't be necessary for us to go anywhere else. No, I want to do the negotiations here in the boss' quarters. Hey, Otomi. The boss here has a pretty good idea of how many scars you have and where they are. But the missus probably doesn't. Give her a good look. In your case, your scars are your fortune.

OTAKI *(Not in the least intimidated):* I don't need to see in any more detail. Indeed, one glance tells me that you're blackmailers, extortionists. *(Chuckles dryly.)* I don't care how many scars you have, how deep, how shallow. For they're only on the surface, and beneath them I can see your heart and the evil schemes it harbors. Yes, I see your scars, but the hiring at a brothel is the job of the mistress of the household. If I were to name a price, I'd say one gold piece per stitch, seventy-five gold pieces for seventy-five stitches. *(Shamisen accompaniment stops.)* If we offer you a whole hundred, you should have no complaints.

YASU *(Angered):* What's that? We "should have no complaints"? *(Shamisen accompaniment resumes. Still facing forward,* YASU *addresses* GENZAEMON*.)* You took your pleasure with this woman, and then when she was of no more use to you, you had her cut up and gave her to me to dispose of. But I couldn't very well "dispose of" someone who wasn't yet dead. So I nursed her back to health. And why? So I could demand money from you, the way I'm doing now. If I'd dumped her body like you said, you'd have her blood on your hands, Boss. She's only sitting here alive before you today because I saved her life. Oh, yes, I've got heaps of things to say, once you get me started.

OTAKI *(Still refusing to be cowed):* If you've got "heaps of things to say," let's hear them, then. Our ears are for listening, after all.

YASU *(Angered in earnest, he taps out the tobacco from his pipe with a clack):* Oh, you couldn't stop me if you tried. *(Begins to crawl over the floor toward* OTAKI.*)* The boss here, he may be a respectable businessman now, but he used to be . . .

OTOMI *(Frantically gesturing for him to stop before he says any more):* Yasu, you should watch what you say in front of the missus.

YASU: Why should I worry about what I say in front of her? I'm telling her because she doesn't know the truth!

> *(YASU and* OTOMI, *ad-libbing, stand up.* YASU *holds up one hem of his kimono, spoiling for a fight.)*

OTOMI: But if you're going to get angry like that . . .

YASU: Of course I'm angry! They won't listen to us! Anyway, as I was saying, the boss used to be . . .

OTOMI: I said wait, Yasu. Why don't you leave things to me?

YASU: But, you . . .

OTOMI: Yasu, didn't you hear me?

YASU: It's not that I didn't hear, but . . .

OTOMI: Well, then, let me take over. You go back and sit down, now.

> *(Shamisen accompaniment stops as she pushes* YASU *back to where he had been sitting.)*

YASU: I don't like this one bit.

> *(Looking highly put out, he flicks up the hem of his kimono, baring his legs, and sits cross-legged. He then takes out a fan and fans himself furiously. Ad-libbing,* OTOMI *walks over to* OTAKI. *When their eyes meet,* OTOMI *gives a self-conscious laugh.* OTAKI *looks away. Shamisen accompaniment resumes.)*

OTOMI: So, you're the mistress of the household here, are you? *(Seats herself next to the couple.)*

OTAKI *(Still without looking at* OTOMI*):* I'm Genzaemon's wife, yes. *(Looks at her angrily.)* What's it to you?

OTOMI: My, my. You don't have to take that tone with me. Well, I don't know when you became the woman of the household *(proudly)*, but I myself was once your husband's mistress. He even promised to make me his wife, but a little indiscretion on my part brought me these seventy-five stitches. I may have been cut up enough to die, but what cannot be cut is the tie that binds a couple, even in the life to come. *(Insinuatingly.)* You may not like the idea, but please think of me as your younger sister.

KISUKE: Hey, lady. If this were some respectable business, your threats might hit their mark. But this is a brothel, and we're used to dealing with women problems.

TASUKE: A mere mistress or lover—some consolation money should take care of that.

KISUKE: Go away! Get out of here, now!

> *(Shamisen accompaniment stops.)*

BOTH *(Shouting):* Get lost! *(Both rise to their knees.)*

OTOMI *(Rising to her knees, she faces them down and makes shushing motions with the hand towel):* Please! Please, keep things down. *(She settles herself down again.)* Although I might not look it, I'm really rather timid. *(In a very loud voice, posing strongly.)* I'll get *scared* if you yell at me like that! *(Continues in a quieter tone. Shamisen accompaniment resumes.)* Now, it may be customary for a mistress who has been kept on three or five gold pieces a month to accept twenty-five pieces of gold as severance pay and sign a receipt to seal the bargain. But my case is somewhat different. If you want me to cut my ties with Genzaemon, then you'll have to make it worth my while. Missus, it's up to you to make the decision here.

OTAKI *(Still not losing her cool demeanor):* In light of the fact that you were once his mistress, my husband is willing to give you a hundred gold pieces. *(Laughs scornfully.)* But if it were up to me, it would be only twenty or thirty. So I'd advise you to say no more, but take the money you've been given and leave.

OTOMI: Come on, now. If this were a rice shop or pawnbroker's, I'd take the hundred gold pieces and leave without another word. *(Her tone darkens.)* But you people are making money out of nothing here. In a case where an ordinary person would be expected to pay one hundred gold pieces, it's only reasonable for you to pay two hundred, especially when you consider how good business is in Miroku, even compared to the other towns along the highway to Kyoto. *(She flings her hand towel insolently over her shoulder and raises her voice.)* So stop making us wait, and fork over the money, now. *(She poses menacingly, raising her left knee and lacing both hands over it.)*

OTAKI *(Finally riled):* Wait just one minute there! On days when we do business to the tune of three or four hundred gold pieces, it must seem that we are indeed making money out of nothing. But there's not a single one of our employees who doesn't cost us money. Each of our girls was purchased for a price. *(Angrily clacks her pipe against the ashtray and puts it down.)* No, I don't think you can say we're making money out of nothing here.

(OTOMI removes the towel from her shoulder and resumes a normal sitting posture.)

OTOMI *(Changing tack and speaking with fake contrition):* Oh, I see. I misspoke. It was wrong to say you're making money out of nothing. But you are only recently married, and you don't know what business your husband used to be engaged in. So of course you got angry. *Now* Genzaemon may be making an honest living as a brothel owner. But in the *past . . . (Shamisen accompaniment stops.* OTOMI *drops her hand towel, then crawls over to* GENZAEMON *on her knees, resting her left hand on his thigh.)* You used to make money out of nothing *then,* didn't you, Genzaemon? *(Sweetly.)* Boss, you don't mind if I have a smoke, do you? *(Shamisen accompaniment resumes as she takes* GENZAEMON*'s tobacco tray*

and pipe, moves back, and begins smoking, left knee raised insolently.) Ah, I used to
share your pipe like this every night. This brings back memories. Shall I give
you a puff, too? *(With a clack of the pipe bowl she empties the ashes in the ashtray,
then puts in some more tobacco and lights it.)*

YASU *(Leaning sideways belligerently, spoiling for a fight):* Watch how you behave in front
of your husband!

OTOMI: Shut up, Yasu. I'm trying to get you your rightful cut as a wronged husband.
(Barely mollified, YASU *sits cross-legged, fanning himself angrily.* OTOMI *returns
to* GENZAEMON *and hands him the lit pipe.)* Boss, thank you kindly.

KISUKE *(Indignantly):* To listen to the way you speak, you'd think you're trying to
imply that the boss here used to be a thief or something. But instead of bad-
mouthing others, why don't you first chase away the flies around your own
heads?

TASUKE: "Scarface" Otomi and "Bat" Yasu—you're nothing more than a pair of
common thieves. The only reason you came today was to extort money out
of us, wasn't it?

KISUKE: That's right!

BOTH: Extortionists! Blackmailers! *(They rise to their knees and pull back their sleeves as if
to attack.)*

OTOMI *(Rising to her knees, she brandishes the hand towel):* Wait just one minute there!
(Shamisen accompaniment ceases.) Extortion? Blackmail? *(Loudly.)* Even without you two spelling it out, anyone can tell that's *precisely* what I'm doing.
*(*OTOMI*'s climactic speech of defiance is in seven-five meter* [shichigochō], *performed in a stylized, declamatory manner. She poses with her right knee raised and
gestures grandly with her hand towel as she speaks. Shamisen plays "*Tana no
Daruma.*")* Mere woman though I be, I am known far and near as the bold and
fearless "Scarface." Yet were it not for these scars, I'd wear painted eyebrows
and set myself up as a geisha, or take a patron. I'd have a lover, too, and enjoy
a life even more rich and stylish than the eels they serve at Wada and Ōwada.
But thanks to the seventy-five stitches of these scars, the world of love and
romance has passed me by, there in my house by the cliff at Satta Pass. Living
on the brink though I do, yet I can pick up money as easily as a hand wet by
the waves picks up grains of millet. But unlike a certain gentleman here,
extortion's the worst of my crimes, and never have I stooped to commit anything so base as theft by night, petty pilfering, or burglary. *(She shifts her position, her back to* GENZAEMON, *raising her left knee and lacing her fingers over
it.)* No, never yet have I sunk so low as to steal.

YASU *(Still smoking, he addresses* GENZAEMON *):* There are plenty of people like you,
who by rights should already have lost their heads to the executioner's sword.
Though they're called "Master" by those around them, wash them well and

"Scarface" Otomi (Kawarasaki Kunitarō V) poses in the extortion scene *(yusuriba)*, insolently dropping her multicolored *haori* from one shoulder: "Mere woman though I be, I am known far and near as the bold and fearless 'Scarface.' " (Tsubouchi Memorial Theatre Museum of Waseda University)

you'll find they're nothing but murderers. Compared to the likes of you, I'm a nobody, a mere accomplice to extortion and blackmail. And even if I did do wrong, this tattoo of mine would soon betray me as "Bat" Yasu. But now, like a bat that's flown blindly into the muck, I'm stuck in a situation for which I'm ill-prepared.

OTOMI *(Still sitting with raised knee, she removes her* haori, *revealing its red lining, and folds it as she speaks):* Though you may hide your true nature under the jacket of a respectable citizen, you cannot do so for long. Put us off though you might, sooner or later the ugly truth will out.

YASU: Perhaps, as you say, you didn't get your money through illegal means. But your packets of money have no official seal, and should that fact come to light, all your money will be as good as naught.

(KŌJŪRŌ comes out from the hall right and eavesdrops at the sliding paper door. His suspicions about GENZAEMON are confirmed by what he hears.)

OTOMI: The less said, the better for you. So, Boss, how about handing over the money we're asking for?

GENZAEMON: I see you're both determined to do me in, even if it means being arrested along with me. Well, although I'm now the honest proprietor of a house of pleasure, in the past, I was . . . *(GENZAEMON looks toward the door where KŌJŪRŌ is eavesdropping and, sensing that he is being overheard, stops what he was about to say. KŌJŪRŌ realizes that he has been detected and retreats.)* But what's the point of dwelling on the past? If you really want to expose me, go right ahead. Whether one dies at fifty or lives to be a hundred, it's all a matter of karma.

OTOMI: In that case, if you give us the sum we're asking for, you won't have to worry about us saying something you'd rather keep secret.

YASU: We'll even sign a contract saying we'll never come here again.

GENZAEMON *(Dryly):* As if a contract would do any good—you're in no more position to go to court than I am. No matter whether a contract be written on Mino paper or Nishinouchi, once it's ripped up, it's no better than scrap. *(To OTAKI.)* Otaki . . . give them another hundred.

OTAKI *(Angrily):* You mean to say that you're going to give them two hundred gold pieces just because they asked for it?

GENZAEMON: Why not? There's more of that where it came from. In any event, I don't have any choice, seeing as they're threatening to open up old wounds. Otaki, give them the hundred gold pieces, quickly.

OTAKI *(Reluctantly):* Even so . . .

GENZAEMON *(Losing his temper):* I said give it to them, will you?

OTAKI: Well, then *(stands up),* hand me the key! *(With barely controlled rage, she takes the key from GENZAEMON and gets the money from the chest of drawers.)*

348   OTOMI: Yasu, the missus here sure is a nice lady.

                (YASU *sits sideways, with one knee raised, at ease now that they have gotten the upper hand.*)

YASU: Yes, all brothel keepers' wives should be so nice.

OTOMI: They say *tatami* and wives are best when new.

YASU: I wish some of Genzaemon's luck would rub off on me!

OTAKI: Here. (*Hands* GENZAEMON *the money.*)

GENZAEMON: Two hundred gold pieces, just as you requested. (*Slides the money over the matting to* OTOMI.) Satisfied?

                (*Shamisen accompaniment stops.*)

OTOMI (*In her joy at getting the money, she momentarily reveals her real feelings*): How could I not be? Now that I have this, I can take it to the man I love . . . (*She goes to reach for the money, but realizing what she has said, stops.*)

YASU (*Looking at her suspiciously*): Eh?

OTOMI: Nothing. I just said that I *love* men who give up their money so freely.

                (*Unfolding her hand towel, she wraps the money in it.* YASU *stands up and straightens his kimono in preparation for leaving.*)

YASU: I'll use this as capital to go straight and set myself up in some small business. When I've done so, we'll come by to thank you again.

GENZAEMON: That won't be necessary. In fact, I'd prefer it if you kept your distance.

OTOMI: Even if you tell us not to come by again, we are bound by the tie of this gift to pay a visit now and again.

TASUKE: You think we'll stand for another "visit" from the likes of you?

KISUKE: We'll send you packing.

OTOMI: But we wouldn't just stop by without a good reason. No, we'll come by when we need some more spending money. Right, Yasu? (*Puts the money in the breast of her kimono.*)

YASU: We'll be by again to beg your favor.

OTAKI: This is too much! (*Rises to her knees as if to attack.*)

GENZAEMON: Otaki, leave them alone. (*Recalling the threat posed by* KŌJŪRŌ.) For, in a moment, they'll be . . .

OTOMI: Eh?

GENZAEMON (*To* OTOMI *and* YASU): Watch out for your lives.

OTOMI: Sorry to have caused such a fuss!

                (OTOMI *and* YASU *get up.*)

YASU: Well, we got what we came for, so we might as well go. (*Ad-libbing as they step through the sliding door, right, and into the hallway.*) My, this hallway is filthy!

OTOMI: I'm going to borrow these sandals. (*Puts on sandals that have been left outside the door.*)

KISUKE and TASUKE: And if you never come again, it'll be too soon!

(KISUKE *pushes* OTOMI *out the door. A single loud* ki *clack is heard.*)

OTOMI: What do you mean, treating us like vermin! *(She faces the door, hand in a fist, as if wanting to continue the fight.)*

YASU: Who cares how they treat us, as long as we got what we wanted? Just leave them be.

(OTOMI *is placated and they move on. To shamisen accompaniment in the sentimental* shinnai *ballad style* [shinnai nagashi] *they proceed to the* hanamichi *and stop at* shichisan, *ad-libbing.*)

YASU: Well, well. Things couldn't have gone better. *(In an expansive mood, he puts both hands inside the breast of his kimono.)* But, be that as it may, aren't you forgetting something, Otomi?

OTOMI: I can't think of anything. *(Checks around her and on her person.)*

YASU: Oh, yeah? What about the money? Hand it over here. *(With his right arm still inside his kimono, he sticks out his hand through the breast opening.)*

OTOMI *(Chuckling):* I've got it, so it's all right.

YASU: All right? It's dangerous for a woman to be carrying all that money around. Give it to me.

OTOMI: What are you saying? We modern women are all strong.

YASU: Otomi! Does this mean you have other plans for the money?

OTOMI *(Flustered):* Of—of course not!

YASU: Well, if that's the case, you should hand it over to me like a good girl. After all, I've never had my hands on two hundred gold pieces. I'd like to see what it feels like to carry around all that money.

OTOMI: But you don't have anything to put the money in.

YASU: You don't have to worry about that—I've brought along my own wallet! *(He puts his hand back in his kimono front and then sticks out both hands, holding a yellow cloth bag.)*

OTOMI: You certainly came well prepared. Well, seeing that you've brought your own wallet, I guess I don't have any choice. *(She removes one of the hundred gold piece packets from the towel and puts it in* YASU's *wallet with obvious reluctance.)*

YASU *(Looking at it in disbelief):* What's this? That's only one hundred.

OTOMI: Isn't one hundred enough? After all, I want to see what it feels like to carry around a hundred gold pieces myself.

YASU: What's yours is mine, and what's mine is yours. When we get home, I'll give it back to you.

OTOMI: You'll really give it back when we get home?

YASU: Of course! Come on, hurry up and put the rest of the money in my wallet.

OTOMI: You'd better mean it. All right, you win. Here you are. *(Taking out the towel again, she reluctantly drops the second packet of money into* YASU's *open bag.)*

YASU: My, I just love that heavy feel in my wallet. *(Puts away the wallet inside the front of his kimono, then slides out his right hand from the front of his kimono again and gestures with it expansively.)* Well, now that's settled, I could really use a drink. How about going to All-Night Kuma's?

OTOMI: No, the service there is so slow.

YASU: All right, then, I'll go on ahead and order before you get there. You can follow along as soon as you can. See you later, Otomi!

OTOMI: Well, then, Yasu!

YASU: Ah, what a business*! (Obviously pleased with himself for having duped* OTOMI, *he rushes off down the* hanamichi *before she has a chance to realize his true intentions.)*

OTOMI: Yasu! I'll be there as quickly as I can! Don't forget that you're to give me the money!

(The music momentarily ceases when YASU *has exited the* hanamichi. OTOMI *ad-libs,* "Don't drop it!," "Make sure you give it back to me, now!," *and the like, hitting the towel against her hand for emphasis. She then looks at the towel and closes her hand over it, suddenly realizing that she's been had. She hits her knee and says,* "Ah!" *Then she immediately puts the towel to her lips to silence herself and looks around to make sure that she has not been overheard. The* shinnai-*style shamisen accompaniment resumes. Holding the towel between her lips, she picks up the front flap of her kimono for ease of movement and begins walking, then running, down the* hanamichi *to* tsuke *beats symbolizing the sound of running* [batabata]. *After* OTOMI *has exited, the music stops.)*

KISUKE and TASUKE *(Still seated.)*: Damned bitch!

OTAKI: Toss some salt after her to purify the place.

KISUKE and TASUKE : Yes, ma'am.

*(*KISUKE *and* TASUKE *exit via the hallway right, and* OKIN *exits through the sliding doors center.* GENZAEMON *and* OTAKI *remain, seated on either side of the charcoal brazier.)*

GENZAEMON: Well, now that you know all about my past, you'll probably be wanting to get rid of me.

OTAKI *(Unperturbed)*: What? If I were the sort to let something like that bother me, I wouldn't be able to survive for a moment in this business of buying and selling human flesh.

GENZAEMON: Ha, ha! Just as they say—the best wife for a demon is a ghoul. *(Both laugh. A sprightly shamisen melody plays, and* KŌJŪRŌ *enters from the hallway.)* Have you mistaken your room?

KŌJŪRŌ: No, that's not it. *(Sits down politely in the middle of the room.)* I was planning to stay the night, but I've suddenly remembered an errand, and I'll have to be leaving now. I'd appreciate it if you would be so kind as to give me back the sword I checked with you earlier. *(Bows politely.)*

GENZAEMON: Oh, I see. Just a moment, then. *(Calls inside.)* Hey, Okin! Bring our guest's sword, will you?

OKIN: Yes, sir. *(She comes from inside carrying KŌJŪRŌ's sword.)* It's a shame that you must be leaving so soon, sir. Here's your sword. *(She hands it to him.)*

KŌJŪRŌ *(To OKIN):* Sorry to trouble you. *(Shamisen accompaniment stops. OKIN bows and exits inside. Holding his sword, KŌJŪRŌ addresses GENZAEMON in a suddenly sinister tone.)* And now, I'd like you to hand over one more sword.

GENZAEMON *(Surprised):* What do you mean?

KŌJŪRŌ: The sword I want you to hand over is none other than the heirloom sword of the Chiba clan, Hokutomaru.

(He stands, putting his sword in his obi, and assumes a threatening pose, with one leg thrust forward. GENZAEMON, still sitting, also assumes a belligerent posture, with his coat held away from his body.)

GENZAEMON: What's that you say—what's that you say?

(The two men pose in a confrontational tableau [hippari mie] to loud double tsuke beats. Shamisen play "Yachiyo Jishi." KŌJŪRŌ puts the back hem of his kimono into his obi for ease of movement. He then takes out his truncheon. Meanwhile, OTAKI surreptitiously goes to the cupboard to get out GENZAEMON's sword. Shamisen accompaniment resumes.)

KŌJŪRŌ: Listen well, bandit Kannon Kyūji. You're the thief who recently broke into the mansion of the Chiba clan and made off not only with their money, but also their heirloom sword. Tonight by sheer coincidence I learned about your past. Now that you've been found out, it's too late for escape. Hand over the sword and submit to the ropes. *(Points his truncheon at GENZAEMON.)*

GENZAEMON: Damn your insolence! I am indeed Kannon Kyūji. Well, seeing that things have come this far, I've got no choice. You'll never take me alive! Wife! *(Shamisen accompaniment stops. GENZAEMON throws his pipe at KŌJŪRŌ to distract him as he takes his sword from OTAKI.)*

KŌJŪRŌ: How dare you!

(Tsuke and drum wind pattern accompany the struggle between KŌJŪRŌ and GENZAEMON. GENZAEMON fends off KŌJŪRŌ's truncheon with his hand. They pose in a mie to a two-beat pattern of the tsuke [batan], KŌJŪRŌ leaning toward GENZAEMON as he points his truncheon at him, and GENZAEMON center with his hand on the hilt of his sword. OTAKI blows out the lantern. GENZAEMON unsheathes his sword and throws the scabbard onto the floor. The three characters grope around in the dark [danmari] to a low and sinister shamisen accompaniment and wind pattern. The three pose in a mie: KŌJŪRŌ right, on one knee and holding his truncheon to one side; GENZAEMON center, holding his sword over his head; and OTAKI kneeling to GENZAEMON's left. A single ki clack signals the impending end of the scene. Double beats of the tsuke. Shamisen

accompaniment and wind pattern resume. The characters continue to grope in the dark as accelerating ki *clacks* [kizami] *accompany the closing of the curtain. The large offstage drum plays a linking pattern* [tsunagi] *representing the sound of rain* [amaoto] *to maintain suspense until the next scene begins.*)

The Chikushōzuka at Kitsunegasaki

(*Rain pattern reaches a climax, growing louder and slower. A single clack of the* ki *sounds, followed by a pause and then a second, softer* ki *clack. Rain pattern continues as a slow and eerie shamisen accompaniment commences. The lonely atmosphere is accentuated by the hollow beating of a wooden block* [mokugyō] *that can occasionally be heard in the background. As the curtain opens, the* ki *clacks accelerate, climaxing in one final sounding of the* ki. *The scene is a lonely graveyard at Kitsunegasaki, or Fox Point. The black backdrop indicates night. Upstage, broken gravestones mingle with willow trees and clumps of overgrown grass. Right is a well over which a wooden bucket is suspended on a pole.* KISUKE *and* TASUKE *enter from right, sharing a single paper umbrella. Shamisen accompaniment continues.*)

KISUKE: That shower we just had was really something. We'd better get a move on before it starts pouring again. But say, Tasuke, it sure was a shock to find out the boss was really Kannon Kyūji.

TASUKE: You can say that again! But be that as it may, we'd better get far away before we get arrested, too.

KISUKE: Right!

(*They exit left. Shamisen, rain pattern, and* mokugyō *cease momentarily as a temple bell sounds ominously in the distance. Shamisen accompaniment and rain pattern resume as* YASU *enters on the* hanamichi, *sheltering himself under a paper umbrella. His kimono, no longer covered by a jacket, has been hitched up over his naked legs, and he wears wooden clogs. The temple bell tolls again, and then again as* YASU *reaches* shichisan.)

YASU (*Turning and looking over his shoulder*): There's a lot of noise coming from the town. I wonder if there's a fight or something going on there. (*Shamisen and rain pattern resume as he proceeds to the stage. He stops right and sticks his hand out from under the umbrella to see if it is still raining. Rain pattern and shamisen stop.*) It looks like the rain's let up. (*He closes the umbrella, flicking water off it, and draws his left arm inside his sleeve, resting it on his chest.*) Oh, that feels good. (*Shamisen accompaniment resumes.*) When I returned home earlier and discovered Otomi with a man, I eavesdropped on their conversation and found out that he was Otomi's lover, Yosaburō, and that he needed two hundred gold pieces in order to redeem a sword. I let myself go along with Otomi's idea of blackmailing the Akamaya, pretending I didn't know why she wanted the money. Otomi doesn't know I'm on to her. Well, ignorance is bliss, they say. Otomi may be clever—as clever as that fellow in the old story who had to crawl out of the nose of the Great Statue of Buddha after getting stuck inside—but after all, she's only a woman. Her luck ran out once she handed me these two hundred gold pieces. *(With his left hand, he takes out the packet of money and considers it briefly, then puts it back.)* From here, I'm going to put some wind in my sails and go by ship over the seventy-five leagues of the Sea of Enshû. Then I'll go overland by the Ise Highway to Kamigata. The faster I make my getaway, the better. *(Looks at the sky.)* I'd better get going, before either the rain or that bitch Otomi catches up with me. *(Wind pattern begins as he starts to go off.)*

OTOMI: Yasu! Yasu!

YASU *(Looking around suspiciously):* Who's calling me?

> *(OTOMI appears from behind a gravestone where she has been hiding. A large straw mat wrapped around her head and shoulders shields her from the rain and hides her identity.)*

OTOMI *(Advancing):* It's me, "Scarface" Otomi.

YASU: Does that mean you . . . ? *(He pulls back his sleeve in preparation for a fight.)*

OTOMI *(Advancing, still hidden by the straw mat):* Yes, I heard everything from where I was hiding. Hand over the money!

YASU: Over my dead body I will!

> *(OTOMI opens the straw mat, revealing that she is now wearing the cotton kimono in bold black-and-white check that she had the palanquin bearers take to All-Night Kuma's. The hem, hitched high and tucked under the obi for ease of movement, exposes her white underskirt. She is barefoot and wears a polka-dot hand towel around her head, tied kerchief-like under her chin. YASU and OTOMI pose in a tense confrontational tableau [hippari mie] to two tsuke beats [batan], YASU right, with his closed umbrella thrust out to the side, and OTOMI left, holding the straw mat open in back of her. Lively festival-style music [shōden] begins, played by shamisen, stick drum, large drum, bamboo flute [shinobue], and metal gong [surigane] struck with a mallet.)*

OTOMI *(Rolling up the straw mat):* For the sake of my lord I made myself hateful and extorted those two hundred pieces of gold. I suspected you wouldn't hand over the money unless I had a weapon to plead my case. So I stole a kitchen knife from that all-night tavern and went through the rice paddies, arriving here before you. As the mosquitoes were eating me alive, I listened from my hiding place to you speak of your plans to escape. But why risk the dangers of a voyage over the seventy-five leagues of the Sea of Enshū when you can be safely delivered across the River of Death by the boat of Buddha's salvation? Closer than the Ise Highway is the shortcut to Hades. Prepare yourself to travel straight to the crossroads of hell!

(OTOMI throws down the rolled-up mat. As YASU speaks, she wrings water from her sleeve and dabs at her wet hair with the towel.)

YASU: So, from your hiding place you heard everything I just said. Well, now that things have come this far, I've got no choice. You outfoxed me and now have me cornered, here at Fox Point. It looks like the dice have rolled against me, but I've a gambler's pride. I won't be killed and forfeit my winnings to the house. No, this time I'm going to break even. *(Facing OTOMI and pointing his closed umbrella at her.)* Otomi, prepare yourself to die!

OTOMI: Shut up and get ready to cross the River of Death!

(Wind pattern crescendos. OTOMI attacks with her bare hands, and YASU, kicking off his clogs, fends her off with his closed umbrella. OTOMI then takes out her knife and slashes YASU in the shoulder. He staggers backward toward the gravestones and collapses beside the well. OTOMI runs to shichisan to loud, rapid tsuke beats [batabata]. She poses in a mie to double tsuke beats and the metallic sound of a gong [hitotsugane] being hit by a hammer. A solo offstage singer begins "Omae no Sode" ["Your Sleeves"]. The plaintive human voice against shamisen accompaniment serves as a sensual counterpoint to the sadistic beauty of the stylized fight scene [tachimawari] that follows. Further sound effects are provided by the single or double beats of the tsuke that mark each blow or fall and sharp beats of the metal gong. OTOMI looks around and notices the knife in her hand, seeming surprised at what she has done. Then, as if determined to finish what she has started, she goes back to the main stage, cautiously looking around to be sure she is not being observed, and advances on YASU, who lies prostrate where he has fallen. His hair is down, and the right side of his kimono is lowered. As OTOMI brandishes the knife, he tries to repel her by throwing stones. Rising, he fends off OTOMI with the half-opened umbrella. The two pose in a mie, YASU resting the closed umbrella over his shoulders like a yoke, OTOMI raising the knife overhead in one hand and grasping the tip of the umbrella in the other. YASU opens the umbrella and pushes OTOMI away. He then falls to the ground, where he opens the umbrella and rolls its edge along the ground, tracing a curve, as he repels OTOMI, who slashes with the knife. YASU gets up and grabs OTOMI from behind as they pose, both standing behind the opened umbrella. OTOMI breaks free and kicks YASU, who falls in a sitting position, facing forward, with the opened umbrella resting over his shoulder. From behind him, OTOMI splits the paper dome of the umbrella down the middle, and, to sounding of the metal gong and tsuke, the two pose in the most dramatic mie in this scene, with OTOMI standing behind the ripped umbrella and brandishing the knife over her head as she looks down at the seated YASU. Breaking free, YASU fends off OTOMI with the closed umbrella, then throws it down and staggers to the well. When OTOMI attacks again, he pushes her down. Half-reclining, with her back to the audience, she points the knife at YASU, who poses, grasping the pole that sup-

"Scarface" Otomi (Sawamura Tosshō V, later Sawamura Sōjūrō IX) and "Bat" Yasu (Bandō Tsurunosuke IV, later Nakamura Tomijūrō V) pose in a powerful *mie* during the murder scene *(koroshiba)*. Otomi rips apart Yasu's paper umbrella and lifts the kitchen knife overhead as she is about to end his life. (Tsubouchi Memorial Theatre Museum of Waseda University)

ports the well bucket, one foot on the side of the well. Powerful tableau [hippari mie] to tsuke and metal gong. The song resumes. OTOMI comes after YASU again, and he staggers away, using gravestones to shield himself. He knocks one over and falls to the ground in front of it, back to the audience. OTOMI poses behind the gravestone, looming over YASU, holding both hands high over head, the knife in her right. YASU recoils, his back to the audience and his right arm held out straight to *repel* OTOMI. *Music changes to* kasai aikata, *a lively tune played by shamisen, stick drum, and small metal bells* [matsumushi] *hit with a hammer. Rapid wind pattern.* Tsuke *beats increase in tempo as* OTOMI *comes at* YASU *again and again, slashing repeatedly.* YASU *uses a wooden grave marker to defend himself, but* OTOMI *cuts the grave marker in two with the knife, leaving him defenseless. Finally, she delivers the fatal blow to* YASU *'s side. The metal gong is struck rapidly. With the knife still in* YASU, OTOMI *removes the wallet with the two hundred gold pieces from inside his kimono. She then pulls out the knife, and, to repeated sounds of the metal gong,* YASU *falls backward into the bushes, his dying hands grasping futilely at the air before he sinks out of view.* OTOMI *collapses center, the knife locked in her grip so tightly she has to strike her hand to release it.)*

OTOMI: The bastard was tougher than I thought. Well, now that I finally have the two hundred gold pieces, I must deliver them to Yosaburō without delay.
(She raises the money to her forehead in a gesture of gratitude, then puts it in the front of her kimono. Wind pattern on the large drum resumes. As she prepares to exit, six POLICE OFFICERS *enter from left and right. Four carry poles and two carry truncheons.)*

FIRST POLICE OFFICER: Otomi!

ALL: You're under arrest!

(As tsuke *accent the action, the* POLICE OFFICERS *shout and surround her. One holds her at bay with his truncheon while the rest pose menacingly. They cry "Stop!" and all pose. They then resume fighting to* hayazen, *played by shamisen, gong* [dora], *and large drum.* OTOMI *first fends off the* POLICE OFFICERS *with poles, forcing their retreat. Then she fights barehanded against the two remaining* POLICE OFFICERS, *who attack with truncheons.* OTOMI *picks up the umbrella where it has fallen center and jabs them with it, immobilizing them. To rain and wind pattern and* batabata OTOMI *escapes to* shichisan, *where she opens the umbrella and poses with it on her shoulder. The two* POLICE OFFICERS *do somersaults, landing on their backs, legs and arms crossed, symbolizing their complete defeat. A soft* ki *clack signals the black curtain upstage to fall, revealing a lonely dawn view of rice paddies.* OTOMI *poses in a* mie *to double* tsuke *beats. Slow festival music,* shichōme, *is played by shamisen, bamboo flute, stick drum, and* surigane, *with the large drum and wooden block in the background.* OTOMI, *trembling with the shock of the fight and pressing a hand to her side as if in pain from the exertion, holds the torn, half-open umbrella over her shoulder as she staggers, then runs, down the* hanamichi. *Curtain.)*

This glossary is restricted to terms used in Volume 3. Glossary entries in other volumes will differ somewhat, as will the wording of some of the definitions. Long vowels are given only for italicized words and not for terms likely to be found in a standard English dictionary. Cross-referenced words are in bold type. A literal translation is given only for selected terms.

agemaku (lift curtain), the curtain at the audience end of the **hanamichi** and the small room to which it leads. It can also refer to the striped curtain on stage right in **nō**-style settings used in **matsubame mono.**

aibiki, stool, either high or low, placed under an actor by a **kōken** or **kurogo** to ease the strain of sitting or standing over a long period. Often it helps to give the actor additional stature.

aikata, any melodic excerpt played during dialogue or action by offstage shamisen to suggest mood or emotional context.

akuba (wicked woman), a female role type developed during the nineteenth century. *Akuba* are rough-edged women, usually once of higher status but now reduced to poverty, who do not hesitate to perform criminal acts if it will help a lover or a former lord. Also known as *dokufu* (poison woman).

akuba mono (wicked-woman play), a kind of play featuring the **akuba** role type. An example is *Scarface Otomi,* in this volume.

amaoto, offstage drum pattern suggesting rain. Also, *ame no oto.*

aragoto (rough business), bravura acting style, specialty of the Ichikawa Danjūrō acting family, particularly in **Kabuki Jūhachiban** plays.

asagimaku (light-blue curtain), large curtain of light-blue cotton rigged downstage in order to cover the full width of the stage. When dropped, a new scene is suddenly revealed.

bakufu, the military government or shogunate that ruled Japan prior to the Meiji Restoration of 1868.

bakumatsu, the late Tokugawa period, roughly from the 1840s to the 1860s, although sometimes extended backward to the earlier years of the nineteenth century.

batabata. See **tsuke.**

batan. See **tsuke.**

bon kyōgen (soul play), play performed during the midsummer Buddhist *bon* festival (or Obon) to honor the souls of the dead, often featuring ghosts of characters who have died tragically or have been murdered. Also, *natsu kyōgen.*

bukkaeri (sudden change), a quick, onstage costume change technique by which stage assistants remove basting threads so that, at the proper moment, the top half of the costume falls about the actor's waist, with the inside lining covering the lower half of the kimono. This lining matches the newly revealed upper half, the effect being as if the entire costume has been changed. The actor strikes a *mie*, and the assistants hold up the rear portion of the dropped fabric to increase the actor's size. See also *hayagawari, hikinuki.*

bungobushi, narrative musical style originated in the eighteenth century and considered the progenitor of such lasting styles as *kiyomoto* and *tokiwazu.*

bunraku, popular term for a commercial puppet theatre form based in Osaka. The term derives from the name of late eighteenth /early nineteenth century producer Uemura Bunrakuen (or Bunrakuken).

buyōgeki (dance drama), play that combines dance and drama, including character development, a plot, and considerable dialogue.

chasen (tea whisk), a wig with a topknot resembling a tea whisk.

chinko yakusha, an adult actor in an Edo children's theatre troupe.

chirashi (scattering), segment of musical composition, usually rapid, played just before the finale *(dangire).*

chobokure, story-telling section of a dance.

chōchin nuke (lantern piercing), trick device that allows a ghost to make a magical entrance through a paper lantern.

chūnori (riding in the air), stage trick *(keren)* of an actor flying, via ropes (or wires) and pulleys, over the stage or audience.

chūshibai (middle theatre), middle-ranking theatre in the Kamigata area from which an actor might graduate to play at a major theatre *(ōshibai).* See also *hamashibai.*

daibyōshi, a festive musical accompaniment using shamisen, large drum, and small drum.

dan, division of a play, most commonly an act within a dialogue play. Also, a section or sequence of a dance play, such as "waving sleeves and stamping" *(momi no dan)* and "bell-tree" *(suzu no dan).*

danmari, scene of nighttime pantomime, usually performed in slow motion by six to eight characters, but sometimes fewer. In most cases, a valuable object is searched for and passed from hand to hand.

darani no kane, prayer bell.

de, the entrance dance found at the beginning of many dance plays.

dokeyaku (fool role), comic male role type and the actor who plays such roles.

dokufu. See *akuba.*

dokugin (solitary recital), solo offstage singing accompaniment. It is designed to heighten the plaintive atmosphere of certain scenes.

donchō, drop curtain used in small theatres **(koshibai)** in place of the striped draw curtain **(hikimaku)** of large theatres. This restriction reflected these small theatres' second-class status.

donchō shibai (drop-curtain theatre), pejorative term for theatres restricted by licensing laws from using draw curtains. See **donchō.**

dora, also *dorabuchi,* a knobbed gong usually struck to mark the hours.

dorabuchi. See **dora.**

dorodoro, onomatopoeic word for an intermittent rolling pattern of the offstage large drum **(ōdaiko)** that denotes tension, mystery, or the supernatural.

dotera, padded dressing gown.

eboshi, lacquered hat of various sizes, usually black. Worn, as a rule, by nobility.

Edo sanza (Edo's three theatres), the three large, officially licensed theatres **(ōshibai)** of Edo: the Nakamura-za, Morita-za, and Ichimura-za. Also, *sanza.*

ekiro, a kind of small bell, such as horses once wore.

enkiri, divorce of a lover or spouse, which became an important plot device after its introduction in the 1790s by playwright Namiki Gohei I.

ero-guro (erotic-grotesque), a modern word coined to designate fascination with things combining qualities of the sensual with the bizarre.

etō, the Chinese classical calendrical system.

fugu (blowfish), a delicacy that can poison the eater if not properly prepared.

"Fuji Ondo" (Wisteria Dance), a musical section heard in *Wisteria Maiden.*

fukiwa (blown circle), elaborate wig worn by high-ranking female character in a **jidaimono.** The topknot is constructed around a large drum of silver or gold.

fumidashi. See **mie.**

fune no sawagi uta, the melody of a lively boatman's song, used in *Three Kichisas.*

furi, gestural patterns in dance, generally of a realistic, rather than abstract, nature.

furisode (hanging sleeve), kimono style worn by young women, so called because of its very long sleeves.

fusuma, papered sliding doors that divide one room from another in traditional Japanese homes.

gagaku, ceremonial music of the imperial court.

gama, a kind of toad associated with black magic that may appear onstage in gigantic form.

gesaku, general term for light fiction of the Tokugawa period. Source of dramatic plots for some kabuki plays.

geta, wooden clogs worn outdoors.

geza (lower seat), offstage musicians' room, located stage right (the "lower" side of a kabuki stage). Also, the shamisen, drum, gong, and flute players and singers who perform here, watching the unfolding stage action through slits in the scenery. Also, the background music and songs performed throughout a play by these offstage musicians.

ginshu. See **kinshu.**

giri to nasake (duty and compassion), a somber musical accompaniment meant to convey the atmosphere of a low-class neighborhood.

gitchō, a kind of rhythmical shamisen accompaniment.

gojūnichi (fifty days), a man's wig, its pate grown in as though the character has not shaved it for several months.

gōkan, a type of nineteenth-century popular literature that inspired many plays.

hachimaki, small cloth, rolled or folded and tied around the head as a headband.

hadanugi, the practice of removing a garment from one or both shoulders, usually to free the arms for action.

hakama, wide, ankle-length, pleated culottes worn over kimono by commoners or together with a vest **(kataginu)** by samurai. **Nagabakama** (long *hakama*), worn by samurai on the most formal occasions, trail behind the wearer six or eight feet and require care when walking.

hamashibai (shore theatres), theatres located on the south, or shore side, of Dōtonbori Canal, Osaka's main theatre district. They were middle-ranking theatres **(chūshibai).**

hame uta, a kind of sea chantey.

hanagushi, a silver flower comb.

hanamichi (flower path), rampway running from the rear of the auditorium, through the audience, and connecting stage right, used for major entrances and exits.

hana shakujō, priest's short stick adorned with cherry blossoms.

hana yoten, a fanciful kind of stage policeman or soldier and the floral-decorated costume he wears. He fights with spears dressed with flowers or flowering branches.

hanten, laborer's short, open work jacket, usually made of indigo-dyed cotton.

haori, thigh-length, open outer robe worn by men over kimono; it is an informal garment for samurai and a formal garment for commoners.

happi, man's work jacket, open at the front.

haragake, a kind of overall garment.

hashiramaki no mie (pillar-wrapping pose), a dramatic pose ***(mie)*** in which the actor wraps his arms and legs around a scenic pillar.

haya daibyōshi, rapid offstage accompaniment using large drum, two-headed lashed drum, and ***nō*** flute.

hayagawari (quick change), any one of a variety of quick-change costume techniques, such as ***hikinuki*** or ***bukkaeri.***

hayariuta, elegant offstage shamisen accompaniment.

hayashi (orchestra), ensemble of three drums and flute, derived from ***nō,*** that often is part of kabuki musical accompaniment.

hayazen (fast zen prayer), accompaniment using shamisen, gong, and large drum.

henge buyō. See ***hengemono.***

hengemono (transformation dance), a kind of dance that evolved during the nineteenth century in which a single actor played up to twelve roles in sequential dance scenes. Only some of the individual scenes from these longer dance works still survive, except for *Six Poet Immortals,* which is sometimes still produced with all five of its original scenes. Also called *henge buyō.*

hifu, a kind of woman's over-robe.

"Higashi Kazusa" ("Eastern Kazusa"), slow and gloomy offstage song and shamisen accompaniment.

hikae yagura (alternative drum towers), the "fall-back" managements that were allowed to operate in the Tokugawa period when a major theatre's management was unable to do so because of financial difficulties. Also, *kari yagura.*

hikimaku (pull curtain), kabuki's standard draw curtain, pulled open and closed by stage assistants.

hikinuki (pulling out), onstage quick costume change in which basting threads are pulled out of an outer kimono so it can be removed instantly to reveal an inner kimono of a different color.

hinadan (doll platform), long, two-step platform covered with a red cloth on which sit the fifteen to twenty instrumentalists and singers of a ***nagauta*** musical ensemble.

hinda bushi, an archaic poetic form in which some lyrics are cast in *Yasuna.*

hiōgi, a large fan with streamers attached.

hippari (no) mie (pulling tableau), group ***mie*** showing tension of unresolved conflict between hero and opponent or additional characters at a play's final curtain.

hitotsugane, medium-sized gong hit with mallet.

honmaku. See ***ki.***

hontsurigane (main bell), large offstage bronze bell and its sound. Struck with a mallet, its long reverberation tolls the time and creates a pensive or expectant mood.

hyakunichi (one hundred days), male wig whose bushy growth suggests the character has not shaved his pate for a long time, often because of illness.

hyōshimaku. See **ki.**

ichibanme (the first part), also *ichibanme mono.* The first half of a Tokugawa-period kabuki play, written as a **jidaimono.** See **nibanme.**

idaten, shamisen music to accompany someone running.

ie no gei (family art), a group of plays or a style of acting associated with a particular acting family. The *ie no gei* of the Ichikawa Danjūrō line is both its **Kabuki Jūhachiban** play collection and its **aragoto** acting style.

inga. See **ingamono.**

ingamono (fate plays), a category of nineteenth-century plays in which the role of fate *(inga)* plays a major role. Kawatake Mokuami was the leading writer of such works.

iroaku, sexy male villain, a type of role that became popular in the nineteenth century.

janome mawashi (bullseye revolve), a revolving stage within a revolving stage; it allowed the set or actors to move in two different directions simultaneously.

jidaimono (period piece), one of the major dramatic genres, a history play concerning rulers, gods, imperial nobility, or samurai. Usually but not necessarily set in the distant, pre–Tokugawa-period past.

jikkan jūnishi (ten calendar signs, twelve horary signs), the Chinese calendar cycle in which hours, months, or years are divided into sixty recurring periods. Each period has its unique characteristic affecting people who are born during that period.

jitsuaku, a type of mature male villain.

jitsu wa (in reality), dramatic situation or action in which a character, previously in disguise or assuming another identity, reveals his or her true nature.

jitte, short metal truncheon held in one hand by police **(torite)** or fighting chorus **(yoten)** that serves as both weapon and symbol of authority.

jōruri, generic term for narrative theatre music, sung-chanted and accompanied by shamisen performed in several styles, including **takemoto, tokiwazu,** and **kiyomoto** in kabuki and *gidayū* (another name for *takemoto*) in the puppet theatre. Often used to refer to the puppet theatre as a whole.

jūnihitoe, a multilayered woman's robe, worn at court.

Kabuki Jūhachiban (Eighteen Famous Kabuki Plays), a group of plays performed mainly in **aragoto** acting style, created by several generations of actors in the Ichikawa Danjūrō family line. Established by Danjūrō VII in 1840, the collection includes *The Medicine Seller* and *Just a Minute!,* translated in Volume 1.

kagen, offstage musical pattern played by **nō** flute, large drum **(ōdaiko),** and shamisen mimicking ancient imperial **gagaku** music, used to suggest impressive grandeur of a court scene in a **jidaimono** play. Sometimes spelled *kangen.*

kagura (god dance), dances associated with the Shinto religion; performed at shrines, the imperial court, or in villages on auspicious occasions.

kaidan mono (ghost play), a category of play that became popular in the nineteenth century and in which vengeful ghosts play a central role. *Ghost Stories at Yotsuya* is the classic example.

kakeai, the convention of two or more different musical ensembles, such as **nagauta** and **kiyomoto,** appearing together in the same play and often performing in alternation during the action.

kakegoe, well-timed shouts directed at the actors by spectators to encourage a performance, or sometimes to criticize it.

kakekotoba (pivot words), a literary convention whereby the final word of a line is linked to the next line, but with a separate meaning.

kakeri, offstage accompaniment of large waist drum, small drum, and flute; used for entrances of mad or deranged persons.

kakikae kyōgen, practice of rewriting familiar plays, often with striking new devices, such as changing a hero into a heroine.

kaminari (thunder), a kind of lively and comical musical accompaniment.

kamishimo (top-bottom), formal samurai male outer garments worn over basic kimono and consisting of stiffened vest **(kataginu)** and wide, ankle-length, pleated culottes **(hakama).**

kamisuki, hair-combing, an intimate domestic action seen in various plays.

kane, a small, metal percussion instrument.

kaneru yakusha, a versatile actor who can play any role.

kankara, a small, barrel-like drum. Also, *kankara taiko.*

kanmuri, tall black cap of state.

kanzashi, decorative hair ornament.

kaomise kyōgen (face-showing play), the first play of the annual theatre season, in the eleventh lunar month (usually mid- or late December), constructed to showcase a troupe's new lineup of stars.

karakuri, mechanical stage devices, which became popular in the early nineteenth century.

kara ni, the single stroke of an open shamisen string.

karasutobi (jumping like a crow), a dance section in *Sanbasō*.

kariginu, a formal garment fashioned after a hunting robe.

kari hanamichi (temporary *hanamichi*), the secondary runway sometimes set up on the audience right side of the auditorium. In the past this was a permanent part of theatre architecture, but in modern productions it is set up only if needed. Formerly *higashi no ayumi*.

kasai aikata, offstage accompaniment using shamisen, stick drum, and small metal bells.

"Kasa o Te ni Mochi" ("With a Reed Hat in My Hand"), a packhorse driver's song, accompanied by shamisen.

kashagata, middle-aged female role type and an **onnagata** who plays such roles.

kata (form, pattern), conventional forms of acting, makeup, or costumes handed down over generations but nonetheless changeable according to each actor's taste.

kataginu (shoulder silk), wing-like vest forming the upper half of a samurai's formal **kami- shimo** garb.

katakiyaku (villain's role), role type, the broadest category of villain; includes Doemon in *Gorozō the Gallant*.

kayaku, in the nineteenth century, the practice of an actor playing a role outside his specialty, for which he was paid a bonus *(yonai)*.

kazaoto. See **kaze no oto**.

kaze no oto (wind sound), also *kazaoto*, a pattern of the offstage large drum **(ōdaiko)** that suggests a strong wind.

kazoe uta, a "counting song."

keren, spectacular stage tricks or special effects, including quick costume changes, character transformations, acrobatic stunts, flying in the air, and stunts using real water.

kesa, a priest's silk surplice.

ki, also *hyōshigi*, two tapered hardwood clappers struck together in the air to produce a clear, musical sound that signals a technical change in a scene. A continuous pattern (either *kizami, honmaku,* or *hyōshimaku*) accompanies the opening or closing of the draw curtain. A single clack signals the start of a scene *(ki o naosu or naoshi)*, the end of a performance *(tomegi)*, a curtain to fall, or the stage to revolve *(itchōgi)*, or it sets up the final moments of a scene *(kigashira or ki no kashira)*.

kihachijō, yellow-and-black plaid fabric design.

ki no kashira. See **ki**.

kinshu (money person), financial backer of a producer **(zamoto, nadai).** Called *ginshu* in Kamigata.

kinuta (fulling block), offstage music suggesting the beating of cloth on a fulling block.

kiyomoto, major musical style that originated in the nineteenth century, for dance plays. The musicians appear on stage when they perform.

kizami. See **ki.**

kizewamono, "raw" or "pure" domestic plays **(sewamono),** a nineteenth-century genre pioneered by Tsuruya Nanboku IV, dealing with contemporary lowlife.

kōdan, a popular form of professional storytelling that influenced and was influenced by kabuki.

kodomo shibai (children's theatre), a popular children's offshoot of kabuki that flourished in Osaka but was also developed in Edo, where it was called *chinko shibai.*

koi-zukushi, the enumeration of puns on the word *"koi,"* meaning "love" or "come here."

kōken (see from behind), acting assistant who, crouching unobtrusively behind an actor, helps him with properties, costumes, or makeup. Wears formal costume **(kamishimo)** and wig in formalistic pieces like *Sanbasō* and *Six Poet Immortals;* in less formal plays, wears black garments (hence the nickname **kurogo**). Some plays employ both types of assistant.

"Kokorozukushi" ("That Letter, Written from the Heart"), lively offstage song accompanied by shamisen, bamboo flute, and stick drum.

kome arai (rinsing the rice), lively, rhythmic offstage melody.

"Komori no Aikata" ("Bat Song"), lively offstage song accompanied by shamisen and stick drum.

koroshiba (murder scene), scenes in which characters are killed, often violently.

koshibai (small theatre), unlicensed minor theatres, usually small in size in contrast to the major theatres **(ōshibai).** Using low-ranking actors, they operated during the Tokugawa period under various restrictions. See also **donchō shibai, miya shibai.**

koshi goromo, priestly black apron.

kōshin, fifty-seventh element of Chinese calendrical system. See **etō.**

kotsuzumi, a small drum held in one hand and struck with the other.

kowakare (child separation), scene of pathos in which a parent and child must part from one another.

kudoki (entreaty or lamentation), plea of a female character to her lover, or expression of pathos or deep sorrow, usually through mime, to sung lyrics in a dance play or to chanted narrative from the puppet theatre.

kugeaku (evil noble), role of an evil imperial court official, such as Kuronushi in *Six Poet Immortals.*

kumadori (following the shadow), highly stylized makeup consisting of a white base on which are applied strong red or blue lines that follow and emphasize bone contours. Primarily used for heroic or supernatural figures in ***aragoto***-style plays.

kumosuke uta, packhorse bearers' song.

kuraiboshi (star of rank), gentle black mark over each eyebrow, worn by imperial court nobles and ladies as a sign of their high status.

kuriage, during a confrontation between two characters an exchange of a repeated word or phrase that rises to a crescendo and ends in a unison line.

kurogo (black clothes), nickname for black-robed and hooded stage assistants. Also, *kuronbo* (black boy). See ***kōken.***

kyahan, small, triangular cloth patch tied beneath each knee. Worn by barelegged messengers.

kyōgen (farcical words), genre of short comic plays performed alternately with ***nō*** plays on a theatre program. In kabuki, generic term for a play, as in ***natsu kyōgen*** (summer play).

kyōgen kakko, offstage music using a combination of ***nō*** flute and stick drum.

maegami (front hair), the forelock worn by adolescent males, a sign of youthful sexual appeal.

mago (no) uta, packhorse drivers' songs.

maku soto no hikkomi (outside-the-curtain exit), lead actor's exit down the ***hanamichi*** after the curtain has been closed behind him; used to conclude an act or play and/or to focus audience attention on the *hanamichi*.

matsubame mono (pine board play), kabuki adaptation of a ***nō*** play staged in a setting that approximates a *nō* stage, showing a pine tree painted on a boardlike backdrop. Although the performance is adapted to kabuki acting and music, it bears a strong resemblance to the original.

matsumushi, small bells played as part of offstage music.

mawari butai (revolving stage), first introduced in 1758 as a large disk that sat atop the stage and, from the 1790s, was built into it. Used to change entire scenes or, as in *The Picture Book of the Taikō*, to partially alter the scene before returning to the original view. The action may continue as the stage revolves, giving the production a cinematic quality.

mesenryō no yakusha (actor with eyes worth a thousand gold pieces), a nickname for the actor Iwai Hanshirō V. An English version might be "actor with the million-dollar eyes."

michiyuki (travel scene), scene in which two characters—usually lovers—travel to their destination, performed as an independent dance or a dance scene within a longer play. Often associated with a double suicide.

midare, offstage drum and flute accompaniment, usually used for formal court entrances.

midori (see and take), the practice of creating a kabuki program from famous dramatic scenes and short plays rather than full-length plays. It first was instituted in the nineteenth century.

mie (pose), powerful acting technique in which the actor makes several rhythmic movements that culminate in a freeze of several seconds. Often one foot may be planted strongly *(fumidashi),* arms are thrust outward, head is rotated *(senuki),* and, at the final moment, one eye is crossed in a glaring expression *(nirami)* that expresses intense feelings. **Tsuke** beats accompany the foot planting and the two-part head rotation. Usually performed by powerful male characters and far less frequently by females. A *mie* may have a technical name.

mitate, the artistic and often game-like convention of subtly likening characters or images in plays to concepts or persons known to the audience.

mitsuburi, a three-part head movement in dance.

mitsu daiko (triple drumbeats), repeated triple beats of the offstage large drum (**ōdaiko**) indicating alarm or impending attack.

miyaji shibai. See **miya shibai.**

miya kagura (shrine music), offstage shamisen and percussion pattern, featuring **ōdaiko, taiko,** bamboo flute, and small bronze cymbals, indicating the precincts of a shrine.

miya shibai (shrine theatre), temporary theatres set up under special licensing arrangements on the grounds of temples and shrines. Also, *miyaji shibai* (shrinegrounds theatre) and *hyakunichi shibai.* They competed with the **ōshibai.** See also **koshibai.**

mizu kyōgen (water play), play in which real water was used, usually to create a cooling atmosphere during summertime performances.

mizu no oto (water sound), pattern of offstage large drum **(ōdaiko)** suggesting flowing water.

mokkin, wooden xylophone.

mokugyō iri, offstage atmospheric accompaniment by the wooden percussion instrument called *mokugyō* and shamisen for scenes in lonely, deserted places.

momi no dan, the "waving sleeves and stamping" section in *Sanbasō.*

momohiki, a kind of leggings.

mon (crest), family crest, worn on clothing or emblazoned on personal items to announce one's lineage. In kabuki a crest can identify either the family of the dramatic character or the actor.

monogatari (narration), solo narrative of an important event from the past by a male character; a major dramatic sequence in kabuki plays derived from the puppet theatre.

nadai (name), in Kyoto and Osaka a manager licensed by the government to produce kabuki plays at a theatre. Other meanings include: the title of a kabuki play, a ranking actor. See also **zamoto.**

nadeshiko (wild pink), a kind of pond blossom.

nagabakama. See **hakama.**

nagauta (long song), music of shamisen and singers with the flute and three drums of the **nō** ensemble that became the basic form of kabuki music. A lyric style as opposed to a narrative style. Played onstage for dance plays or offstage **(geza)** as background music during dialogue plays.

nagori kyōgen (farewell play), also *onagori kyōgen,* productions given in the season-ending tenth month, in which actors made their farewells before joining a new company. Plays were often restrained and autumnal in feeling.

naimaze, the playwriting practice of mixing several **sekai** in the same play. This became a fairly complex procedure in the writing of Tsuruya Nanboku IV.

nami no oto (wave sound), drumbeat pattern of offstage large drum **(ōdaiko)** that suggests continuous swelling and falling of waves.

nami nuno (wave cloth), a groundcloth resembling waves for scenes near or on the sea.

nanori, the convention of having a character announce his name, usually in a formal speech. See **tsurane.**

naoshi. See **ki.**

narimono, the general term for offstage percussion and flute music played singly or in combination by **nō** drums and flute **(hayashi),** large drum **(ōdaiko),** bells, and gongs, as well as other instruments. *Narimono* music may be played by itself or together with offstage shamisen and/or song.

natsu kyōgen. See **bon kyōgen.**

netori (roosting bird), eerie rising and falling of an offstage flute melody suggesting the supernatural. Also, *netoribue.*

netoribue. See **netori.**

nezumi kabe (mouse walls), realistic looking grey-painted walls of poor farmers' domiciles.

nezumi naki (squeaking of a rat), the ritual of striking wooden tags on the floor to signal start of business at a brothel.

nibanme (the second part), also *nibanme mono,* the second half of a play or program; consists of a **sewamono** play or scene, in contrast to the **jidaimono** play or scenes of the first half **(ichibanme).**

nimaime, roles of handsome and romantic young men, often played in the gentle style called *wagoto.*

ninja, thief or spy, dressed completely in black, believed to possess the magical power to suddenly appear or disappear, as well as the ability to leap or fly.

ninjō banashi. See **rakugo.**

nō, austere, classical genre of theatre, predating kabuki. During the Tokugawa period, *nō* was made the official theatre of the samurai class, while kabuki catered to commoners.

noren, the split curtains that hang in the doorways of traditional Japanese homes and shops.

nōshi, a silk outer gown.

nuigurumi (sewed wrapping), costume worn by an actor portraying an animal.

nureba (moist scene), a love scene.

ochappi, a tomboy role that preceded the creation of the **akuba** role type.

ōdaiko (large drum), large offstage drum played with a pair of either thick or light sticks to provide a wide range of atmospheric rhythmic patterns.

odoriji (dance section), lively concluding section of a dance or dance play using rhythmic and often abstract movements. Also, lively offstage shamisen melody.

ōiri (big entrance), full or sold-out house. An actor may write in the air the simple three-stroke character for "large" *(ō)* and the two-stroke character for "enter" *(iri)* as a symbol of good fortune.

ōji (prince), wig on which hair hangs loose from a shaved pate to below the shoulders. Worn by aristocratic villains **(kugeaku)** in **jidaimono.**

"Oki no Susaki Uta" ("Shoals in the Offing"), title of a sea chantey.

okiuta, introductory song passage in a dance.

"Omae no Sode" ("Your Sleeves"), solo song.

"Omae Sono Yō Ni" ("When You Drink Like That"), song sung to accompaniment of shamisen, stick drum, and gong.

ondo, type of folk or dance song.

ongaku, offstage accompaniment of bells, large drum, and **nō** flute, usually heard in temple scenes.

onnagata (female form), male actor of female roles.

onna ōgi, a woman's small fan.

ōshibai (large theatre), major licensed theatre in Edo, Kyoto, or Osaka, in contrast to a middle-ranking theatre **(chūshibai** or **hamashibai)** or small theatre **(koshibai** or **miya shibai).** See also **Edo sanza.**

Oshichi-Kichisa mono, plays about the love of greengrocer's daughter Oshichi and Kichi-saburō.

otokodate (chivalrous commoner), virtuous Tokugawa-period commoners who acted as protectors of the townsmen against samurai abuse. Sometimes called "street knights." Gorozō in *Gorozō the Gallant* is an example.

"Ōtsu-e Aikata" ("Ōtsu Pictures"), offstage shamisen accompaniment indicating gloomy atmosphere.

ōzatsuma, early type of narrative music used in Edo for **aragoto**-style plays. Usually performed by onstage musicians.

rakugo, popular story-telling art that provided stories of kabuki plays.

renga, popular form of linked verse, often composed during competitions.

rokkasen, six poetic sages: Ariwara Narihira, Ono no Komachi, Henjō, Ōtomo Kuronushi, Bunya (Funya)Yasuhide, and Kisen.

rōnin (wave man), an unemployed, dismissed, or otherwise masterless samurai.

roppō (six directions), stylized bravura masculine walk, usually performed on the **hanamichi** as an exaggerated way of exiting. One type is the *tobi roppō* (flying in six directions), a leaping, bounding exit, as in *Tokubei from India.*

ryō, oblong gold coin of high, but varying, value, translated in the plays as "gold piece."

ryōgin, offstage accompaniment of shamisen, drum, and two voices.

ryū, a "school," used to distinguish, for example, one school of dance from another, as in the Fujima *ryū* or the Bandō *ryū.*

sagariha, offstage accompaniment using **nō** instruments for solemn scenes.

sajiki, side galleries in kabuki playhouses, usually considered first-class seating.

sakoku, the policy of isolating Japan from the rest of the world, introduced in the 1630s.

sandan, the three steps at the front of a **nō** stage.

sanjū, a kind of dramatic shamisen accompaniment.

sankin kōtai, the Tokugawa-period policy of making daimyo and their retinue maintain a household in Edo while returning periodically to their home fiefs and—to prevent rebellions—keeping their families in Edo as hostages.

sanmaime, comic role.

sanza no miya shibai, the three Edo **miya shibai** that were considered the leaders in their field during the Tokugawa period. They were the minor-league equivalents of the **Edo sanza.**

sarashi, fight scene accompaniment using shamisen, large drum, **nō** flute, and stick drum.

sashidashi (thrust forth), long, thin pole with a candle at one end used by **kurogo** or **kōken** to light an actor's face. Still used in certain plays to recapture the feeling of old-time kabuki.

sashigane (thrust metal), long, thin pole used by **kurogo** or **kōken** to bring to magical life a butterfly, bird, or other object attached by a wire to its tip.

sashinuki, pantaloon-like trousers.

sekai (world), well-known cluster of characters and situations from the past from which a playwright fabricates a plot *(shukō)* to create a new play.

semeba (torture scene), a kind of scene in which important characters are tortured.

seppuku (cut belly), ritual suicide by disembowelment, an honorable means of dying. Also, colloquially, *harakiri* (belly cutting).

seri, stage elevator to raise or lower scenery and/or actors. See also **suppon.**

sewamono (domestic piece), a play concerning commoners of any period, although usually set during the Tokugawa period.

sharebon (smart book), story, usually about the licensed quarters, popular in the third quarter of the eighteenth century.

shibai jaya (theatre teahouse), teahouse, usually adjoining a theatre, that served as restaurant and lounge for theatregoers. Tickets could also be purchased at them.

shibai shōden, festive music of large drum, stick drum, flute, and gong.

shichigochō (seven-five meter), verse written for puppet performance or dialogue written for kabuki composed in alternating phrases of seven and five syllables. Usually sung in puppet-derived plays and spoken in rhythmic style in pure kabuki plays.

Shichi-go-san no Owai (Seven-five-three Celebration), shrine visits by children at the auspicious ages of seven, five, and three.

shichisan (seven-three), an actor's strongest position on the **hanamichi,** located in the midst of the audience, seven units from the stage and three from the back of auditorium. An actor entering or exiting the *hanamichi* stops at this position in order to shift focus toward or away from the scene onstage. In the twentieth century, with the advent of projecting balconies, *shichisan* was moved forward to a position three units away from the stage and seven units from the back of the auditorium so an actor in this position may be seen by all audience members.

shichōme (fourth ward), slow festival music of flute, large drum, stick drum, gong, and shamisen.

shimada, a hairstyle worn by geisha and younger women.

shin-e (death pictures), portraits of actors published soon after their death. Thousands were sold after the deaths of the most popular actors.

shinjū mono (double-suicide plays), dramas in which the hero and heroine are a young couple in love driven by forces beyond their control to commit suicide together.

shinnai nagashi, sentimental ballad in the musical style called *shinnai.*

shinobi sanjū, musical accompaniment of staccato shamisen notes.

shinobue, a **nō**-style flute.

shinoiri no aikata, languorous offstage music of flute and shamisen.

shiranami mono (white-wave plays), plays—like *Three Kichisas*—about romanticized bandits and outlaws, a specialty of playwright Kawatake Mokuami, the *"shiranami* playwright *(shiranami sakusha),"* and Ichikawa Kodanji IV, the *"shiranami* actor *(shiranami yakusha)."* The term *"shiranami"* comes from a Chinese word for a gang of robbers whose hideout was in "White Wave Valley."

shiranami sakusha. See **shiranami mono.**

shite (doer), main character in a **nō** play, often masked.

"Shito Kokoro" ("Longing Heart"), a festive offstage song accompanied by shamisen, drum, and flute that sets a lively mood.

shōden, festival-like music.

shōji, sliding doors of latticed framework covered with white paper, used to divide rooms or serve as entrance and exit doors to a residence.

shosabutai (dance stage), polished cypress platforms placed over the main stage and **hanamichi** for dance or **aragoto**-style plays. The platforms facilitate smooth sliding steps and reverberate when stamped on.

shosagoto (posture business), a dance play, with little or no dramatic plot, that emphasizes skill in dance and elegance of appearance, normally featuring an **onnagata** role. See also **buyōgeki.**

sōban, an offstage gong hung from a wooden stand and struck with a hammer.

sogimen, a comical trick mask used to suggest the inside of a face after its front has been sliced off in battle.

Sōgo shinkō (Sōgo new sect), a newly formed religious sect in which Sōgo (of *Martyr of Sakura*) is honored as a deity.

suberiashi (sliding steps), small, heel-toe steps whereby the actor moves from widely spread legs into a straight standing position. Also, *jiri-jiri.*

sugomi, menacing tune played on offstage shamisen.

suō, voluminous outer robe worn by samurai in a **jidaimono.**

suppon (snapping turtle), small stage elevator ***(seri)*** located at **shichisan** on the **hanamichi,** used for appearance or disappearance of a single character, usually a ghost or other supernatural figure.

surigane, an offstage metal bell struck with a mallet.

sutezerifu (thrown-away dialogue), dialogue not written in the script, but ad-libbed or extemporized by actor.

suzu, a short, rod-like instrument to which bells are attached.

suzu no dan, a scene in *Sanbasō* in which the dancer shakes a **suzu.**

tabi, bifurcated socks for men or women of all stations, worn indoors, or outdoors with sandals ***(zōri)*** or clogs ***(geta).***

tachimawari (standing and turning), stylized fight scene consisting of choreographed movement sequences ***(kata)*** that culminate in **mie.** It may involve two or three major characters, or it may pit a hero against a mass of opponents, in which case it may also be called *tate.*

tachiyaku (standing role), originally a term that distinguished actors, who stood and moved, from seated musicians. Now a leading male role of various types.

taiko, stick drum, adapted in kabuki from the **nō** musical ensemble.

takageta, tall wooden clogs, worn mainly by courtesans, such as Ōshū in *Gorozō the Gallant,* but also worn by a few male characters, in order to greatly increase their height.

takemoto, emotional, highly dramatic style of narrative music ***(jōruri)*** adapted to kabuki from the puppet theatre (where it is called *gidayū*). Performed by a team of one chanter-singer *(tayū)* and one shamisen player for dialogue plays and by a large ensemble for dance plays.

tanabata mie, pose performed in *Ghost Stories at Yotsuya* in which two lovers incline toward each other, like the separated lovers celebrated in the Weaver and the Cowherd festival.

"Tana no Daruma" ("Daruma on a Shelf"), a shamisen melody.

"Tanda Ute Ya" ("Just Beat the Drums"), song accompanied by shamisen, bamboo flute, and stick drum.

tatami, straw-covered mats used for residential flooring.

tatesakusha (head playwright), chief playwright of a theatre company and supervisor of second-ranking playwright *(nimaime sakusha)*, third-ranking playwright *(sanmaime sakusha)*, and writing and rehearsal assistants *(kyōgen kata* or *kyōgen sakusha)* attached to the company.

tate ya no ji, a formal style of tying the obi so that the knot resembles the *hiragana* symbol for *ya.*

Tenpō no kaikaku (Tenpō Reforms), social and economic reforms instituted during the Tenpō period, including many that had a heavy impact on kabuki. The most famous was the forced move of the **Edo *sanza*** to Saruwaka-chō.

tenugui, hand towel ubiquitously carried by commoners; second only to the fan in its variety of uses as a theatrical hand property.

terakane, offstage gong pattern suggestive of a temple scene.

teuchi (hand clapping), rhythmic, unison celebratory hand clapping used by actor fan clubs *(renchū).*

tobi roppō. See ***roppō.***

toita. See ***toitagaeshi.***

toitagaeshi (rain door switch), a famous stage trick in *Ghost Stories at Yotsuya* in which two bodies, nailed to opposite sides of a rain door *(toita),* float down a river. Through quick-change techniques, the same actor plays each corpse when the board is flipped over.

toki no kane, an offstage bell tolling the time.

tokiwazu, one of the major forms of kabuki narrative musical accompaniment ***(jōruri),*** played by an ensemble of six to ten shamisen players and singers who appear onstage dressed in formal **kamishimo.** Most commonly used as a dance accompaniment, its narrative properties are secondary to the beauty of its singing.

tomimoto, early style of highly emotional narrative music created in kabuki to accompany dances. Now defunct.

tōri kagura, shamisen and vocal melody underlain with quiet percussion.

torite, policeman or constable, usually in a group and charged with arresting a miscreant.

tosaka, a female wig style worn by ***akuba,*** like Otomi in *Scarface Otomi.* The forelock is cut in such a way that it can be combed to either side.

tōshi (full play), performance of an entire, or nearly entire, play text. Most programs are composed of selected scenes from several plays; these are called ***midori.***

tōshi kyōgen (straight-through play), performance of an entire, or nearly entire, all-day play. Today, usually acts from several plays are performed on a program ***(midori).***

tsujiuchi, lively offstage music with shamisen and stick drum.

tsuke, two wood blocks beat alternately on a wooden board placed on the floor near the stage left proscenium. *Tsuke* beats *(tsuke uchi)* accompany and emphasize stage action: a single beat *(hiro te)* for a small action, a double beat *(batan)* for a strong action or a **mie;** a continuous pattern *(batabata)* to accompany running; and a rising and falling pattern *(uchiage)* to highlight a climactic *mie.* A three-beat pattern *(battari)* may also be used to emphasize *mie.*

tsukechō, cue book for offstage music; it contains starting and stopping cues and the titles of all offstage music to be played during one play.

tsukkake, musical accompaniment for strong entrances in battle scenes played by the large drum **(ōdaiko)** and sometimes the flute and stick drum **(taiko).**

tsunagi (tie together), quiet music or **tsuke** beats played during the brief interval in which a set is changed, usually with house lights dimmed.

tsurane (in succession), bravura monologue normally delivered by a hero in a **jidaimono** to boast of his virtues and power. Formerly composed by the actor, playwrights have developed elaborate speeches in **shichigochō** with puns, word play, insults, lists of related words, and other entertaining verbal devices. May also refer to less flamboyant but nevertheless dramatic speeches of self-introduction in **sewa-mono,** as, for example, Oroku's *tsurane* in *Osome and Hisamatsu.*

tsurane no aikata, a shamisen accompaniment heard during Oroku's **tsurane** in *Osome and Hisamatsu.*

tsurieda (hanging branches), decorative border of cherry or plum blossoms, maple leaves, lightning flashes, or other features of nature that frames an outdoor setting.

uchiage. See **tsuke.**

uchidashi (beating out), a rousing offstage pattern of the large drum played after the final curtain. It sends the departing audience off in a lively mood.

uchikake, woman's elegantly trailing outer robe worn over kimono on formal occasions, usually padded and heavily embroidered and left open at the front.

ueshita aikata (upper and lower music), alternation of shamisen music played by an "upper" **takemoto** ensemble, who are seated on a platform onstage, and the "lower" **geza** musicians seated offstage right, as in *Martyr of Sakura.*

uma no shippo, a ponytail wig style worn by **akuba.**

usudorodoro, light drumbeat pattern to create an ominous mood. See **dorodoro.**

utaigakari, nō-style formal chanting.

utazaimon, a kind of broadsheet providing news of the latest scandals; its contents were publicized by itinerant balladeers during the Tokugawa period.

wakaonnagata (young female form), an actor of youthful or unmarried female roles.

wakashu (young man), role type of an adolescent. Also, adolescent actors who were important in early kabuki.

waki (beside), secondary character in **nō** who is the unmasked questioner of the main character **(shite).**

warizerifu (divided dialogue), also *kakeai zerifu,* antiphonally spoken dialogue, usually by two characters and usually composed in phrases of seven and five syllables **(shichigochō)** with the final phrase spoken in unison.

warumi, comic mimicry or parody of feminine actions by a male character, as in the "Kisen" section of *Six Poet Immortals.*

wataribyōshi (passing rhythm), lively offstage percussion music often employing shamisen and song and used to accompany a courtesan procession or crowd entrance.

watarizerifu (passed-along dialogue), a long speech divided among a group of characters who speak in sequence, joining together to deliver the last phrase or line in unison.

yachiyojishi (lion dance of eight thousand ages), name of a shamisen and koto accompaniment.

yagō (house name), the name of an actor's house, family, shop, or "guild," which audience members shout to show appreciation (see *kakegoe*). Used as a kind of nickname for a kabuki actor.

yakko (footman), attendant who, in spite of his lowly position, is dynamic and independent. Often featured in dance scenes that call for vigorous movement.

yakubarai. See *yakuharai.*

yakugara (role type), categorization of role types, including basic role types of *tachiyaku,* *onnagata,* comic, villain, and elderly characters.

yakuharai, also *yakubarai,* an ornate form of dialogue using many plays on words and usually spoken by a leading character in a *sewamono.*

yakusha hyōbanki (actor critique), annual listing of actors, with their rankings and critical commentary on their personal and professional lives, that provides an unparalleled source of documentation for Tokugawa-period kabuki. Published separately for actors of, respectively, Edo, Osaka, and Kyoto.

yamadai (mountain platform), single-level platform covered with a red cloth and placed onstage to seat a *takemoto, kiyomoto, tokiwazu,* or *ōzatsuma* narrative musical ensemble in a dance play.

"Yamanba" ("Mountain Witch"), name of a shamisen accompaniment.

yamaoroshi, beating of large offstage drum to suggest being deep in the heart of mountains.

"Yasuna," offstage musical selection named for the dramatic character Yasuna.

yatai kuzushi (house collapse), stage device of making a palace seem to collapse before the audience's eyes.

yomena, a kind of wild chrysanthemum with edible leaves.

yomihon (reading book), stories with Buddhist or Confucian didactic content, published in five or more volumes *(kan)* popular from 1750 to the end of the Tokugawa period.

yomiuri, a kind of Tokugawa-period scandal sheet.

yonai. See *kayaku.*

yose, variety theatres where **rakugo** and **kōdan** are performed.

yosogoto (somewhere-else business), or *yosogoto jōruri* (somewhere-else music), offstage music played by one of kabuki's major musical performers in a **sewamono,** realistically justified as being nearby musicians rehearsing. A technique developed by Kawatake Mokuami.

yoten, wide-sleeved garment with hems split at the sides worn by minor samurai or by groups of policemen or constables in fight scenes. Also, the characters who wear these costumes. *Hana yoten* (flower *yoten*) wear colorful costumes of this type and wield branches of cherry blossoms as weapons, as in *Six Poet Immortals.*

yotsudake (bamboo castanets), or *yotsudake aikata,* accompaniment of shamisen and bamboo sticks.

yugao (evening faces), a kind of white flower.

yukata, lightweight, cotton summer kimono.

yuki (no) aikata (snow melody), large drum and shamisen, used in snowy scenes.

yuki no oto (snow sound), offstage pattern of the large drum **(ōdaiko)** suggesting falling snow. Also, *yuki oroshi* (snowstorm).

yuki nuno (snow cloth), a white groundcloth used to suggest snow.

yuki oroshi. See **yuki no oto.**

yusuriba (extortion scene), a kind of scene found in many nineteenth-century **kizewamono** in which characters try to blackmail others out of large sums of money, often unsuccessfully.

zagashira (troupe head), in Edo, the actor-manager of a troupe. Called **zamoto** in Kamigata.

zamoto (troupe/theatre foundation), in Edo, the person licensed by the government to produce kabuki plays at a theatre. In Kamigata, the actor-manager of a troupe.

zankoku no bi (aesthetic of cruelty), quality of beauty arising in scenes of torture or death that are performed in stylized, musicalized fashion.

zen no tsutome, offstage music played by knobbed gong **(dora)** and large drum **(ōdaiko)** for entrance or exit of temple priests or for a scene on a lonely embankment.

zōri, straw sandals with thongs.

SELECTED BIBLIOGRAPHY

Apart from a small number of standard English-language works about kabuki and even fewer about classical Japanese theatre in general, the bibliography is limited to sources used in the preparation of this volume's introductions and translations. Sources related to specific plays are given with an abbreviation for the play following their listing. Works without abbreviations apply to more than one play.

GG	Gorozō the Gallant
GS	The Ghost Stories at Yotsuya on the Tōkaidō
K	Kasane
M	Masakado
MS	The Tale of the Martyr of Sakura
OH	The Scandalous Love of Osome and Hisamatsu
SA	Sanbasō with His Tongue Stuck Out
SO	Scarface Otomi
SPI	The Six Poet Immortals
SU	The Execution Ground at Suzugamori
TK	The Three Kichisas and the First New Year's Visit to the Pleasure Quarters
TTI	The Tale of Tokubei from India
WM	The Wisteria Maiden
Y	Yasuna

Bowers, Faubion. *Japanese Theatre*. New York: Hermitage House, 1952. Reprint, Rutland, Vt.: Tuttle, 1974.

Brandon, James R., trans. *Kabuki: Five Classic Plays*. Cambridge, Mass.: Harvard University Press, 1975. Rev. ed., Honolulu: University of Hawai'i Press, 1992.

———, ed. *Chūshingura: Studies in Kabuki and the Puppet Theatre*. Honolulu: University of Hawai'i Press, 1982.

380

Brandon, James R., William P. Malm, and Donald Shively. *Studies in Kabuki: Its Acting, Music, and Historical Context.* Honolulu: University of Hawai'i Press, 1978.

Cavaye, Ronald. *Kabuki: A Pocket Guide.* Rutland, Vt.: Tuttle, 1993.

Ernst, Earle. *The Kabuki Theatre.* Rev. ed., Honolulu: University of Hawai'i Press, 1974.

Fujio Shinichi, ed. *Tsuruya Nanboku Zenshū* (Collection of Tsuruya Nanboku). Vol. 5. Tokyo: Sanichi Shobō, 1971. OH

Gunji Masakatsu. *Kabuki.* John Bester, trans. 2d ed. Tokyo and New York: Kodansha, 1985.

———, ed. *Tōkaidō Yotsuya Kaidan: Shinchō Nihon Koten Shūsei* (The Ghost Stories at Yotsuya on the Tōkaidō: New Revised Japanese Classics). Vol. 41. Tokyo: Shinchōsha, 1981. GS

———. *Iromoyō Chotto Karimame* (Sensual Colors, Going to Cut Beans) and *Shitadashi Sanbasō* (Sanbasō with His Tongue Stuck Out). In *Buyōshū* (Dance Anthology). *Kabuki On-Sutēji* (Kabuki Onstage series). Vol. 25. Tokyo: Hakusuisha, 1987. K, SA

Halford, Aubrey S., and Giovanna M. *Kabuki Handbook.* Tokyo and Rutland, Vt.: Tuttle, 1961.

Imao Tetsuya, ed. *Sannin Kichisa Kuruwa no Hatsugai: Shinchō Nihon Koten Shūsei* (The Three Kichisas and the First New Year's Visit to the Pleasure Quarters: New Revised Japanese Classics). Vol. 65. Tokyo: Shinchōsha, 1984. TK

Kawatake Itojo and Kawatake Shigetoshi, eds. *Mokuami Zenshū* (The Collected Works of Mokuami). Vol. 7. Tokyo: Shunyōdō, 1926. SO

Kawatake Mokuami. *Musume Gonomi Ukina no Yokogushi* (Scarface Otomi). Kokuritsu Gekijō Kabuki Kōen Jōen Daihon (National Theatre Kabuki Production Script). Tokyo: Kokuritsu Gekijō, January 1992. SO

Kawatake Shigetoshi. *Kabuki: Japanese Drama.* Tokyo: Foreign Affairs Association of Japan, 1958.

Kawatake Toshio. *Japan on Stage: Japanese Concepts of Beauty as Shown in the Traditional Theatre.* P. G. O'Neill, trans. Tokyo: 3A Corporation, 1990.

Kincaid, Zoe. *Kabuki: The Popular Stage of Japan.* London: Macmillan, 1925.

Kokuritsu Gekijō Geinō Chōsa Shitsu, ed. *Ya no Ne, Sannin Kichisa Kuruwa no Hatsugai* (The Arrow Sharpener, The Three Kichisas and the First New Year's Visit to the Pleasure Quarters). Edited by Rikura Kōichi. Kokuritsu Gekijō Kōen Jōen Daihon. Tokyo: Nihon Geijutsu Bunka Shinkōkai, 1972. TK

———. *Arigataya Megumi no Kagekiyo, Tsumoru Koi Yuki Seki no To, Sannin Kichisa Kuruwa no Hatsugai* (The Lucky Kagekiyo, The Barrier Gate, The Three Kichisas and the First New Year's Visit to the Pleasure Quarters). Kokuritsu Gekijō Kōen Jōen Daihon. Tokyo: Nihon Geijutsu Bunka Shinkōkai, 1978. TK

———. *Kokuritsu Gekijō Jōen Shiryōshū 399. Sakura Giminden* (Production Research Materials Collection 399: The Tale of the Martyr of Sakura). Tokyo: Nihon Geijutsu Bunka Shinkōkai, October 1989. MS

———. *Kokuritsu Gekijō Jōen Shiryōshū 322: Gedatsu/Shinobi Yoru Koi wa Kusemono/Musume Gonomi Ukina no Yokogushi* (Production Research Materials Collection 322: Spiritual Awakening, Thieving Night When Love Is Blind, A Female Version of the Boxwood Comb Lover's Scandal). Tokyo: Nihon Geijutsu Bunka Shinkōkai, January 1992. KO

Leiter, Samuel L., trans. and comm. *The Art of Kabuki: Famous Plays in Performance.* Rev. ed., Mineola, N.Y.: Dover, 2000.

———. *New Kabuki Encyclopedia: A Revised Adaptation of* Kabuki Jiten. Westport, Conn.: Greenwood, 1997.

———. *Frozen Moments: Writings on Kabuki, 1996–2001.* Ithaca, N.Y.: Cornell East Asia Series, forthcoming.

———, ed. *A Kabuki Reader: Essays on Japanese Theatre History and Performance.* Armonk, N.Y.: M. E. Sharpe, 2002.

Malm, William P. *Nagauta: The Heart of Kabuki Music.* Tokyo and Rutland, Vt.: Tuttle, 1963.

Matsui Kōji. *Rokkasen Sugata no Irodori* (The Six Poet Immortals in Colorful Guises). Kokuritsu Gekijō Jūgatsu Jōen Daihon (National Theatre October Production Script). Tokyo: Kokuritsu Gekijō, 1985. SPI

Mochizuki Tainosuke. *Kabuki no Geza Ongaku* (Kabuki Backstage Music). Tokyo: Engeki Shuppansha, 1975.

Morisada Ichirō. *Nihon Buyō Kyokushūran* (Collection of Japanese Dances). Chiba: Kashiwa Shuppan, 1975. WM

Ortolani, Benito. *The Japanese Theatre: From Shamanistic Ritual to Contemporary Pluralism.* Rev. ed., Princeton, N.J.: Princeton University Press, 1995.

Raz, Jacob. *Audience and Actors: A Study of Their Interaction in Japanese Traditional Theatre.* Leiden: E. J. Brill, 1983.

Scott, A. C. *The Kabuki Theatre of Japan.* Reprint, Mineola, N.Y.: Dover, 1999.

Shaver, Ruth. *Kabuki Costume.* Rutland, Vt.: Tuttle, 1966.

Toita Yasuji et al. *Meisaku Kabuki Zenshū* (Collection of Kabuki Masterpieces). Vol. 9. Tokyo: Sōgensha, 1969. GS, SU

——— et al., eds. *Meisaku Kabuki Zenshū* (Collection of Kabuki Masterpieces). Vol. 10. Tokyo: Sōgensha, 1968. TK

———. *Meisaku Kabuki Zenshū* (Collection of Kabuki Masterpieces). Vol. 11. Tokyo: Sōgensha, 1969. GG

———. *Meisaku Kabuki Zenshū* (Collection of Kabuki Masterpieces). Vol. 15. Tokyo: Sōgensha, 1970. OH

382 ———. *Meisaku Kabuki Zenshū* (Collection of Kabuki Masterpieces). Vol. 19. Tokyo: Sōgensha, 1970. K, M, SA, SPI, Y

———. *Meisaku Kabuki Zenshū* (Collection of Kabuki Masterpieces). Vol. 23. Tokyo: Sōgensha, 1972. SO

Tsubouchi Shōyō and Atsumi Seitarō, eds. *Ō Nanboku Zenshū* (Collection of the Great Nanboku). Vol. 6. Tokyo: Shunyōdō, 1926. OH

Tsubouchi Shōyō and Yamamoto Jirō. *History and Characteristics of Kabuki, the Japanese Classical Drama.* Ryōzō Matsumoto, trans. Yokohama: Heiji Yamagata, 1960.

Urayama Masao and Matsuzaki Hitoshi, eds. *Nihon Koten Bungaku Taikei* (Outline of Japanese Classical Literature). Vol. 54. Tokyo: Iwanami Shoten, 1961. OH

Yoshida Yukiko et al., eds. *Nihon Buyō Zenshū* (Collection of Japanese Dances) series. Vols. 2, 5, 8. Tokyo: Nihon Buyōsha, 1978, 1981, 1988. SPI

EDITORS

James R. Brandon

Professor Emeritus and former Chair of the Department of Theatre and Dance at the University of Hawai'i at Manoa, Honolulu. Ph.D. in Theatre and Television, University of Wisconsin-Madison. Translator-director of eleven English-language kabuki productions in the United States and Europe, including *Sukeroku: Flower of Edo, Narukami the Thundergod, The Subscription List,* and *The Scarlet Princess of Edo.* Founding editor, *Asian Theatre Journal* (1984–1971) and author/editor/translator of sixteen books, including *Kabuki: Five Classic Plays* (1975; 2d ed. 1992); *Chūshingura: Studies in Kabuki and the Puppet Theater* (1982); *Two Kabuki Plays:* The Subscription List *and* The Zen Substitute (with T. Niwa, 1966); *Kabuki Dancer* (trans. of Ariyoshi Sawako's *Izumo no Okuni,* 1994); *Studies in Kabuki, Its Acting, Music and Historical Context* (with W. Malm and D. Shively, 1978); *Nō and Kyōgen in the Modern World* (1997); *Cambridge Guide to Asian Theatre* (1993); and the forthcoming *The Death of Kabuki and Other Myths: Kabuki under American Occupation.* Among honors are the Order of the Rising Sun–Gold Rays with Rosette from the Japanese government; the Uchimura Prize of the International Theatre Institute; the John D. Rockefeller III Award in Asian Arts; and Outstanding Theatre Teacher of the Year of the Association for Theatre in Higher Education.

Samuel L. Leiter

Head, Graduate Program, Department of Theatre, Brooklyn College, City University of New York, and faculty member, Ph.D. Program, City University of New York. Ph.D., Dramatic Art, New York University. Author/editor/translator of seventeen books on American theatre, international stage directors, and Japanese theatre, including *The Art of Kabuki: Plays in Performance* (1979; rev. ed. 2000); *Kabuki Encyclopedia: An English-language Adaptation of* Kabuki Jiten (1979); *New Kabuki Encyclopedia: A Revised Adaptation of* Kabuki Jiten (1997); *Japanese Theatre in the World* (1997); *Zeami and the Nō Theatre in the World* (with Benito Ortolani, 1998); *Japanese Theatre and the International Stage* (with Stanca Scholz-Cionca, 2000); *The Man who Saved Kabuki: Faubion Bowers and Theatre Censorship in Occupied Japan* (trans./adapt. of Okamoto Shiro's *Kabuki o Sukutta Otoko,* 2001); *A Kabuki Reader: History and Performance* (2002); *Frozen Moments: Writings on Kabuki, 1966–2001* (2002); etc. Founding editor, *Asian Theatre Bulletin;* editor, *Asian Theatre Journal* (1992 to present); and editorial board member, *Theatre Symposium.* Honors include East-West Center Fellowship (1962–1964), Fulbright Fellowship to Japan (1974–1975), Claire and Leonard Tow Professorship (1997–1998), Wolfe Fellowship in the Humanities (1999–2000), Broeklundian Professorship (2001–2006), Brooklyn College Award for Creative Achievement (2001), seven CUNY Research Foundation grants, and Visiting Scholar at Waseda University (1994, 1995).

TRANSLATORS

Ronald Cavaye

Professor of piano at the Musashino Academy of Music in Tokyo between 1979–1986; concert pianist who studied in London, Hannover, and Budapest. Now living in London and returns to Japan several times a year for concerts, teaching, and lectures. Founder/narrator of the English "Earphone Guide" at Tokyo kabuki theatres. Lectures regularly on Japanese theatre for the Central School of Speech and Drama in London. Author of *Kabuki: A Pocket Guide* (1993).

Alan Cummings

M.A., Waseda University. Specialist in kabuki of late Tokugawa and Meiji periods. Ph.D. candidate, University of London; dissertation topic: "Mokuami and Meiji Kabuki." Commentator/translator for English "Earphone Guide," Kabuki-za and Kokuritsu Gekijō, Tokyo.

Valerie L. Durham

M.A. and Ph.D., Japanese literature, Ochanomizu University, Tokyo. Currently associate professor, Tokyo Keizai University; also teaches at International Christian University. Research focus: representations of evil women in the fiction and theatre of the late Edo and early Meiji periods. Commentator/translator of English "Earphone Guide," Kabuki-za and Kokuritsu Gekijō, Tokyo, since 1982.

Paul M. Griffith

Associate Professor, Education Faculty, Saitama University. Ph.D. candidate, St. Antony's College, Oxford University, with focus on Tokugawa-period art history. Worked in Far Eastern Department, Victoria and Albert Museum (London), on their kabuki woodblock print collection. Recipient of Japanese Ministry of Education fellowship (1981–1983) and Japan Foundation Scholarship (1985–1987) for study in Japan. Translator for NHK bilingual program *Traditional Japanese Performing Arts*. Producer and translator/commentator for the English "Earphone Guide," Kabuki-za and Kokuritsu Gekijō, Tokyo. Studies *nihon buyō* under Fujima Hideka.

Kei Hibino

Lecturer, Faculty of Humanities, Seikei University, Tokyo. Formerly an adjunct in the Department of Area Studies at Tokyo University. M.A., English Literature, University of Tokyo. Ph.D. candidate, Theatre, City University of New York. Author of recently published essay "Family, Society and the Individual in Modernity: The Representation of the Family in Eugene O'Neill's *Mourning Becomes Electra*" (1999). Presented papers at various conferences.

Paul B. Kennelly

Ph.D., University of Sydney. Under a Japan Foundation fellowship, conducted research at Waseda University Theater Museum, Tokyo, from 1998–2000. Author of a number of articles on the major plays of Tsuruya Nanboku IV; translation of and commentary on Nanboku's *Ehon Gappō ga Tsuji* appears in the fall 2000 issue of *Asian Theatre Journal*.

Mark Oshima

Instructor, Sophia University, Tokyo. Teaches Japanese theatre, with focus on kabuki and bunraku. A.B., East Asian Studies, Harvard University. Ph.D. candidate, East Asian Languages and Civilizations, Harvard University; dissertation topic on kabuki. Resident of Japan for thirteen years. Professional singer of *kiyomoto* (stage name Kiyomoto Shimatayū) at

Kabuki-za and Kokuritsu Gekijō. Student of *nihon buyō* (stage name Fujima Toyaki). Extensive touring experience, Europe and South America, with international fusion theatre and dance groups. Translator/commentator for English "Earphone Guide," kabuki and *bunraku* performances, Tokyo; writer of English-language programs for the Kabuki-za; and performance translator for NHK Television. Translator of Nakamura Matazō's *Kabuki Backstage, Onstage: An Actor's Life* (1990) and the kabuki plays *Yotsuya Ghost Stories* and *A Maiden at Dōjōji* (1998). Author of *Konnichiwa Kabuki Dance: Heaven and Earth, the World of Contradictions* (1992).

Anne Phillips

Honors Degree (B.A.), Japanese Studies, University of Adelaide. Currently completing an M.A. at Meiji University, Tokyo, specializing in the plays of kabuki dramatist Kawatake Mokuami. Translator/ commentator for the English "Earphone Guide," Kabuki-za and Kokuritsu Gekijō.

Leonard C. Pronko

Professor and former Chair of the Theatre Department, Pomona College, California. Ph.D., Tulane University. Author of seven books, including *Theater East and West: Perspectives Toward a Total Theater* (1967; rev. ed. 1974) and *Guide to Japanese Drama* (1984). Accepted as a student in the first class of the Kabuki Training Program of the Kokuritsu Gekijō (National Theatre of Japan) (1970–1971) and subsequently directed eighteen productions of kabuki plays in English. Translator of more than a dozen kabuki plays over a period of twenty-five years. Honors include the Order of the Sacred Treasure, Third Degree, awarded by the Japanese government, and the Award for Outstanding Theatre Teacher of the Year, presented by the Association for Theatre in Higher Education.

This index includes terms, plays, and actors found in the editors' and translators' introductions.